ANTIOCHUS AND PERIPATETIC ETHICS

This book offers a fresh analysis of the account of Peripatetic ethics in Cicero's *On Ends* 5, which goes back to the first-century BCE philosopher Antiochus of Ascalon. Georgia Tsouni challenges previous characterisations of Antiochus' philosophical project as 'eclectic' and shows how his reconstruction of the ethics of the 'Old Academy' demonstrates a careful attempt to update the ancient heritage, and predominantly the views of Aristotle and the Peripatos, in the light of contemporary Stoic-led debates. This results in both a hermeneutically complex and a philosophically exciting reading of the old tradition. A case in point is the way Antiochus grounds the 'Old Academic' conception of the happy life in natural appropriation (*oikeiōsis*), thus offering a naturalistic version of Aristotelian ethics.

GEORGIA TSOUNI is a post-doctoral researcher and lecturer (Assistentin) to the Chair of History of Philosophy at the University of Bern. She has published extensively on Aristotelian/Peripatetic and Stoic ethical and political philosophy, including a new edition and translation of Didymus' *Summary of Peripatetic Ethics*, which survives in the Byzantine anthology of Stobaeus.

T0382053

CAMBRIDGE CLASSICAL STUDIES

ANTIOCHUS AND PERIPATETIC ETHICS

GEORGIA TSOUNI

University of Bern, Switzerland

CAMBRIDGE
UNIVERSITY PRESS

CAMBRIDGE
UNIVERSITY PRESS

Shaftesbury Road, Cambridge CB2 8EA, United Kingdom

One Liberty Plaza, 20th Floor, New York, NY 10006, USA

477 Williamstown Road, Port Melbourne, VIC 3207, Australia

314–321, 3rd Floor, Plot 3, Splendor Forum, Jasola District Centre, New Delhi – 110025, India

103 Penang Road, #05–06/07, Visioncrest Commercial, Singapore 238467

Cambridge University Press is part of Cambridge University Press & Assessment, a department of the University of Cambridge.

We share the University's mission to contribute to society through the pursuit of education, learning and research at the highest international levels of excellence.

www.cambridge.org
Information on this title: www.cambridge.org/9781108412612

DOI: 10.1017/9781108354790

© Faculty of Classics, University of Cambridge 2019

First published 2019
First paperback edition 2023

A catalogue record for this publication is available from the British Library

Library of Congress Cataloging-in-Publication data
NAMES: Tsouni, Georgia, author.
TITLE: Antiochus and peripatetic ethics / Georgia Tsouni.
DESCRIPTION: Cambridge, United Kingdom ; New York, NY : Cambridge University Press, 2019. | Series: Cambridge classical studies | Includes bibliographical references and index.
IDENTIFIERS: LCCN 2018039852 | ISBN 9781108420587
SUBJECTS: LCSH: Antiochus, of Ascalon, approximately 130 B.C.-69 or 68 B.C. | Peripatetics. | Philosophy, Ancient.
CLASSIFICATION: LCC B535.A774 T76 2019 | DDC 186/.2–dc23
LC record available at https://lccn.loc.gov/2018039852

ISBN   978-1-108-42058-7   Hardback
ISBN   978-1-108-41261-2   Paperback

CONTENTS

Contents

ACKNOWLEDGEMENTS

This is a substantially revised version of my PhD thesis submitted in May 2010 to the Faculty of Classics at the University of Cambridge for the degree of Doctor of Philosophy. Although the core objective of the thesis remains intact in this book, namely the identification and appreciation of the Peripatetic dimension in Antiochus' teaching, my initial objective has been refined and enlarged during the years of revision; in particular the book argues for a more nuanced thesis of the way Platonic and Stoic elements interact with Antiochus' Peripateticism. Chapter One has been added in order to place Antiochus' activity in its larger historical and cultural context but also in order to highlight Cicero's contribution as a *Vermittler* of Antiochean philosophy. The chapter on *oikeiōsis* towards theoretical virtue is partly based on a chapter which appears in D. Sedley (ed.), *The Philosophy of Antiochus* (Cambridge, 2012).

During my studies in Cambridge, I was fortunate enough to be a PhD student at the Arts and Humanities Research Council-funded project entitled 'Greco-Roman Philosophy in the First Century BC' (2006–2009) under the direction of Professor D. Sedley and Professor M. Schofield. I am most grateful to both of them for their comments and support during this period. I also wish to thank the post-doctoral investigators of the project, Dr M. Hatzimichali and Dr R. Polito, for valuable advice and comments. The volume *The Philosophy of Antiochus* (the only one in English to have been entirely dedicated to Antiochus), which emerged from a conference of the 'First Century BC' project, has provided an important context for the development of my own views.

The Arts and Humanities Research Council honoured me with a fees-only award, whereas the Greek State Scholarships Foundation covered the living costs during my doctoral studies in Cambridge. The Faculty of Classics and Newnham College, Cambridge, have both provided financial help for living and travel funds during these years. To all these bodies I am most grateful. Special thanks are also due to the examiners of my PhD thesis, Professor Malcolm Schofield and Professor Christopher Gill, for their detailed comments on the PhD thesis.

The revision of the manuscript of this book started during a post-doctoral research stay at the Central European University and, subsequently, at the University of Bern, where I currently hold the position of post-doctoral researcher and lecturer (Assistentin) to the Chair of History of Philosophy. I wish to thank all the individuals who contributed with their comments, encouragement and support in the past years to the writing of the book, and especially Professor Gábor Betegh and Professor Richard King. I owe many thanks also to Professor Bill Fortenbaugh who offered constant valuable advice and guidance during the period of preparation of the edition and translation of Didymus' *Outline of Peripatetic Ethics* (published in the Rutgers Series in Classical Humanities), which coincided with the preparation of this book. Parts of this translation are used in this book to illuminate Antiochus' views. I also wish to thank Katja Vogt who provided valuable comments for a paper on Antiochean/ Peripatetic *oikeiōsis* which was presented at the Princeton Classical Philosophy Colloquium in December 2014. The comments of the two reviewers for Cambridge University Press have significantly helped me to ameliorate the book and to decide on its final shape. Above all, I wish to thank my Cambridge supervisor Professor David Sedley without whom this book would never have been written. I owe him gratitude for being a great supervisor during my graduate studies and generous in so many ways. I also owe him thanks for providing comments on all the individual topics in the book as also for reading the final draft and providing suggestions for improvement until the very last stage. His scholarly example has provided the inspiration needed to bring the task to completion. Of course, I take the responsibility for any omissions and mistakes that remain.

Acknowledgements

I dedicate this book to Anastasios Kalogirou. Many of our discussions have centred around the value of self-love for happiness, a topic discussed by Antiochus as well.

ABBREVIATIONS

ANRW   *Aufstieg und Niedergang der Römischen Welt: Geschichte und Kultur Roms im Spiegel der neueren Forschung.* Ed. H. Temporini and W. Haase. Berlin, 1972–

DG   *Doxographi Graeci.* Ed. Hermann Diels. Berlin, 1879

Dörrie   *Der Platonismus in der Antike,* Begr. Von H. Dörrie, fortgeführt von M. Baltes unter Mitarbeit von F. Mann Bd. 1–7. Stuttgart, 1987

FHS&G   Theophrastus of Eresus. *Sources for His Life, Writings, Thought and Influence.* Ed. and trans. W.W. Fortenbaugh, P.M. Huby, R.W. Sharples and D. Gutas. 2 vols. Leiden, 1992

LS   A.A. Long and D.N. Sedley, *The Hellenistic Philosophers.* Vol. 1: *Translations of the Principal Sources with Philosophical Commentary.* Volume 2: *Greek and Latin Texts with Notes and Bibliography.* Cambridge, 1987

LSJ   H.G. Liddell, R. Scott and H.S. Jones, *A Greek-English Lexicon with a Revised Supplement.* Oxford, 1996

RUSCH   Rutgers University Studies in Classical Humanities

SVF   *Stoicorum Veterum Fragmenta.* Ed. J. von Arnim, vols. 1–3, Stuttgart, 1903–05; vol. 4 (indexes) by M. Adler

Überweg   *Grundriss der Geschichte der Philosophie,* 13th edn, vol. 1–., Ed. H. Flashar et al. Basel and Stuttgart, 1983–

Wachsmuth	*Ioannis Stobaei Anthologii.* Books 1 and 2 (*Eclogai*), ed. C. Wachsmuth, Berlin, 1884; Books 3 and 4, ed. O. Hense, Berlin, 1894–1909
Wehrli	*Die Schule des Aristoteles.* Texte und Kommentar, Hrsg. von F. Wehrli, 2nd edition, Bände I–X, Basel/Stuttgart, 1967–1969

All Latin citations of Cicero's *De Finibus* follow the text of the OCT edition by Reynolds (1998). Fragments and Testimonia of Antiochus follow Mette's 1986 edition, which is also reproduced in Sedley (ed.), *The Philosophy of Antiochus* (2012b). Translations of original sources, unless otherwise indicated, are mine.

INTRODUCTION

Antiochus from the city of Ascalon, a philosopher who at the end of the second century BCE moved to Athens from the periphery of the Greek-speaking world in order to become a member of the Academy, stands at the crossroads of many important developments. During his lifetime, Rome conquered Athens and the rest of the Eastern Mediterranean; as a consequence of this development, Athenian philosophical schools closed down and Greek-speaking intellectuals moved to Rome popularising philosophical discourse among the Romans. Favoured by the Roman interest in Greek culture, the original writings of Plato and Aristotle received renewed attention. Amid these developments, Antiochus professed to recover in his lectures and writings the original teaching of the early (fourth century BCE) Academy.[1]

Part of Antiochus' philosophical activity is revealed by the titles of works that are attributed to him by ancient authors. Thus, Sextus mentions a treatise *Canonica*, a doxographical work, where Antiochus laid down diverse views on the criterion of truth; Sextus twice makes reference to Antiochus as a source, once in the part of the doxography which conveys the views of the Academic Carneades,[2] and a second time when referring to the

---

[1] It is not clear whether Antiochus officially called his school Old Academy as Glucker (1978) 106 suggests, or whether he professed to be merely recovering in his lectures and writings the teaching of the early Academy.

[2] Antiochus *F*2 = Sextus Empiricus *Against the Professors* 7.162–63: οἷον προσβλέψαντές τινι, φησὶν ὁ Ἀντίοχος, διατιθέμεθά πως τὴν ὄψιν, καὶ οὐχ οὕτως αὐτὴν διακειμένην ἴσχομεν ὡς πρὶν τοῦ βλέψαι διακειμένην εἴχομεν. κατὰ μέντοι τὴν τοιαύτην ἀλλοίωσιν δυεῖν ἀντιλαμβανόμεθα, ἑνὸς μὲν αὐτῆς τῆς ἀλλοιώσεως, τουτέστι τῆς φαντασίας, δευτέρου δὲ τοῦ τὴν ἀλλοίωσιν ἐμποιήσαντος, τουτέστι τοῦ ὁρατοῦ. καὶ ἐπὶ τῶν ἄλλων αἰσθήσεων τὸ παραπλήσιον. ὥσπερ οὖν τὸ φῶς ἑαυτό τε δείκνυσι καὶ πάντα τὰ ἐν αὐτῷ, οὕτω καὶ ἡ φαντασία, ἀρχηγὸς οὖσα τῆς περὶ τὸ ζῷον εἰδήσεως, φωτὸς δίκην ἑαυτήν τε ἐμφανίζειν ὀφείλει καὶ τοῦ ποιήσαντος αὐτὴν ἐναργοῦς ἐνδεικτικὴ καθεστάναι. References to Antiochus' fragments follow Mette (1986), as reproduced also in Sedley (2012b).

epistemological views of Asclepiades the medic.[3] Another testimony mentions a (lost) Antiochean treatise *On the Gods*.[4] This information is the most that we can get from the sole verbatim fragment that may securely be ascribed to Antiochus in Sextus Empiricus[5] and from *testimonia* about the philosopher which survive independently of Cicero.

It is only in Cicero that Antiochus emerges as more than a name and as a key player on the Roman philosophical scene. If one takes at face value Cicero's explicit remarks about the authorship of the speeches that he puts in the mouths of his interlocutors, then we can be confident that three of the speeches that appear in his dialogues from 45 BCE contain major Antiochean content, with only minor Ciceronian interventions in the philosophical ideas that they express.[6] In the *Lucullus* (11–62), the homonymous character

---

[3] Antiochus *F*2 = Sextus Empiricus *Against the Professors* 7.201: ὅτι γὰρ ἐγένοντό τινες τὸ τοιοῦτο ἀξιοῦντες, προῦπτον πεποίηκεν Ἀντίοχος ὁ ἀπὸ τῆς Ἀκαδημίας, ἐν δευτέρῳ τῶν Κανονικῶν ῥητῶς γράψας ταῦτα ʼἄλλος δέ τις, ἐν ἰατρικῇ μὲν οὐδενὸς δεύτερος, ἁπτόμενος δὲ καὶ φιλοσοφίας, ἐπείθετο τὰς μὲν αἰσθήσεις ὄντως καὶ ἀληθῶς ἀντιλήψεις εἶναι, λόγῳ δὲ μηδὲν ὅλως ἡμᾶς καταλαμβάνειν.ʼ

[4] Antiochus *T*7 = Plutarch *Life of Lucullus* 28.8: ταύτης τῆς μάχης Ἀντίοχος ὁ φιλόσοφος ἐν τῇ Περὶ θεῶν γραφῇ μνησθεὶς οὔ φησιν ἄλλην ἐφεωρακέναι τοιαύτην τὸν ἥλιον.

[5] Although *F*2 contains the only sentences in Sextus that may be guaranteed to originate from Antiochus, some scholars have defended the view that larger parts of the doxographical account of epistemology in Sextus' *Against the Professors* 7 is dependent upon Antiochus. Both Tarrant (1985) and Sedley (1992); (2012a) 88–93 have defended the view that Antiochus is the main source of Sextus Empiricus *Against the Professors* 7. 141–260, whereas Tarrant claims an Antiochean influence for the paragraphs 7.89–140 as well. Against this view, see Brittain (2012) 109–13. The doxographical part of Sextus' book contains summaries, in Stoic terminology, of Plato's views (7.141–44) but also of a position attributed jointly to Aristotle and Theophrastus (7.217–26). If genuinely Antiochean, the accounts may be taken to show how Antiochus interpreted the epistemological views of the old tradition in light of his Stoic commitments in this domain of philosophy, as endorsed in the *Lucullus* as well. Sedley (2012a) 88–101 argues that Antiochus followed in these accounts (belonging to his early phase) the aim of 'maximising the continuity between the early Academy and Stoicism'.

[6] Despite Cicero's explicit markers of Antiochean authorship, the identification of Ciceronian texts that can with security be attributed to Antiochus has been disputed in scholarship. Luck (1953) 73–94 identifies eighty-six fragments as Antiochean choosing only passages in Cicero which contain explicit references to Antiochus' name; however, in his commentary he seems to adopt a more 'loose' criterion for the identification of Antiochean material, which leads to the inclusion of passages whose connection to Antiochus is only vague. Giusta (1964) 93 expresses scepticism about the Antiochean origin of Piso's account in *On Ends* 5 and takes Cicero to have combined Antiochean views on the *telos* with a Peripatetic doxographical source. Mette (1986) on the other hand, reduces the number of fragments that may be ascribed to Antiochus to eleven but includes there extensive passages from the *Academic Books*, the *Lucullus* and the *On Ends*; still, he takes Piso's account at *On Ends* 5.24–70 not to be securely

conveys Antiochean views on epistemology. The Roman general becomes the mouthpiece of the epistemological views of Antiochus by virtue of the fact that the latter served as his philosophical advisor for many years; accordingly, the fact that Lucullus heard the doctrines of the school at first hand is invoked in *Lucullus* 10 as a guarantee of the trustworthiness of the account.[7] Cicero's authorial remarks seem to point to an Antiochean work as a source, one which set out to defend the Stoic criterion of truth against the criticisms of Academic sceptics.

The other two major Ciceronian sources for Antiochus are more doxographical in character: they are contained in Piso's speech in *On Ends* 5 (9–74) and Varro's account in the fragment that survives from the second book of the *Academic Books* (15–42). In these accounts, the two Antiochean spokespersons explicitly offer an account of the ethics of the Old Academy and of the main points of the Old Academic system in all three branches of philosophy, respectively. Cicero goes to great lengths in the last book of *On Ends* to show the book's Antiochean credentials; thus, Piso is chosen as the mouthpiece of Antiochus because he had the Peripatetic philosopher Staseas of Naples in his household for many years, but also because he *himself* heard the lectures of Antiochus in Athens.[8] Cicero in addition asks Brutus, the

---

Antiochean and only paraphrases the bulk of the account. Barnes (1989) takes Piso's speech in *On Ends* 5, Lucullus' speech in *Lucullus* and Varro's report in the *Academic Books* to be securely reporting Antiochean views. He is followed by Fladerer (1996) xiii; cf. also Karamanolis (2006) 44 n.1. The newest collection of Antiochean fragments and testimonies by Sedley (2012b), on which the present study is based, contains eleven fragments, including the entire speeches of Piso, Varro and Lucullus in the *On Ends, Academic Books* and *Lucullus* respectively. Fragment 10 also includes material from the *Tusculan Disputations* (3.59–60; 5.21–3) and fragment 11 from *On the Nature of the Gods* (1.11;1.16). A further category of texts, without being assigned explicit Antiochean authority, may be deemed Antiochean on the basis of their content, e.g. by references to Antiochus' (exclusive) thesis that the Academy and the Peripatos form part of the same tradition. The critique of Stoicism by the 'sceptic' Cicero in *On Ends* 4 may count among these passages. For a defence of the Antiochean pedigree of *On Ends* 4, see Sedley (2012a) 80.

[7] *Lucullus* 10: *tamen expecto ea quae te pollicitus es Luculle ab Antiocho audita dicturum.* Later on, Lucullus stresses that he heard Antiochus 'undistracted and with great interest, more than once on the same topic': *vacuo animo illum audiebam et magno studio, eadem de re etiam saepius.*

[8] *On Ends* 5.8: *censemus autem facillime te id explanare posse, quod et Staseam Neapolitanum multos annos habueris apud te et compluris iam menses Athenis haec ipsa te ex Antiocho videamus exquirere.* Note how Cicero is keen to stress at *On Ends*

dedicatee of the dialogue, to be particularly attentive and check the accuracy of Piso's presentation of Antiochean philosophy, with which Brutus became acquainted through attending the lectures of Antiochus' brother, Aristus.[9] We are thus invited to take the claim of Antiochean authority at face value and assume that Piso's account presents accurately the Antiochean positions which, in the case of *On Ends* 5, are taken to represent the ethical theory of the Peripatos as well. Varro finally is chosen as a spokesperson for the Antiochean material in the revised version of the *Academic Books* because he is himself a well-known follower of Antiochus.[10]

The picture of Antiochus that emerges from the study of Piso's and Varro's accounts is going to be the main focus of the book.[11] It is only in these two latter sources that we encounter a key

5.75 that Piso gave an account of the Peripatetic *telos* which in some significant points diverges from that of Staseas of Naples who favoured a more 'Theophrastean' line. On the latter Chapter 3, *infra*. For a discussion of the few surviving evidence on Staseas see Moraux (1973) 217–21. Cicero signals with this that he conveys Antiochus' *own* reconstruction of Peripatetic ethics, which in some points diverges from that of other contemporary Peripatetics: '*quod quidem eo probavi magis, quia memini Staseam Neapolitanum, doctorem illum tuum, nobilem sane Peripateticum, aliquanto ista secus dicere solitum, adsentientem iis qui multum in fortuna secunda aut adversa, multum in bonis aut malis corporis ponerent.*' '*Est, ut dicis,*' inquit; '*sed haec ab Antiocho, familiari nostro, dicuntur multo melius et fortius quam a Stasea dicebantur.*' However, for an alternative view on the role of Staseas see Inwood (2014) 72 who speculates that Cicero could have adopted the theory of 'Aristotelian naturalism' that features in Piso's speech in *On Ends* 5 from Staseas.

[9] *Ibid.* 5.8: *cuius oratio attende, quaeso, Brute, satisne videatur Antiochi complexa esse sententiam, quam tibi, qui fratrem eius Aristum frequenter audieris, maxime probatam existimo.* See also Cicero's remarks in *Academic Books* 1.12 that Brutus studied under Antiochus' brother Aristus. For the importance of Cicero's reference to Brutus for the Antiochean pedigree of Piso's speech, see Görler (2011) 333. For a more sceptical reading of these remarks, see Giusta (1964) 98 who believes that Cicero combines in *On Ends* 5 Antiochean views with a (separate) Peripatetic doxographical source.

[10] Numerous remarks on the choice of Varro as a suitable dramatic character to convey Antiochus' views in Cicero's new edition of the *Academic Books* survive in Cicero's letters; see *F6a–6e = Letters to Atticus* 13.12.3; 13.16.1–2;13.19.3–5;13.25.3; *Letters to Friends* 9.8.1 (which contains the dedicatory letter of the second edition to Varro): *tibi dedi partis Antiochinas, quas a te probari intellexisse mihi videbar, mihi sumpsi Philonis.*

[11] Instead I will have less to say about Antiochus' views as they are expressed in the *Lucullus*. The reason for this is that the Antiochean speech in the *Lucullus* largely reflects Stoic views about epistemology. One may hypothesise that Lucullus' account is based on a work belonging to a different phase of Antiochus' philosophical activity than the works which formed the basis for Piso's speech in *On Ends* 5 and for Varro's speech in the *Academic Books*. A developmental view about Antiochus' philosophical activity is advocated in Sedley (2012a).

hermeneutical assumption of Antiochus' reconstruction of the philosophy of the 'ancients', namely that the philosophical traditions of the Academy and the Peripatos represent a single, harmonious body of doctrines. In these sources we also encounter the idea that the Stoa merely modified (on the level of terminology) the views that it received from the old tradition. Consequently, Antiochus' views, as they appear in the accounts of Piso and Varro, require a subtle approach, which does justice to the complex allegiance of the Old Academy.

The scholarship on Antiochus reflects this complexity as well: here, we may notice two tendencies. The one is a reductive approach which wishes to ascribe to Antiochus an exclusive identity, whether Stoic, Platonic or Peripatetic. Another approach sees in Antiochus an eclectic, or syncretist, philosopher who combined different, and perhaps even incompatible, views in his Old Academic system.

The interpretation of a 'Stoic' Antiochus has been known since Antiquity; according to this view, Antiochus, although claiming to be recovering Platonic and Aristotelian views, is in reality a 'most faithful Stoic'.[12] This seems to largely match Antiochus' defence of Stoic views in the domain of epistemology—an area where perhaps Antiochus recognised the Stoics as making a positive contribution, and even going beyond the 'ancients'. If Antiochus recognised Stoic authority in this one area of philosophical discourse, the polemic of Cicero, who attacks Antiochus in the second part of the *Lucullus* as abandoning his professed

---

[12] See *Lucullus* 132: *per ipsum Antiochum, qui appellabatur Academicus, erat quidem si perpauca mutavisset germanissimus Stoicus.* For the most clear expression of this accusation, see Antiochus *F*1 = Sextus Empiricus *Outlines of Pyrrhonism* 1.235: ἀλλὰ καὶ ὁ Ἀντίοχος τὴν Στοὰν μετήγαγεν εἰς τὴν Ἀκαδημίαν, ὡς καὶ εἰρῆσθαι ἐπ' αὐτῷ ὅτι ἐν Ἀκαδημίᾳ φιλοσοφεῖ τὰ Στωικά· ἐπεδείκνυε γὰρ ὅτι παρὰ Πλάτωνι κεῖται τὰ τῶν Στωικῶν δόγματα. Since the reference to Antiochus is preceded in Sextus by the exposition of Philo of Larissa's epistemological views, we may infer that Antiochus' 'Stoic identity' addresses primarily the epistemological views he advanced. Cf. Antiochus *T*5a = Plutarch *Cicero* 4.1–2 (which notes, more carefully, that Antiochus switched to favouring the Stoic account 'in most matters'): τὸν Στωικὸν ἐκ μεταβολῆς θεραπεύων (sc. ὁ Ἀντίοχος) λόγον ἐν τοῖς πλείστοις. Aenesidemus who attempted a revival of Pyrrhonist philosophy in the first century BCE also attacked contemporary Academics for adopting Stoicism, clearly with Antiochus in mind; see Photius *Library* 212.170a: Οἱ δ' ἀπὸ τῆς Ἀκαδημίας, φησί, μάλιστα τῆς νῦν, καὶ Στωικαῖς συμφέρονται ἐνίοτε δόξαις, καὶ εἰ χρὴ τἀληθὲς εἰπεῖν, Στωικοὶ φαίνονται μαχόμενοι Στωικοῖς.

school, seems to be based on the assumption that Antiochus is a 'Stoic' in *all* areas of philosophy.[13] However, this does not fit with the obvious anti-Stoic staging of the Antiochean account in Cicero, when it comes to the domain of ethics;[14] in *On Ends* the Antiochean speech is offered as an *alternative* to Stoicism and as representative of a different school of thought, namely that of the Platonic-Peripatetic camp of the Old Academy. A 'Stoic' reading of Antiochus in this domain is also not supported by the polemic against Stoicism which is expressed in both Piso's and Varro's accounts; such a polemic is primarily motivated by the aim of subsuming Stoicism under the old tradition as a derivative school of thought. Thus, even if an interpretation traces 'Stoicising' features in Antiochus' ethical account (in line with the abundant appropriation of Stoic terminology by Antiochus), it should also show how such features are connected with the reconstruction of the Platonic and Peripatetic doctrines that Antiochus professes to offer.

On the other hand, a strand of modern scholarship has emphasised Antiochus' Platonic identity. There, Antiochus appears as the precursor of a series of Platonists who attempted to revive the dogmatic teaching of Plato in the first two centuries CE; thus, according to Theiler, Antiochus was the 'founder of Platonism in the Imperial period' and Dillon ranks him as the first among the 'Middle Platonists'.[15] An important qualification, however, is

---

[13] See e.g. *Lucullus* 134, where Cicero traces an inconsistency between the Stoic and the Old Academic conception of the *telos: ecce multo maior etiam dissensio. Zeno in una virtute positam beatam vitam putat. quid Antiochus? 'etiam' inquit 'beatam, sed non beatissimam'.* Conversely, the 'sceptic' Cicero at *On Ends* 5.76 assumes that Piso does not defend Stoic epistemological views, since he advocates Peripatetic views in ethics: *itaque haec cum illis (sc. Stoicis) est dissensio, cum Peripateticis nulla sane.* Antiochus could, however, admit Stoic authority solely in the domain of epistemology, whereas assuming a different stance in the domain of ethics; see Chapter 2, *infra.*

[14] This is underlined also in Schofield (2012b) 241–42.

[15] See, for example, Theiler (1930) 51 and Luck (1953) 27 who speak of an association of Antiochus with the Alexandrian Eudorus. However, as Barnes (1989) 52 notes, 'no text associates the two men'; cf. Glucker (1978) 90–7. Sedley (2012a) 81 also maintains a distance from the view that Antiochus 'anticipated the main Middle Platonists'. Another line of scholarship has focused on the way Antiochus *influenced* later Platonists, especially by co-opting Aristotle for the understanding of Plato: thus, Karamanolis (2006) 45 takes Antiochus to be the first in a series of Platonists 'to draw attention to the value of Aristotle's philosophy as a means for accessing that of Plato' and Bonazzi (2012) 311 claims that 'Antiochus' contribution to the development of

needed in the presentation of Antiochus as the precursor of Platonists who were active in the first centuries CE. Even if later Platonists incorporated Aristotelian ideas and terminology into their work, they did it with the primary goal of interpreting Plato and his dialogues, since the latter represented for them the highest wisdom.[16] In line with this, one of the hallmarks of Platonists became a strong claim of the infallibility of Plato's words *in their own right*, against a lesser authority of Aristotle and subsequent philosophers.[17] This claim of infallibility but also the thesis of the exclusivity of Platonic authority is missing in Antiochus who believes that Platonic views can and should be supplemented by Academic, Aristotelian and, in some cases, even Stoic ideas, in order to meet contemporary, systematic standards of philosophical debate.[18]

Furthermore, one should acknowledge the significant shift in philosophical focus attested in later Platonists: whereas metaphysics and the independent ontological status of Platonic forms is not (explicitly at least) discussed in Antiochean passages,[19] much of the identity of a Platonist in the subsequent centuries is connected with a quest for intelligible principles.[20] Forms acquire thereby central importance and feature in the scheme of Middle Platonic 'first principles',

imperial Platonism is evident when it is considered that he was the first to insist both on Aristotle's Academic credentials and on his importance for a correct assessment of Plato's philosophy.' Cf. Tarrant (2007).

[16] Cf. Atticus *ap.* Eusebius, *Preparation for the Gospel* 11.2.4.

[17] Cf. Boys-Stones (2001) 103: 'Platonists were able to commit themselves to the truth of a proposition *on the grounds that* Plato had said it, and, it might be, even before they themselves understood *why* it was true.' Plotinus and Simplicius co-opt Aristotle but only in so far as it serves the understanding of the 'divine' Plato; see also Karamanolis (2006) 4.

[18] Sedley (2012a) 81 points in the same direction when he says: '[I]t is no accident that he (sc. Antiochus) calls himself an Academic rather than a Platonist, because his interest is in realigning himself with the mainstream tradition of the Academy as a school, not with the thought of Plato in particular.' Cf. *ibid.*: 'For Antiochus, Plato's unique importance as founder of the school did not imply his infallibility.' As Boys-Stones (2001) 143 notes Antiochus' position is 'an argument *from* the consensus established by Plato, not *to* the authority of Plato'. On the idea that Antiochus' 'Academic' project also involved an attempt to incorporate Stoicism into the Academic tradition, cf. Gerson (2013) 184 n.15.

[19] Cf. Karamanolis (2006) 63: 'Antiochus does not share the strong metaphysical concerns of later Platonists, concerns which will give rise to objections of a different order.'

[20] For Eudorus' role as the first 'Platonist' to turn attention to metaphysics see Karamanolis (2006) 84.

alongside god and matter.[21] In the domain of ethics, 'assimilation to god', a formulation which does not yet have special importance in Cicero, becomes identified for later Platonists with the Platonic *telos*.[22] Emphasis on such ideas, which proved to be hallmarks of Platonism in the subsequent centuries, seems to be missing in Antiochus. What we find in Antiochus, instead, is a reading of Plato which conforms largely to the Stoic agenda and focuses predominantly on the domains of ethics and epistemology.[23] Finally, taking Antiochus to represent exclusively Platonic authority has come at the cost of disregarding the importance of the Peripatetic elements of his philosophy and has turned scholarly attention away from evaluating them in their own right; that such Peripatetic elements play an important role in Piso's account at *On Ends* is suggested by the frequent references in the account to Aristotle and Theophrastus and by Cicero's own characterisation of the work as a 'Peripatetic' treatise.[24] While Antiochus would have probably defended the view that the Platonic Academy and the Peripatos agree on all essential ethical points, the explicit Peripatetic character of *On Ends* 5 strongly suggests that the Peripatos had for Antiochus a special authority, at least in the domain of ethics. This, as we shall see, is compatible with the use of occasional 'Socratic' elements in

---

[21] See e.g. Alcinous' theological chapters in his *Handbook of Platonism* 8–10.

[22] The formula appears, perhaps for the first time, in the anonymous commentary to Plato's *Theaetetus*, see Sedley (1997) 127. Other early occurrences include a passage in the first part of the chapter of ethical doxography in Stobaeus' *Selections*, 49.8–50.10 Wachsmuth and in Alcinous' *Handbook of Platonism* 28.1. Boys-Stones (2014) highlights how post-Hellenistic Platonists reacted to the Stoic and Peripatetic (or Antiochean) attempt to ground ethics in οἰκείωσις and how they appeal instead to 'assimilation to god' as an ethical principle.

[23] This is exemplified by the way Antiochus reads the Platonic *Timaeus* along largely Stoic lines, omitting any reference in his physical account to the transcendent Ideas. See Chapter 2, *infra*.

[24] This is explicitly stated in *Letters to Atticus* 13.19.4: *ita confeci quinque libros* περὶ Τελῶν *ut Epicurea L. Torquato, Stoica M. Catoni,* Περιπατητικὰ *M. Pisoni darem.* The Aristotelian/Peripatetic character of Piso's account has sometimes been ignored in scholarship. Suggestive is that Moraux (1973) in his seminal work on the revival of Aristotelianism in the first century BCE does not devote a chapter to Antiochus. However, the Peripatetic character of Piso's account has recently been reappraised by Inwood (2014) 17, who deems *On Ends* 5 to be perhaps 'the peak of neo-Aristotelian thinking before Alexander'.

Piso's ethical account, which seem to derive from the Platonic aporetic dialogues.

Another camp in modern scholarship attempts to rehabilitate the historicity of Antiochus' claims by tracing in his views original Peripatetic teaching, thus doing justice to Cicero's remarks that the Antiochean account can even be, at least with regard to ethics, *identified* with a Peripatetic position. Dirlmeier's 1937 seminal study *Theophrastus' Theory of Oikeiosis* (*Die Oikeiosislehre Theophrasts*) has seen in Theophrastus a major inspiration for Antiochus' ethical views in Cicero's dialogue *On Ends*. Dirlmeier has gone so far as to ascribe a whole theory of natural appropriation (*oikeiōsis*) to Theophrastus, which was allegedly reproduced by Antiochus in the last book of *On Ends*.[25] In more recent years, Gigon has argued that *On Ends* 5.24–70 (esp. 24–58) is 'a rather precise excerpt' from Theophrastus' *On Happiness*.[26] However, the attempt to identify a single Greek source for Antiochus' teaching, or even an exclusive Peripatetic identity, brings with it the danger of a reductionist account. Whereas it is a plausible hypothesis that Theophrastus was, alongside Plato and Aristotle, a major inspiration for Antiochus' theses (and this hypothesis will be explored in this book), the dialectical context against which the Peripatetic views are expressed in Antiochus give them a new shape and make them respond to novel philosophical challenges which did not form part of the intention of their originators. As the analysis which follows will attempt to show, Antiochus was able to select among the sources of the 'ancients' the ones that were most relevant for his purposes and the ones that could respond most to the demands raised by a contemporary (predominantly Stoic) philosophical agenda. We may conclude that he did not passively preserve the material he revived but

---

[25] See especially Dirlmeier (1937) 66; 73. There is not, however, enough evidence in Theophrastus' fragments to support this hypothesis; still, the word οἰκείωσις appears for the first time in a philosophical text in Theophrastus' *Fr.* 435 FHS&G but belongs there to the context of natural science rather than to ethics.

[26] Gigon (1988) 263; 269. Gigon also adds that paragraphs 5.77 and 5.86–95 are a free adaptation from the same source. For a refutation of the idea that Theophrastus' *On Happiness* is the sole source of *On Ends* 5, see Görler (1998) 324. At least on the point of the sufficiency of virtue for a happy life, Antiochus (at *On Ends* 5.85) clearly keeps a distance from the views expressed in the Theophrastean treatise.

shaped it into a new form. Thus, while one should attempt to do justice to the 'historic' view that Antiochus reconstructed genuine Academic philosophy (of which a major part may be ascribed to the Peripatos), one needs to retain an open attitude as to the methods and sources that he used in order to do so. Such an interpretative stance should also be able to accommodate the fact that Antiochus, while aiming at giving a reconstruction of Platonic and Peripatetic views, is operating within a largely Stoic terminological and classificatory framework.[27] This need not, however, compromise the Peripatetic, and for that matter Platonic, character of his ethical philosophy.

The Peripatetic character of Antiochus' teaching is supported by the comparison of the Antiochean ethical account in Cicero's *On Ends* 5 with a doxographical source which follows a similar project and explicitly attempts to convey the main points of the ethical theory of the Peripatos: the summary of Peripatetic ethics entitled *Of Aristotle and the Rest of the Peripatetics on Ethics* (*Aristotelous kai tōn loipōn Peripatētikōn peri tōn ēthikōn*)[28] in Stobaeus' *Selections* 2.7.[29] The summary forms part of an epitome written by a certain philosopher Didymus, who has been customarily, but perhaps falsely, identified with Arius Didymus, the court-philosopher of Augustus.[30] Similarities between the two

---

[27] In a similar vein Gill (2016) 228–29 cautions against an exclusive focus on the Aristotelian character of Antiochus' *oikeiōsis* theory.

[28] All references to Didymus' text henceforth are given following the pagination in Wachsmuth (1884). Deviations from Wachsmuth's text, and English translations, follow the edition and translation by Tsouni in Fortenbaugh (2017).

[29] There are two titles attributed to Didymus in Stobaeus. The first is a 'Summary' or an 'Epitome' (see the lemma Ἐκ τῆς Διδύμου Ἐπιτομῆς in Book 4, chapter 39.28); the second is a work 'On Philosophical Sects' (Διδύμου ἐκ τοῦ Περὶ αἱρέσεων in Book 2, chapter 1.17). One may assume that they both refer to a single work belonging to the doxographical genre περὶ αἱρέσεων. In this work, Didymus seems to have collected the views of the most important sects of his time, and most probably those of Plato, Aristotle and the Stoics, presumably on all three branches of philosophy, i.e. physics, ethics and dialectic. The doxographical piece entitled Ἀριστοτέλους καὶ τῶν λοιπῶν Περιπατητικῶν περὶ τῶν ἠθικῶν belongs to the ethical part of philosophy (Περὶ τοῦ ἠθικοῦ εἴδους τῆς φιλοσοφίας) and marks the transition from epistemological to ethical topics. It is the third of three ethical doxographies in a row and is often designated in scholarship as 'Doxography C'; see Hahn (1990) 2945.

[30] Since the publication of Diels' *Doxographi Graeci*, the prevailing hypothesis has been that the author of the Peripatetic and Stoic doxographies in Stobaeus' *Selections* 2.7 is Arius Didymus, a Stoic philosopher who lived in the time of Augustus. See Diels (1879)

accounts in both content and terminology have been already noticed in scholarship, and even a suggestion of common authorship has been formulated.[31]

Didymus' text constitutes an attempt to reconstruct the main 'headings' (*kephalaia*) in the ethical and political domain of philosophy, drawing on the two authoritative heads of the Peripatetic school, Aristotle and Theophrastus. The exposition draws on original material found in the Peripatetic treatises but also makes ample use of Stoic terminology (as in the case of the adoption of the term *oikeiōsis*) and attempts to offer in some cases alternative theses to the ones advanced by the Stoa on the topics at hand.[32] Pursuing a similar aim,[33] Piso's account in *On Ends* 5 may well derive from an ethical treatise of Antiochean origin which set out to present the views of the Old Academy, and especially of Aristotle and the Peripatetics,

---

80. Diels followed Meineke on this point. Cf. Meineke (1860) CLV. This hypothesis is taken for granted in most modern scholarship after Diels. See, for instance, Giusta (1964) 81, Moraux (1973) 259 and Hahm (1990) 3047. The only exception known to me is Göransson (1995) 203–18. An alternative source from the *Suda* makes reference to an Academic philosopher Didymus with the cognomen Atteius, see *Suda* s.v. 'Didymus' (δ 871 Adler); he could provide an alternative authorship for the text, and one which would connect the writer of the epitome with the Academic milieu, see also Tsouni (2016) 121. Since I wish to keep the question of the authorship of the text open, I will refer to the writer of the doxography throughout this book as Didymus, and not, as has been customary until now, as Arius Didymus. Less clear is the authorship of the first doxography in Stobaeus' *Selections* 2.7, the so-called Doxography A; that Arius Didymus (*sic*) is the author of the 'prolegomena' to the two ethical doxographies in Stobaeus' *Selections* 2 is defended by Huby (1983) 122. Hahm (1990) 3011–12 also defends the hypothesis of common authorship for all three doxographical parts in Stobaeus' *Selections* 2.

[31] Due to profound similarities in their approach, a common authorship has been suggested for both texts: see Madvig (1876) 848 and Strache (1909). Hirzel (1882) 695ff. and Arnim (1926) were the first to argue that, despite the similarities in their approach, the two accounts have different authors; cf. Giusta (1964) 79; 81. The issue is also discussed in Tsouni (2016).

[32] See, for example, the discussion of the justification of suicide at Didymus *ap.* Stobaeus *Selections* 2 126.2 11 Wachsmuth.

[33] Suggestive is the use of the characterisation 'ancients' in both texts to refer to the authorities whose thought they reconstruct. See Didymus *ap.* Stobaeus *Selections* 2 129. 4–6 Wachsmuth: 'The choiceworthy and the good seemed to be the same thing to the ancients' (τὸ δ᾽ αἱρετὸν καὶ ἀγαθὸν ταὐτὸν ἐδόκει τοῖς ἀρχαίοις εἶναι); cf. *ibid.* 131.2–4 Wachsmuth: 'But we should follow the custom of the ancients and say that the end is "that for the sake of which we do everything but it for the sake of nothing"' (ἀκολουθητέον μέντοι τῇ τῶν ἀρχαίων συνηθείᾳ καὶ λεκτέον τέλος εἶναι οὗ χάριν πάντα πράττομεν αὐτὸ δὲ οὐδενός). Antiochus refers to the ancients (*antiqui*) as well: see e.g. *On Ends* 5.7.

on the main topics of ethics,[34] with a view to offering an alternative account to that offered by the Stoa. Of particular interest are the common hermeneutical strategies both accounts develop in an attempt to present Aristotelian/Peripatetic thought in a 'modern' light influenced by the agenda of Stoic philosophy. This may be seen in particular by a comparison between the first part of Didymus' doxography (Stobaeus *Selections* 2 116.19–124.14 W.) and the Antiochean account in *On Ends* 5, which shows an attempt by both authors to ground the *telos* in natural appropriation towards the bodily and psychic virtues.

Still, Didymus (especially in the second part of the epitome) appears to work more closely with the Aristotelian and Peripatetic ethical treatises[35] and on some points, such as on the nature of the practical virtues and the sufficiency of virtue for the happy life, he clearly offers divergent views from Antiochus.[36] This suggests that the two accounts were composed independently of each other.

---

[34] Barnes (1989) 65–66 takes Piso's speech to contain Antiochean views but he believes that Cicero's model was not a particular treatise by Antiochus on the *telos*. See *ibid.*: '[W]e can suppose that *Fin.* v tells us something about Antiochus' views: we should not suppose that we are reading Antiochus in Latin translation, nor even that Cicero is paraphrasing a work of Antiochus.' Cf. also Fladerer (1996) 139: 'Eine Lehrschrift mit dem Titel περὶ τέλους stand offenbar nicht zur Verfügung.' Giusta (1964–67) vol. 1, 64ff., on the other hand, takes the source of the Antiochean passages in Cicero to be not Antiochus himself but another doxographical source, organised around the major topics of ethics, which he identifies with the *vetusta placita* of Arius Didymus (*sic*). For a critique of Giusta's hypothesis, see Moraux (1973) 264–68. For a defence of the view that a single Antiochean treatise forms the basis of Piso's speech at *On Ends* 5, see Görler (2011) 333: 'Die Quelle für Pisos Rede (8–75) ist also Antiochos von Askalon, wahrscheinlich eine einzelne zusammenhängende Schrift'. For a more recent reaction against the (exclusive) Antiochean authorship of Piso's speech in *On Ends* 5 see Inwood (2014) 71–72.

[35] A significant amount of material that we find in the doxography (especially in the sections on human happiness and virtue as a mean) maps onto what can be found in the school treatises transmitted under Aristotle's name, namely the *Nicomachean Ethics,* the *Eudemian Ethics,* and the *Magna Moralia.* For example from 145.11 Wachsmuth onward, Didymus offers definitions of all major ethical virtues; the list and order of exposition here follows closely *Magna Moralia* 1.20, 1190b9-32. The epitome closes with a synoptic account of the chief points from the domains of household management and politics. In these two last parts of the outline, Didymus abandons Stoic vocabulary and restricts himself to his Peripatetic sources, and mainly to what has come down to us in Aristotle's *Politics.*

[36] On the differences with regard to philosophical doctrine between Didymus and Antiochus, see also Hirzel (1882) 714–17. Whereas Antiochus opts for an intellectualist reading of the virtues at *On Ends* 5 (see Chapter 3, *infra*), Didymus refers to reason and passion as the two principles of the virtues (128.11–25 Wachsmuth).

Passages from the doxography of Didymus will be adduced in the following analysis in order to illuminate better Antiochus' views and show how in some cases similar strategies were followed in an attempt to offer a reconstruction of the views of Aristotle and the Peripatos. Points of difference between the two accounts may highlight cases in which Antiochus diverged from the Aristotelian/Peripatetic line in order to draw from the 'richer' Academic tradition, as for example from the Platonic dialogues.

The considerations presented above seem to favour a reading of Antiochus which resists tendencies towards reductionism and attempts to do justice to the inclusive nature of his project. Such an interpretative line is also pursued in strands of modern scholarship which present Antiochus as an 'eclectic' philosopher: the label of eclecticism was attached to Antiochus already in the influential nineteenth-century history of philosophy of Zeller.[37] After Zeller, Hans Strache gave his 1921 monograph on Antiochus the telling title *The Eclecticism of Antiochus of Ascalon* (*Der Eklektizismus des Antiochus von Askalon*). The use of the term, however, when applied to Antiochus' project, seems problematic, since eclecticism is more appropriate to characterising the activity of philosophers who eschew allegiance to a particular school of thought and choose their doctrines (deliberately) from heterogeneous sources. In the case of Antiochus the 'eclectic' interpretation seems anachronistic, since Antiochus' project predates the consolidated identities of 'Platonism' and 'Aristotelianism' and views both traditions not as different schools but as representing the same harmonious set of doctrines.[38] Furthermore, in the case of ethics, Antiochus does not combine Stoic positions with Old Academic ones but shows how the 'ancients' offered better

---

[37] See e.g. Zeller (1868): 624. Cf. Giusta (1964) 80.

[38] For the rejection of eclecticism in connection with Antiochus see Donini (1988) 32, who recognises Antiochus' position as idiosyncratic and *sui generis*. Cf. also Karamanolis (2006) 81, who, however, takes Antiochus to be committed to the reconstruction of, specifically, Plato's philosophy. Similarly, Moraux (1973) 442 rejects the application of the terms syncretism and eclecticism in connection with the philosophical project of (Arius?) Didymus, which is in important respects similar to that of Antiochus. Eclecticism as an explicit marker of ancient philosophical identity postdates Antiochus and appears for the first time with the Alexandrian philosopher Potamo in the first century CE. For an analysis of Potamo's 'eclectic' stance, see Hatzimichali (2011) 175–78.

alternatives to Stoic theses; thus the adoption of Stoic material in this case serves the defence of the Academic tradition and not the creation of a composite system.

Even if the attribution of eclecticism was in the course of the twentieth century abandoned, the majority of recent scholars have opted for the understanding of Antiochus' thought in terms of a synthesis of views, suggesting a combination of heteroclite elements. Thus Dillon characterises it an 'amalgam of Stoicism and Platonism',[39] Barnes in his seminal article on Antiochus calls him a 'syncretist'[40] and Annas talks, with relation to Antiochus, about a 'hybrid theory, drawing on several sources'.[41] While, such characterisations help us to keep an open eye with regard to the way Antiochus relates to a wide variety of sources, it should not lead us to a dismissal of his philosophical project. A syncretistic viewpoint may have a positive or a negative ring to it; in the former case it is, as Inwood notes, 'philosophically respectable and intellectually defensible',[42] but it may also suggest an opportunistic, incoherent or even distorting merging of ideas.

The present study aims at showing that Antiochus' attempt to reconstruct the ethical views of the Old Academy, in Piso's so-called Peripatetic account at *On Ends* 5, does not result in an arbitrary collection of ancient views, nor does it distort the old tradition by imposing on it foreign terms of analysis—other than merely terminological ones. It will rather transpire from the discussion that shall ensue that the Antiochean account in ethics demonstrates a careful attempt to update the old material in the light of contemporary (Hellenistic) debates.[43] Thus, the choice of a Stoic terminology and a Stoic agenda will be shown to serve the

---

[39] Dillon (1977) 77.
[40] Barnes (1989) 79; 87. Cf. Sedley's (2012a) 103 references to Antiochus' 'syncretistic agenda' in the domain of epistemology (which he takes, however, to have been mitigated in his later phase recorded in Varro's account in the *Academic Books*) and Inwood (2012) 218.
[41] Annas (1993) 180. Cf. Annas and Woolf (2001) ix.   [42] Inwood (2012) 218.
[43] See e.g. Annas and Woolf (2001) xx: 'Antiochus produced an ethical theory which restated Aristotle's ethics in the terms of contemporary debate, and so produced an updated version.' See also Inwood (2012), who in his discussion of Antiochean physics talks about a 'creative reappropriation of the tradition' on Antiochus' part. In the case of Antiochean ethics, such an approach is sketched in Inwood (2014) 67–72.

Antiochean credo that the 'old authorities' provide *alternative* positions to the ones offered by the Stoa. This seems to be indicative of a period when Antiochus read the ancient tradition *in its own right* but still in close juxtaposition to the Stoic tradition.[44]

Another line pursued in the study shall be that Antiochus' reconstruction of Old Academic ethics contains hitherto neglected *dominant* elements of Peripatetic origin, which seem to stem from Aristotelian/Peripatetic treatises on natural science but also from the ethical treatises of this tradition. Finally, it will be suggested that Antiochus' thesis of the unity of the Academy and the Peripatos allows him occasionally to supplement his Aristotelian/Peripatetic account in ethics with Platonic elements. The latter will be shown to amount primarily to ideas ascribed to the character Socrates in the aporetic Platonic dialogues. From the related discussion of all these different strands of thought in Piso's account, it will (hopefully) transpire that the latter offers novel and, most importantly, philosophically interesting readings of the ethics of the old tradition, and especially of Aristotle and the Peripatos.

---

[44] For a developmental hypothesis with regard to Antiochus' philosophical production, see Sedley (2012a) 103, who highlights the distinctive, more historically sensitive, approach adopted in Varro's account in the *Academic Books*. The line adopted in Piso's account in *On Ends* 5 may be indicative of yet another, intermediate stage in Antiochus' approach towards the old tradition.

PART I

ANTIOCHUS IN ROME AND OLD ACADEMIC HISTORY OF PHILOSOPHY

ANTIOCHUS IN ROME

The involvement of Athens in the First Mithridatic War (89–84 BCE) and the ensuing siege of the city by Sulla in 86 BCE brought about the end of a centuries-long continuity of philosophical institutions in Athens. This initiated a process of decentralisation of philosophical activity from its traditional headquarters to a new Roman context.[1] In many cases, this process was accompanied by the migration of philosophers to the new centres of political power. Greek-speaking philosophers, such as Diodotus the Stoic, Phaedrus the Epicurean, Staseas of Naples and, the best known due to the survival of his works, the Epicurean Philodemus, were active in Italy in the first half of the first century BCE, assuming new roles as educators and advisors to Roman patrons.[2] Philo of Larissa, the last head of the Platonic Academy and teacher of Antiochus, had already fled from Athens to Rome in 88 BCE, and his lectures in Rome at this time were attended by the young Cicero.

Antiochus of Ascalon followed this trend and sought to assume a new role in the political context which followed the Roman conquest of Athens. His association with two powerful Romans, the general Lucius Licinius Lucullus and Cicero,[3]

---

[1] This development is highlighted and sketched in Sedley (2003).

[2] The creation of a Greek-speaking intellectual diaspora in the Roman world was well under way in the middle of the second century BCE, when intellectuals like Polybius and Panaetius were commissioned as advisors to members of the Roman political élite. For Panaetius' association with Scipio Africanus Aemilianus, see Panaetius *Fr.* 14 Van Straaten. Another intellectual associated with Scipio the Younger is Clitomachus who also dedicated books to L. Censorinus in 149 BCE; see Momigliano (1975) 5.

[3] Varro was another influential Roman who belonged to Antiochus' circle; see Augustine *City of God* 19.3; cf. Plutarch *Life of Lucullus* 42 and *Life of Brutus* 2.2. For Antiochus' influence on Varro's philosophical development, see Blank (2012). Significant of the authority that the circle of Antiochus enjoyed, Cicero reported that in 51 BCE he visited Antiochus' brother Aristus (supposedly his successor in the Academy and teacher of M. Brutus), writing that Aristus was the most interesting voice of philosophy at Athens; see *Letters to Atticus* 5.10.5: *philosophia sursum deorsum. si quid est, est in Aristo, apud quem eram.* For Brutus' relation to Antiochus, see Lévy (2012).

who preserves in his philosophical dialogues from 45 BCE the most important testimonies of Antiochus' philosophical activity, attests Antiochus' new role as a Greek-speaking intellectual in Rome and highlights the way in which the resurrection of the philosophy of the 'ancients' (advertised by Antiochus' frequent references to the Old Academy) was crucially supported by Roman interest in the appropriation of the Greek philosophical heritage.

Around the time of the Roman conquest of Athens, Antiochus fled from the city and entered the service of the Roman general Lucius Licinius Lucullus, an associate of Sulla, who had played an important role in the military victories that led Rome to the conquest of the Eastern Mediterranean in the first century BCE. Antiochus became Lucullus' philosophical advisor[4] and died while at his service.[5] It seems that the displacement of both Philo and Antiochus from the Athenian philosophical headquarters encouraged the adoption of radical new theses. According to the testimony of Cicero, Antiochus, while in the service of Lucullus at Alexandria in 87/6 BCE, got hold of two books of Philo, written when the latter was already in Rome.[6] In his 'Roman books' Philo seems to have advanced some novel epistemological positions, where he defended the view that reality is knowable, while rejecting the (Stoic) criterion of infallibility as a necessary

---

[4] See Antiochus T6a = Plutarch *Life of Lucullus* 42.3: τὸν Ἀσκαλωνίτην Ἀντίοχον, ὃν πάσῃ σπουδῇ ποιησάμενος φίλον ὁ Λεύκολλος καὶ συμβιωτήν; cf. Antiochus T6b = Aelian, *Historical Miscellany* 12.25. Antiochus and Lucullus met most probably in Greece after Sulla's siege, see Glucker (1978) 21. According to Glucker (1978) 27 the approach of the two was based on predominantly political preoccupations: 'Lucullus' choice of Antiochus (...) was made for reasons more immediately relevant to his political and military activities at the time.' On the wider political benefits of acquiring a Greek-speaking philosopher–advisor for Roman statesmen operating in the Hellenistic East, see *ibid.* 24–27. Cf. Rawson (1985) 81. On the symbolic capital associated with the pursuit of philosophical studies among the late-republican Roman élite, see Crawford (1978).

[5] According to the testimony of Cicero in *Lucullus* 61, Antiochus died in the company of Lucullus during a campaign in Syria. The evidence from Antiochus T3 = Philodemus *History of the Academy* (*PHerc.* 1021) c. xxxiv.35–43 also states that Antiochus spent most of his life in Rome and the eastern provinces in the service of generals and died in Mesopotamia following Lucullus. For a recent analysis of all the biographical evidence related to Antiochus, see Hatzimichali (2012).

[6] *Lucullus* 11: *et quidem isti libri duo Philonis, de quibus heri dictum a Catulo est, tum erant allati Alexandriam tumque primum in Antiochi manus venerant.*

requirement of knowledge.[7] Antiochus reacted vehemently against his former teacher by writing a polemical work entitled *Sosus*; there, he must have offered a defence of Stoic epistemology against Academic scepticism, expressing openly his 'dogmatic' turn and his defection from the (New) Academy.[8]

After his break with Philo, Antiochus appears as the representative of the Old Academy, a denomination referring collectively to the Platonic Academy (before Arcesilaus took over the headship of the school) and the Peripatos.[9] Thus, at the prologue of *On Ends* 5 (with the dramatic date of 79 BCE), Antiochus appears giving lectures at the Roman gymnasium of the city and teaching the views of the old tradition of the Academy and the Peripatos.[10] The prologue presents Antiochus as the only representative of ancient philosophical wisdom in Athens[11] and attests the

---

[7] The most important evidence for Philo's views is found in Sextus Empiricus *Outlines of Pyrrhonism* 1.235: Οἱ δὲ περὶ Φίλωνά φασιν ὅσον μὲν ἐπὶ τῷ Στωικῷ κριτηρίῳ, τουτέστι τῇ καταληπτικῇ φαντασίᾳ, ἀκατάληπτα εἶναι τὰ πράγματα, ὅσον δὲ ἐπὶ τῇ φύσει τῶν πραγμάτων αὐτῶν, καταληπτά. For an extensive discussion of Philo's epistemological views, see Brittain (2001) 129–168; cf. Sedley (2012a) 85 for an alternative reading of the epistemological view ascribed to Philo.

[8] *Lucullus* 12: *nec se tenuit quin contra suum doctorem librum etiam ederet, qui Sosus inscribitur.* For the reaction of Antiochus to Philo's claims, see *Lucullus* 18: *Philo autem dum nova quaedam commovet, quod ea sustinere vix poterat quae contra Academicorum pertinaciam dicebantur, et aperte mentitur ut est reprehensus a patre Catulo, et ut docuit Antiochus in id ipsum se induit quod timebat.* The *Sosus* may have been the source for the Antiochean account in the *Lucullus*. For evidence of an eminent Stoic called Sosus, see Antiochus *T4b* = Stephanus of Byzantium, *Ethnica* p.132.3 Meineke. For Antiochus' break with Philo and his endorsement of Stoic positions, see Antiochus *T1* = Numenius *Fr.* 8 Leemans/*Fr.* 28 des Places: Φίλωνος δὲ γίνεται ἀκουστὴς Ἀντίοχος, ἑτέρας ἄρξας Ἀκαδημίας. Μνησάρχῳ γοῦν τῷ Στωικῷ σχολάσας ἐναντία Φίλωνι τῷ καθηγητῇ ἐφρόνησε μυρία τε ξένα προσῆψε τῇ Ἀκαδημίᾳ. According to Glucker (1978) 20 Antiochus' defection from Philo must have taken place already before the Alexandrian episode 'some time in the nineties of the first century BC'. For an alternative view about the dating of Antiochus' secession, see Polito (2012) 32–34.

[9] It is not clear whether Antiochus officially founded a school with the denomination Old Academy or whether he merely professed to be recovering in his lectures and writings the teaching of the old tradition. Polito (2012) 38 seems right in saying that what is meant by that name is the 'philosophical outlook' of the faction led by Antiochus rather than an official Old Academic institution.

[10] *On Ends* 5.1 Evidence that Cicero visited Antiochus' lectures in Athens is provided in Antiochus *T5a–5c* and in *Brutus* 315.

[11] Suggestive on this point is Cicero's description in the prologue of *On Ends* 5 of the deserted Platonic Academy. Cicero presents himself as the only follower of Carneades, alluding to the way he revives the Academic sceptic method of philosophising through his dialogues. *On the Nature of the Gods* 1.6 also suggests that the New Academy was already regarded as an obsolete philosophical option at the time of the writing of the

reputation that he had assumed in the first century BCE as a mediator of ancient philosophical wisdom in Rome.

Antiochus' association with Lucullus highlights the Roman context within which his project of 'recovery' of the ancient Greek Academic tradition took place. Plutarch's portrait of Lucullus suggests that the Roman general held pretensions to Greek wisdom[12] and belonged to a circle of leading Romans who defended the value of Greek *paideia*. Plutarch refers especially to Lucullus' library, which was housed in his hereditary estate in Tusculum and contained a valuable collection of books. Scholarly research on the rich collection was encouraged by Lucullus, whose mansion became, according to Plutarch's testimony, 'a home and prytaneium' for Greek intellectuals who arrived at Rome;[13] among them one may count the grammarian Tyrannion, who, according to the testimony of both Plutarch and Strabo, worked on the school treatises of Aristotle and Theophrastus, after the treatises were on Roman soil, but was also associated with Cicero and the arrangement of his library at Tusculum.[14]

Cicero alludes to Lucullus' library complex in the prologue to *On Ends* 3 (7–10); the dialogue features Cicero going to the mansion of Lucullus in his search for some Aristotelian treatises (*commentarii*) and finding there Cato the Younger studying the

---

dialogue (and after the death of Philo), in contrast to the Old Academy of Antiochus. Cf. *ibid.* 1.11.

[12] According to the testimony of Plutarch, Lucullus by associating himself with Antiochus opposed Cicero, who was Philo's student and held opposing views on key philosophical issues, such as the possibility of secure knowledge, see Plutarch *Life of Lucullus* 42: ὃν (sc. Ἀντίοχον) πάσῃ σπουδῇ ποιησάμενος φίλον ὁ Λούκουλλος καὶ συμβιωτὴν ἀντετάττετο τοῖς Φίλωνος ἀκροαταῖς, ὧν καὶ Κικέρων ἦν.

[13] Plutarch *Life of Lucullus* 42.1–3: σπουδῆς δ' ἄξια καὶ λόγου τὰ περὶ τὴν τῶν βιβλίων κατασκευήν. καὶ γὰρ πολλὰ καὶ γεγραμμένα καλῶς συνῆγεν, ἥ τε χρῆσις ἦν φιλοτιμοτέρα τῆς κτήσεως, ἀνειμένων πᾶσι τῶν βιβλιοθηκῶν, καὶ τῶν περὶ αὐτὰς περιπάτων καὶ σχολαστηρίων ἀκωλύτως ὑποδεχομένων τοὺς Ἕλληνας, ὥσπερ εἰς Μουσῶν τι καταγώγιον ἐκεῖσε φοιτῶντας καὶ συνδιημερεύοντας ἀλλήλοις, ἀπὸ τῶν ἄλλων χρειῶν ἀσμένως ἀποτρέχοντας. (...) καὶ ὅλως ἑστία καὶ πρυτανεῖον Ἑλληνικὸν ὁ οἶκος ἦν αὐτοῦ τοῖς ἀφικνουμένοις εἰς τὴν Ῥώμην. Plutarch refers to Lucullus' admiration for the grammarian Tyrannion at *Life of Lucullus* 19.7. On Lucullus' library see also Rawson (1985) 40.

[14] Cicero possessed a rich library, whose books were at some point arranged by the grammarian Tyrannion; see *Letters to Atticus* 4.4a.1: *offendes dissignationem Tyrannionis mirificam librorum meorum, quorum reliquiae multo meliores sunt quam putaram*. See also Rawson (1985) 41.

Stoics.[15] The availability of Aristotelian treatises in Lucullus' estate suggests that it was a repository of material coming from Greece, and perhaps preserved part of the booty that Sulla brought from Athens; according to the 'official' story that has been preserved in Strabo and Plutarch, among this booty were also the school treatises of the Peripatos.[16] One may assume that through his association with Lucullus, Antiochus also gained access to his library and was engaged into the collection and interpretation of the texts that were available there. It is suggestive that Piso's account in *On Ends*, which explicitly transmits the Antiochean reconstruction of Old Academic, and in particular Peripatetic ethics, starts by giving a catalogue of some of the 'esoteric' works of the Peripatos, according to the threefold division of physics, ethics and dialectic (5.9–11).[17] This signals that Antiochus' doxographical account which occupies the bulk of *On Ends* 5 is based on authentic material and 'first hand' contact with the original treatises of the Old Academy. This again links Antiochus with the early phase of resurrection of interest in the school treatises of the Peripatos in Rome,[18] suggesting that his project of the Old Academy was supported by the strong

---

[15] See *On Ends* 3.7: *nam in Tusculano cum essem vellemque e bibliotheca pueri Luculli quibusdam libris uti, veni in eius villam ut eos ipse, ut solebam, depromerem. Quo cum venissem, M. Catonem, quem ibi esse nescieram, vidi in bibliotheca sedentem, multis circumfusum Stoicorum libris* and *ibid.* 3.10: (Cicero speaking:) '*Commentarios quosdam*' inquam '*Aristotelios, quos hic sciebam esse, veni ut auferrem, quos legerem dum essem otiosus.*' *Commentarii* is a word used to characterise the 'school treatises' of the Peripatos at *On Ends* 5.12.

[16] The 'official' story based on the evidence of both Strabo and Plutarch suggests that after the conquest of Athens, Sulla confiscated Apellicon's library, which contained the school treatises of both Aristotle and Theophrastus, and brought it as booty to Rome, see Strabo *Geography* 13.1.54: εὐθὺς γὰρ μετὰ τὴν Ἀπελλικῶντος τελευτὴν Σύλλας ἦρε τὴν Ἀπελλικῶντος βιβλιοθήκην ὁ τὰς Ἀθήνας ἑλών, δεῦρο δὲ κομισθεῖσαν Τυραννίων τε ὁ γραμματικὸς διεχειρίσατο φιλαριστοτέλης ὤν. Cf. Plutarch *Life of Sulla* 26: ἀναχθεὶς δὲ πάσαις ταῖς ναυσὶν ἐξ Ἐφέσου τριταῖος ἐν Πειραιεῖ καθωρμίσθη καὶ μυηθεὶς ἐξεῖλεν ἑαυτῷ τὴν Ἀπελλικῶνος τοῦ Τηΐου βιβλιοθήκην, ἐν ᾗ τὰ πλεῖστα τῶν Ἀριστοτέλους καὶ Θεοφράστου βιβλίων ἦν, οὔπω τότε σαφῶς γνωριζόμενα τοῖς πολλοῖς. Λέγεται δὲ κομισθείσης αὐτῆς εἰς Ῥώμην Τυραννίωνα τὸν γραμματικὸν ἐνσκευάσασθαι τὰ πολλά. The historical claim of Strabo's story receives important new corroboration in Primavesi (2007).

[17] This catalogue is discussed in Chapter 2, *infra*.

[18] This interest seems to have culminated in a new 'edition' of the Peripatetic treatises by Andronicus; since there is no evidence of the activity of Andronicus in Cicero, we may assume that the editorial activity took place in the last half of the first century BCE. For

Roman interest in the collection and study of Greek philosophical treatises and in the recovery of the 'ancient' wisdom that they contained.[19]

Antiochus in Cicero

Cicero belonged to the members of the Roman elite in the late Republican period who most powerfully defended the importance of introducing Greek philosophy to the Roman audience. Being himself a student of philosophy under various teachers both in Greece and Rome, he became particularly associated with the Academy and Academic scepticism under Philo of Larissa.[20] It was only later in his life, and after experiencing various disappointments with politics, that Cicero turned to the writing of philosophical dialogues, introducing thereby a new genre to Latin literature. The philosophical works written in the period 46–44 BCE, where we find an abundance of Antiochean material, had the ambitious aim of rendering into the Latin language technical terminology and modes of argumentation first introduced by the Greeks. The aim was not just a linguistic appropriation of the Greek philosophical modes of expression into Latin[21] but also

---

a recent discussion of Andronicus' engagement with the Aristotelian corpus, see Hatzimichali (2013) 19–23.

[19] This is matched by Roman interest in ancestral practice (*mos maiorum*) and by a movement of antiquarianism in the first century BCE, see Wallace-Hadrill (2008) 213–58.

[20] See *Academic Books* 13. See also evidence at *Lucullus* 115 for Cicero's association with the Stoic Diodotus and *Letters to Friends* 13.1.2 for his Epicurean teacher Phaedrus. At *On Ends* 5.1 Cicero is depicted at Athens attending the lectures of Antiochus. At *Brutus* 306, Cicero states that he 'devoted himself entirely' to the teachings of Philo of Larissa with which he became acquainted when the latter visited Rome in 88 BCE.

[21] Suggestive in this respect are Atticus' remarks at *On Ends* 5.96, who praises Piso for expressing the Old Academic views in Latin in appropriate words and 'with no less clearness than the doctrines have in Greek': *quae enim dici Latine posse non arbitrabar, ea dicta sunt a te verbis aptis nec minus plane quam dicuntur a Graecis.* Cf. similar remarks of Atticus at *Academic Books* 14. A preoccupation with the right translation of 'technical' philosophical vocabulary from Greek into Latin is ubiquitous in Cicero's philosophical dialogues; see e.g. Varro's remarks in *Academic Books* 25 on the translation of Greek termini pertaining to physics and Cicero's remarks at *On Ends* 3.15 on the translation of ethical termini. For Cicero's practice as a translator of philosophy from the Greek, see also Powell (1995).

the attempt to show that the Romans could excel in a characteristically Greek activity.[22]

There are various aspects of the Ciceronian dialogues which attest an attempt at 'Romanisation' of the genre of philosophical discourse:[23] The philosophical views of the dominant Greek schools of philosophy are put, for instance, into the mouth of prominent Roman politicians.[24] Thus, the Roman general Lucullus presents the Antiochean epistemological views in the homonymous dialogue, whereas Marcus Porcius Cato, who committed suicide after being defeated by Caesar at the battle of Thapsus in 46 BCE, is chosen as the spokesperson for the Stoic ethical account in *On Ends* 3. Furthermore, the setting of the dialogues is meant to place philosophical dialectic in a framework which on the one hand strongly evokes a Greek context but on the other hand is familiar to the elite Roman audience: thus Cicero's dialogues almost always take place in country villas, places dedicated to leisure and retreat away from the laborious political and military arena.[25] It is suggestive that Cicero's own villa at Tusculum had two *gymnasia*, the 'Academy' and the 'Lyceum', where many of the philosophical dialogues that he stages take place.[26] The suggestive choice of these names by Cicero stands for the transposition of the Greek philosophical schools (where the views that Cicero discusses were debated) to the private

---

[22] Especially telling with regard to this aspect of Cicero's philosophical project are the prefaces at *Tusculan Disputations* 1.1, *On Ends* 1.1–10 and *On Appropriate Actions* 1. 1–3. Cf. *Lucullus* 6 for the glory adduced through excel in philosophy. See also how at *On Ends* 5.8 Piso takes great pride in talking philosophy as a Roman in the Academy: *dat enim id nobis solitudo, quod si qui deus diceret, numquam putarem me in Academia tamquam philosophum disputaturum.*

[23] 'Romanisation' is a term that is applied mostly to material culture; as a counterpart to 'Hellenisation' it may be understood as the active appropriation of Hellenic culture, in this case of the intellectual tradition of philosophy, on the part of the Romans. For a nuanced discussion of the reciprocating form of cultural appropriation during the Roman contact with Greek modes of thinking, see Wallace-Hadrill (2008) 9ff.

[24] Cf. Gildenhard (2007) 31: 'Cicero's marginalization of Greek intellectuals is a prerequisite for his intellectual empowerment of Roman *nobiles*.'

[25] E.g., the discussion in the *Academic Books* is set in Hortensius' villa, see *Academic Books* 9. The discussion in the first book of *On Ends* takes place at Cicero's country house at Cumae.

[26] See e.g. *Tusculan Disputations* 2.9; *ibid.* 3.7.

setting of a Roman villa, where such views were now discussed by Roman noblemen during their period of *otium*.[27]

The Roman appropriation of Greek philosophical discourse serves Cicero's idea that philosophy is an important educational tool for the Romans.[28] The prologue to *On Ends* 5, which contains Antiochus' 'Peripatetic' ethical account, offers a good example of the way Cicero in his dialogues presented philosophy as a worthy object of pursuit by his contemporary noblemen. Away from the usual setting of other Ciceronian philosophical works, at the beginning of the book we are transferred in time and place to the Athens of 79 BCE (as against 52 BCE in the rest of the work).[29] Cicero and his companions are depicted in a nostalgic mood, associating places in Athens with great figures of the past. Cicero himself, following his philosophic inclinations, remembers Carneades,[30] whereas Piso shows his preference for the old tradition of the Academy by calling to mind Plato and the scholarchs who succeeded him.[31] The nostalgic mood is suggestive of a return to old authority, a motif most intimately connected with Antiochus' Old Academy. The reason for the debate, cast through the personae of Cicero and Piso as a rivalry between Carneades and the Old Academy of Antiochus, is the education of Cicero's young cousin, Lucius.[32] The latter is being trained to become a politician, and like many members of the Roman elite of his time he is on an educational trip to Greece, before returning to Rome to take up public office. Piso urges the young Lucius to engage with the philosophy of Antiochus, i.e. that of the

---

[27] For the evocations connected to the architectural form of the *gymnasium* in Cicero, cf. Wallace-Hadrill (2008) 171–73.

[28] This is explicitly referred to as one of Cicero's main reasons for engaging in philosophy at *Academic Books* 11: *aut etiam ad nostros cives erudiendos nihil utilius*. Cf. *On Ends* 1.10. This aspect of Cicero's philosophical production is especially underlined in Gildenhard (2007) 30–34.

[29] *On Ends* 5 is the only surviving philosophical dialogue of Cicero that takes place on Greek soil. The only other case of a Greek setting in Cicero is probably the incomplete *Timaeus*, whose prologue is set in Ephesus.

[30] *On Ends* 5.4: *etsi multa in omni parte Athenarum sunt in ipsis locis indicia summorum virorum, tamen ego illa moveor exhedra. Modo enim fuit Carneadis.*

[31] *On Ends* 5.2: *venit enim mihi Platonis in mentem, quem accepimus primum hic disputare solitum; cuius etiam illi hortuli propinqui non memoriam solum mihi adferunt sed ipsum videntur in conspectu meo ponere. Hic Speusippus, hic Xenocrates, hic eius auditor Polemo, cuius illa ipsa sessio fuit quam videmus.*

[32] See *On Ends* 5.6.

'ancients', since their writings contain all liberal teaching (*doctrina liberalis*), which is especially important for a career in the political sphere.[33] Consequently, the account of Piso serves not only as an introduction to Antiochean, that is in this case Aristotelian/Peripatetic, ethical doctrine, but also as an exhortation to philosophy in general, addressed to a young man who is about to enter the public sphere. The very dramatic framework of the dialogue serves in this case to show that philosophy may provide the ideal intellectual training for Roman youth.

Ciceronian interventions in the Greek philosophical material are not restricted to the level of the *personae* and the setting against which the dialogue takes place, but extend to the presentation of the philosophical ideas which constitute the main topic of the dialogues. Thus, Cicero supplements the philosophical material with examples chosen either from literary works or from Roman history. In the former case, the examples are drawn from works adapted into Latin from Greek originals, suggesting a similar process of 'Romanisation' in the field of poetry, as the one undertaken by Cicero himself in the field of philosophy.[34] For example, at *On Ends* 5.28, Cicero uses a quotation attributed to the character Menedemus from Terence's Latin translation of Menander's comedy, the 'Self-Tormentor' (in Greek *Heautontimoroumenos*), in order to show that all actions are ultimately based on self-love. Again, in Piso's account, a quotation from Accius' Latin version of Sophocles' *Philoctetes* serves the same point by showing that fear of death is

---

[33] *On Ends* 5.7: *ad eos igitur converte te, quaeso. Ex eorum enim scriptis et institutis cum omnis doctrina liberalis, omnis historia, omnis sermo elegans sumi potest, tum varietas est tanta artium ut nemo sine eo instrumento ad ullam rem inlustriorem satis ornatus possit accedere. Ab his oratores, ab his imperatores ac rerum publicarum principes exstiterunt. Ut ad minora veniam, mathematici poëtae musici medici denique ex hac tamquam omnium artificum officina profecti sunt.* The prioritisation of a political career over a 'scientific' one in the above passage suggests that Cicero has an audience of Roman noblemen in mind. This order is reversed in Piso's exposition, which expresses the Old Academic views on the best *bios*, in *ibid.* 5.58. On the educational value of the Old Academy see also *ibid.* 5.74: *ita relinquitur sola haec disciplina digna studiosis ingenuarum artium, digna eruditis, digna claris viris, digna principibus, digna regibus.*

[34] For a parallelism of Cicero's activity in philosophy with that of the Latin poets Ennius, Pacuvius and Accius, see *Academic Books* 10: *quid enim causae est cur poetas Latinos Graecis litteris eruditi legant, philosophos non legant? an quia delectat Ennius Pacuvius Accius multi alii, qui non verba sed vim Graecorum expresserunt poetarum – quanto magis philosophi delectabunt, si ut illi Aeschylum Sophoclem Euripidem sic hi Platonem imitentur Aristotelem Theophrastum.* Cf. *On Ends* 1.5.

27

universal and, thus, yet another proof of the fundamental character of love for oneself, which is itself an outcome of natural appropriation.[35] At times, Cicero supplements Greek philosophical material with his own translations, as in the case of a passage from the *Odyssey* at *On Ends* 5.49, which, interpreted in an allegorical way, is meant to support the view that intellectual pursuits are inherently valuable.[36] The *Tusculan Disputations* offers the most ample examples of such Ciceronian interventions, quoting more translations from both Greek poetry and prose than any other of Cicero's works.[37]

In other cases, Cicero uses examples from Roman history in order to show that a philosophical idea is already 'alive' in the attitude and behaviour of the Roman people. A suggestive case study for this is offered at *On Ends* 5.64, where Cicero counters the Greek superiority in the excellence of the intellectual virtues (shown at *ibid.* 5.50 by such examples as Pythagoras, Plato and Democritus) with Roman superiority in the moral domain.[38] Thus, Cicero uses such examples as Lucretia, who decided to commit suicide in order to expiate the shame inflicted on her as a result of rape, or the two consuls Gaius Fabricius Luscinus and Quintus Aemilius Papius, who revealed to their foe, the Greek king Pyrrhus, the plans of a traitor to poison him, in order to show that Roman history provides ample examples which show that morality (*honestas*) is inherently choice worthy, independently of advantage.[39] This is matched by Cicero's remarks at the beginning

---

[35] *On Ends* 5.32.

[36] *o decus Argolicum, quin puppim flectis, Ulixes,/ Auribus ut nostros possis agnoscere cantus!/ Nam nemo haec umquam est transvectus caerula cursu,/ Quin prius adstiterit vocum dulcedine captus,/ Post variis avido satiatus pectore musis/Doctior ad patrias lapsus pervenerit oras./ Nos grave certamen belli clademque tenemus,/ Graecia quam Troiae divino numine vexit,/ Omniaque e latis rerum vestigia terris.* The translation is from Homer's *Odyssey* 12.184–91.

[37] See Schofield (2013) 82.

[38] Note the emphasis placed at *On Ends* 5.64 on the fact that the Romans provide not only fictional examples of moral behaviour but 'living' examples from their own history: *talibus exemplis non fictae solum fabulae, verum etiam historiae refertae sunt, et quidem maxime nostrae.*

[39] *Ibid.* 5.64: *nostri consules regem inimicissimum moenibus iam appropinquantem monuerunt a veneno ut caveret, nostra in re publica [Lucretia] et quae per vim oblatum stuprum voluntaria morte lueret inventa est et qui interficeret filiam ne stupraretur. Quae quidem omnia et innumerabilia praeterea quis est quin intellegat et eos qui fecerint dignitatis splendore ductos immemores fuisse utilitatum suarum nosque, cum ea laudemus, nulla alia re nisi honestate duci?* Additional examples of the devotion of

of the *Tusculan Disputations* which purport to show that Latin *mores* are superior to Greek ways of behaviour.[40] This seems to suggest that Romans are the most suitable audience for all the ethical theories, including that of the Old Academy, underlining the importance of virtue (the *honestum*) for the happy life.

Bringing the philosophical views expressed nearer to 'collective' Roman experience is meant to serve the idea that philosophy is an important vehicle of liberal education, worthy of a Roman nobleman. Far from being incompatible with a political career, philosophy appears to supplement it in a way that fosters the kind of intellectual attitude which is necessary to serve the Roman republic. Its service, however, is not shown by practical results but by providing 'cultivation of the mind' (*cultura animi*)[41] and fostering the qualities that befit an (ideal) human being; this set of qualities is conveyed in Cicero by the newly emerging concept of *humanitas*.[42] Cicero is shown here to follow Greek ideas about the intrinsic value of intellectual pursuits[43] and to integrate them into a distinctive educational and behavioural ideal that corresponds to his time.

The argument that philosophy, as the 'liberal pursuit' *par excellence*, is worthwhile in its own right as a tool of education is supplemented by another line of reasoning which is found in the prologues of Cicero's philosophical dialogues. According to this line, philosophy provides an ideal alternative to someone who is deprived of political activity but still seeks an 'honourable' occupation. In this case philosophy acts as therapy (*medicina*) or, as he puts it at *On Ends* 5.53, as a 'mitigation of wretchedness' (*levamentum miseriarum*).[44] An example used to illustrate this in the

leading Roman men to *honestas* are provided at *ibid.* 5.70 (with references to Scipio Africanus and Scipio Aemilianus).

[40] Cf. Wallace-Hadrill (2008) 34.

[41] See e.g. *Tusculan Disputations* 2.13; *On Ends* 5.54.

[42] For a discussion of the concept as a Roman alternative to the Greek *paideia*, see Wallace-Hadrill (2008) 34–35.

[43] Such ideas on the intrinsic value of intellectual pursuits are put into the mouth of Piso at *On Ends* 5.48–58. Cicero may have used similar arguments in his defence of philosophy in the lost *Hortensius*.

[44] *On Ends* 5.53: *nos autem non solum beatae vitae istam esse oblectationem videmus sed etiam levamentum miseriarum; itaque multi cum in potestate essent hostium aut tyrannorum, multi in custodia, multi in exsilio dolorem suum doctrinae studiis levaverunt.* Cf. *Academic Books* 1.11: *nunc vero et fortunae gravissimo percussus vulnere et*

29

above passage is Demetrius of Phaleron, who when in exile at the court of King Ptolemy at Alexandria devoted himself to studies which did not have any practical use but were merely 'food for the kind of attitude which befits a human being' (*humanitatis cibus*).[45] Demetrius appears in some Ciceronian passages as the ideal combination of statesman and intellectual, an ideal which Cicero wished to vindicate for himself. Thus, in his prologues to the philosophical dialogues Cicero's image of a great statesman who at one point saved the republic from disaster is supplemented by the image of the writer who when cut off from the political arena turned to another noble activity, that of philosophy. This is deemed by Cicero an alternative contribution to the republic and its values.[46]

Although Cicero places Greek philosophy in a particularly Roman context, and supplements his material with examples as he sees fit, he aspires to offer an accurate view of the Greek philosophical ideas that he presents in his dialogues. Cicero's reliability as a source for the philosophical theories that he conveys, including that of the Old Academy, seems to be corroborated by his own philosophical identity. His aim is, following the line of the New Academy, to offer with his dialogues the greatest 'approximation to truth' (*veri simile*). This may be done through the juxtaposition of the most important opposing viewpoints on a particular subject of inquiry. For these purposes, Cicero creates a genre which exemplifies in writing the dialectical practice of the New Academy;[47] there, the views of the most important philosophical schools are presented and then critically scrutinised (from

---

administratione rei publicae liberatus doloris medicinam a philosophia peto et otii oblectationem hanc honestissimam iudico.

[45] *On Ends* 5.54: *princeps huius civitatis Phalereus Demetrius, cum patria pulsus esset iniuria, ad Ptolomaeum se regem Alexandream contulit. Qui cum in hac ipsa philosophia ad quam te hortamur excelleret Theophrastique esset auditor, multa praeclara in illo calamitoso otio scripsit, non ad usum aliquem suum, quo erat orbatus, sed animi cultus ille erat ei quasi quidam humanitatis cibus.*

[46] On writing philosophy as an alternative contribution to the republic, see especially *On Divination* 2.1.

[47] For the genre of the Ciceronian philosophical dialogue, see Schofield (2008). The characterisation of the 'dialogue treatise' fits best the dialogue *On Ends. Tusculan Disputations* uses another type of 'Socratic' discourse, that of a 'lecture' (*schola*) and Cicero's last work *On Appropriate Actions* is not a dialogue at all but a continuous exposition with Cicero's son Marcus as the addressee.

the viewpoint of an opposed school).[48] In this process, Cicero is clear in separating exposition of the theory from critical engagement with that theory. Critical engagement (often undertaken by the character Cicero himself) may contain elements of polemic and distort some of the premises of the particular school which is under attack (most often from the viewpoint of a competing school).[49] Since, however, the aim of Cicero's works is not to advocate a particular theory as better than others, the critical engagement itself may contribute to the approximation of truth only if accompanied by an accurate exposition of the theory which is under attack.[50] In this way the reader is able to view a topic from two different perspectives and exercise his judging faculty in evaluating the competing arguments. This is in line with the description that Cicero gives of his own philosophical activity in *On Ends* 1.6: he preserves (*tueri*) the views of the various philosophers, while imposing his own order of exposition (*scribendi ordinem*) with a view to the exercise of 'free judgement' (*iudicium*).[51]

---

[48] This reflects the method of *disputatio in utramque partem*, i.e. of 'arguing on both sides of a question', endorsed by Carneades and his followers as the best way to achieve approximation to truth. Schofield (2013) 79 highlights Cicero's indebtedness to Carneades for this 'comprehensive approach'.

[49] This is the case e.g. at *On Ends* 4, where Cicero adopts Old Academic views in order to combat Stoicism. See also the way Cicero from *On Ends* 5.76ff. subjects the Old Academic views on the *telos* to critical scrutiny.

[50] One of the most clear expressions of this Ciceronian practice is contained in a passage from *Letters to Atticus* 13.19.5, where Cicero comments on the way he took care to 'set out faithfully' (*diligenter a me expressa*) Varro's Old Academic position in the *Academic Books* and make it appear 'utterly convincing', despite it being against his own Academic sceptic position: *itaque ut legi tuas de Varrone, tamquam ἕρμαιον adripui. aptius esse nihil potuit ad id philosophiae genus quo ille maxime mihi delectari videtur eaeque partes ut non sim consecutus ut superior mea causa videatur. sunt enim vehementer πιθανὰ Antiochia; quae diligenter a me expressa acumen habent Antiochi, nitorem orationis nostrum, si modo is est aliquis in nobis.* See also Cicero's remarks prefacing the exposition of Epicurean ethics at *On Ends* 1.13, which separate search of truth from adversarial refutation: *verum enim invenire volumus, non tamquam adversarium aliquem convincere.*

[51] *si nos non interpretum fungimur munere, sed tuemur ea quae dicta sunt ab iis quos probamus eisque nostrum iudicium et nostrum scribendi ordinem adiungimus, quid habent cur Graeca anteponant iis quae et splendide dicta sint neque sint conversa de Graecis?* On the exercise of the free judgement of the audience (*iudicium audientium relinquere integrum ac liberum*) as the aim of (New) Academic practice, see especially *On Divination* 2.150.

The main philosophical ideas discussed in Cicero's dialogues stem from the major Hellenistic schools of Epicureanism and Stoicism; to them Cicero adds the Old Academy of Antiochus, which is granted in his dialogue *On Ends* equal importance to the two major Hellenistic philosophical schools. In particular, Cicero presents the Old Academy of Antiochus as offering an alternative to Stoicism, a theory which, due to its emphasis on the inherent value of virtue, was particularly attractive to Cicero.[52] Apart from the philosophical theses that he put forward in his reconstruction of the views of the Old Academy, the importance assigned to Antiochus in Cicero may well be linked to the fact that his teaching offered access to ancient philosophical wisdom, and especially to the 'original' treatises of the Academy and the Peripatos; even though these treatises were gaining major importance as capital of ancient wisdom, access to them, in terms of both content and linguistic style, remained difficult. Thus, a school which claimed to offer a systematic presentation of the alleged doctrines that these treatises represented could gain in importance. In the absence of a 'living' representative of the ancient views after the closure of the philosophical schools in Athens, Antiochus thus becomes in Cicero the main vehicle of transmission of Academic and Peripatetic philosophical wisdom, coming to supplement Cicero's own preoccupation with the old authorities, and especially with Plato.[53]

The resurgence of interest in the writings of the old philosophical tradition in the last decades of the Roman republic, major evidence of which is provided by the Antiochean passages in Cicero, is suggestive of a yet further development: the views of the representatives of the old tradition appear in them to have a value which commends their approval. This value is conveyed in Cicero by the use of the word *auctoritas*, which combines the notions of 'authorship' and 'authority'. The word bears also,

---

[52] For Cicero's own preference to an ethical system which acknowledges the primary importance of virtue, see e.g. *On Ends* 5.95 (which shows a preference for the Old Academic view of the *telos* on the condition that it is able to stand dialectical scrutiny with regard to its logical consistency).

[53] Evidence of Cicero's own preoccupation with Plato is the incomplete translation of the *Timaeus* as also various translations of Platonic passages in the *Tusculan Disputations* (1.53–54; 97–99, 5.35–36). For Cicero's preoccupation with Plato see also Long (1995).

particularly Roman, connotations of dignity and (in a legal context) trustworthy testimony, which must have resonated with Cicero's audience. It is suggestive that the Senate is invested with symbolic authority in the republican constitution;[54] although not bound by law to obey its decrees, it was expected that the magistrates would follow the advice of its senior members, as of a universally recognised pillar of the republican constitution.[55] The association of *auctoritas* on the political level with the aristocratic element of the republican constitution explains why denigrating remarks against philosophical schools which did not draw their origin from the Platonic line are cast at times in Cicero in particularly social terms; for example, in the first book of the *Tusculan Disputations* Cicero contrasts (old) Academics with 'plebeian' philosophers,[56] who lack the venerable pedigree of their Academic peers.

Finally, the example of ancestral practice (*mos maiorum*) is in Roman society invested with special authority offering reliable guidance for action, which could be trusted without the need to be critically scrutinised.[57] Reflecting the acknowledgment of the value of 'ancient ways', the investment of Antiochus with the *auctoritas* of the 'ancients' appears as an additional reason for a positive evaluation of his views in Cicero. Thus, Cicero in some cases transforms the Antiochean reliance on ancient wisdom into an argument from authority and exploits in his dialogues the rhetorical implications that the invocation of the 'ancients' has for his audience. This invocation serves, for example, the Antiochean purpose of downgrading the Stoic school in favour of a return to the study of the 'ancients': at *On Ends* 4.61 Cato is asked to change his allegiance from the Stoics to the school of Plato and

---

[54] See e.g. *On Laws* 3.28.
[55] However, the standard phrase *senatus auctoritas* denotes mostly decrees of the Senate which became invalidated (e.g. through tribunician veto), in contrast to the *senatus consultum*, an effective resolution which received approval by the appointed magistrate. For the development of the notion of *auctoritas* in the juridical and political fields, see Heinze (1925) and Balsdon (1960).
[56] *Tusculan Disputations* 1.55: *licet concurrant omnes plebei philosophi – sic enim i qui a Platone et Socrate et ab ea familia dissident appellandi videntur –*.
[57] See e.g. *On Invention* 1.101.

his pupils, provided that the criterion of decision is the authority associated with those thinkers.[58] In other passages which bear Antiochean influence, such as at *Tusculan Disputations* 5.34, Stoic doctrines like the defence of the self-sufficiency of virtue for a happy life, are explicitly traced back to Platonic texts, their importance being ascribed to Plato's *auctoritas* rather than to the Stoics themselves.[59] Association with ancient authority legitimises the Old Academic stance also in a passage in the first book of the *Tusculan Disputations*, where authority and antiquity are associated with a privileged route to truth.[60]

Antiochus' reliance on authority is balanced by Cicero's own warnings in his dialogues to resist consenting to anything but what is presented as persuasive to reason. The very structure of the Ciceronian dialogue is meant to serve the open-ended research for truth, and defend freedom of judgement from the danger of dogmatism and reliance on authority.[61] In a suggestive passage from *On the Nature of the Gods*, Cicero asserts that one should not attempt to find in his dialogues his own dogmatic opinion on matters. For one, he adds, should not seek in debate so much the weight of authority as that of reason:

Those, on the other hand, who ask what I myself feel about each topic are being more inquisitive than the case demands. For in debate it is not so much the weight of authority that should be sought as that of reason [*non enim tam auctoritatis in disputando quam rationis momenta quaerenda sunt*]. (*On the Nature of the Gods* 1.10)[62]

---

[58] *sin te auctoritas commovebat, nobisne omnibus et Platoni ipsi nescio quem illum anteponebas?*

[59] *et, si Zeno Citieus, advena quidam et ignobilis verborum opifex, insinuasse se in antiquam philosophiam videtur, huius sententiae gravitas a Platonis auctoritate repetatur.*

[60] *Tusculan Disputations* 1.26: *auctoribus quidem ad istam sententiam quam vis obtineri uti optimis possumus, quod in omnibus causis et debet et solet valere plurimum, et primum quidem omni antiquitate quae quo propius aberat ab ortuet divina progenie, hoc melius ea fortasse quae erant vera cernebant.*

[61] See e.g. *Lucullus* 9 for a critique of rash assent to authority without previous examination of all the positions available. Cf. also *Tusculan Disputations* 5.83: *utamur igitur libertate, qua nobis solis in philosophia licet uti, quorum oratio nihil ipsa iudicat, sed habetur in omnis partis ut ab aliis possit ipsa per sese nullius auctoritate adiuncta iudicari.*

[62] *qui autem requirunt quid quaque de re ipsi sentiamus, curiosius id faciunt quam necesse est; non enim tam auctoritatis in disputando quam rationis momenta quaerenda sunt.*

Here, Cicero reveals his New Academic credentials and rejects authority as a guarantee of truth: Contrary to devotees of particular masters, the New Academic retains his power of judgement intact and experiences the freedom which results from not committing to a particular authority.[63] At the other end of the scale, Cicero vehemently criticises the Pythagoreans who, when asked to justify their opinions, responded always with the formula 'He (sc. Pythagoras) said so' (*ipse dixit*). As Cicero notes, this seems to be a case of 'authority having value without the aid of reason' (*sine ratione valeret auctoritas*).[64] Similarly, at *On the Nature of the Gods* 3.10 the New Academic Cotta juxtaposes following religion on the basis of the tradition of the forefathers or 'founders' (*auctoritates*) and proving divine existence by the use of philosophical argument (*ratio*).[65] In the opposition between *ratio* and *auctoritas*, Antiochus seems to occupy a middle position, by supplementing his appeals to the *auctoritas* of the Old Academy with an exposition of its doctrines which is amenable to reasoned argument. Cicero thus assigns to the 'ancients' and to Antiochus a major role in his dialogues as representatives of a venerable tradition, while at the same time subjecting Old Academic views to dialectical challenges, showing his critical engagement with that very tradition.

---

[63] See especially *Lucullus* 8.
[64] *On the Nature of the Gods* 1.10: *nec vero probare soleo id quod de Pythagoreis accepimus, quos ferunt, si quid adfirmarent in disputando, cum ex iis quaereretur quare ita esset, respondere solitos 'ipse dixit'; ipse autem erat Pythagoras: tantum opinio praeiudicata poterat, ut etiam sine ratione valeret auctoritas.*
[65] *mihi enim unum sat erat, ita nobis maioris nostros tradidisse. Sed tu auctoritates contemnis, ratione pugnas.*

OLD ACADEMIC HISTORY OF PHILOSOPHY

The invocation of the Old Academy for the new sect that
Antiochus initiated at some point in the 90s BCE signals the
revisionary spirit of his movement;[1] for reference to the old
tradition of the Academy was challenging the institutional authority of Academics contemporary with Antiochus (deemed henceforth the New Academy) to represent Plato and his views.[2] This, as
will be shown, was linked to a new reading of Plato based on the
assumption that he held doctrines that could be reconstructed from
his dialogues. The Stoic school supplied Antiochus with the epistemological tools for the justification of his dogmatic reading of
the old tradition, which were lacking in the writings of the
'ancients'.

The adoption of this radical new approach towards the philosophical orientation of the Platonic Academy was made possible by
incorporating into the tradition of Plato and his followers other
strands of philosophical development. In particular, Antiochus'

---

[1] For the denomination 'Old Academy' (παλαιά Ἀκαδήμεια), see Antiochus *T6a* = Plutarch
Life of Lucullus 42.3: φιλοσοφίαν δὲ πᾶσαν μὲν ἠσπάζετο (sc. ὁ Λεύκολλος) καὶ πρὸς
πᾶσαν εὐμενὴς ἦν καὶ οἰκεῖος, ἴδιον δὲ τῆς Ἀκαδημείας ἐξ ἀρχῆς ἔρωτα καὶ ζῆλον ἔσχεν, οὐ
τῆς νέας λεγομένης, καίπερ ἀνθούσης τότε τοῖς Καρνεάδου λόγοις διὰ Φίλωνος, ἀλλὰ τῆς
παλαιᾶς and Antiochus *T8* = Plutarch *Life of Brutus* 2.2–3: τῶν δ᾽ Ἑλληνικῶν φιλοσόφων
οὐδενὸς μὲν ὡς ἁπλῶς εἰπεῖν ἀνήκοος ἦν οὐδ᾽ ἀλλότριος, διαφερόντως δ᾽ ἐσπουδάκει πρὸς
τοὺς ἀπὸ Πλάτωνος· καὶ τὴν νέαν καὶ μέσην λεγομένην Ἀκαδήμειαν οὐ πάνυ προσιέμενος,
ἐξήρτητο τῆς παλαιᾶς, καὶ διετέλει θαυμάζων μὲν Ἀντίοχον τὸν Ἀσκαλωνίτην, φίλον δὲ καὶ
συμβιωτὴν τὸν ἀδελφὸν αὐτοῦ πεποιημένος Ἄριστον.
[2] On Antiochus' establishment of 'another' Academy, see Antiochus *T1* = Numenius *Fr.* 8
Leemans/*Fr.* 28 des Places: Φίλωνος δὲ γίνεται ἀκουστὴς Ἀντίοχος, ἑτέρας ἄρξας
Ἀκαδημίας. For the classification of different phases of the Academy and the view that
Antiochus represents a distinct phase of Academic history, see Antiochus *F1* = Sextus
Empiricus *Outlines of Pyrrhonism* 1.220: Ἀκαδημίαι δὲ γεγόνασιν, ὡς φασὶν οἱ πλείους,
τρεῖς, μία μὲν καὶ ἀρχαιοτάτη ἡ τῶν περὶ Πλάτωνα, δευτέρα δὲ καὶ μέση ἡ τῶν περὶ
Ἀρκεσίλαον τὸν ἀκουστὴν Πολέμωνος, τρίτη δὲ καὶ νέα ἡ τῶν περὶ Καρνεάδην καὶ
Κλειτόμαχον· ἔνιοι δὲ καὶ τετάρτην προστιθέασι τὴν περὶ Φίλωνα καὶ Χαρμίδαν, τινὲς δὲ
καὶ πέμπτην καταλέγουσι τὴν περὶ [τὸν] Ἀντίοχον. Cf. also Antiochus *T2* = [Galen],
On the History of Philosophy 600.1–4.

peculiar approach was based on the idea that Aristotle and the Peripatetic tradition (down to Theophrastus) but also the Stoics, the most dominant philosophical school of Antiochus' time, formed part of the same tradition and, with some qualifications, could be shown to espouse the same doctrines in key philosophical issues. Such an inclusive view justifies Antiochus' engagement with a wide variety of sources, the influence of which flows into his proposed reconstruction of the doctrines of the Old Academy. In this chapter, I will discuss Antiochus' engagement with the various traditions which he wished to incorporate into the Old Academy, as also the hermeneutical strategies that supported his theses on the history of philosophy. The analysis will focus mostly on the Antiochean accounts of Piso and Varro in *On Ends* 5 and the *Academic Books* respectively, which give ample evidence of Antiochus' views on the history of philosophy. Especially Varro's account at the *Academic Books* is said to draw on a work of Antiochus, which explicitly set out to defend the thesis that the Academy underwent a radical shift of orientation from dogmatism to (Academic) scepticism, against the competing view of Antiochus' former teacher Philo, who traced his epistemological stance back to Socrates and the beginnings of the Academic tradition.[3]

Antiochus and Socrates

After Arcesilaus became head of the Academy in 267 BCE, Plato's school was dedicated to the dialectical examination of diverse philosophical ideas with a view to showing that no definitive claim may be espoused which represents absolute truth.[4] This

---

[3] See *Academic Books* 13–14: *'est' inquit 'ut dicis; sed ignorare te non arbitror quae contra Philonis Antiochus scripserit.' 'Immo vero et ista et totam veterem Academiam, a qua absum tam diu, renovari a te nisi molestum est velim', et simul 'adsidamus' inquam 'si videtur.'*

[4] Arcesilaus developed the criterion of the 'reasonable' (*eulogon*) for claims that, although deprived of absolute certainty, could admit of a good justification, see Sextus Empiricus *Against the Professors* 7.158. Such claims are according to Arcesilaus sufficient to regulate the conduct of life. Carneades on the other hand deemed certain impressions 'convincing' (*pithanon*) and held that the approval of such impressions constitutes the criterion of action and of (fallibilist) truth. The epistemological positions of the Academic Sceptics are presented in *Against the Professors* 7.176ff. (perhaps part of

practice was thought to be rooted in the Academic tradition itself; for it was thought to embody and develop further the dialectical methodology that Plato ascribes to Socrates in some of his dialogues.[5] For Arcesilaus and Carneades, down to Philo of Larissa, the technique of cross-examination, the so-called *elenchus*, as practised by the character Socrates in the aporetic Platonic dialogues, was indicative of the aporetic character of the Platonic Academy as a whole. It is suggestive that in a passage from Cicero's *On the Orator* 3.67 which reflects the Antiochean version of the history of philosophy, the 'sceptic turn' of Arcesilaus is explained through the influence of some 'Platonic writings and Socratic dialogues':

> There remain the Peripatetics and the Academics, though the latter are really two schools of thought under one name. For Plato's nephew Speusippus and his pupil Xenocrates and Xenocrates' pupils Polemo and Crantor did not seriously disagree on any point of opinion from Aristotle, their fellow-pupil under Plato, although possibly they were not his equals in fullness and variety of style; whereas Polemo's pupil Arcesilas, to begin with, adopted from the various writings of Plato and the Socratic dialogues [*ex variis Platonis libris sermonibusque Socraticis*] the view that nothing can be apprehended with certainty either by the senses or by the mind [*nihil esse certi quod aut sensibus aut animo percipi possit*].[6] (Transl. Rackham (1942) with alterations)

---

a doxography of Antiochean origin). The technique of 'arguing on both sides of a question' (εἰς ἑκάτερα ἐπιχείρησιν) is connected with the practice of Arcesilaus and Carneades in Eusebius' *Preparation of the Gospel* 14.7.15.1–5 and was used as a method to reach the greatest approximation to truth. See e.g. *Lucullus* 7: *neque nostrae disputationes quicquam aliud agunt nisi ut in utramque partem dicendo et audiendo eliciant et tamquam exprimant aliquid quod aut verum sit aut ad id quam proxime accedat.*

5 Suggestive in this respect is a text from *On Divination* 2.150 which presents the dialectical practice of the (New) Academy as having been inherited by Socrates: *cum autem proprium sit Academiae iudicium suum nullum interponere, ea probare quae simillima veri videantur, conferre causas et quid in quamque sententiam dici possit expromere, nulla adhibita sua auctoritate iudicium audientium relinquere integrum ac liberum, tenebimus hanc consuetudinem a Socrate traditam eaque inter nos, si tibi, Quinte frater, placebit, quam saepissime utemur. Mihi vero, inquit ille, nihil potest esse iucundius.*

6 *Reliqui sunt Peripatetici et Academici; quamquam Academicorum nomen est unum, sententiae duae; nam Speusippus Platonis sororis filius et Xenocrates qui Platonem audierat, et qui Xenocratem Polemo et Crantor, nihil ab Aristotele, qui una audierat Platonem, magno opere dissensit; copia fortasse et varietate dicendi pares non fuerunt: Arcesilas primum, qui Polemonem audierat, ex variis Platonis libris sermonibusque Socraticis hoc maxime adripuit, nihil esse certi quod aut sensibus aut animo percipi possit.*

38

The passage suggests that the epistemological credo of Arcesilaus, which it presents as a form of 'negative dogmatism', was crucially influenced by Socratic practice, as the latter was illustrated in the Platonic writings. Indeed, the New Academy used Socrates' disavowal of knowledge in the *Apology*, and the associated Socratic aporetic methodology, to justify its own dialectical practice and epistemological views.[7] Plato was read, in line with this, as endorsing the Socratic attitude and exemplifying it through the use of the dialogue form.[8] For these thinkers then Plato was not committed to any positive doctrine, but only to free enquiry into truth through dialectic. Accordingly, Academics who espoused this interpretation of Plato developed an adversarial philosophical practice to conduct their philosophical inquiry, a technique adopted by Cicero himself for the construction of his own dialogues.

Antiochus by establishing a movement of revival of the Old Academy testifies to an *alternative* understanding of the Academic tradition which connects the Socratic and the Platonic pedigree with constructive philosophical aims. Antiochus traced such aims in a more articulated form in the followers of Plato in the Academy, in the Peripatos and in the Stoa. Since this was presented not as a new orientation, but just as a return to a previous phase of the school, Antiochus was able to claim that he was representing the *original* Academy, thus strongly differentiating himself from those who were taken to have deviated from it, i.e. the New Academics. This resulted in identifying a rift between a pre-Arcesilean and a post-Arcesilean era in the history of the Academy, which presented Academics contemporary with Antiochus as dissidents and heterodox thinkers. In line with this,

---

[7] The Socratic *confessio ignorationis* is referred to at the beginning of the account of the New Academic history of philosophy in *Academic Books* 44, where Socrates is placed in a 'sceptic' lineage alongside Democritus, Anaxagoras and Empedocles: *'cum Zenone' inquam 'ut accepimus Arcesilas sibi omne certamen instituit, non pertinacia aut studio vincendi ut quidem mihi videtur, sed earum rerum obscuritate, quae ad confessionem ignorationis adduxerant Socratem.* Cf. *On Ends* 2.2; *Tusculan Disputations* 1.8; *On the Nature of the Gods* 1.11.

[8] See for example *Academic Books* 46: *si quidem Platonem ex illa vetere numeramus cuius in libris nihil affirmatur et in utramque partem multa disseruntur, de omnibus quaeritur nihil certi dicitur.*

Antiochus referred in his attack against Philo of Larissa to 'two Academies'.[9]

Linked to Antiochus' alternative reading of Academic history was his attempt to integrate the Socratic heritage into a dogmatic Academic tradition. Interestingly enough this is connected in Antiochean passages with a historically sensitive reading of Socrates (as he appears in Plato), which subtly differentiates Socratic methodology from Socratic intentions. A major move in this direction is a distinction in Antiochean passages between Socrates and Plato himself; this seems to answer to the New Academic attempt to conflate the two figures.[10]

The separation of Plato and Socrates in Antiochus' presentation of the Academic tradition rests on considerations relating both to their philosophical interests and to their chosen methodology. Thus, Socrates, according to Varro at *Academic Books* 15, was the first to abandon enquiry into natural phenomena pursued by all previous (pre-Socratic) philosophers and turn to ethics.[11] Socrates' lack of interest in physical enquiry is attributed either to the difficulty of acquiring knowledge about 'heavenly things' (*caelestia autem vel procul esse a nostra cognitione censeret*), or, alternatively, to the conviction that such a knowledge is irrelevant to a happy life (*vel, si maxime cognita essent, nihil tamen ad bene vivendum*).[12] Plato is shown, by contrast, to have supplemented the Socratic interest in ethics with enquiries into the other branches of philosophy.

---

[9] See *Academic Books* 13: (Cicero speaking) *quamquam Antiochi magister Philo, magnus vir ut tu existimas ipse, †negaret in libris, quod coram etiam ex ipso audiebamus, duas Academias esse, erroremque eorum qui ita putarent coarguit.* For Philo as a defender of the unity of the Academy down to his day, see Sedley (1997) 120.

[10] The distinction between Socrates and Plato may be traced back to Aristotle and his followers, see e.g. Aristotle *Metaphysics* 1.1078b22–32; *Magna Moralia* 1.1182a15–26.

[11] *Academic Books* 15: *Socrates mihi videtur, id quod constat inter omnes, primus a rebus occultis et ab ipsa natura involutis in quibus omnes ante eum philosophi occupati fuerunt avocavisse philosophiam et ad vitam communem adduxisse ut de virtutibus et de vitiis omninoque de bonis rebus et malis quaereret.* This tallies with our evidence on Socrates from other sources, e.g. Xenophon's *Memoires* 1.11–3; Aristotle's *Metaphysics* 1.987b1; *On the Parts of Animals* 1.642a28.

[12] *Academic Books* 1.15: *caelestia autem vel procul esse a nostra cognitione censeret vel, si maxime cognita essent, nihil tamen ad bene vivendum.* This is consistent with the testimony of Xenophon, *Memoirs* 1.13. Cf. Sextus Empiricus, *Against the Professors* 7.8.

Thus, at *On Ends* 5.87, Plato is presented as having gained scientific knowledge about numbers and celestial phenomena (*numeros et caelestia*) through his contact with Egyptian priests and Pythagoreans like Archytas and Timaeus.[13] In his dialogues, he is subsequently said to have combined the Pythagorean *disciplina* and its 'theoretical' elements with the Socratic interest in ethics.[14] This may point to a hermeneutical principle, according to which certain views which show Pythagorean influence in Plato's dialogues should not be attributed to Socrates himself but to the author Plato and his attempt to combine the views of his teachers.

Further, it seems that Antiochus in his presentation of Old Academic ethics separated Socratic philosophical methodology from Socrates' philosophical commitments on ethical matters. Thus, Varro at *Academic Books* 16 refers to the 'elenctic' nature of Socrates' method, as it appears in writings of members of the Socratic school, alluding, in particular, to the aporetic Platonic dialogues: there, 'he (sc. Socrates) discusses in such a way that he himself does not assert anything but refutes others' (*ita disputat ut nihil adfirmet ipse, refellat alios*) and 'affirms that he knows nothing besides the mere fact that he does not know anything' (*nihil se scire dicat nisi id ipsum*).[15] Socratic aporetic methodology, as also the concession that Socrates was sincere in his disavowal of knowledge, is, however, carefully supplemented in this passage by

---

[13] *Nisi enim id faceret, cur Plato Aegyptum peragravit ut a sacerdotibus barbaris numeros et caelestia acciperet? cur post Tarentum ad Archytam? cur ad reliquos Pythagoreos, Echecratem, Timaeum, Arionem, Locros, ut, cum Socratem expressisset, adiungeret Pythagoreorum disciplinam eaque quae Socrates repudiabat addisceret?* Cf. also *Tusculan Disputations* 1.39. The same picture of Plato is conveyed also in Diogenes Laertius *Lives of Eminent Philosphers* 3.6 and Augustine's *City of God* 8.4. Already Aristotle informs us that Plato 'followed the Italians (i.e. the Pythagoreans) in most things'; see *Metaphysics* 1.987a30.

[14] *On Ends* 5.87. Cf. *On the Republic* 1.16. See also Tarrant (1985) 129 and Karamanolis (2006) 52.

[15] *Academic Books* 1.16: *hic in omnibus fere sermonibus qui ab is qui illum audierunt perscripti varie copioseque sunt ita disputat ut nihil adfirmet ipse, refellat alios, nihil se scire dicat nisi id ipsum, eoque praestare ceteris quod illi quae nesciant scire se putent, ipse se nihil scire id unum sciat, ob eamque rem se arbitrari ab Apolline omnium sapientissimum esse dictum quod haec esset una hominis sapientia, non arbitrari sese scire quod nesciat.* The last clause of the text maps onto Socrates' presentation in *Apology* 23b. Cf. ibid. 1.17: *illam autem Socraticam dubitanter de omnibus rebus et nulla adfirmatione adhibita consuetudinem disserendi reliquerunt.*

a reference to Socrates' concern for the cultivation of virtue.[16] Suggestive for Antiochus' interpretation of Socrates' philosophical aims (as presented in Plato's dialogues) is one passage from *Academic Books* 16,[17] which, if one admits the reading *tamen* in the main clause,[18] contrasts Socratic *agnoia* with the fact that Socrates' discourse was spent 'in praising virtue and in exhorting people to the pursuit of it'. This seems to be an explicit reminder of the Socratic exhortation to the 'care for virtue' as a way to exercise care for one's soul, as we find it, for example, in Plato's *Apology*.[19] There, as also in other Platonic aporetic dialogues which focus on the investigation of virtue, Socrates aims explicitly at convincing the people he is conversing with that excellence is dependent solely upon the state of one's soul, and not upon material possessions such as wealth.[20] Although nowhere in the aporetic dialogues does Socrates claim to possess ethical expertise that may be taught, or a philosophically founded theory for his interest in virtue, his practice, as depicted in Plato, may be taken to imply a commitment to certain positive beliefs. Such beliefs would include the supreme value of psychic virtue for happiness, as also the belief that excellence of the soul may be developed through the reasoning process of philosophical dialectic.[21] Since these are both

---

[16] On the other hand, *Lucullus* 15 puts more emphasis on Socrates' confession of ignorance for the purposes of refutation: *Socrates autem de se ipse detrahens in disputatione plus tribuebat is quos volebat refellere.* Socrates' 'irony' consists, according to the passage, in drawing a distinction between 'what he said and what he believed': *ita cum aliud diceret atque sentiret, libenter uti solitus est ea dissimulatione quam Graeci* εἰρωνείαν *vocant.* Following Reid (1885), Brittain (2001) 183 explains away the alleged divergence between the two reports of Socrates by ascribing the Socratic interpretation in the *Academic Books* to the historical Varro. Sedley (2012a) 82–83, by contrast, traces in the presentation of Socrates in the *Lucullus* an earlier phase of Antiochean history of philosophy, when Socrates was still understood as forming part of the doctrinal Platonic tradition. On the other hand, Varro's speech in the *Academic Books* represents, according to Sedley, a later Antiochean phase and a more historically sensitive reading which took Socrates' disavowal of knowledge at face value.

[17] *quae cum diceret* (sc. Socrates) *constanter et in ea sententia permaneret, omnis eius oratio tamen in virtute laudanda et in hominibus ad virtutis studium cohortandis consumebatur ut e Socraticorum libris maximeque Platonis intellegi potest.*

[18] The reading is supported by Reid (1885) 111 and Rackham (1933), against the mss. reading *tam.* Plasberg (1922) on the other hand prints *tantum.* By contrast, see Sedley (2012a) 83, who reads the passage as not involving a contrast between methodology and Socratic beliefs and, thus, as supporting a non-doctrinal reading of Socrates.

[19] See *Apology* 31b.   [20] See *Apology* 30a–b.

[21] This seems to be also confirmed by Piso's exposition on the previous history of philosophy at *On Ends* 5.88, where Socrates' discussions are connected with the idea

views that Antiochus ascribes to the Old Academy in his ethical account of *On Ends* 5,[22] we may assume that for him the difference between Socrates (as depicted in the aporetic dialogues of Plato) and the subsequent Academics may not have consisted in their ethical beliefs, but in the systematic treatment of their views and in their style of philosophising.[23]

Antiochus and Plato's Academy

Plato is regarded by Antiochus as the one who laid the foundations of the single philosophical *system* of the Old Academy, and therefore in Antiochean accounts of Academic history receives a special place, as its 'leader' and 'originator' (*auctor*). Antiochus believes that in Platonic dialogues one may find the seeds of all subsequent philosophical developments. The special place granted to Plato by Antiochus comes to the fore in a passage from Varro's account at *Academic Books* 17:

Originating with Plato [*Platonis ... auctoritate*], a thinker of manifold variety and fertility [*qui varius et multiplex et copiosus fuit*], there was established a philosophy that, though it had two appellations, was really a single and uniform system [*una ... philosophiae forma*], that of the Academic and the Peripatetic schools, which while agreeing in doctrine differed in terminology.[24]

---

that 'all our hope for a good and happy life depends on virtue': *post enim haec in hac urbe primum a Socrate quaeri coepta, deinde in hunc locum delata sunt, nec dubitatum quin in virtute omnis ut bene sic etiam beate vivendi spes poneretur.* Cf. Fladerer (1996) 30: 'In der Ethik, wo ihm ein Urteil möglich ist, fordert Sokrates zum Streben nach *virtus* auf, ohne von skeptischer Zurückhaltung beeinflusst zu sein.'

[22] Piso at *On Ends* 5 (e.g. 5.38) seems to espouse an intellectualist reading of the virtues, which is reminiscent of views ascribed to Socrates in Plato, see Chapter 5, *infra*. Antiochus seems to borrow also from the 'Socratic' dialogues (especially the *Alcibiades*) the motif of self-knowledge which plays a central role in the ethical account of *On Ends* 5 (e.g. 5.44); see Chapter 4, *infra*.

[23] In his exposition, Varro remarks that these thinkers abandoned the Socratic aporetic custom of discussing (*consuetudinem disserenti*) and created a certain defined method of teaching (*certam quandam disciplinae formulam*). See also Fladerer (1996) 34: 'Lediglich die *dissimulatio* des Wissens als methodisches Spezifikum des Sokrates erfuhr keine Aufnahme in den Philosophiebetrieb (sc. der 'Alten Akademie')' und *ibid*. 35: 'Der Elenktik des ironischen Sokrates steht die von Platon betriebene Systematisierung und Verschriftlichung (...) gegenüber'.

[24] *Platonis autem auctoritate, qui varius et multiplex et copiosus fuit, una et consentiens duobus vocabulis philosophiae forma instituta est Academicorum et Peripateticorum qui rebus congruentes nominibus differebant.*

The creation of a new philosophical teaching which received its starting point with Plato is also characterised with expressions like *ars philosophiae, rerum ordo* and *descriptio disciplinae*.[25] The idea of a philosophical system conveyed by all these expressions should not be understood in a strong sense as the deductive derivation of all doctrines from a limited number of first principles, but in a more loose sense, referring primarily to the classification of the various philosophical topics into distinct areas of enquiry and to a particular order of exposition. This emphasis on philosophy as an *ars* suggests that Antiochus' reconstruction of the philosophy of the 'ancients' was informed by contemporary models and, in particular, Stoicism;[26] accordingly, origination in the above text may not mean necessarily that Plato is the sole contributor to the Old Academic system.

An area where the philosophical 'order' (*ordo*) of the Old Academy manifests itself is the delineation of distinct areas of philosophical discourse. Thus, Antiochus traces back to the Old Academy a threefold classification of philosophy (*philosophandi ratio triplex*) comprising three clearly defined branches: that of ethics, physics and dialectic. According to Varro, at *Academic Books* 19, the threefold classification was already inherited by Plato (*iam accepta a Platone*) and was retained later by Zeno, who took it over from his predecessors.[27] The first deals with forms of life and ethics (*de vita et moribus*), the second with the physical world and things not accessible to the senses (*de natura et rebus occultis*), whereas the third encompasses dialectic and what is right and wrong in both reasoning and expression (*tertia de disserendo et quid verum quid falsum, quid rectum in oratione*

---

[25] *Academic Books* 17: *ita facta est quod minime Socrates probabat ars quaedam philosophiae et rerum ordo et descriptio disciplinae*. Cf. *Lucullus* 15. On the notion of *disciplina* as a 'school of thought' or a 'philosophical system', see Karamanolis (2006) 53.

[26] Elsewhere, the same expressions are used to characterise the Stoic philosophical system, see for example *On Ends* 3.74: *verum admirabilis compositio disciplinae (sc. Stoicorum) incredibilisque rerum me traxit ordo*. On the influence of the Stoic conception of philosophy as a system of doctrines on Antiochus, see Karamanolis (2006) 12–13.

[27] *Fuit ergo iam accepta a Platone philosophandi ratio triplex, una de vita et moribus, altera de natura et rebus occultis, tertia de disserendo et quid verum quid falsum quid rectum in oratione pravumve quid consentiens quid repugnet iudicando*. Cf. also *On Ends* 4.4. The tripartite division of the philosophical *logos* is, however, hailed as an innovation of Zeno in Diogenes Laertius' *Lives of Eminent Philosophers* 7.39.

pravumve quid consentiens quid repugnet iudicando).[28] It is the same threefold division of a *forma disciplinae* that is attributed explicitly to Aristotle and the Peripatetics at *On Ends* 5.9.[29] It is instructive to compare the ascription of a threefold philosophical system to Plato with a passage from Sextus' *Against the Professors* 7.16,[30] whose main idea resembles strongly the Antiochean views, as found in the *Academic Books*:

These thinkers (sc. Xenophanes and Archelaus), however, seem to have handled the question incompletely, and, in comparison with them, the view of those who divide philosophy into Physics, Ethics, and Logic is more developed. Of these Plato is *potentially* the originator [ὧν δυνάμει μὲν Πλάτων ἐστὶν ἀρχηγός], as he discussed many problems of physics and of ethics, and not a few of logic; but those who most explicitly [ῥητότατα] adopt this division are the followers of Xenocrates and the Peripatetics, and also the Stoics. (Sextus Empiricus *Against the Professors* 7.16 = *Fr.* 1 Isnardi Parente [Xenocrates])[31]

Noteworthy in the above-mentioned testimony is the expression the 'followers of Xenocrates', which is generally held to mean no more than the person referred to, i.e. Xenocrates himself, but it is also broad enough as to include other members of the Academy, such as Polemo. It is also noteworthy that the Stoics are adduced at the end of the passage, as a kind of supplement to the Academic line. The inclusion of both Academics and Peripatetics alongside Plato as precursors of an idea found in the Stoics may well point to Antiochus as a source of the text in Sextus. For Plato is presented in Varro's (Antiochean) account in the *Academic Books* (in the

---

[28] In the first ethical doxography in Stobaeus' *Selections* 2.7, the division of the philosophical *logos* into three parts is again 'projected' onto Plato, with the additional classification of specific Platonic dialogues into the three branches. Thus, the author maintains that Plato applied a tripartite division of philosophy, whereby the *Timaeus* stands for physics, the *Republic* for ethics and the *Theaetetus* for dialectic. Stobaeus *Selections* 2 49.18–23 W.: εἴρηται δὲ παρὰ Πλάτωνι κατὰ τὸ τῆς φιλοσοφίας τριμερές, ἐν Τιμαίῳ μὲν φυσικῶς (προσθήσω δὲ καὶ Πυθαγορικῶς), σημαίνοντος ἀφθόνως τὴν ἐκείνου προεπίνοιαν· ἐν δὲ τῇ Πολιτείᾳ ἠθικῶς· ἐν δὲ τῷ Θεαιτήτῳ λογικῶς.

[29] *On Ends* 5.9: *sed est forma eius disciplinae (sc. Peripateticorum), sicut fere ceterarum, triplex: una pars est naturae, disserendi altera, vivendi tertia.*

[30] The passage is found at the beginning of a doxographical piece on epistemology, which may partly draw on Antiochus' work Κανονικά as a source, see Introduction, *supra*.

[31] πλὴν οὗτοι μὲν ἐλλιπῶς ἀνεστράφθαι δοκοῦσιν, ἐντελέστερον δὲ παρὰ τούτους οἱ εἰπόντες τῆς φιλοσοφίας τὸ μέν τι εἶναι φυσικὸν τὸ δὲ ἠθικὸν τὸ δὲ λογικόν· ὧν δυνάμει μὲν Πλάτων ἐστὶν ἀρχηγός, περὶ πολλῶν μὲν φυσικῶν, [περὶ] πολλῶν δὲ ἠθικῶν, οὐκ ὀλίγων δὲ λογικῶν διαλεχθείς· ῥητότατα δὲ οἱ περὶ τὸν Ξενοκράτη καὶ οἱ ἀπὸ τοῦ Περιπάτου, ἔτι δὲ οἱ ἀπὸ τῆς Στοᾶς ἔχονται τῆσδε τῆς διαιρέσεως.

passage already examined) as possessing the *auctoritas* of a full and consistent system which was developed after him by all philosophers in the Old Academic line, from Speusippus down to the Stoics, including Aristotle and Theophrastus as well.[32] Furthermore, one may discern in Sextus' passage two assumptions about Platonic *auctoritas* found in Antiochus as well. The first such assumption is that it is *transferable*. This is linked to the fact that Antiochus' dogmatic reconstruction of the views of the 'ancients' is committed to a Hellenistic model of school allegiance. The paradigmatic case here is the Epicurean commitment to Epicurus as the founder of the school.[33] Projecting the Hellenistic model of a philosophical school onto the 'ancients', Antiochus argued that the Old Academy had Plato as its founder, whose (dogmatic) teaching has been faithfully handed down through lines of master-pupil relationships.

Furthermore *auctoritas*, as it emerges from the Antiochean passages, is dynamic and admits of *progress*; Plato may have provided the building blocks of the whole tradition, but the philosophical system of the Old Academy was elaborated by his successors.[34] This allows for the supplementation and systematisation of Platonic ideas with material coming from the subsequent tradition. This loose attitude towards Platonic authority also reveals that the aim of Antiochus' project is not to explicitly offer an exegesis of Plato but to present a coherent system which entails

---

[32] See e.g. *Academic Books* 17. Note, however, that Varro's exposition of the Old Academic system of philosophy in the *Academic Books* follows a different order of the philosophical disciplines than the one presented in the Sextan passage, starting with ethics followed up by physics and dialectic. Again, in *On Ends* 5.9–11, which presents the 'Peripatetic' system of philosophy, the order is 'physics, logic, ethics'.

[33] See Sedley (1989).

[34] By contrast, Karamanolis (2006) 37 dissociates from 'Platonists', to whom he counts Antiochus as well, the idea that Aristotle's views constitute progress over those of Plato (an idea that he ascribes to later Peripatetics). Still, when reconstructing Antiochus' own view *ibid.* 54, he ascribes to him the idea that the Old Academic philosophical system 'was in need of articulation and reconstruction, which the Academics and the Peripatetics were happy to provide'. See also *ibid.* 58 for the idea that, according to Antiochus, Plato's philosophy is a 'project amenable to further development'. The idea of an elaboration of an old philosophical doctrine by subsequent developments is in line with Peripatetic philosophical historiography as well; it appears for example in the doxography on Anaxagoras in the first book of Aristotle's *Metaphysics* 1.989a30–33: Ἀναξαγόραν δ' εἴ τις ὑπολάβοι δύο λέγειν στοιχεῖα, μάλιστ' ἂν ὑπολάβοι κατὰ λόγον, ὃν ἐκεῖνος αὐτὸς μὲν οὐ διήρθρωσεν, ἠκολούθησε μέντ' ἂν ἐξ ἀνάγκης τοῖς ἐπάγουσιν αὐτόν.

the best philosophical solutions to (contemporary) philosophical problems.

The Antiochean idea of an Academic philosophical *forma* is premised on the view that the writings of the members of the Old Academy contain specific doctrines, namely clearly articulated theoretical positions, in every branch of the philosophical discourse. Plato's work, due to its dialogical form and rhetorical style, must have presented particular problems to the Antiochean thesis. A characterisation here deserves special attention: the word *multiplex*, in Varro's account at *Academic Books* 17, hints at the versatility of Plato's thought,[35] although it is not clear whether the characterisation applies to Plato's doctrine, ingenuity or literary form.[36] As it stands, however, it is supplemented by the one and uniform philosophical 'system' (*philosophiae forma*) of the Old Academy. The Antiochean reference to Plato finds a parallel in Stobaeus' *Selections* 2.7. The hermeneutical strategy followed in this piece of doxography on the *telos* is suggestive of the way in which Plato was read at least from the time of Antiochus onwards:

Plato's variety in expression does not amount to variety in doctrine [τὸ δέ γε πολύφωνον τοῦ Πλάτωνος οὐ πολύδοξον]. Now his views concerning the *telos* are said in many ways [πολλαχῶς]. On the one hand his expression is versatile [ποικιλίαν τῆς φράσεως] due to his erudition and grandness [λόγιον καὶ μεγαλήγορον], but on the other hand it contributes to the doctrinal sameness and concord [εἰς δὲ ταὐτὸ καὶ σύμφωνον τοῦ δόγματος συντελεῖ]. And this is living in accordance with virtue [κατ' ἀρετὴν ζῆν]. The latter is both the possession and the use [κτῆσις ἅμα καὶ χρῆσις] of perfect virtue. (Stobaeus *Selections* 2 50.1–6 Wachsmuth)

As in the Antiochean passage, the versatility of Platonic style and mode of expression is contrasted here with agreement in doctrine, expressed through the musical metaphors of 'polyphony' (*polyphōnon*) and 'concord' (*symphōnon*) respectively.[37] Further

---

[35] The same word characterises Socrates' method of discussion (*ratio disputandi*) at *Tusculan Disputations* 5.11.

[36] The word *multiplex* can apply to all these cases; see Reid (1885) 111 s.l. Bonazzi (2012) 309 notes with regard to the 'manifold' character of Plato's philosophy: 'The assumption seems to be that Plato's philosophy was doctrinal in nature and yet the literary form of his dialogues partially obscured the details of the system.'

[37] On the conception of 'polyphony' in the so-called doxography A in Stobaeus' *Selections* 2, see Hahm (1990) 3003–4.

it is argued, using the principle that something 'is said in many ways', that, although Plato used different formulations of the *telos*, they all amount to the same meaning, namely the ideal of a 'life according to virtue';[38] again the latter encompasses, in Aristotelian fashion, 'both the possession and the use of perfect virtue'.[39] We may compare this strategy to the way Antiochus in *On Ends* 5 ascribes to the Old Academy as a whole (and implicitly to Plato himself) the *telos* formula of a 'life according to nature' (*On Ends* 5.24; 26), which he interprets in his own way along Aristotelian/Peripatetic lines.[40]

Further, the immediate followers of Plato are also co-opted in Antiochean passages for the support of the thesis of a unified dogmatic Old Academy. As already discussed above, Antiochus claimed that the idea of a philosophical system took its lead from Plato but was articulated by his successors; these included the scholarchs of the Academy during the eighty years that followed upon Plato's death, namely Speusippus, Xenocrates and Polemo. These figures (along with Aristotle and Theophrastus) are often invoked, besides Plato himself, when there is reference to the Old Academy in Cicero, as for example at *On Ends* 5.2 and 5.7. The invocation of these Academic authorities alongside Plato clearly differentiates Antiochus from all later Platonists who professed explicitly a return to Plato *himself* as the source of ultimate truth.[41] Such an inclusion of Plato's successors reveals, by contrast, a belief in philosophical progress on Antiochus' part which was not shared by later Platonists.

At *Academic Books* 34, Varro, acting as the Antiochean spokesman, stresses the fact that Speusippus and Xenocrates were first to receive the teaching and *auctoritas* of Plato (*primi Platonis rationem auctoritatemque susceperant*), whereas all the rest of the Academics, i.e. Polemo, Crates and Crantor, in their turn preserved 'attentively the doctrines that they received from their

---

[38] The same principle is employed by the doxographer to account for the different divisions of goods in Plato, see Stobaeus *Selections* 2 55.5–21 W.

[39] See the *telos* formula ascribed to Aristotle at *ibid.* 50.11–12 W.: Ἀριστοτέλης χρῆσιν ἀρετῆς τελείας ἐν βίῳ τελείῳ προηγουμένην.

[40] See Chapters 3 and 8, *infra*.

[41] See Boys-Stones (2001) 143. Cf. Bonazzi (2012) 309.

predecessors' (*diligenter ea quae a superioribus acceperant tuebantur*).[42] Although there is evidence to suggest that at least some of the successors of Plato in the Academy, like Xenocrates and Crantor, were involved in the reinterpretation and defence of ideas expounded in Platonic works like the *Timaeus*,[43] it is suggestive that Varro seems to ignore the differences between the views of different leaders of the post-Platonic Academy, attested in other sources.[44] No trace, for instance, is found of Speusippus' innovations in the domain of metaphysics and his theory of numbers.[45] What seems important for the Antiochean reading is rather that the successors of Plato abandoned the dialogue form and chose a dogmatic style of philosophising. In line with this, the available material from the post-Platonic Academy could be read with a view to confirming the Antiochean thesis of a single Academic tradition, which agrees on a set of fundamental doctrines. The lack of sufficient independent evidence on these writers does not allow us to check the validity of Antiochus' formulations. It is striking, however, that no reference to particular treatises of the Academics after Plato is made in the Antiochean passages, in the way that, as we shall see, this is attested for Aristotle and Theophrastus. We may speculate then that the inclusion of the list of immediate successors of Plato in the Antiochean canon has, partly at least, a rhetorical force.[46]

Polemo, the last major head of the Academy before its 'sceptical turn', deserves perhaps particular attention. The importance of Polemo, in his role as a teacher of both Zeno and Arcesilaus, is

---

[42] This may be contrasted with the unfavourable view of Numenius *ap.* Eusebius' *Preparation for the Gospel* 14.5.1, according to which the first successors of Plato deserted their master and misrepresented his views: Ἐπὶ μὲν τοίνυν Σπεύσιππον τὸν Πλάτωνος μὲν ἀδελφιδοῦν, Ξενοκράτη δὲ τὸν διάδοχον τὸν Σπευσίππου, Πολέμωνα δὲ τὸν ἐκδεξάμενον τὴν σχολὴν παρὰ Ξενοκράτους (...) ἐπεὶ εἴς γε τὰ ἄλλα πολλαχῇ παραλύοντες, τὰ δὲ στρεβλοῦντες, οὐκ ἐνέμειναν τῇ πρώτῃ διαδοχῇ.

[43] In Proclus' *Commentary on Plato's Timaeus* 1.76.1–2, Crantor is referred to as the first 'exegete' of Plato: τὸν περὶ τῶν Ἀτλαντίνων σύμπαντα τοῦτον λόγον οἳ μὲν ἱστορίαν εἶναι ψιλήν φασιν, ὥσπερ ὁ πρῶτος τοῦ Πλάτωνος ἐξηγητὴς Κράντωρ. As Karamanolis (2006) 2 n.4 notes, it is not clear what form his commentary had.

[44] Dörrie (1987) 327 refers also to a fictitious Academic continuity fabricated by Antiochus.

[45] Speusippus *Fr.* 92–122 Isnardi Parente.

[46] Dörrie (1987) 327 defends a similar view and claims that Antiochus' allusions to the successors of Plato in the Academy could not possibly have been refuted, since no writings of those Academics had survived by Antiochus' time.

shown by the frequent use of his name in references to the *vetus Academia* in Cicero.[47] The master–pupil relationship between Zeno and Polemo was crucial for the Antiochean unitary thesis, which ventured to include Stoicism in its territory, since such a connection could corroborate the idea that Zeno received the main doctrines of his philosophy from his teacher and did not initiate a novel philosophical school;[48] we are going to see that this is one of the key (polemical) strategies used by Antiochus in his attempt to present the Old Academy as a better alternative to the dominant Stoic school in the domain of ethics. Accordingly Cicero, wearing his Antiochean hat, claims at *On Ends* 4.3 that Zeno, having been a pupil of Polemo, 'had no reason to dissent from his own master and from those who went before him' by founding a new school,[49] and, in the same vein, at *On Ends* 4.14, it is stated that Polemo, among the *superiores*, was the one who most obviously (*planissime*) held the view that the 'highest good' consists in 'living according to nature', something which is meant to confirm the thesis that Zeno inherited his principal doctrines from the Old Academy.[50]

The most significant evidence to suggest possible Polemonian influence on Antiochean ethical views is in Clement, where Polemo is reported to have written some 'books on the life according to nature' (*en tois peri tou kata physin biou syntagmasi*).[51] This may support the thesis that Polemo was the first to introduce the *telos* formula that is ascribed in *On Ends* 5.24 to the Old Academics, and which is espoused by the Stoics as well.

---

[47] See e.g. *Lucullus* 131.

[48] This is expressed at *Academic Books* 35, at *On Ends* 4.51 and *ibid.* 4.61. Cf. also Diogenes Laertius *Lives of Eminent Philosophers* 7.25.

[49] *non esset causa Zenoni, cum Polemonem audisset, cur et ab eo ipso et a superioribus dissideret.* See also the ironic remark at *On Ends* 4.21: *o magnam vim ingenii causamque iustam, cur nova existeret disciplina!*

[50] Cf. *On Ends* 4.45 with reference to Zeno's receiving the idea of the 'first things according to nature' (*prima naturae*) from Polemo. Cf. *ibid.* 4.60.

[51] Clement of Alexandria *Miscellanies* 7.6.32.9 Stählin = Polemo *Fr.* 112 Gigante: δοκεῖ δὲ Ξενοκράτης ἰδίᾳ πραγματευόμενος Περὶ τῆς ἀπὸ τῶν ζώων τροφῆς καὶ Πολέμων ἐν τοῖς Περὶ τοῦ κατὰ φύσιν βίου συντάγμασι σαφῶς λέγειν, ὡς ἀσύμφορόν ἐστιν ἡ διὰ τῶν σαρκῶν τροφή, <ἢ> εἰργασμένη ἤδη καὶ ἐξομοιοῖ ταῖς τῶν ἀλόγων ψυχαῖς. The fragment seems to suggest that Polemo's books entailed a defence of vegetarianism on the basis of Pythagorean and Platonic views, but we have no existing evidence about the ethical views espoused there.

Doxographical evidence on the *telos* defended by Polemo, which survives in Clement, suggests that his views were similar to the ones put forward by the Antiochean spokesperson at *On Ends* 5. Thus, whereas he held that an utterly self-sufficient life is comprised not only of virtue but also of non-psychological goods (among which he counted both bodily and external goods),[52] he also maintained, like Antiochus, the 'robust' view that virtue is under all circumstances sufficient for happiness.

Still, a word of caution with regard to the importance of Polemo for Antiochus is in order. Polemo's views, are never clearly distinguished in Antiochean texts from those of the Peripatetic members of the Old Academy: at *On Ends* 2.34, for example, where Cicero represents the Antiochean position, Polemo is said to have used the notion of 'first things according to nature' (*prima secundum naturam*), an idea which is, however, said to have been *already* used by Aristotle himself (*Polemoni et iam ante Aristoteli ea prima visa sunt, quae paulo ante dixi*).[53] That Polemo's views coincided with those of Aristotle is stated again at *On Ends* 5.14.[54] An additional difficulty comes from the fact that the importance assigned to Polemo by Antiochus is not confirmed by evidence in sources independent of Cicero.[55] Diogenes Laertius in his chapter on Polemo concentrates almost exclusively on biographical details, and although he states that Polemo left behind him a considerable amount of works,[56] he does not include a catalogue of them or mention any specific doctrines that Polemo held. Thus, Polemo's surviving fragments from other sources are unable on their own to sustain the claim that he was a major

---

[52] Clement of Alexandria *Miscellanies* 2.22.133.7 Stählin = Polemo *Fr.* 123 Gigante: ὁ γὰρ Ξενοκράτους γνώριμος Πολέμων φαίνεται τὴν εὐδαιμονίαν αὐτάρκειαν εἶναι βουλόμενος ἀγαθῶν πάντων, ἢ τῶν πλείστων καὶ μεγίστων. δογματίζει γοῦν χωρὶς μὲν ἀρετῆς μηδέποτε ἂν εὐδαιμονίαν ὑπάρχειν, δίχα δὲ καὶ τῶν σωματικῶν καὶ τῶν ἐκτὸς τὴν ἀρετὴν αὐτάρκη πρὸς εὐδαιμονίαν εἶναι. Cf. the Old Academic *telos* in *Academic Books* 22.

[53] The idea of *principia naturae* is attributed to Polemo also at *On Ends* 4.45.

[54] *antiquorum autem sententiam Antiochus noster mihi videtur persequi diligentissime, quam eandem Aristoteli fuisse et Polemonis docet.*

[55] Cf. Gigon (1989) 166. Karamanolis (2006) 72 is cautious as well: '[T]he slight evidence that we have about Polemo's ethics (...) makes it difficult to see how much of Piso's account goes back to Polemo.'

[56] *Lives of Eminent Philosophers* 4.20.

source for Antiochus' Old Academic system, at least in the domain of ethics.[57]

Finally Crantor, a contemporary of Polemo in the Academy, is known for cultivating a rhetorical style of philosophy and for the use of metaphors and illustrations to convey philosophical messages. In one such illustration which survives in Sextus, his imagery conveys the idea of a plurality of goods with virtue, represented by courage, ranking first, followed by the less significant goods of health, pleasure and wealth. Such passages could be read by Antiochus as compatible with the reconstructed value system of the Old Academy, according to which virtue is primary and bodily goods only of secondary importance for the acquisition of happiness;[58] as we shall see, however, Antiochus adopts a more nuanced position with regard to the components of *eudaimonia*, making use of the idea that nature appropriates us both to the psychic and bodily virtues.[59]

Antiochus and the Peripatos

Although Antiochus chose for his movement the name 'Old Academy', Aristotle and Theophrastus are, alongside Plato, the central figures in the tradition that he attempts to resurrect.[60] In Antiochus' understanding of history of philosophy, the Peripatos was just a branch of the Academy. Thus, Aristotle is, perhaps strikingly for modern readers, consistently regarded in Antiochean texts as a faithful disciple of Plato, who inherited and

---

[57] For the view that Polemo is a major source for Antiochus' views in ethics, see Dillon (1977) 57–9; (2003) 159–66 and Sedley (1997) 122. Cf. also Sedley (2012a) 81 who ascribes to Polemo 'summative' authority by virtue of being the final major head of the 'Academy proper' in its early phase, i.e. before Arcesilaus' accession to the headship. In particular Sedley (2002) has defended strongly the Polemonian influence on Old Academic physics, arguing that Varro's account in *Academic Books* 24–9 reflects the physical theory of the Academy in the time of Polemo.

[58] Sextus indeed prefaces the illustration of Crantor with the staple reference to the Old Academy by joining in the same phrase 'the followers of the Academy and the Peripatos', see *Against the Professors* 11.51: ἀγαθὸν δ' εἶπαν αὐτὴν ὑπάρχειν, οὐ μὴν καὶ πρῶτον, οἵ τε ἀπὸ τῆς Ἀκαδημίας καὶ οἱ ἀπὸ τοῦ Περιπάτου. δεῖν γὰρ ὑπέλαβον ἑκάστῳ τῶν ἀγαθῶν τὴν οἰκείαν τάξιν τε καὶ ἀξίαν ἀπονέμειν. ἔνθεν καὶ ὁ Κράντωρ εἰς ἔμφασιν τοῦ λεγομένου βουλόμενος ἡμᾶς ἄγειν πάνυ χαρίεντι συνεχρήσατο παραδείγματι.

[59] See Chapter 8, *infra*.

[60] For the novelty of Antiochus' move to attach Aristotle (and Theophrastus) to the Academic lineage, see Sedley (1989) 118.

elaborated further Platonic ideas.[61] Varro, using the Carneadean distinction of *res* and *verba*, stresses in *Academic Books* 17 that Academics and Peripatetics build a single philosophical system, although they apply to themselves different names (*qui rebus congruentes nominibus differebant*).[62] Varro seeks thereby to underplay any doctrinal differences between the two schools by attributing their distinctive designation merely to the fact that Academics and Peripatetics used to assemble at different locations in Athens—the Peripatetics in the Lyceum, the Academics in the Academy.[63]

In sharp contrast to the vague references to the followers of Plato, Antiochean passages demonstrate some first-hand acquaintance with Peripatetic treatises. The importance assigned to the availability of the written texts of the Peripatetic authorities becomes evident by the way Piso, the Antiochean spokesperson in *On Ends* 5 (9–12), goes to great lengths to advertise his knowledge of the Peripatetic corpus, and in particular of the *commentarii* (translating in all probability the Greek *hypomnēmata*) of the Peripatos, treating the latter as authoritative material for the reconstruction of the Old Academic ethical doctrines. This may also give credence to the hypothesis that Antiochus was under the influence of the resurgence of interest in the school treatises of the Peripatos, which followed upon the transfer of the texts from Greece to Rome in the time of Sulla.[64]

---

[61] Cf. Diogenes Laertius, *Lives of Eminent Philosophers* 4.67. On historical evidence regarding the engagement of Aristotle and early Peripatetics with Plato, see Karamanolis (2006) 331–36. Such evidence hardly justifies though the strong Antiochean claim that the Academy and the Peripatos held the same doctrines.

[62] *Academic Books* 17: *una et consentiens duobus vocabulis philosophiae forma institute est Academicorum et Peripateticorum, qui rebus congruentes nominibus differebant.* Cf. *ibid.* 18: *quae quidem erat primo duobus ut dixi nominibus una; nihil enim inter Peripateticos et illam veterem Academiam differebat.*

[63] *Ibid.* 17: *nam cum Speusippum sororis filium Plato philosophiae quasi heredem reliquisset, duo autem praestantissimo studio atque doctrina, Xenocratem Calchedonium et Aristotelem Stagiritem, qui erant cum Aristotele Peripatetici dicti sunt quia disputabant inambulantes in Lycio, illi autem quia Platonis instituto in Academia quod est alterum gymnasium coetus erant et sermones habere soliti e loci vocabulo nomen habuerunt.*

[64] This may not mean that Aristotelian writings were unavailable before that time. The list of Aristotelian writings in Diogenes Laertius' *Lives of Eminent Philosophers* 5.22–27 suggests the availability of, at least, some Aristotelian writings in Alexandria during the Hellenistic period and before the editorial activity of Andronicus, see Moraux (1973) 4

The Peripatetic philosophical system is organised in Piso's account according to the Stoic threefold division of philosophy into physics, dialectic and ethics; a division which leaves aside the domain of metaphysics.[65] In the domain of physics, Piso refers to topics on the physical elements and on the universe, alluding also to the use in these domains of demonstrative proofs as a methodological tool.[66] Particular stress is put on Aristotelian works on animals with Piso's references perhaps alluding to such works as *On the Generation of Animals* and *On the Parts of Animals*, and the Theophrastean ones on plants with what sounds like an explicit reference to the treatise *On the Causes of Plants* at *On Ends* 5.10.[67] In the part of the catalogue which refers to

n.2, Gottschalk (1987) 1085 and Barnes (1997) 13–16. The event of the 'rediscovery' of the Peripatetic school treatises after a long period of neglect is mainly known through the two anecdotal reports in Strabo 13.1.54 and Plutarch's *Life of Sulla* 26. The credentials of the rediscovery story have more recently received important support from the evidence discussed in Primavesi (2007) 51–77.

[65] There is no evidence that Antiochus knew of the treatises which came to form the collection of the *Metaphysics*. A reference to Aristotle's 'undermining' of the Platonic 'ideas' (*species*), as part of the 'innovations' to the Old Academic system that need to be excised, at *Academic Books* 33 (*Aristoteles igitur primus species quas paulo ante dixi labefactavit, quas mirifice Plato erat amplexus ut in iis quiddam divinum esse diceret*) may be a (vague) reference to the Aristotelian critique of Ideas at *Metaphysics* 1.9 (990a32–993a11), or to the fragmentary Aristotelian treatise *On Ideas*. However, Varro presents Platonic ideas in *Academic Books* 30 merely from an epistemological perspective, namely as mental objects of knowledge. Accordingly, he moves from a reference to Platonic 'ideas' to a reference to 'concepts of the soul' (*animi notionibus*) in *ibid*. 32. I thus follow Karamanolis (2006) 63–65 and Boys-Stones (2012) 226 in understanding the objection made at *Academic Books* 33 as purporting to have mainly an epistemological relevance. For a reconstruction of the Aristotelian position which is attacked by Antiochus, in the context of first century BCE Aristotelianism, see Boys-Stones (2012) 225–27. See also *ibid*. 228 for the choice of the word *labefactare* on Antiochus' part. Furthermore, the *Categories* are nowhere explicitly referred to in the Antiochean accounts; given the flourishing of commentaries on this treatise in the next generation of Aristotelian commentators, this absence of reference seems even more striking. For evidence of Boethus' and Andronicus' engagement with the *Categories*, see Simplicius *On Aristotle's Categories* 29.28–30.5.

[66] *On Ends* 5.9: *natura sic ab iis investigata est, ut nulla pars caelo, mari, terra, ut poëtice loquar, praetermissa sit; quin etiam, cum de rerum initiis omnique mundo locuti essent, ut multa non modo probabili argumentatione, sed etiam necessaria mathematicorum ratione concluderent, maximam materiam ex rebus per se investigatis ad rerum occultarum cognitionem attulerunt.* The text is discussed briefly at Sharples (2010) 107.

[67] *Ibid*. 5.10: *persecutus est Aristoteles animantium omnium ortus, victus, figuras, Theophrastus autem stirpium naturas omniumque fere rerum, quae e terra gignerentur, causas atque rationes.* Cf. also Cicero's references, most probably reproducing Antiochean views, at *On Ends* 4.13: *quam multa ab iis (sc. antiquis) conquisita et collecta sunt de omnium animantium genere, ortu, membris, aetatibus! quam multa de rebus iis, quae gignuntur e terra!*

dialectic, Aristotle is explicitly referred to as the first who 'initiated the practice of speaking on either side concerning individual matters' (*de singulis rebus in utramque partem dicendi*); this may well point to material contained in the *Topics*, although the emphasis lies in Piso's catalogue on the dialectical activity, and not on a particular treatise.[68] The Antiochean spokesman is keen in this case on differentiating the Aristotelian practice from that of New Academics, since the latter were using this method in order to arrive at suspension of judgement and not in order to defend a specific thesis or arrive at knowledge.[69]

It is in the domain of ethics that we find the most explicit references in Piso's account to writings of the early Peripatos. Thus, at *On Ends* 5.12 we encounter the earliest allusion to what is known to us as the *Nicomachean Ethics,* although the authorship of those 'books on ethics' (*scripti de moribus libri*) is connected with Nicomachus, Aristotle's son, and not with Aristotle himself; this perhaps suggests that the Aristotelian *corpus* was not yet securely established through a standard edition.[70] A vague

---

[68] *Ibid.* 5.10: *ab Aristoteleque principe de singulis rebus in utramque partem dicendi exercitatio est instituta, ut non contra omnia semper, sicut Arcesilas, diceret, et tamen ut in omnibus rebus, quicquid ex utraque parte dici posset, expromeret.* Aristotle refers to the method of arguing on both sides of a question in the context of 'problems' (προβλήματα) i.e. questions as to whether a statement is so or not, see e.g. *Topics* 1.104b1–18. Evidence for the origin of the practice comes from yet another source: Alexander of Aphrodisias refers to the practice of εἰς ἑκάτερον μέρος ἐπιχείρησις as involving arguing for and against a specific thesis for reasons of training (γυμνασία). Alexander affirms that there are books of Aristotle and Theophrastus with examples of this practice and adds that this method was used a lot by the 'ancients', see Alexander *On the Topics* 27.11–18: ἢ γυμνασίαν λέγοι ἂν τὴν εἰς ἑκάτερον μέρος ἐπιχείρησιν. ἦν δὲ σύνηθες τὸ τοιοῦτον εἶδος τῶν λόγων τοῖς ἀρχαίοις, καὶ τὰς συνουσίας τὰς πλείστας τούτων ἐποιοῦντο τὸν τρόπον, οὐκ ἐπὶ βιβλίων ὥσπερ νῦν (οὐ γὰρ ἦν πω τότε τοιαῦτα βιβλία), ἀλλὰ θέσεώς τινος τεθείσης εἰς ταύτην γυμνάζοντες αὐτῶν τὸ πρὸς τὰς ἐπιχειρήσεις εὑρετικὸν ἐπεχείρουν, κατασκευάζοντές τε καὶ ἀνασκευάζοντες δι' ἐνδόξων τὸ κείμενον. καὶ ἔστι δὲ βιβλία τοιαῦτα Ἀριστοτέλους τε καὶ Θεοφράστου γεγραμμένα ἔχοντα τὴν εἰς τὰ ἀντικείμενα δι' ἐνδόξων ἐπιχείρησιν.

[69] The Aristotelian 'constructive' manner and the 'destructive' one of Arcesilaus and Carneades are contrasted also in a passage from On the *Orator* 3.80, where Crassus refers to the ideal orator: the ideal orator should combine both manners, arguing for and against a thesis, and not adopt only the 'eristic' one of opposing every thesis.

[70] *On Ends* 5.12: *quare teneamus Aristotelem et eius filium Nicomachum, cuius accurate scripti de moribus libri dicuntur illi quidem esse Aristoteli, sed non video cur non potuerit patri similis esse filius.* Piso seems here to treat the text as authoritative for the Old Academic conception of the *telos* that he expounds in *On Ends* 5. On the other hand Hirzel (1882) 718–20 sees in the ascription of the work to Nicomachus a deliberate

---

reference to the *Nicomachean Ethics* may also be contained in Piso's allusion to a 'most illustrious' discourse (*inlustris oratio*) dedicated to the defence of the intellectual life at *On Ends* 5.11.[71] To the *commentarii* in the domain of ethics, Piso adds the so-called exoteric works of the Peripatos;[72] this seems to tally with evidence in Piso's account, suggesting the use of some examples from the *Protrepticus*[73] for the defence of the value of theoretical virtue.[74] Finally, Piso refers in his exposition to works of both early Peripatetic authorities on politics, alluding to, among others, the collections of constitutions and laws from various cities, but also to a treatise on the best constitution (*optimus rei publicae status*).[75]

The exposition offered, with its allusions to the biological and botanical investigations of the Peripatos, highlights Aristotle and Theophrastus as experts in the domain of natural science; this corresponds to the way empirical observations about plants and animals are integrated into the ethical account of *On Ends* 5.[76] It may well be the case that Antiochus regarded the study of the behaviour of living organisms (including plants) as the particular contribution of the Peripatos to the system of the Old Academy.

---

attempt on Antiochus' part to take a distance from the conception of *eudaimonia* advocated in the *Nicomachean Ethics*. Rawson (1985) 290 espouses the view that Piso's reference to Nicomachus suggests that the work was read in a pre-Andronican edition. For a discussion of Andronicus' edition, see Gottschalk (1987) 1095 and Barnes (1997) 28–44. Cicero's lack of references to Andronicus may function as an argument *ex silentio* for the suggestion that the edition took place in the second half of the first century BCE.

[71] *Vitae autem degendae ratio maxime quidem illis placuit quieta, in contemplatione et cognitione posita rerum, quae quia deorum erat vitae simillima, sapiente visa est dignissima. Atque his de rebus et splendida est eorum et inlustris oratio.*

[72] *On Ends* 5.12: *de summo autem bono, quia duo genera librorum sunt, unum populariter scriptum, quod ἐξωτερικόν appellabant, alterum limatius, quod in commentariis reliquerunt, non semper idem dicere videntur.*

[73] 'Exoteric' works, like the *Protrepticus*, are alluded to in the 'Antiochean' account at *On Ends* 4.6: *itaque quae sunt eorum (sc. antiquorum) consolationes, quae cohortationes, quae etiam monita et consilia scripta ad summos viros.*

[74] These are discussed in Chapter 6, *infra*.

[75] *Ibid.* 5.11: *omnium fere civitatum non Graeciae solum sed etiam barbariae ab Aristotele mores instituta disciplinas, a Theophrasto leges etiam cognovimus. Cumque uterque eorum docuisset qualem <esse> in re publica principem conveniret, pluribus praeterea conscripsisset qui esset optimus rei publicae status, hoc amplius Theophrastus, quae essent in re publica rerum inclinationes et momenta temporum quibus esset moderandum utcumque res postularet.* The latter must be a reference to the Theophrastean work Πολιτικὰ πρὸς τοὺς καιρούς, see Diogenes Laertius, *Lives of Eminent Philosophers* 5.45. Cf. *On Ends* 4.61.

[76] See Chapter 9, *infra*.

The Peripatos' treatises in this domain put human behaviour into a larger naturalistic context and gave ample examples of the way teleology operates in the natural world. Their observations in this regard provided valuable material for the construction of a thesis of natural appropriation, which, similarly to an equivalent theory advanced by the Stoa, extended to other living forms as well.[77] This theory is advocated as the main idea in Piso's account at *On Ends* 5 and helps to explain the explicit Peripatetic character of this Antiochean account.

The second domain of expertise assigned to the Peripatos seems to be the ethical part of philosophy, a domain intimately connected in Antiquity with political philosophy as well. Antiochus could find in the ethical treatises of the Peripatos defence for the over-riding importance of virtue for a happy life, which he integrated into his account of the Old Academic *telos*. He also seems to borrow from Peripatetic sources the idea that happiness is a kind of activity (*actio*, translating the Greek *energeia*).[78] Still, Antiochus' use of the Peripatetic texts is not an exegetical one, but serves primarily the reconstruction of the main Old Academic doctrines along the lines of a later, specifically Stoic, agenda.[79]

A striking feature of Antiochus' views on the history of philo-sophy is the central role ascribed to Theophrastus as an *equal* authority alongside Aristotle in the Old Academic canon; as we saw their school treatises are presented in Piso's catalogue as supplementing one another.[80] There is no hint that Theophrastus elaborated on or improved in any way on what Aristotle said, as for example in the domain of logic or metaphysics, and the Antiochean spokesman is keen to stress that 'as far as essentials

---

[77] See Chapter 3, *infra*.   [78] See Chapter 8, *infra*.

[79] In line with this, the exact *lexis* of the texts of Aristotle and Theophrastus seems not to be of primary importance and is only vaguely alluded to in the Antiochean passages in Cicero, without explicit indication of sources. There is a clear difference in this respect between Antiochus and the Peripatetics Boethus and Xenarchus who lived in the second half of the first century BCE; the latter drew for their reconstruction of Aristotelian thought explicitly on Aristotelian treatises, see e.g. Alexander, *Mantissa* 17 151.7–13. Even Didymus, who may be chronologically closer to Antiochus, shows more clear signs of a closer engagement with Peripatetic texts, see Introduction, *supra*.

[80] Compare also the title of Didymus' summary of Peripatetic ethics 'Of Aristotle and the Rest of the Peripatetics on Ethics' (Ἀριστοτέλους καὶ τῶν λοιπῶν Περιπατητικῶν περὶ τῶν ἠθικῶν) in the second book of Stobaeus' *Selections*.

are concerned there are no contradictions to be found in the writings of the two leading Peripatetics, nor did they disagree among themselves' (*nec in summa tamen ipsa aut varietas est ulla apud hos quidem quos nominavi aut inter ipsos dissensio*).[81] The view of a harmonious relationship between the two heads of the Peripatos only breaks when it comes to their conception of the happy life, and more explicitly on the issue whether adverse external circumstances can ruin happiness. Here, Theophrastus is shown, as Antiochus puts it, to succumb to the 'weak' view that a virtuous person will not be happy, if bad luck befalls on him. The Theophrastean treatise *On Happiness* is referred to in this context as departing from Aristotle's 'true' opinion on this matter; the thesis that seems to have been expressed in the treatise is that (extremely) unfavourable circumstances can ruin happiness.[82] Accordingly, Theophrastus' opinion is described in Varro's account in the *Academic Books* as 'making a breach in the authority of the old tradition' (*fregit quodam modo auctoritatem veteris disciplinae*).[83] Still Piso attests that he consults Theophrastus 'on most points' (*pleraque*) for the reconstruction of the ethics of the Old Academy.[84]

The favourable attitude towards Theophrastus, in all but the issue of the role of fortune in one's life, can be contrasted with the dismissive references in *On Ends* 5 to other scholarchs of the Peripatetic school from Strato down to nearly contemporary Peripatetic philosophers of Antiochus' own time, like Critolaus.[85] Piso goes so far as to say that the successors of Aristotle within the

---

[81] *On Ends* 5.12

[82] See especially *On Ends* 5.12: q*uod maxime efficit Theophrasti de beata vita liber, in quo multum admodum fortunae datur; quod si ita se habeat, non possit beatam vitam praestare sapientia* and *Academic Books* 33: *Theophrastus autem, vir et oratione suavis et ita moratus ut prae se probitatem quandam et ingenuitatem ferat, vehementius etiam fregit quodam modo auctoritatem veteris disciplinae; spoliavit enim virtutem suo decore imbecillamque reddidit, quod negavit in ea sola positum esse beate vivere.* Cf. *On Ends* 5.77; 5.85.

[83] For all the evidence on Theophrastus' views on fortune, see *Frs.* 487–501 *FHS&G*.

[84] On Ends 5.12: *Theophrastum tamen adhibeamus ad pleraque, dum modo plus in virtute teneamus, quam ille tenuit, firmitatis et roboris.*

[85] Antiochus' dismissive attitude towards the Hellenistic Peripatos matches the views of modern scholars on this period of the school. References to the decline of the Peripatos are made in Moraux (1973) 16 and Lynch (1972) 135. A critical distance from the decline thesis is expressed in White (2004).

Hellenistic Peripatos were so disconnected from the old tradition that Antiochus revives that, as stated at *On Ends* 5.13, they seem to 'have given birth to themselves' (*ut ipsi ex se nati esse videantur*). The reference to the Peripatetics after Theophrastus follows the chronological 'succesion' (*diadochē*) of the school. First in the line is Strato, who is repeatedly accused of neglecting ethics and concentrating on physical science, for which reason he acquired the epithet 'physicist' (*physikos*).[86] A further pair of philosophers, Lyco, scholarch of the Peripatos for almost forty years in the late third century BCE, and Aristo, are rejected by virtue of lacking the authority connected with the school, without, however, any special reference to the (divergent) doctrines they held.[87] Antiochus' dismissive attitude towards the Hellenistic Peripatos finds a match in Strabo, who presents the period after Theophrastus as a decadent phase of the school by virtue of the unavailability of the 'esoteric' treatises of its founding fathers. The rhetorical style that the members of the Peripatos cultivated during this period, with its emphasis on the defence of set propositions and proper recitation, is ridiculed accordingly as not 'proper' philosophising.[88]

A second group of younger Peripatetics, namely Hieronymus of Rhodes (the only one among the Peripatetics that Antiochus discusses who did not hold the official title of a scholarch) and Diodorus of Tyre, are rejected by virtue of the conception of the *telos* they put forward, since both of them are said to have either identified absence of pain with the *telos*,[89] or to have included it on a par with virtue in their formulation of the final end, respectively. Thus, according to the Carneadean classificatory scheme of ethical

---

[86] *On Ends* 5.13: *primum Theophrasti, Strato, physicum se voluit; in quo etsi est magnus, tamen nova pleraque et perpauca de moribus.* Cf. *Academic Books* 34.

[87] *On Ends* 5.13: *huius, Lyco, oratione locuples, rebus ipsis ieiunior. Concinnus deinde et elegans huius, Aristo, sed ea quae desiderata a magno philosopho gravitas in eo non fuit; scripta sane et multa et polita, sed nescio quo pacto auctoritatem oratio non habet.*

[88] Strabo *Geography* 13.1.54: συνέβη δὲ τοῖς ἐκ τῶν Περιπάτων τοῖς μὲν πάλαι τοῖς μετὰ Θεόφραστον οὐκ ἔχουσιν ὅλως τὰ βιβλία πλὴν ὀλίγων, καὶ μάλιστα τῶν ἐξωτερικῶν, μηδὲν ἔχειν φιλοσοφεῖν πραγματικῶς, ἀλλὰ θέσεις ληκυθίζειν. These views have been taken to reflect the attitude of the first generation of 'Aristotelians' in Strabo's time, who viewed Aristotle's text as the proper source of philosophising, see Moraux (1973) 24–5 and Hahm (2007) 99.

[89] The Greek ἀλυπία or ἀοχλησία, and the corresponding *telos* formulas ἀλύπως ζῆν and ἀοχλήτως ζῆν, are rendered variously in Latin through the expressions *vacuitas doloris, non dolere* and *sine ulla molestia vivere*, see *On Ends* 2.8; 2.16; 5.20; 5.73.

views, from which Antiochus seems to derive his information on these Peripatetics, Hieronymus identified the 'good life' with a life lacking pain, whereas Diodorus put forward a composite formula of the 'highest good', whereby the latter consists of a combination of virtue with the absence of pain.[90] Some passages in the Aristotelian ethical treatises which seem to support the view that a life can be deemed happy only if 'unobstructed' and free from the pain associated with adverse circumstances[91] may be taken to support the formulation of the *telos* advanced by these thinkers. Whether Hieronymus and Diodorus in developing their ethical views also committed themselves to a certain conception of the *telos* is something that we cannot conclusively confirm, since no independent evidence on their ethics survives.

Antiochus' rejection of these Peripatetics as 'heterodox' reveals his own favoured interpretation of the Old Academic *telos*. According to this, virtue and a good bodily condition are both inherently desirable and the only constituents of the *telos*.[92] The virtues of the soul, both theoretical and practical, are thereby of predominant importance for *eudaimonia*, to the extent that Antiochus claims that they are sufficient for a happy life. A good bodily condition, for which he counts absence of pain as one among multiple parameters, may contribute only minimally to the happy life, to so limited an extent that it does not in itself determine whether a life is happy or not.[93] As a result of this, Antiochus rejects not only Hieronymus'

---

[90] *On Ends* 5.14: *praetereo multos, in his doctum hominem et suavem, Hieronymum, quem iam cur Peripateticum appellem nescio. Summum enim bonum exposuit vacuitatem doloris; (. . .) Diodorus, eius auditor, adiungit ad honestatem vacuitatem doloris.* For the *telos* conception assigned to the two Peripatetics in the *Carneadea divisio*, see also *On Ends* 2.35: *ita tres sunt fines expertes honestatis, unus Aristippi vel Epicuri, alter Hieronymi, Carneadi tertius, tres, in quibus honestas cum aliqua accessione, Polemonis, Calliphontis, Diodori, una simplex, cuius Zeno auctor, posita in decore tota, id est in honestate.* Cf. *ibid.* 2.8; 2.16; 5.14; 5.20–21; 5.73 and Clemens *Miscellanies* 2.21.127: ὅ τε Ἱερώνυμος ὁ Περιπατητικὸς τέλος μὲν εἶναι τὸ ἀοχλήτως ζῆν, τελικὸν δὲ ἀγαθὸν μόνον τὴν εὐδαιμονίαν.

[91] See e.g. *Nicomachean Ethics* 1.1100b25-30: πολλὰ γινόμενα μὲν εὖ μακαριώτερον τὸν βίον ποιήσει (καὶ γὰρ αὐτὰ συνεπικοσμεῖν πέφυκεν, καὶ ἡ χρῆσις αὐτῶν καλὴ καὶ σπουδαία γίνεται), ἀνάπαλιν δὲ συμβαίνοντα θλίβει καὶ λυμαίνεται τὸ μακάριον· λύπας τε γὰρ ἐπιφέρει καὶ ἐμποδίζει πολλαῖς ἐνεργείαις.

[92] This conception of the *telos* will be discussed in Chapter 8, *infra*.

[93] For the inclusion of absence of pain among the bodily goods in Antiochus' account, see *On Ends* 5.47. For the view that virtue is sufficient for happiness, see *ibid.* 5.71.

telos, as neglecting the dominant component of the happy life, namely virtue,[94] but also the equal inclusion of absence of pain alongside morality in the *telos* formula ascribed to Diodorus, since that would make happiness too dependent upon external conditions.[95] This Peripatetic 'controversy' between Antiochus and earlier representatives of the school may also be viewed in the light of the dialectical context within which Antiochus formulated his Old Academic views.

In this context, the diversity of the views on the *telos* within the Peripatos was made a tool in the hands of the Academic sceptics, who wished to show the inconsistency of the dogmatic tradition.[96] It is suggestive in this respect that Hieronymus' view that absence of pain is not synonymous with pleasure is used by Cicero to attack Epicurus' position. Hieronymus is presented along these lines as holding an alternative hedonistic theory to that of Epicurus.[97] Through juxtaposition to Hieronymus' view, Epicurus was misleadingly presented by the Academic sceptics as promoting a conception of pleasure as the highest end, which corresponds to the neutral state of tranquillity or absence of pain, and is at odds with a 'positive' conception of pleasure (the *voluptas*) which again, allegedly, Epicurus, alongside Aristippus, advocated as the first object of pursuit at the beginning of our lives. In this case, the comparison with both Hieronymus and Aristippus attempted to reduce the Epicurean thesis to a repetition of the *telos* formula of one or other of these two thinkers, who put forward a neutral and a 'positive' understanding of pleasure

---

[94] See Piso's remarks at *On Ends* 5.21, that a conception of the *telos* which makes both pleasure and absence of pain the *sole* ends of human conduct should be rejected on the grounds that 'human beings are born to a certain higher destiny': *sed quoniam non possunt omnia simul dici, haec in praesentia nota esse debebunt, voluptatem semovendam esse, quando ad maiora quaedam, ut iam apparebit, nati sumus. De vacuitate doloris eadem fere dici solent quae de voluptate.* A similar polemic is attributed to Chrysippus at *Lucullus* 140. For Chrysippus' anti-hedonistic polemics, see Algra (1997) 116.

[95] With regard to composite conceptions of the *telos*, which include morality alongside pleasure or freedom from pain (without, however, suggesting the primacy of virtue), see Piso's remarks at *On Ends* 5.22: *coniunctio autem cum honestate vel voluptatis vel non dolendi id ipsum honestum quod amplecti vult, id efficit turpe. Ad eas enim res referre quae agas, quarum una, si quis malo careat, in summo eum bono dicat esse, altera versetur in levissima parte naturae, obscurantis est omnem splendorem honestatis, ne dicam inquinantis.*

[96] Cf. Hahm (2007) 75.   [97] *On Ends* 2.9; 2.16.

respectively.[98] The alleged contradiction of Epicurus rested on the false assumption that there is a neutral state of pleasure disconnected from a 'positive' conception of pleasure; accordingly, negative terms such as 'lack of pain' (*aponia*) are viewed as conceptually distinct from the concept of pleasure (*hēdonē*), rather than as different aspects of it.[99] By contrast, Antiochus wishes to present the Old Academy as part of a different 'debate', i.e. as an alternative to Stoicism and as a tradition which uncompromisingly recognises the overriding value of virtue for a happy life, without at the same time wholly neglecting the bodily aspects of human nature.

Furthermore, by accusing the Peripatetics of deviating from the teaching of the Old Academy, Antiochus seems to import a standard which was perhaps foreign to the practice of the Hellenistic Peripatos. Members of the latter seem to have been allowed to explore different aspects of Aristotle's philosophy in response to contemporary concerns, without perceiving this as a threat to their Peripatetic philosophical identity.[100] An explanation for this could be that the Aristotelian text was not seen as a repository of fixed doctrines that needed to be preserved, but as a basis for critical investigation and further debate. The Antiochean attitude towards these thinkers reveals a different approach which puts centre stage the recovery of established views, namely doctrines, which make up the identity of a philosophical school.[101]

---

[98] See especially *On Ends* 2.35, where the role of the Academic sceptic is assumed by the *persona* of Cicero himself: *Epicurus autem cum in prima commendatione voluptatem dixisset, si eam, quam Aristippus, idem tenere debuit ultimum bonorum, quod ille; sin eam, quam Hieronymus, <ne> fecisset idem, ut voluptatem illam Aristippi in prima commendatione poneret*. The Epicurean distinction between 'kinetic' and 'katastematic' pleasure, which is introduced at passages such as *On Ends* 2.9, appears as a late Epicurean attempt to answer this New Academic critique. The distinction is attacked by 'Cicero' at *ibid.* 2.16 by reference again to Hieronymus.

[99] Epicurus, however, refers to pleasure using both positive and negative terms, see, for example, *On Ends* 1.37, where we find both, on the one hand, *vacuitate omnis molestiae* and, on the other hand, *detractio molestiae* and *doloris amotio* as descriptions of pleasure (*voluptas*). For the idea that the differentiation between 'kinetic' and 'static' pleasure was attributed to Epicurus for polemical purposes, see Nikolsky (2001).

[100] In this respect, Inwood (2014) 29 speaks about 'the latitude inherent in Aristotelianism'. Cf. *ibid.* 44.

[101] Cf. Sharples (2010) 1.

We do not possess much evidence for the period from the death of Lyco to Critolaus (around 150 BCE) and the silence of Diogenes Laertius on this period contributes a lot to our ignorance. Antiochus declared that Critolaus 'wished to imitate the ancients' (*imitari voluit antiquos*), especially in terms of his philosophical style and diction, something which perhaps suggests an attempt at revival of ancient thought already in his time.[102] In the domain of physics, Critolaus seems to have claimed that the mind is made out of the so-called fifth substance,[103] a view which is presented as Aristotelian doctrine in Varro's account in *Academic Books* 26.[104] In another case, Antiochus seems to be borrowing the Critolaan metaphor of the scales of a balance in order to illustrate the overriding value of the goods of the soul in relation to bodily goods.[105] Still, the reference to Critolaus in the Antiochean excursus at *On Ends* 5.14 ends with the verdict that he did not remain faithful to the doctrines of the 'ancients' (*ac tamen <ne> is quidem in patriis institutis manet*), suggesting that he fell short of being an heir to the Peripatetic tradition. The rationale of this rejection is not given explicitly in the text but may be connected to Critolaus' view that the *telos* is a 'joint completion' (*symplērōma*) of all three types of goods. Antiochus most probably thought that such a position does not recognise in a lucid way the primacy of virtue with regard to the other categories of goods by failing to make relevant distinctions. To answer such problems, Antiochus offers his own theory about 'two degrees' of happiness.[106]

---

[102] *On Ends* 5.14. [103] See Critolaus *Frs.* 16–18 Wehrli.

[104] *quintum genus, e quo essent astra mentesque, singulare eorumque quattuor quae supra dixi dissimile Aristoteles quoddam esse rebatur.*

[105] *On Ends* 5.91–92. Cf. *Tusculan Disputations* 5.50 = Critolaus *Fr.* 21 Wehrli: *quo loco quaero quam vim habeat libra illa Critolai qui cum in alteram lancem animi bona imponat, in alteram corporis et externa, tantum propendere illam bonorum animi lancem putet, ut terram et maria deprimat.* For a discussion of this image, see Hahm (2007) 66 and Inwood (2014) 58.

[106] For the same reason Critolaus is criticised in Didymus' epitome of Peripatetic ethics. For a dicussion of this controversy, see Chapter 8, *infra*. Hahm (2007) 95, on the other hand, suggests that Antiochus concealed the similarities between Critolaus' views and his own, 'so that he himself could claim the distinction of reviving Peripatetic philosophy in the guise of his "Old Academic" philosophy'. Although their views are similar, at least on the importance of external goods for happiness, Antiochus seems to diverge from Critolaus, see Chapter 8, *infra*.

Critolaus' pupils are also referred to as 'heterodox' Peripatetics in Piso's account; these include Diodorus of Tyre, Critolaus' successor and last head of the Peripatos after Sulla's siege of Athens, and also Callipho and Aristo the younger. No information is, however, given in Antiochean passages on their respective doctrines. We may conclude by saying that the narrative of a degenerate post-Theophrastean Peripatos, as it is found in the Antiochean account at *On Ends* 5, primarily serves Antiochus' aim of showing that the doctrines of the Peripatos are contained exclusively in the writings of Aristotle and Theophrastus, and not in their successors. The claim that Antiochus seems to make is that he is the one who recovers these (original) doctrines by appropriately linking Aristotle and Theophrastus to the tradition of the Academy; the latter also incorporates the Stoa, the school that was flourishing in the same period as the Peripatos had fallen into decadence.[107]

Antiochus and the Stoa

Although Antiochus drew the material for his reconstruction of Old Academic ethics from Academic and Peripatetic writings, something attributed to Carneades in Diogenes Laertius can be rightly said of him too: without the Stoa, there would be no Antiochus.[108] First of all, the Stoa supplied the epistemological basis for Antiochus' conversion to dogmatism. In the *Lucullus* (11–61), which contains an exposition of Antiochean epistemology, Antiochus emerges not as a defender of the Old Academy but as an ardent follower of Stoic epistemological views.[109] Thus, the homonymous Antiochean spokesperson

---

[107] See *On Ends* 5.14: *antiquorum autem sententiam Antiochus noster mihi videtur persequi diligentissime, quam eandem Aristoteli fuisse et Polemonis docet.*

[108] Diogenes Laertius *Lives of Eminent Philosophers* 4.62: Καρνεάδης Ἐπικώμου ἢ Φιλοκώμου, ὡς Ἀλέξανδρος ἐν Διαδοχαῖς, Κυρηναῖος. οὗτος τὰ τῶν Στωικῶν βιβλία ἀναγνοὺς ἐπιμελῶς <καὶ μάλιστα> τὰ Χρυσίππου, ἐπιεικῶς αὐτοῖς ἀντέλεγε καὶ εὐημέρει τοσοῦτον, ὥστε ἐκεῖνο ἐπιλέγειν· εἰ μὴ γὰρ ἦν Χρύσιππος, οὐκ ἂν ἦν ἐγώ.

[109] Antiochus' favourable attitude towards Stoicism in the *Lucullus* may be also explained on the grounds that the *Lucullus* is based on a different kind of Antiochean work than the one which formed the basis for the ethical account at *On Ends*; rather than being a doxographical work which explicitly attempts to offer a reconstruction of the views of the 'ancients', the main source of the *Lucullus* seems to be an Antiochean work,

explicitly sets out in this account to defend Zeno's so-called *cataleptic* impressions as a reliable foundation to our epistemic access to truth.[110] In his epistemology, as laid out in the *Lucullus*, Antiochus proves himself to be a *germanissimus Stoicus*, to borrow Cicero's expression.[111] Varro's short discussion of Old Academic epistemology in the *Academic Books*, on the other hand, shows an appreciation of the way Platonic views differed from those of the Stoics on some key epistemological points, such as the reliability of the senses for the acquisition of knowledge.[112]

The short account of Old Academic physics, again in *Academic Books* (24–9), attests Antiochus' engagement with Plato's account of the creation of the world in the *Timaeus*. Here, we can discern an attempt to fit Platonic views, as expressed in the *Timaeus* creation story, into a doxographical scheme of an active and passive principle, as part of a dualist interpretation of the Platonic account.

---

possibly the *Sosus*, which contained an explicit polemic against the former associates of Antiochus, the Academic sceptics.

[110] See *Lucullus* 18, where Lucullus states that he will put his attack on the New Academy there at the service of defending Zeno's definition of the cataleptic impression, including the condition of infallibility tied to Zeno's definition; according to the latter, true impressions should always be distinguishable from false ones, see e.g. *Lucullus* 18: *visum igitur inpressum effictumque ex eo unde esset quale esse non posset ex eo unde non esset.*

[111] *Lucullus* 132. The strongest recent expression of Antiochus' Stoic credentials in epistemology may be found in Brittain (2012). Cf. Sharples (2010) 106.

[112] The different nature of Varro's account is reflected in the way it diverges from the philosophical doctrines conveyed in the *Lucullus*. Thus, the short epistemological remarks of Varro in the *Academic Books* 30–32 focus on the deficiency of the senses offering an anti-empiricist interpretation of early Academic epistemology. For example, Varro's reference to the continual flux of perceptible things (*quia continenter laberentur et fluerent omnia*) seems to point to some views found in Plato's *Theaetetus* (152e), see Long (1995) 46 n.18. On the other hand, we also find in the passage a clear expression of the two-world view found at *Timaeus* 27d–28a, with a reference to the perceptible realm as what is 'an object of opinion' (*itaque hanc omnem partem rerum opinabilem appellabant*); for a relevant discussion of Antiochus' reference to the *Timaeus*, see Sedley (2012a) 85. By contrast, the Antiochean spokesman in the *Lucullus* passes a favourable judgement with regard to the epistemic role of the senses, saying that they are able to make 'clear and certain judgements' (*clara iudicia et certa*) with regard to their individual subject-matter. Such views seem to signal Antiochus' commitment to Stoic doctrines in the domain of epistemology. A vindication of the senses as reliable is also explicitly attributed by Varro to Zeno in *Academic Books* 1.40–2. For the suggestion of a different 'historical model' used in the two Antiochean accounts found in the *Lucullus* and the *Academic Books*, see Sedley (2012a) 84.

The reconstruction offered points to an approximation between Platonic and Stoic views in this domain.

Varro begins his summary of Old Academic physics by postulating a pair of primary contrary principles. According to this, everything is made from a formative (*efficiens*) and a passive (*se praebens*) principle or power; the two Latin terms must translate the Greek pair *poiētikos* and *pathētikos*.[113] The active principle is further specified as a form of power (*vis*), the passive with matter (*materia*).[114] These primary principles do not derive from each other, nor from anything else, whereas everything else that exists derives from them. Varro's account suggests that the primary principles, the formative one and the material one, are in theory independent of each other, but in the physical world they are necessarily bound to each other in order to form the physical reality; as Varro puts it *in utroque … utrumque*: the active force is the presupposition for the coherence and unity of the material substratum, whereas, on the other hand, the formative force is necessarily manifested in a material substratum.[115] Following the identification of the primary principles, Varro gives an account of their interaction for the formation of substances. Thus, the affection of (passive) matter by the formative principle leads to the creation of bodies (*corpora*), which are also called 'qualities' (*qualitates*), or at *Academic Books* 28 'qualified things' (*qualia*),

---

[113] *Academic Books* 24: *de natura autem (id enim sequebatur) ita dicebant ut eam dividerent in res duas, ut altera esset efficiens, altera autem quasi huic se praebens, eaque efficeretur aliquid.* The pair of an active and a passive principle defined as δύναμις τοῦ ποιεῖν καὶ πάσχειν makes its first appearance in Plato's *Sophist* as a suggestion of the Eleatic Stranger, see *Sophist* 247e: Λέγω δὴ τὸ καὶ ὁποιανοῦν [τινα] κεκτημένον δύναμιν εἴτ' εἰς τὸ ποιεῖν ἕτερον ὁτιοῦν πεφυκὸς εἴτ' εἰς τὸ παθεῖν καὶ σμικρότατον ὑπὸ τοῦ φαυλοτάτου, κἂν εἰ μόνον εἰς ἅπαξ, πᾶν τοῦτο ὄντως εἶναι· τίθεμαι γὰρ ὅρον [ὁρίζειν] τὰ ὄντα ὡς ἔστιν οὐκ ἄλλο τι πλὴν δύναμις. For the occurrence of the pair in relation to first principles, see also Aristotle's *Physics* 1.189b14: τὰ δύο μὲν ποιεῖν τὸ δὲ ἓν πάσχειν. Such a pair of principles deemed τὸ ποιοῦν and τὸ πάσχον is attributed to the Stoics as well, see e.g. Diogenes Laertius *Lives of Eminent Philosophers* 7.134 = *SVF* 1.85 (from Zeno's *On Substance*): δοκεῖ δ' αὐτοῖς ἀρχὰς εἶναι τῶν ὅλων δύο, τὸ ποιοῦν καὶ τὸ πάσχον· τὸ μὲν οὖν πάσχον εἶναι τὴν ἄποιον οὐσίαν τὴν ὕλην, τὸ δὲ ποιοῦν τὸν ἐν αὐτῇ λόγον τὸν θεόν.

[114] *Academic Books* 24: *in eo quod efficeret vim esse censebant, in eo autem quod efficeretur tantum modo materiam quandam.*

[115] *Academic Books* 24: *neque enim materiam ipsam cohaerere potuisse si nulla vi contineretur, neque vim sine aliqua materia.* As Inwood (2012) 209 notes the interdependence of formative force and matter relates specifically to their 'independent, spatially determinate existence'.

namely things of a certain sort.[116] The bodies created by the interaction of formative force and matter in Antiochus' account include both the primary (*principes*) substances (the principles or elements),[117] also called 'simple bodies' (*simplices*), and the macroscopic, derivative (*ex his ortae*), or composite, bodies, which are deemed varied (*variae*) and of 'many kinds' (*multiformes*).[118] The 'simple bodies' consist in the four traditional elements (air, water, fire and earth), of which air and fire themselves play an active role, whereas earth and water act as passive elements.[119] Out of the interaction of these come about living organisms, both animate and inanimate.[120] Using a verbal echo from the *Timaeus*, in the sentence *nihil est enim quod non alicubi esse cogatur* in *Academic Books* 24, the Antiochean spokesperson further identifies matter with space.[121]

Making a transition at *Academic Books* 29, Varro says that the 'power' (namely the formative principle) is a mind and perfected wisdom, which the 'ancients' call god (*quam vim ... esse mentem sapientiamque perfectam, quem deum appellant*). In this way the divine principle is identified with the formative one.[122] In his brief

---

[116] *Academic Books* 24: *sed quod ex utroque, id iam corpus et quasi qualitatem quandam nominabant*. However, in *ibid*. 28 the word *qualitas* is reserved for the active principle, whereas the body resulting from the interaction between an active and a passive principle is called *quale: et cum ita moveatur illa vis quam qualitatem esse diximus, et cum sic ultro citroque versetur, et materiam ipsam totam penitus commutari putant et illa effici quae appellant qualia.*

[117] See *Academic Books* 26: *ergo illa initia et ut e Graeco vertam elementa dicuntur*. This translates the Greek ἀρχαί καὶ στοιχεῖα.

[118] *Ibid.*: *earum igitur qualitatum sunt aliae principes aliae ex his ortae. Principes sunt unius modi et simplices; ex his autem ortae variae sunt et quasi multiformes*. For the differentiation between simple and composite bodies, see also Aristotle *Physics* 1. 189b32–34: φαμὲν γὰρ γίγνεσθαι ἐξ ἄλλου ἄλλο καὶ ἐξ ἑτέρου ἕτερον ἢ τὰ ἁπλᾶ λέγοντες ἢ τὰ συγκείμενα; cf. *On Heavens* 268b26ff; *Metaphysics*, 1028b8–13. For the characterization of 'macroscopic' bodies as πολυειδῆ, see *Phaedo* 80b4.

[119] *Academic Books* 26: *e quibus aer et ignis movendi vim habent et efficiendi, reliquae partes accipiendi et quasi patiendi, aquam dico et terram.*

[120] *Ibid.*: *ex his autem ortae animantium formae earumque rerum quae gignuntur e terra.*

[121] Varro's sentence echoes *Timaeus* 52b: φαμὲν ἀναγκαῖον εἶναί που τὸ ὂν ἅπαν ἔν τινι τόπῳ καὶ κατέχον χώραν τινά. Cf. Reid (1885) 125, n.9. The Antiochean account may contain also other echoes of the *Timaeus*, according to Sedley (2002) 55.

[122] The juxtaposition of the Old Academy with Stoic physics in *Academic Books* 39 suggests that the formal (or efficient) cause is understood by Antiochus as being of immaterial nature: *discrepabat (sc. Zeno) etiam ab isdem, quod nullo modo arbitrabatur quicquam effici posse ab ea quae expers esset corporis, cuius generis Xenocrates et superiores etiam animum esse dixerant, nec vero aut quod efficeret aliquid aut quod efficeretur posse esse non corpus.*

exposition of Antiochean physics, Varro also favours a *continuum* theory of matter; accordingly, he denies at *Academic Books* 27 that there is an absolute minimum in nature which does not admit of division (*cum sit nihil omnino in rerum natura minimum quod dividi nequeat*).[123] In line with this, matter, or the passive principle, on which the formative principle acts is further analysed into a primary matter which is indestructible and entirely devoid of any specification; this kind of matter underlies any kind of substance, including the simple substances of the four elements, and admits of indefinite alteration and division, through the action of the active principle.[124] The active principle is further identified with the 'world soul' (*animus mundi*), a rational divine principle,[125] which is also deemed 'necessity' (*necessitas*).[126]

Although Varro's account of the natural world matches in its general features the *Timaeus'* emphasis on the way an active principle 'establishes order' through form and shapes a material substrate for the creation of the visible cosmos, it also silences the role of transcendent Ideas,[127] which serve in the narrative of the *Timaeus* as the intelligible paradigms of perceptible reality. The picture that emerges from Varro's account reflects, by contrast, an immanentist view of the formative principle. The interpretative choices sketched above seem to support the view that Antiochus, while explicitly relying on Plato's text,

---

[123] *Academic Books* 27: *quae autem moveantur omnia intervallis moveri, quae intervalla item infinite dividi possint.* The doctrine that matter is divisible *ad infinitum* is attributed to the Stoics at Diogenes Laertius *Lives of Eminent Philosophers* 7.150. Cf. also *SVF* 2.482–491.

[124] *Academic Books* 27: *sed subiectam putant omnibus sine ulla specie atque carentem omni illa qualitate (. . .) materiam quandam, ex qua omnia expressa atque effecta sint, quae tota omnia accipere possit omnibusque modis mutari atque ex omni parte eoque etiam interire, non in nihilum sed in suas partes, quae infinite secari ac dividi possint.*

[125] *Ibid.* 29: *quam vim animum esse dicunt mundi, eandemque esse mentem sapientiamque perfectam, quem deum appellant.*

[126] *Ibid.* 29: *quam interdum eandem necessitatem appellant, quia nihil aliter possit atque ab ea constitutum sit, (. . .) quasi fatalem et immutabilem continuationem ordinis sempiterni.* The wording used here largely reflects Stoic formulations, see *SVF* 2.917–21.

[127] This is corroborated by reference to Platonic Ideas (merely) as *animi notiones* in *Academic Books* 32. One may, however, find in a further reference to the 'divine' character of Platonic Forms *ibid.* 33 acknowledgement on Antiochus' part of their special status. Bonazzi (2012) 323, n.49 speaks on the basis of this reference of the 'ontological transcendence' of Forms in Antiochus, although he admits that evidence is scarce for a complete reconstruction of Antiochus' interpretation of Platonic Forms.

advanced a reading of the *Timaeus* along lines which were defined by the Stoic philosophical agenda in the domain of physics.[128] By contrast the Antiochean ethical account of *On Ends* 5 reveals another strategy towards Stoicism. In this domain, Antiochus sets out explicitly to offer an *alternative* account to the one offered by the Stoa on the basis of ideas that he traces back to the Academic and the Peripatetic tradition. A crucial part of this strategy is to present the Stoic views in ethics as derivative in comparison with the ones found in the old tradition. On this point, Antiochus seems to have been crucially influenced by the dialectical approach of the New Academy. A large part of the activity of the New Academy (especially when Carneades was head of the school) was dedicated to the dialectical refutation of the dominant school of the Hellenistic period, namely Stoicism. Stoics were

---

[128] Fladerer (1996) 40–43 treats Varro's summary as an attempt to faithfully represent the Platonic views in the *Timaeus* and views the silence of the role of the Ideas as a shift of emphasis, see e.g. *ibid.* 43: 'Sein Schweigen über das wahrhaft Seiende soll nicht als Widerspruch zu Platon interpretiert werden, sondern ist Ausdruck eines anders gelagerten Problembewusstseins.' For an advocacy of the Stoic influences on this passage, see Inwood (2012). Sedley (2002) 43, by contrast, takes this passage to reflect historical views of the Early Academy, which subsequently functioned as a model for the development of the Stoic physical theory. He relies for this on the emphasis with which Antiochus' version of Academic physics rejects the Xenocratean thesis of indivisibles, i.e. of minimal geometrical lines as the ultimate constituents of physical reality. In particular, he connects the views expressed in Varro's passage with the Academy in the time of Polemo. On this interpretation, Zeno's historical link with Polemo may serve to explain the strong similarities of the views attributed to the Old Academy with Stoic theses in physics. This view is also endorsed by Dillon (2003) ch. 4. For criticisms against this line of interpretation, see Inwood (2012) 215–17. The 'historical' interpretation of Varro's passage may be corroborated, as Sedley (2002) points out, by evidence of an interpretation of Plato's *Timaeus* along the lines of a two-principle doxographical scheme which is found already in a Theophrastean fragment, see Theophrastus *Fr.* 230 FHS&G = Simplicius *Commentary on Aristotle's Physics* CAG t.9 p.26.5–15 Diels: ὁ μέντοι Θεόφραστος τοὺς ἄλλους προϊστορήσας "τούτοις, φησίν, ἐπιγενόμενος Πλάτων, τῇ μὲν δόξῃ καὶ τῇ δυνάμει πρότερος τοῖς δὲ χρόνοις ὕστερος καὶ τὴν πλείστην πραγματείαν περὶ τῆς πρώτης φιλοσοφίας ποιησάμενος, ἐπέδωκεν ἑαυτὸν καὶ τοῖς φαινομένοις ἁψάμενος τῆς περὶ φύσεως ἱστορίας ἐν ᾗ δύο τὰς ἀρχὰς βούλεται ποιεῖν τὸ μὲν ὑποκείμενον ὡς ὕλην ὃ προσαγορεύει πανδεχές, τὸ δὲ ὡς αἴτιον καὶ κινοῦν, ὃ περιάπτει τῇ τοῦ θεοῦ καὶ τῇ τοῦ ἀγαθοῦ δυνάμει." In some more recent remarks Sedley (2012a) 102–3 suggests that an 'unhistorical retrojection of Stoic physics onto the early Academy' on Antiochus' part would be in line with his early interpretative practices. He suggests that Antiochus' (alleged) epistemological doxography of Platonist views on the criterion in Sextus' *Against the Professors* 7 (see Introduction, *supra*) may serve as an example of this interpretative practice, although he also argues that Varro's account, in which the passage on physics occurs, derives from Antiochus' later work, which distances itself from such distortions and contains more historically sensitive readings of the old tradition.

forced to answer to the Carneadean critique and revise their original doctrines in the light of such attacks. Some of the polemical strategies of Carneades were inherited by Antiochus as well, and were used for the defence of the primacy of the philosophical tradition of the Old Academy against the Stoa, in the domain of ethics. At *On Ends* 3.41, for example, the position that the difference between Stoics and Peripatetics is merely terminological, and not substantial, is explicitly ascribed to Carneades,[129] but it is repeatedly used in Antiochean passages in Cicero as well.[130] Antiochus uses the same technique in order to defend his 'unitary' Academy by arguing that although Academics and Peripatetics differed in name, they agreed on the same philosophical doctrines.[131]

Another Carneadean technique inherited by Antiochus is that of the division and classification of different ethical views that is explicitly referred to in the fifth book of *On Ends* (5.16). The scheme was meant to help to trace inconsistencies or disagreement (*diaphōnia*) across ethical traditions by comparing their respective conception of the ultimate end of action (*telos*). The notion of *diaphōnia* within a tradition was used by Academic sceptics as a tool in order to discredit the view held by the founder of that tradition, showing how one could reach different

---

[129] *Carneades tuus egregia quadam exercitatione in dialecticis summaque eloquentia rem in summum discrimen adduxit, propterea quod pugnare non destitit in omni hac quaestione, quae de bonis et malis appelletur, non esse rerum Stoicis cum Peripateticis controversiam sed nominum.* The differentiation is itself based on the Aristotelian methodological principle of 'what is said in many ways' (πολλαχῶς λεγόμενον), which is referred to in the *Topics* in order to distinguish an argument which is factual (κατ' αὐτὸ τὸ πρᾶγμα) and not merely terminological (μὴ πρὸς τὸ ὄνομα), see Aristotle's *Topics* 108a18–20.

[130] For an expression of this thesis by Antiochus, as part of his polemical strategy against the Stoics, see e.g. *On Ends* 5.22: *restant Stoici, qui, cum a Peripateticis et Academicis omnia transtulissent, nominibus aliis easdem res secuti sunt*; see also ibid. 5.89: *quid interest nisi quod ego res notas notis verbis appello, illi nomina nova quaerunt quibus idem dicant?* and *ibid.: dum res maneant, verba fingant arbitratu suo.* According to *On the Nature of the Gods* 1.16, Antiochus included the view that Stoics and Peripatetics disagree (in the domain of ethics) only in words but not in substance in a book with Balbus as addressee: *Antiocho enim Stoici cum Peripateticis re concinere videntur verbis discrepare; quo de libro Balbe velim scire quid sentias.* The same polemical move is employed also by Cicero against the Stoics at *On Ends* 4.21. Cf. Schofield (2012b) 242 who notes that 'in ethics Antiochus was paradoxically no less anti-Stoic than Carneades'.

[131] See e.g. *Academic Books* 17.

conclusions from the same premises. It ultimately served the goal of showing that no doctrine can stand critical scrutiny and claim to represent absolute truth.[132] As transpires from the Antiochean account in *On Ends* 5.16, Antiochus adopted this framework, but used it in order to serve his own dogmatic aim of defending the ethical theory of the 'ancients' against the rival theory of the Stoa.[133] In this way, dialectical techniques stemming from Academic scepticism were put to use by Antiochus for the reconstruction of the doctrines of the Platonic and Aristotelian tradition in opposition to the Stoa.

Still, the agenda of the alternative account that Antiochus offers in the domain of ethics, as also some of its key concepts, are borrowed from the Stoa. Suggestive is, for example, the way Antiochus attempts to show at *On Ends* 5 that the 'ancients', and especially the Peripatos, used to ground their view of the *telos* in natural appropriation (*oikeiōsis*), a term introduced into the philosophical discourse by the Stoics.[134] The hermeneutical credo that underlies Antiochus' approach is that the 'ancients' did not have the particular terminology which was introduced by the Stoa but they did possess the equivalent concepts. The reverse side of the defence of the origination of Stoic ethical views in the ancient Academic tradition is a polemical approach towards Stoicism, which sets out explicitly to downgrade the originality of the Stoic school. Thus, the Stoics are presented in Varro's account at *Academic Books* as forming part of the same tradition that Antiochus wishes to resurrect, and the presentation of their doctrines follows up on those of the 'ancients'.

Belonging together with the Old Academics to the dogmatic camp, Zeno, according to Varro, undertook a reform (*correctio*) of

---

[132] For the way in which the *Carneadea divisio* served this 'destructive' aim by relying on the διαφωνία among the philosophical schools, see Algra (1997) 131–38.

[133] The use of the *Carneadea divisio* on the part of Antiochus will be further discussed in Chapter 3, *infra*.

[134] Suggestive is the way Piso starts his exposition of the argument from *oikeiōsis* by stating that also the Stoics follow the example of the 'old thinkers' (i.e. start their exposition of ethics with *oikeiōsis*), *On Ends* 5.23: *ergo instituto veterum, quo etiam Stoici utuntur, hinc capiamus exordium*. For an analysis of the argument of natural appropriation in Piso's account, see Chapter 3, *infra*. Something similar may be claimed about the intellectualist reading of the virtues proposed at *On Ends* 5.38, see Chapter 5, *infra*.

the school.[135] The word *correctio* used to describe the Zenonian activity is ambiguous between suggesting genuine improvement in doctrine, on the one hand, and mere word substitution on the other.[136] This ambiguity is reflected in the way Antiochus both makes ample use of Stoic terminology for the presentation of Old Academic views and, at the same time, reduces such terminology to a repetition of ancient ideas. For example, in the domain of ethics, the peculiar Stoic idea that some objects of choice have only relative value and are 'preferred indifferents' (*praeposita*) is reduced in some Antiochean passages to a mere terminological quibble with no substantial message. Thus, for Antiochus the meaning of 'preferred' is co-extensive with that of 'good' and does not constitute an innovation in value theory.[137] The same applies to the Stoic term *oikeiōsis*, which is used in the Antiochean presentation of Old Academic ethics in *On Ends* 5 in order to convey the species-specific Peripatetic teleology. The corollary of this attitude is that Stoic ethical terms are not treated in Antiochean passages in their own right, but only as a medium for conveying the views of the 'ancients'.[138] We may contrast with this the way a positive Stoic contribution is recognised in the domain of epistemology in Varro's account of the Old Academic system in the *Academic Books*; thus, Varro grants that the terms 'apprehension' (*katalēpsis*, translated in Latin as *comprehensio* and *perceptio*) and 'mental assent' (*synkatathesis*, translated in Latin as *adsensio* or

---

[135] *Academic Books* 35: *sed Zeno, cum Arcesilam anteiret aetate valdeque subtiliter dissereret et peracute moveretur, corrigere conatus est disciplinam.*

[136] Cicero, wearing his Antiochean hat, uses with reference to Zeno's 'reforms' also the word *emendatio* at *On Ends* 4.21: *haec videlicet est correctio philosophiae veteris et emendatio, quae omnino aditum habere nullum potest in urbem, in forum, in curiam.* At *On Ends* 1.17, *correctio* refers to the changes that Epicurus brought about to the teaching of Democritus. In rhetorical theory *correctio* has the meaning of the Greek ἐπανόρθωσις, i.e of the recalling of a word in order to use a more significant one in its place. See e.g. *On the Orator* 3.204: *correctio est quae tollit id quod dictum est, et pro eo, id, quod magis idoneum videtur reponit.* Bonazzi (2012) 313–14 takes *correctio* to bear no positive value; this does not, however, appear to do justice to Varro's positive attitude towards Stoic innovations in epistemology.

[137] See *Academic Books* 37: *atque ut haec non tam rebus quam vocabulis commutaverat.* Equivocation is explored for polemical purposes also at *On Ends* 4.56; cf. *ibid.* 4.72.

[138] Bonazzi's idea (2012) 314 that Antiochus' aim was a 'subordinated integration' of Stoicism may be apt to describe Antiochus' strategy towards Stoicism in the domain of ethics.

adprobatio) were introduced first by the Stoics to give expression to 'novel things' (*nova*), suggesting that, at least in this domain, Antiochus ascribed to the Stoics conceptual and not mere terminological innovation.[139]

In some Antiochean passages we also find a strategy of exclusion towards the Stoa, suggesting that in some cases Antiochus took the Stoics to be departing from ancient doctrine, and not just to be 'refashioning' ancient ideas. At worst, the Stoics are presented in some Antiochean passages as 'forgers' of the Academic tradition, who changed the names of the doctrines that they appropriated, just as thieves change the marks of the objects which they have stolen, so that they may not be detected.[140] This polemical reproach found its way also into an anecdote in Diogenes Laertius, where Zeno appears as someone who cunningly enters from the 'back door' of the Academy and steals the doctrines of the school, disguising them with a Phoenician dress.[141] A stronger accusation that emerges from such polemical passages is that the Stoics with their use of elaborate technical terminology not only changed the names of the ideas they inherited but also diverged from some of the doctrines of the Old Academy.[142] The value distinction

---

[139] See especially *Academic Books* 41: *plurimisque idem* (sc. Zeno) *novis verbis (nova enim dicebat) usus est.* Cf. Karamanolis (2006) 57: 'Antiochus thus admits that Stoic epistemology was not strictly speaking a reconstruction of Plato's views, but rather a genuinely Stoic theory, which, however, did justice to Plato's spirit.' The acknowledgment of (positive) Stoic innovations in the *Academic Books* may be due to the fact that Varro's account reflects the later phase of Antiochus' philosophical production, presumably a phase characterised by more historically sensitive readings of the ancient texts. For this developmental hypothesis, see Sedley (2012a) 103. The ascription of 'novelty' to Zeno by Varro need not have the exclusive negative connotations that Bonazzi (2012) 313 suggests.

[140] See *On Ends* 5.74: *Stoici restant. Ei quidem non unam aliquam aut alteram <particulam> a nobis, sed totam ad se nostram philosophiam transtulerunt; atque ut reliqui fures earum rerum quas ceperunt signa commutant, sic illi, ut sententiis nostris pro suis uterentur, nomina tamquam rerum notas mutaverunt.*

[141] Diogenes Laertius, *Lives of Eminent Philosophers* 7.25. There, it is reported that Polemo addressed Zeno with the following words: "οὐ λανθάνεις, ὦ Ζήνων, ταῖς κηπαίαις παρεισρέων θύραις καὶ τὰ δόγματα κλέπτων Φοινικικῶς μεταμφιεννύς"; Cf. also *On Ends* 4.56 (from Cicero's 'Antiochean' polemic): *postea tuus ille Poenulus (scis enim Citieos, clientes tuos, e Phoenica profectos), homo igitur acutus, causam non optinens repugnante natura verba coepit.*

[142] See e.g. how the Stoics are said to express 'boastful' (*gloriosa*) things in connection with their failing to grant some, even minimal, value to bodily goods at *On Ends* 5.72: *est enim philosophi non tam gloriosa quam vera quaerentis nec pro nihilo putare ea quae secundum naturam illi ipsi gloriosi esse fatebantur, et videre tantam vim virtutis*

73

between 'preferred indifferents' and 'goods' appears to be a case in point here as well,[143] as also the accusation that the Stoics offered an unintuitive ethical theory by granting, contrary to the 'ancients', no importance whatsoever to the bodily aspect of human nature.[144]

Even if Antiochus adopts a different strategy towards the Stoa in the domain of ethics, we may still say that the Stoa gives the greatest impetus to Antiochus' reading of the ethics of the Old Academy. For the terminological apparatus and the main agenda of the Stoa provides in *On Ends* 5 the framework around which the old material is arranged with a view to offering a (better) alternative to contemporary (i.e. Hellenistic) problems in ethics.

---

tantamque, ut ita dicam, auctoritatem honestatis <*esse*> *ut reliqua non illa quidem nulla, sed ita parva sint ut nulla esse videantur.*

[143] See e.g. Piso's polemical remarks against the Stoics in his exchange with the 'sceptic' Cicero at *On Ends* 5.78: *quae enim mala illi non audent appellare, aspera autem et incommoda et reicienda et aliena naturae esse concedunt, ea nos mala dicimus, sed exigua et paene minima.* Cf. *ibid.* 5.88; 5.90–91; *Academic Books* 37.

[144] See e.g. the anti-Stoic critique at *On Ends* 5.94.

PART II

THE ETHICS OF THE OLD ACADEMY

3

OIKEIŌSIS AND THE TELOS

In line with his peculiar hermeneutical assumptions discussed in the previous chapter, Antiochus adopts Stoic terminology and integrates it into his account of the Old Academic philosophical system. Perhaps the most striking case of philosophical appropriation on Antiochus' part is the way he adopts the Stoic idea of *oikeiōsis* (translated by Cicero into Latin as *commendatio* and *conciliatio*)[1] in his presentation of Old Academic ethics. My discussion in this chapter will centre around the implications of grounding ethics in *oikeiōsis*. In particular, after a discussion of the Stoic argument from *oikeiōsis* and of the dialectical context surrounding this notion, I will present Antiochus' own attempt to ground the Old Academic *telos* in natural appropriation. In the following chapter, I will show how Antiochus assigns to self-love a central role in the manifestation of *oikeiōsis*, by presenting a fundamental feeling of self-love as the psychological principle which motivates us to pursue the *telos* appropriate to our nature. Finally, after discussing *oikeiōsis*, in terms of its bodily and psychic objects, I will analyse how Antiochus understood the role of the different categories of goods in his formulation of the 'happiest' life.

---

[1] Since Pohlenz (1940) 16ff., and Brink (1956) there is a consensus in scholarship that the concept in its philosophical use is genuinely Stoic. It is ascribed specifically to Chrysippus in Diogenes Laertius *Lives of Eminent Philosophers* 7.85–86, see *infra*. It is not clear, however, if Chrysippus was the first one to establish it as *terminus technicus* in Stoic theory. Inwood (1985) 185 ascribes it to Zeno; however, nowhere in the surviving evidence is the idea of οἰκείωσις ascribed *specifically* to Zeno and the expression οἱ ἀπὸ Ζήνωνος in Porphyry's *On Abstinence* 3.19 = *SVF* 1.197 need not mean anything more than 'the Stoics': τὴν δὲ οἰκείωσιν ἀρχὴν τίθενται δικαιοσύνης οἱ ἀπὸ Ζήνωνος. Still, the first attested occurrence of the term is in Theophrastus *Fr.* 435 FHS&G. = Photius *Library* 278, 529b11–23 in a fragment from a lost treatise *On Types of Honey*. This motivated Dirlmeier's theory in *Die Oikeiosis-Lehre Theophrasts* (1937) that Theophrastus had already developed an *oikeiōsis* theory. There is, however, no evidence of such a theory in the Peripatos prior to Antiochus and Didymus.

The main source for the reconstruction of the ethics of Antiochus is the last book of Cicero's *On Ends*; although the account has an explicitly Aristotelian/Peripatetic character (and perhaps goes back to an Antiochean doxography of the ethics of the Peripatos), it will be shown to have some important Platonic/Academic traits as well. The cases where Antiochus diverges from the Aristotelian tradition for the sake of Plato (and the Academy) will be shown to be attempts on his part to offer an interpretation of the ancient tradition which would fit the Hellenistic philosophical agenda and would offer a philosophically interesting alternative to Stoicism.

The *oikeiōsis* is a derivative of the adjective *oikeios*, which means both something descriptively belonging or related to something (it is thus used in a colloquial sense in the context of the household and family relationships)[2] and also, in a strongly normative sense, it means what is appropriate to an entity by virtue of its very nature; this latter is the particular meaning the adjective has in the philosophical texts under discussion here.[3] *Oikeiōsis*, the corresponding *nomen actionis*, conveys the kind of relation that obtains between an entity and what belongs to it or is appropriate to it by virtue of its very nature;[4] it may thus be translated as

---

[2] The relationship of intimacy is conveyed also by the abstract noun *oikeiotēs*, which applies primarily to kinship or generally to intimate relations.

[3] The word appears in its normative sense in the expression οἰκεία ἀρετὴ in Plato's *Republic* 1.353c and 353e, as the proper virtue which belongs to the human soul by virtue of its *ergon* (which according to 353d is 'living'). This line of argumentation is also reflected in Aristotle's so-called function argument, which relies on the notion of *ergon* in order to derive conclusions about the constituents of human *eudaimonia*. Thus, at *Nicomachean Ethics* 1.1098a15 there is reference to a human being's 'proper excellence' (οἰκεία ἀρετή), which corresponds to the human *ergon* being 'activity of soul and actions accompanied by reason'. For a precedent of the *oikeion* as object of desire, see Plato's *Lysis* 221e3–5: τοῦ οἰκείου δή, ὡς ἔοικεν, ὅ τε ἔρως καὶ ἡ φιλία καὶ ἡ ἐπιθυμία τυγχάνει οὖσα, ὡς φαίνεται, ὦ Μενέξενέ τε καὶ Λύσι, and *ibid.* 222a5–6: τὸ μὲν δὴ φύσει οἰκεῖον ἀναγκαῖον ἡμῖν πέφανται φιλεῖν.

[4] The noun derives from the active verb οἰκειοῦν which is often supplemented by two objects in the accusative and dative. The middle-passive form (συν-)οικειοῦσθαι, complemented by a dative or the preposition πρὸς + acc., expresses the (existing) relationship towards something regarded as appropriate. In accordance with Cicero's usual practice, there are two alternatives offered for the rendering of the term *oikeiōsis* in Latin: *commendatio* and *conciliatio;* thus, *conciliari* and *commendari* are presented as translations of *oikeiousthai pros* in *On Ends* 3.16. As for the rendering of the cognate *oikeion*, Cicero chooses the Latin participle *accommodatum*. We find an explicit translation of *oikeion* at *Lucullus* 38: *nam quo modo non potest animal ullum non adpetere id quod accommodatum ad naturam adpareat (Graeci id* οἰκεῖον *appellant).* This is not a lexically exact rendering: the meaning of the verb *accommodo*, from which the translation derives,

appropriation,[5] a word which preserves in English the link to the normative notion of the 'appropriate', in the same way that *oikeiōsis* contains the adjective *oikeion*.

In Hellenistic philosophy *oikeiōsis* becomes linked to a being's *telos*, i.e. the appropriate end-point of development which, as such, is the highest goal for the being at hand, a common assumption of all ancient eudaimonistic theories. In particular, *oikeiōsis* explains the way living organisms relate from the beginning of their lives to their own nature (as members of a certain species) and to things which are appropriate to their nature, with a view to achieving the fulfilment of their nature, i.e. their *telos*. Before embarking on the way Antiochus used the notion of the *oikeion* to ground an Aristotelian/Peripatetic account of *eudaimonia*, we should have a look at the 'prototype' of the *oikeiōsis* argument in the Stoic school. This shall allow us to see both how closely Antiochus modelled his account on the Stoic argument and how he adjusted it to fit an Aristotelian/Peripatetic conception of *eudaimonia*, which employs *oikeiōsis* as the foundation of the best possible state of a human being. It will transpire that Antiochus presented an *alternative* argument from *oikeiōsis* from the one the Stoics used by proposing novel theses: First, his account of human *oikeiōsis* is structured around a division of goods into psychic and bodily goods, something which reflects his commitment to a pluralistic account of *eudaimonia*. Secondly, his *oikeiōsis* theory attempts to underline the unity of human ethical development by suggesting that pre-rational desires at the beginning of our lives *ground* the rational desires of the fully developed agent. In order to appreciate the innovations involved, we need to turn to the 'prototype' Stoic argument, as also to the Hellenistic dialectical context, which influenced Antiochus' formulation of an Aristotelian/Peripatetic account of *oikeiōsis*.

---

does not bear the connotation of the *oikos*, but rather that of 'fitting' or 'adjusting' something. Thus the participle *accommodatus* and the adjective *aptus* (which is also used as an alternative translation of *oikeios* in Cicero's Antiochean account) denote something which is suited or adapted to something else. For a semantic analysis of the verb *oikeioun* and its cognates, see Görgemanns (1983) 181–87.

5 A translation endorsed by Long and Sedley (1987) vol. 1, 351. Inwood (1985) chooses the term 'orientation' to convey *oikeiōsis*.

The Stoic Argument from *Oikeiōsis*

Early Stoics defended the (perfect) rationality of the cosmos (identical to nature, or divine will) in relation to the partial rationality of human beings.[6] The rationality of the cosmos was taken by the Stoics to entail the further assumption that the cosmos *qua* nature is a providential force, which exhibits care and forethought in the way it generates and preserves all living beings which form its parts. Humans, as also plants and animals, are beneficiaries of this providence.

The Stoics took reasoning ability to be the defining characteristic of human beings. The corresponding appropriation to reason which grounds the proper way of life for a human being is conveyed in Stoic theory by means of an argument from *oikeiōsis*. Arguably the best evidence that we have for the reconstruction of an argument from *oikeiōsis* in the early Stoa comes from Diogenes Laertius' *Lives of Eminent Philosophers* 7.85 (= *SVF* 3.178 = LS 57A) and contains evidence from Chrysippus' book *On Ends* (*Peri Telōn*).[7] The relevant passage reads as follows:

The Stoics say that an animal's primary impulse [πρώτην ὁρμήν] is towards preserving itself [τηρεῖν ἑαυτό], since nature appropriated it to itself [οἰκειούσης αὐτὸ <ἑαυτῷ> τῆς φύσεως][8] from the start, as Chrysippus says in the first book of *On Ends*, when saying that the primary thing which belongs to each animal [πρῶτον οἰκεῖον] is its own constitution and the awareness thereof [τὴν αὑτοῦ σύστασιν καὶ τὴν ταύτης συνείδησιν];[9] for it was not likely that nature should either alienate it from itself, nor, after having created it, neither alienate it nor

---

[6] See *SVF* 2.633–645.

[7] Even though the text explicitly contains a quotation from Chrysippus' Περὶ τελῶν, it is not entirely clear which bits are later doxographical additions, or how the original quotations fitted into their context, cf. the remarks in Brunschwig (1986) 133, n.39. For the defence of Diogenes Laertius' doxography as the most important expression of (early) Stoic ethics in general, and the theory of οἰκείωσις in particular, see Inwood (1985) 186; 188, Lee C-U. (2002) 49 and Klein (2016) 151.

[8] Following Dorandi (2013).

[9] Συνείδησιν is the ms. reading which is also printed in Dorandi (2013). The word συναίσθησις, suggested as conjecture by Dyroff (1897) 37, would be, however, more appropriate in this context, since, according to Stoic theory, animals cannot claim to 'know' their constitution, by virtue of not having the rational cognition that is characteristic of human beings. For a defence of the ms. reading, see also Inwood (1984) 313, n.42. One may argue that the term συνείδησις is here applied in a catachrestic way to other animals except human beings, covering both propositionally structured and non-rational cognition. As it stands, however, the term supports the point that the primary aim of the passage is to offer a justification of the human *telos* (of which συνείδησις is the sole

affiliate it to itself. We have to conclude then that nature, after having constituted the animal, affiliated it to itself [οἰκειῶσαι πρὸς ἑαυτό]; for in this way the animal repels things that are detrimental to itself and accepts ones that are appropriate to itself.[10]

We may reconstruct from the testimony of Diogenes Laertius a general Stoic argument from *oikeiōsis* in the form of a *reductio* argument:

Premise 1 Nature either appropriates its creatures to themselves or alienates them from themselves, or neither appropriates its creatures to themselves nor alienates them from themselves.

Premise 2 If nature alienates its creatures from themselves or neither alienates them from themselves nor appropriates them to themselves, then nature does not exercise providence for its creatures.

Implicit premise If creatures were alienated from themselves or neither appropriated to themselves nor alienated from themselves, they wouldn't be able to discern what is appropriate for them, and, as a result of this, they wouldn't survive.

Premise 3 Nature is providential, and exercises forethought for its creatures.

Premise 4 (As a result of 3) Living creatures are not alienated from themselves nor neither appropriated to themselves nor alienated from themselves by nature.

Premise 5 Therefore, living creatures are appropriated to themselves by nature.

As reconstructed above, the idea of *oikeiōsis* in Stoic theory, understood as the process whereby every creature becomes appropriated to itself, i.e. to its peculiar nature, rests on heavy metaphysical assumptions regarding the role of cosmic nature as a creative force which acts intentionally and providentially in bringing about

constitutive part). Unfortunately, no extensive treatment of the term συνείδησις survives in Stoic sources.

[10] τὴν δὲ πρώτην ὁρμήν φασι τὸ ζῷον ἴσχειν ἐπὶ τὸ τηρεῖν ἑαυτό, οἰκειούσης αὐτὸ <ἑαυτῷ> τῆς φύσεως ἀπ' ἀρχῆς, καθά φησιν ὁ Χρύσιππος ἐν τῷ πρώτῳ Περὶ τελῶν, πρῶτον οἰκεῖον λέγων εἶναι παντὶ ζῴῳ τὴν αὑτοῦ σύστασιν καὶ τὴν ταύτης συνείδησιν· οὔτε γὰρ ἀλλοτριῶσαι εἰκὸς ἦν αὐτὸ <αὑτῷ> τὸ ζῷον, οὔτε ποιήσασαν αὐτό, μήτ' ἀλλοτριῶσαι μήτ' [οὐκ] οἰκειῶσαι. ἀπολείπεται τοίνυν λέγειν συστησαμένην αὐτὸ οἰκειῶσαι πρὸς ἑαυτό· οὕτω γὰρ τά τε βλάπτοντα διωθεῖται καὶ τὰ οἰκεῖα προσίεται.

the constituents of the cosmos. As a good craftsman would have to care for the longevity of his products, in the same way nature manages living things most effectively by means of *oikeiōsis*. Now, the Stoics moved from establishing this to the justification of the peculiar *telos* of living beings by means of *oikeiōsis*.[11]

The Stoic discussion of the way nature appropriates living beings to their peculiar life form seems to have involved references to the earliest manifestation of *oikeiōsis* from the beginning of life. Thus, the Diogenes text starts by making a reference to a 'primary impulse' (*prōtēn hormēn*) towards 'preserving oneself' (*tērein heauto*) as a result of *oikeiōsis*. Although reference to the impulse for self-preservation precedes in the account, the primary object of *oikeiōsis* is identified (in a passage which seems to be a direct quotation from Chrysippus) with 'awareness' (*syneidēsin*) of oneself, and more specifically of one's 'constitution' (*systasis*). Reading these two statements together, we may advance a 'cognitive' reading according to which the primary impulse to preserve oneself, i.e. one's constitution results from awareness of oneself.

The link in Stoic theory between one's *systasis* and a cognitive understanding of oneself is best described in what survives from the *Ethical Elements* (*Ēthikē Stoicheiōsis*) of the late Stoic Hierocles. At the beginning of the treatise, Hierocles states that every perception of external objects from the earliest stage of our lives is accompanied by a perception of the self as well and gives a physical explanation of the phenomenon. Thus, *synaisthēsis* is spelled out in the treatise of Hierocles as the awareness of all the parts of our body and soul or of one's constitution (*systasis*) understood as

---

[11] This is corroborated by evidence which attests the derivation of the Stoic value theory from arguments about the 'common nature' and the cosmic administration, see esp. Plutarch *On Stoic Self-Contradictions* 1035c–d = *SVF* 3.68: πάλιν ἐν ταῖς Φυσικαῖς Θέσεσιν 'οὐ γάρ ἐστιν ἄλλως οὐδ' ἐπελθεῖν ἐπὶ τὸν τῶν ἀγαθῶν καὶ κακῶν λόγον οὐδ' ἐπὶ τὰς ἀρετὰς οὐδ' ἐπ' εὐδαιμονίαν, ἀλλ' <ἢ> ἀπὸ τῆς κοινῆς φύσεως καὶ ἀπὸ τῆς τοῦ κόσμου διοικήσεως.' προελθὼν δ' αὖθις· 'δεῖ γὰρ τούτοις συνάψαι τὸν περὶ ἀγαθῶν καὶ κακῶν λόγον, οὐκ οὔσης ἄλλης ἀρχῆς αὐτῶν ἀμείνονος οὐδ' ἀναφορᾶς, οὐδ' ἄλλου τινὸς ἕνεκεν τῆς φυσικῆς θεωρίας παραληπτῆς οὔσης ἢ πρὸς τὴν περὶ ἀγαθῶν ἢ κακῶν διάστασιν.' γίνεται τοίνυν ἅμα πρόσω καὶ ὀπίσω τῶν ἠθικῶν ὁ φυσικὸς λόγος κατὰ Χρύσιππον.

the relation between mind/soul and body:[12] as Hierocles states 'the first proof (*pistis*) of every animal's perceiving itself is the joint-perception (*synaisthēsis*) of its parts and the functions for which they were given'.[13] This, as he explains, is a result of the way affections from the outermost parts of the body become registered in the leading faculty of the soul of an animal bringing about 'grasping' (*antilēpsis*) of all the parts of body and soul.[14] This constant interaction between body and soul resulting in awareness of oneself is explained in Hierocles' account as *prior* to the perception and impulse the animal experiences for things appropriate to it in its environment, and as the presupposition of the latter.[15] Accordingly, Hierocles makes awareness of oneself and not the impulse for external things the most fundamental manifestation of *oikeiōsis*. Hierocles' discussion of *synaisthēsis* may corroborate the reading of the Diogenes text proposed above, according to which the 'primary impulse' to preserve oneself results from awareness of one's constitution. This is suggestive of a theory which places cognition of some kind (not necessarily a propositionally structured one) as the cause of impulse along the lines of an 'internalist' reading of motivation.

Although Hierocles' account regrettably breaks off before a transition to the rational stage of human development is made, we may assume that in the lost part of the treatise he defended the view that awareness of oneself, and the corresponding 'appropriate actions' that ensue as a result of self-awareness, alter once we

---

[12] *Synaisthēsis* has been linked to the modern psychological notion of 'proprioception', whereby an infant comes to perceive e.g. that this is *her* hand, see Brunschwig (1986) 137. Bastianini and Long (1992) 421 point to the difference between the *synaisthēsis* discussed by Hierocles and the modern term 'consciousness': 'la percezione di sé dovrebbe essere considerata una funzione vitale, che è insieme più ampia della "coscienza" e meno intellettualistica nelle sue connotazioni'. On *systasis*, see the definition in Seneca *Letter* 121.10: *principale animi quodam modo se habens erga corpus.*

[13] Hierocles Ἠθικὴ στοιχείωσις col. 2.1–3.

[14] *Ibid.* 4.45–53. On the controlling function of the ἡγεμονικόν, see Aetius 4.21.1 = *SVF* 2.836.

[15] This is explicitly stated in Hierocles Ἠθικὴ στοιχείωσις col. 6.1–3. As empirical proof for the priority of self-perception it is argued in *ibid.* 4.53–5.30 that self-perception takes place even during sleep.

83

have reached the rational stage of our development.[16] This would give support to the view that *oikeiōsis* manifests itself not only at the beginning of life but remains operative throughout our development leading, in the case of human beings, to the pursuit of *oikeia* by means of reason.[17] Accordingly, *oikeiōsis* may explain not only the earliest impulse for one's own survival but also the motivational structure of the fully developed rational agent whose choices encompass other-regarding concerns as well.[18]

In Diogenes' text the link between *oikeiōsis* and the *telos* is supported by the use of a *scala naturae* which underlines the analogical similarities which obtain between all natural kinds in the pursuit of what is appropriate to their nature. Thus, the view that is attributed to the Stoics in Diogenes' doxography is that plants no less than animals grow as a result of the 'management' of nature through processes that are present in human beings as well.[19] Animals on the other hand are meant to pursue what is appropriate to their nature by means of the additional faculties of perception (*aisthēsis*) and impulse (*hormē*). Accordingly, the Stoics suggest that a life according

---

[16] See also Bastianini and Long (1992) 297 who hypothesise that in the part of the papyrus that is lost Hierocles treated, among others, the topic of appropriate actions (καθήκοντα).

[17] Accordingly one may read the reflexive pronoun contained in the phrase *tērein heauto* ('preserving oneself') in a broad way as encompassing the impulse to act upon the rational knowledge of one's constitution. See Klein (2016) for a reconstruction of the Stoic argument which makes rational knowledge central to the account.

[18] Cato in his Stoic account in Cicero's *On Ends* 3.63 presents grasping oneself as part of humanity as a whole as the outcome of the specifically human *oikeiōsis*. The understanding of oneself as part of the human *genos* results from the affiliation of oneself to *logos*, i.e. the best part of oneself. These passages suggest that the Stoics did not consider a conflict between pursuing one's interest and acting with regard to the common benefit. Both seem to be entailed in and be justified by means of the human being's *oikeiōsis* towards reason. The idea that *oikeiōsis* in the case of rational beings results in action for the common benefit appears also in later Stoics. See especially Epictetus *Discourses* 1.19.13–15: καθόλου τε τοιαύτην <τὴν> φύσιν τοῦ λογικοῦ ζῴου κατεσκεύασεν, ἵνα μηδενὸς τῶν ἰδίων ἀγαθῶν δύνηται τυγχάνειν, <ἂν> μή τι εἰς τὸ κοινὸν ὠφέλιμον προσφέρηται. οὕτως οὐκέτι ἀκοινώνητον γίνεται τὸ πάντα αὐτοῦ ἕνεκα ποιεῖν. ἐπεὶ τί ἐκδέχῃ; ἵνα τις ἀποστῇ αὐτοῦ καὶ τοῦ ἰδίου συμφέροντος; καὶ πῶς ἔτι μία καὶ ἡ αὐτὴ ἀρχὴ πᾶσιν ἔσται ἡ πρὸς αὐτὰ οἰκείωσις;

[19] Diogenes Laertius *Lives of Eminent Philosophers* 7.86: οὐδέν τε, φασί, διήλλαξεν ἡ φύσις ἐπὶ τῶν φυτῶν καὶ ἐπὶ τῶν ζῴων, ὅτι χωρὶς ὁρμῆς καὶ αἰσθήσεως κἀκεῖνα οἰκονομεῖ καὶ ἐφ' ἡμῶν τινα φυτοειδῶς γίνεται.

to nature for animals equals to 'being administered according to impulse' (*dioikeisthai kata tēn hormēn*).[20]

The transition to human beings in this scheme is marked by the view that humans possess reason as a result of provisions on nature's part for a 'more accomplished protection' of their kind.[21] In their case 'reason supervenes as the craftsman of impulse', which seems to support the thesis that all human impulses are utterly rational by virtue of being 'crafted' by reason.[22] Finally, this comes to support a conception of the human *telos* as 'living according to reason' (*kata logon zēn*), which equals a life according to nature for human beings. That the Stoics argued for the *telos* on the basis of natural appropriation is corroborated by the remarks which relate to Zeno's conception of the *telos* in Diogenes' doxography. In his work 'On Human Nature' (*Peri anthrōpou physeōs*) Zeno is said to have defended the view that the *telos* is 'living in agreement with nature' (*homologoumenōs tēi physei zēn*), which is said to be equal to 'living according to virtue'.[23] It is important for the Stoic position that the 'agreement' characterising the mindset of the virtuous person extends beyond mere human nature to encompass the cosmic rational principle. The Stoic *telos* seems thereby to imply that the virtuous agent comes to align his or her decisions and actions with the plans of the cosmic *logos*.[24] This presupposes some understanding of cosmic and not merely of human nature for the achievement of *eudaimonia*.

---

[20] *Ibid.*: ἐκ περιττοῦ δὲ τῆς ὁρμῆς τοῖς ζῴοις ἐπιγενομένης, ᾗ συγχρώμενα πορεύεται πρὸς τὰ οἰκεῖα, τούτοις μὲν τὸ κατὰ φύσιν τῷ κατὰ τὴν ὁρμὴν διοικεῖσθαι.

[21] On the particularity of human nature, by virtue of its possession of *logos*, in comparison with other animals, see also Origen *On Principles* 3.1.2–3 p. 196.3–197.11 Koetschau = *SVF* 2.988.

[22] Diogenes Laertius *Lives of Eminent Philosophers* 7.86: τοῦ δὲ λόγου τοῖς λογικοῖς κατὰ τελειοτέραν προστασίαν δεδομένου, τὸ κατὰ λόγον ζῆν ὀρθῶς γίνεσθαι <τού>τοις κατὰ φύσιν· τεχνίτης γὰρ οὗτος ἐπιγίνεται τῆς ὁρμῆς.

[23] See also Stobaeus *Selections* 2 77.16–19 Wachsmuth

[24] See Diogenes Laertius Lives of Eminent Philosophers 7.88 (most probably deriving from Chrysippus' Περὶ τελῶν): διόπερ τέλος γίνεται τὸ ἀκολούθως τῇ φύσει ζῆν, ὅπερ ἐστὶ κατά τε τὴν αὐτοῦ καὶ κατὰ τὴν τῶν ὅλων, οὐδὲν ἐνεργοῦντας ὧν ἀπαγορεύειν εἴωθεν ὁ νόμος ὁ κοινός, ὅσπερ ἐστὶν ὁ ὀρθὸς λόγος, διὰ πάντων ἐρχόμενος, ὁ αὐτὸς ὢν τῷ Διί, καθηγεμόνι τούτῳ τῆς τῶν ὄντων διοικήσεως ὄντι· εἶναι δ᾿ αὐτὸ τοῦτο τὴν τοῦ εὐδαίμονος ἀρετὴν καὶ εὔροιαν βίου, ὅταν πάντα πράττηται κατὰ τὴν συμφωνίαν τοῦ παρ᾿ ἑκάστῳ δαίμονος πρὸς τὴν τοῦ τῶν ὅλων διοικητοῦ βούλησιν.

The doxographer supplies also a concise rationale for Zeno's conception of the *telos*: 'for nature leads us towards it (sc. virtue)'.[25] This points to the idea that *oikeiōsis* in Stoicism functioned as the metaphysical/naturalistic foundation of the *telos* conceived as a life according to reason. At the same time it served to describe the psychological mechanisms by virtue of which organisms are equipped in a suitable way from the beginning of their lives in order to achieve the *telos* that is ordained for them by nature's plan. This relates primarily, as we have already seen, to the cognitive basis for the experience of impulses towards things appropriate to nature. Although particular emphasis is put in the Diogenes text on the 'primary impulse' towards self-preservation understood as the earliest manifestation of *oikeiōsis,* we may assume that the Stoics meant to justify by means of *oikeiōsis* the rational impulses which are characteristic of the fully developed agent as well.

The main assumptions of the Stoic argument from *oikeiōsis*, as reconstructed above on the basis of the testimony of Diogenes, seem to be corroborated by the ethical account at *On Ends* 3, which also purports to offer a concise presentation of the ethics of the Stoic school. *Oikeiōsis* (*commendatio, conciliatio*) assumes also here a foundational role and is related both to the earliest impulse towards self-preservation but also to the rational impulses which are characteristic of the fully developed agent. Thus, the Stoic account at *On Ends* 3 sketches the way the ideal agent comes to perceive by virtue of his or her appropriation to reason the difference between value on the one hand and goodness on the other: thus, the Stoic account states that, for the perfectly rational agent, things 'according to nature' are merely 'valuable' (*aestimabiles*), i.e. have only a *selective* value. This selectivity grounds fundamental 'appropriate actions' (*kathēkonta*) towards oneself and others (for example, the fundamental 'appropriate action' of keeping oneself alive is grounded in the selective value of life as opposed to

---

[25] *Ibid.* 7.87: Διόπερ πρῶτος ὁ Ζήνων ἐν τῷ Περὶ ἀνθρώπου φύσεως τέλος εἶπε τὸ ὁμολογουμένως τῇ φύσει ζῆν, ὅπερ ἐστὶ κατ' ἀρετὴν ζῆν· ἄγει γὰρ πρὸς ταύτην ἡμᾶς ἡ φύσις.

death).[26] In the case of the ideal agent this is accompanied by grasping a higher-order rational principle of nobility and goodness (rendered in Latin as the *honestum*).[27] The higher-order principle of goodness is in Stoic theory the *only* aim that is recognised as being choice worthy for its own sake and the only one able to incite the sort of rational impulse called *hairesis*.[28] It is in accordance with this higher-order principle that the fully developed rational agent decides what is the appropriate thing to do in particular circumstances and is motivated to act accordingly. Such an ability to choose rationally among appropriate actions features among the Stoic formulations of the *telos*.[29] Furthermore, living according to virtue, formulated as 'agreement' or 'consistency' with reason, rendering the Greek term *homologia*,[30] is for the Stoics the singular locus of human happiness. A consequence of this is that virtue, i.e. the cognitive state that is characterised by systematic knowledge of what should be chosen and avoided, is both necessary and sufficient for human *eudaimonia*.

However, the Stoic account at *On Ends* 3 may also seem to diverge from Diogenes' account in significant ways. In particular, the role of cosmic nature as the source of *oikeiōsis* does not become equally clear in Cato's account, where emphasis is laid

---

[26] See *On Ends* 3.20: *initiis igitur ita constitutis, ut ea quae secundum naturam sunt ipsa propter se sumenda sint contrariaque item reicienda, primum est officium – id enim appello* καθῆκον –, *ut se conservet in naturae statu, deinceps ut ea teneat quae secundum naturam sint pellatque contraria.*

[27] Cato suggests in *On Ends* 3.33 that the concept of the 'moral good' is an outcome of logical inference (*collatio rationis*): *cum enim ab iis rebus quae sunt secundum naturam ascendit animus collatione rationis, tum ad notionem boni pervenit.* In *ibid.* 3.21 it is associated with perceiving order and harmony in things 'to be done': *simul autem cepit intellegentiam vel notionem potius, quam appellant* ἔννοιαν *illi, viditque rerum agendarum ordinem et, ut ita dicam, concordiam, multo eam pluris aestimavit quam omnia illa, quae prima dilexerat.* Engberg-Pedersen (1986) 169 connects the grasp of the particular value of the *honestum* in Cicero's Stoic account with 'rational justifiability'.

[28] The difference between an agent's relation to value and the good is captured terminologically by the Stoics as follows: the good is *haireton* (an object of choice); value is *lēpton* (to-be-taken) and it is the object of *eklogē* (selection), see Stobaeus *Selections* 2 75.1–6 Wachsmuth. For the Stoic ethical terminological distinctions, see Inwood (1985) 117–18.

[29] See especially Archedemus' *telos* formulation at Diogenes Laertius *Lives of Eminent Philosophers* 7.88: Ἀρχέδημος δὲ τὸ πάντα τὰ καθήκοντα ἐπιτελοῦντα ζῆν.

[30] The Stoic *telos* is rendered in *On Ends* 3.31 as *convenienter congruenterque naturae vivere.*

87

on the way *oikeiōsis* is manifested as, mainly, a cognitive and psychological phenomenon, rather than as a cosmic one; this is reinforced by the use of middle-passive forms of the verb *oikeioun* (*sibi conciliari, commendari, alienari*) for the description of the process at *On Ends* 3.16.[31] Still, this may be understood as a shift in emphasis which is not incompatible with the thesis about the rationality of the cosmos and the dependency of human action upon it that we find in the text of Diogenes, and even in other instances in Cato's account itself.[32] Another peculiar feature of the Stoic ethical account in Cicero is the way it introduces self-love as an additional manifestation of *oikeiōsis* alongside the impulse that ensues from awareness of one's constitution (*sensus sui*); as we shall see in the following chapter self-love plays a primary role in Antiochus' reconstruction of the ethics of the Old Academy, as the motivational force which underpins all our desires, including the desire to reach our *telos*.[33]

---

[31] The Stoic account in *On Ends* 3 has served as evidence for an 'Aristotelising' version of Stoic ethics, as represented by Annas (1993). Οἰκείωσις as a primarily psychological phenomenon has been at the centre also of Inwood's analysis of Stoic ethics in Inwood (1985), although he also underlines *ibid.*: 212 that the ultimate standard of goodness and happiness in (early) Stoicism is 'harmony with the will of Zeus'. Striker (1983) 161 takes Cicero's Stoic account to be showing only the 'psychological development' of how one comes to adopt *homologia* as the only (appropriate) goal without offering an argument to support this. She adds, however, that if we want an argument proper for the Stoic *telos*, we should consider the account in Diogenes Laertius 'from the design of nature'. Engberg-Pedersen (1990) locates the foundation of Stoic ethics in 'a subjective or internal viewpoint' and takes *On Ends* 3 as grounding this supposition. On the other hand, the idea that the foundation of Stoic ethics is to be sought not in the specifically human but in the universal, cosmic nature (which includes the human one) has been highlighted by Cooper (1995) 587–598, Lee (2002) and Klein (2016).

[32] The psychological account of οἰκείωσις is supplemented in the Stoic account of *On Ends* 3 with references to the way the process of appropriation is embedded within a larger providential framework, see especially *On Ends* 3.23: *atque ut membra nobis ita data sunt, ut ad quandam rationem vivendi data esse appareant, sic appetitio animi, quae* ὁρμή *Graece vocatur, non ad quodvis genus vitae, sed ad quandam formam vivendi videtur data, itemque et ratio et perfecta ratio.* Cf. *ibid.* 3.62; 3.73.

[33] Thus, self-love features in the analysis at *On Ends* 3.16, while it is absent in Diogenes Laertius' account of Stoic *oikeiōsis*. According to the Ciceronian passage, as an outcome of *oikeiōsis,* 'any sentient creature feels affection for its own constitution, and for all that tends to maintain that constitution, while it recoils from destruction, and from all that seems to induce destruction' (*eaque quae conservantia sint eius status diligenda, alienari autem ab interitu iisque rebus quae interitum videantur adferre*). It is this primary love towards one's constitution, as an expression of *oikeiōsis,* that prescribes actions which promote the preservation of oneself and the avoidance of one's destruction. The fundamental love for one's constitution is further in Cato's account premised

Finally, the account at *On Ends* 3 uses numerous empirical examples from the behaviour of children in order to show the manifestation of *oikeiōsis* from the beginning of our lives.[34] This gives to the theory an empirical aspect which is missing in the Diogenes account.[35] The same applies to the *oikeiōsis* accounts of the later Stoics Seneca and Hierocles. In these accounts the early stage of human development occupies a most important role for the empirical manifestation of *oikeiōsis*.[36] Perhaps the best way to understand the emphasis on the developmental features and the empirical manifestations of *oikeiōsis* in the Ciceronian and later Stoic accounts is as an attempt on the part of later Stoics to enter into a debate with other Hellenistic schools, which also used *oikeiōsis* in order to ground their respective ethical theories.[37] Before moving to the presentation of Antiochus' *oikeiōsis* argument, as attested in Cicero's *On Ends* 5, we should have a brief look at Carneades' incorporation of *oikeiōsis* into his discussion of

upon an awareness of the self which is prior to the generation of self-love (*fieri autem non posse ut appeterent aliquid nisi sensum haberent sui eoque se diligerent*), in line with the Stoic evidence from Diogenes Laertius and Hierocles. One should note that Hierocles and Seneca, in the same way as *On Ends* 3, make use of the concept of self-love in their presentation of Stoic οἰκείωσις, see Seneca *Letters* 121.24: *primum hoc instrumentum in illa natura contulit ad permanendum, [in] conciliationem et caritatem sui* and Hierocles Ἠθικὴ στοιχείωσις col. 6.40–41: εἰ μὴ μέλλει τὸ ζῷον εὐθὺ γενόμενον ἀρέσειν ἑαυτῷ, cf. also the reference to φιλαυτία at *ibid.* col. 7.23–24. Schmitz (2014) 26–33 suggests that the Stoic account of *oikeiōsis* at *On Ends* 3 shows signs of 'contamination' from Peripatetic ideas and the use of the concept of self-love serves as an example of this. Brunner (2010) has defended the view that Cicero's presentation of Stoic ethics in *De Finibus* is influenced by Antiochus' views. For an interpretation of Stoic *oikeiōsis* which makes self-love an integral part of the Stoic account, see Engberg-Pedersen (1986).

[34] See e.g. *On Ends* 3.16 (containing a polemical remark against the Epicureans): *id ita esse sic probant, quod antequam voluptas aut dolor attigerit, salutaria appetant parvi aspernenturque contraria* and *ibid.* 3.17: *id autem in parvis intellegi potest quos delectari videamus etiamsi eorum nihil intersit, si quid ratione per se ipsi invenerint*. Schmitz (2014) 50–54 notes that the ascription of *ratio* to children in the latter 'cradle argument' contradicts Stoic theory and reflects Peripatetic influence.

[35] Cf. Brunschwig (1986) 129 who states that in the version of the *oikeiōsis* argument surviving in Diogenes Laertius *Lives of Eminent Philosophers* 7.85 '*a priori* argument is much more important than empirical data' and *ibid.* 133. For the lack of interest in the development of children in the Early Stoa, see Inwood (1985) 187: 'In keeping with the Old Stoa's almost exclusive concern with the role of reason in altering animal nature, Chrysippus neglected any serious study of the gradual growth of the human (or animal, for that matter) from birth to maturity'.

[36] See e.g. the way Seneca describes a child's attempt to stand upright as an outcome of *oikeiōsis* at *Letters* 121.8.

[37] A similar view is suggested by Brunschwig (1986) 133–34.

diverse ethical theories and at the rich dialectical context against which Antiochus formulated his own *oikeiōsis* argument. This may help us appreciate better the originality of his account.

The Dialectical Context of *Oikeiōsis* Arguments

The Stoic argument from *oikeiōsis*, as reconstructed in the previous section, was targeted by Academic sceptics, and more specifically by Carneades, who provided an important intermediate step to the Aristotelian/Peripatetic version of the *oikeiōsis* theory, which is represented by Antiochus. In fact the Aristotelian-Peripatetic account of *oikeiōsis* at *On Ends* 5 is prefaced by an exposition of Carneades' division of ethical theories, suggesting the strong influence this scheme exercised on Antiochus.[38] In Carneades' classificatory scheme, *oikeiōsis* features among the variables which form the basis of the identification of different conceptions of the *telos*. Further, it appears to be a normative requirement built into the Carneadean classificatory scheme, at least in the form in which it has come down to us in *On Ends* 5, that the *oikeiōsis* posited by every philosophical school *should* correspond to the conception of the *telos* of the school at hand. This provides a standard to measure disagreement among and within the ethical accounts of the various schools.[39] In line with the Stoic argument, Carneades understood *oikeiōsis* in a developmental way as well; thus *oikeiōsis* becomes in his scheme associated with pre-rational motivation manifested at the beginning of our lives and with the requirement that the *telos* (and the motivation which characterises the end-point of our development) be in conformity with our pre-rational motivation.[40] The following passage, which prefaces the

---

[38] For Antiochus' use of the *Carneadea divisio*, see *On Ends* 5.16: *quod quoniam in quo sit magna dissensio est, Carneadea nobis adhibenda divisio est, qua noster Antiochus libenter uti solet.*

[39] See e.g. *On Ends* 5.19: *ita fit ut quanta differentia est in principiis naturalibus, tanta sit in finibus bonorum malorumque dissimilitudo.*

[40] For the requirement of congruence between the 'first *oikeiōsis*' and the *telos*, see *On Ends* 5.19: *ex eo autem quod statuerit esse quo primum natura moveatur exsistet recti etiam ratio atque honesti, quae cum uno aliquo ex tribus illis congruere possit.*

Antiochean account in Cicero's *On Ends* 5, contains the methodological requirement of Carneades' scheme, as also his commitment to a developmental reading of *oikeiōsis*:

Now almost all have admitted that the object with which wisdom is concerned and what it desires to attain should be in conformity and agreement with nature and such that in itself it entices and allures that mental impulse which the Greeks call *hormē* [*constitit autem fere inter omnes id in quo prudentia versaretur et quod assequi vellet aptum et accommodatum naturae esse oporteret et tale ut ipsum per se invitaret et adliceret appetitum animi, quem* ὁρμὴν *Graeci vocant*]. But what that object is which exercises this attraction and is in this way sought by nature at the very moment of birth [*in primo ortu*] is not agreed, and on this matter great divergence appears among philosophers during the search for the supreme good. But as concerns the whole enquiry which is carried on about the limits of good and evil, when we debate with regard to them, what is their end, we must discover some source in which are contained the earliest attractions of nature [*fons reperiendus est in quo sint prima invitamenta naturae*]; and when this has been found, the whole discussion about good and evil takes its rise from this as from a fountain head. *On Ends* 5.17)

The developmental emphasis on the first stages of our lives (signified by the phrase *in primo ortu*) in Carneades' scheme, opens up the possibility of lack of continuity between the starting point and the end-point of human ethical development, a possibility that Carneades was keen to use for the purposes of refutation. In line with this, the developmental understanding of *oikeiōsis* became a powerful tool in the hands of Academic sceptics against the consistency of the Stoic argument; according to this critique, the Stoics violate the normative demand for correspondence between the earliest and the fully developed rational impulses because they postulate a break in the development of a human being.[41] One may argue that the *oikeiōsis* accounts of later Stoics, and most notably Seneca and Hierocles, are targeting precisely such a polemic, which attempted to prove that the Stoic argument

---

[41] Suggestive of this polemic is especially *On Ends* 4.33–41, where Cicero defends the Antiochean position against the Stoics, and Plutarch *On Common Conceptions* 1069e–f: πόθεν δ᾽ Ἀριστοτέλης, ὦ μακάριε, καὶ Θεόφραστος ἄρχονται; τίνας δὲ Ξενοκράτης καὶ Πολέμων λαμβάνουσιν ἀρχάς; οὐχὶ καὶ Ζήνων τούτοις ἠκολούθησεν ὑποτιθεμένοις στοιχεῖα τῆς εὐδαιμονίας τὴν φύσιν καὶ τὸ κατὰ φύσιν; ἀλλ᾽ ἐκεῖνοι μὲν ἐπὶ τούτων ἔμειναν ὡς αἱρετῶν καὶ ἀγαθῶν καὶ ὠφελίμων, καὶ τὴν ἀρετὴν προσλαβόντες <ἐν> αὐτοῖς ἐνεργοῦσαν οἰκείως χρωμένην ἑκάστῳ τέλειον ἐκ τούτων καὶ ὁλόκληρον ᾤοντο συμπληροῦν βίον καὶ συμπεραίνειν, τὴν ἀληθῶς τῇ φύσει πρόσφορον καὶ συνῳδὸν ὁμολογίαν ἀποδιδόντες.

is inconsistent if viewed from a developmental perspective. Thus, Seneca in *Letters* 121.14–16 goes to great lengths in order to show that a developmental view of a human being as going through different stages of development from childhood down to old age is not at odds with the Stoic argument of *oikeiōsis*.[42]

The Carneadean move also seems to incorporate elements of the rich dialectical context surrounding the notion of *oikeiōsis* in the Hellenistic period. In particular, the emphasis on the developmental aspect found in Carneades' discussion of *oikeiōsis*, attests the influence of the Epicureans, who attempted to deduce the idea that pleasure is the 'highest good' from the way pleasure acts as an object of impulse at the beginning of a living being's life.[43] In the

---

[42] See e.g. 121.15: *unicuique aetati sua constitutio est, alia infanti, alia puero, alia adulescenti, alia seni: omnes ei constitutioni concilliantur in qua sunt.* On Seneca's argument of 'analogical continuity' to counter objections based on a developmental understanding of human nature, see Inwood (1985) 1965–96. Klein (2016) 148 n.11 traces the continuity of the Stoic account in the pursuit of the integrity of the organism's ἡγεμονικόν and the appropriate functions (καθήκοντα) this secures.

[43] Although absent in the popular writings of Epicurus that have come down to us, an argument from *oikeiōsis* is attributed to the Epicurean sect in Cicero's *On Ends* 1.30 with the explicit confirmation on the part of Cicero that this is the way Epicurus himself 'set out to establish his teaching' (*idque instituit* sc. Epicurus *docere sic*): *omne animal, simul atque natum sit, voluptatem appetere eaque gaudere ut summo bono, dolorem aspernari ut summum malum et, quantum possit, a se repellere.* The foundational character of feelings of pleasure and pain in Epicurean theory is suggested by their characterisation as 'first' and 'congenital' in *Letter to Menoeceus* 129: καὶ διὰ τοῦτο τὴν ἡδονὴν ἀρχὴν καὶ τέλος λέγομεν εἶναι τοῦ μακαρίως ζῆν. ταύτην γὰρ ἀγαθὸν πρῶτον καὶ συγγενικὸν ἔγνωμεν, καὶ ἀπὸ ταύτης καταρχόμεθα πάσης αἱρέσεως καὶ φυγῆς, καὶ ἐπὶ ταύτην καταντῶμεν ὡς κανόνι τῷ πάθει πᾶν ἀγαθὸν κρίνοντες. Καὶ ἐπεὶ πρῶτον ἀγαθὸν τοῦτο καὶ σύμφυτον, διὰ τοῦτο καὶ οὐ πᾶσαν ἡδονὴν αἱρούμεθα, ἀλλ' ἔστιν ὅτε πολλὰς ἡδονὰς ὑπερβαίνομεν, ὅταν πλεῖον ἡμῖν τὸ δυσχερὲς ἐκ τούτων ἕπηται. In the same vein, the goodness of pleasure is cast in terms of its 'appropriate nature' with regard to our constitution, see *ibid.* 129: πᾶσα οὖν ἡδονὴ διὰ τὸ φύσιν ἔχειν οἰκείαν ἀγαθόν. The term *oikeios* does not presuppose here a metaphysically loaded theory of nature, as a principle which entails aims and functions, but relates rather to a mechanical sense of appropriateness: pleasure is the aim of our desires and actions because our senses are able to perceive the sensation that pleasure is and our sense organs may offer infallible information about their perceived objects, cf. Brunschwig (1986) 124, n.30. A developmental version of *oikeiōsis* could have been influenced by the examples of children and animals that Epicureans were keen to use in order to show that pleasure is the 'highest good'. Suggestive in this respect is Diogenes Laertius *Lives of Eminent Philosophers* 10.137 = *Fr.* 66 Usener which uses the 'fact' that animals upon birth delight in pleasure and avoid pain as a proof (ἀπόδειξις) for identifying the final end of life with pleasure: ἀποδείξει δὲ χρῆται τοῦ τέλος εἶναι τὴν ἡδονὴν τῷ τὰ ζῷα ἅμα τῷ γεννηθῆναι τῇ μὲν εὐαρεστεῖσθαι, τῷ δὲ πόνῳ προσκρούειν φυσικῶς καὶ χωρὶς λόγου. Notice that ἀπόδειξις is substituted by πίστις in the Cyrenaic version of the *oikeiōsis* argument in Diogenes Laertius *Lives of Eminent Philosophers* 2.88: πίστιν δ' εἶναι τοῦ τέλος εἶναι τὴν ἡδονὴν τὸ ἀπροαιρέτως ἡμᾶς ἐκ παίδων ᾠκειῶσθαι πρὸς αὐτήν, καὶ

case of ethics, the primary observable (psychological) fact was identified by the Epicureans with the pursuit of pleasure and the avoidance of pain. In order to secure that the value of pleasure is not only one belief among others but grounded in nature herself, Epicurus suggested that new-born infants are the domain where one should look in order to observe the 'primitives' of human behaviour. Thus, in a passage from Sextus conveying Epicurean doctrine, the example adduced to make this point is that of the propensity of infants to cry as soon as they are separated from the womb by virtue of the pain they feel when coming in contact with the cold air in the environment.[44]

On the basis of this allegedly infallible evidence from the senses, some Epicureans concluded that pleasure is a thing 'to be chosen' (*haireton*).[45] The Epicurean views on the *oikeion* seem thus to fit the requirement of the Carneadean *divisio* suggesting a strong continuity between the first and last stages of our ethical development: just as at the beginning of our lives we seek pleasure by means of pre-rational desires, we continue pursuing the same sole object, namely pleasure, once we have reached the final stage of our development, albeit by means of rational desire. What moves our desire in both stages of our lives is pleasure, reason being assigned an instrumental role in its attainment. This has as the consequence that the Epicureans do not admit into their account of the *telos* desires motivated by objects other than pleasure, and in particular desires motivated by virtue.

τυχόντας αὐτῆς μηθὲν ἐπιζητεῖν μηθέν τε οὕτω φεύγειν ὡς τὴν ἐναντίαν αὐτῇ ἀλγηδόνα. Cf. Sextus Empiricus *Outlines of Pyrrhonism* 3.194: ὅθεν καὶ οἱ Ἐπικούρειοι δεικνύναι νομίζουσι φύσει αἱρετὴν εἶναι τὴν ἡδονήν· τὰ γὰρ ζῷα φασιν ἅμα τῷ γενέσθαι, ἀδιάστροφα ὄντα, ὁρμᾶν μὲν ἐπὶ τὴν ἡδονήν, ἐκκλίνειν δὲ ἀλγηδόνας and *On Ends* 1.30: *omne animal, simul atque natum sit, voluptatem appetere eaque gaudere ut summo bono, dolorem aspernari ut summum malum et, quantum possit, a se repellere, idque facere nondum depravatum, ipsa natura incorrupte atque integre iudicante.*

44 Sextus Empiricus *Against the Professors* 11.96: ἀλλ' εἰώθασί τινες τῶν ἀπὸ τῆς Ἐπικούρου αἱρέσεως πρὸς τὰς τοιαύτας ἀπορίας ὑπαντῶντες λέγειν ὅτι φυσικῶς καὶ ἀδιδάκτως τὸ ζῷον φεύγει μὲν τὴν ἀλγηδόνα, διώκει δὲ τὴν ἡδονήν· γεννηθὲν γοῦν καὶ μηδέπω τοῖς κατὰ δόξαν δουλεῦον ἅμα τῷ ῥαπισθῆναι ἀσυνήθει ἀέρος ψύξει ἔκλαυσέ τε καὶ ἐκώκυσεν. εἰ δὲ φυσικῶς ὁρμᾷ μὲν πρὸς ἡδονήν, ἐκκλίνει δὲ τὸν πόνον, φύσει φευκτόν τί ἐστιν αὐτῷ ὁ πόνος καὶ αἱρετὸν ἡ ἡδονή.

45 See *On Ends* 1.71: *si infantes pueri, mutae etiam bestiae paene loquuntur magistra ac duce natura nihil esse prosperum nisi voluptatem, nihil asperum nisi dolorem, de quibus neque depravate iudicant neque corrupte.*

After considering the Carneadean dialectic surrounding *oikeiōsis*, let us move now to Antiochus and his Aristotelian/ Peripatetic version of the *oikeiōsis* argument. In the following sections, I will focus on three aspects in which the Antiochean account seems to diverge from the Stoic model of *oikeiōsis*: (a) the way species-specific nature and not cosmic nature acts as the agent of *oikeiōsis*; (b) the role of self-love as the main manifestation of *oikeiōsis,* acting as the principal motivational force from the beginning of life and until an agent has reached his or her latest stage of ethical development, i.e. has acquired virtue (c) the idea that there are plural objects of *oikeiōsis*, a view which supports a pluralistic account of the *telos.* Antiochus attempts to give an account of this view of the *telos* with his distinction between a happy and a happiest life (*vita beata-vita beatissima*), a view which he projects onto the Old Academy.

The Antiochean-Peripatetic Argument from *Oikeiōsis*

Closely modelling the methodology of the Stoic accounts in Diogenes Laertius and in Cicero's *On Ends* 3, the Antiochean spokesperson Piso starts his exposition of Aristotelian/ Peripatetic ethics with an *oikeiōsis* argument. The argument is introduced in *On Ends* 5.24–27 in three steps: after an introduction which states that the account purports to support a conception of the *telos* of all living organisms, a second part contains the developmental aspect of the Antiochean argument, whereas a third part contains an analogical argument which shows how *oikeiōsis* is meant to manifest itself in all living forms according to the requirements of their peculiar nature, with special reference to human beings. My analysis will highlight the strong similarities in terminology between the Stoic and the Antiochean/Peripatetic accounts but will mostly focus on the way Antiochus adapts the Stoic argument in order to offer a different model of how the *telos* is grounded in natural appropriation. Finally, I will refer to some Aristotelian (and Platonic) views which may well have functioned as corroborative for Antiochus' reconstruction of the ethics of the Old Academy.

Let us focus first on the way the Antiochean spokesperson introduces *oikeiōsis* as part of an argument which grounds the *telos* in natural appropriation. The relevant text reads as follows:

Every animal loves itself [*se ipsum diligit*] and upon its birth [*simul et ortum est*] it acts for its self-preservation [*se ut conservet*]; for [*quod*] this impulse is given to it from the beginning by nature for the sake of the protection of its whole life [*quod hic ei primus ad omnem vitam tuendam appetitus a natura datur*] and in order for it [*ut*] to preserve itself and to be able to be in the best condition in accordance with nature [*ut optime secundum naturam affectum esse possit*].

At the beginning [*initio*] this arrangement is vague and uncertain [*institutionem confusam ...... et incertam*] so that it merely preserves itself as whatever kind of being it is [*qualecumque sit*], as it doesn't comprehend [*intellegit*] what it is or what it can become or what its own nature is [*quid ipsius natura sit*]. But when it has grown somewhat older [*cum processit paulum*] and begins to grasp [*perspicere*] to what extent anything affects and relates to it [*se attingat ad seque pertineat*], then it gradually [*sensim*] begins to progress [*progredi*] and know itself [*seseque agnoscere*] and to comprehend for what reason [*intellegere quam ob causam*] it has the desire of the mind [*animi appetitum*] we referred to, and finally it begins to strive after [*appetere*] the things that it perceives to be suited [*apta*] to its nature and to repel their opposites. Therefore [*ergo*] for every animal its object of desire [*illud quod appetit*] is to be found in what is appropriate to its nature [*naturae ...... accommodatum*]. Hence [*ita*] the ultimate good [*finis bonorum*] (sc. of an animal) consists in living in accordance with nature [*secundum naturam vivere*] in that state which is the best possible one and the most appropriate to its nature [*ut optime affici possit ad naturamque accommodatissime*]. (*On Ends* 5.24)

The first part of the account contains Antiochus' commitment to a teleological understanding of nature as the presupposition for a living being's attainment of its *telos*. The Antiochean argument could be reconstructed in the following way:

Premise 1 A living being would be unable to attain its best possible condition according to nature (namely its *telos*), if it did not have self-love.

Premise 2 (Implicit Premise) Nature secures that each living being is able to attain its respective *telos*. [Teleological Commitment]

Conclusion Therefore, each living being is provided by nature with self-love.

In a strikingly similar way to the Diogenes text which contains the 'canonical' version of Stoic *oikeiōsis*, Piso makes, at the beginning of his account, reference to a 'primary impulse for self-preservation'. *Primus appetitus* and *se conservet* stand here for the *prōtē hormē* and *tērein heauto* in the Greek text. Like in the Stoic source, the 'primary impulse' provides a justification for the *telos*, which is here cast in a generic way as the 'best state according to nature'. However, it is significant that Antiochus in his attempt to offer an Aristotelian/Peripatetic variant of the Stoic theory opts for an *affective* starting-point for the impulse which is the primary manifestation of *oikeiōsis*. This starting point is identified with self-love (*se diligere*, translating most probably the Greek *philein heauton*), which is understood as a desire to be in the best state of oneself. This motivational principle which serves self-preservation and, ultimately, the attainment of our *telos* is not shown to be, at least in its primary manifestation, dependent upon a cognitive principle like the *synaisthēsis* or the *syneidēsis* of the Stoic accounts.

The 'primary' character of the impulse towards self-preservation, which serves as a manifestation of *oikeiōsis*, is here of great importance as well. Sharing the Stoic idea of a *prōtē hormē* but also the framework adopted by Carneades, Antiochus introduces into *oikeiōsis* a developmental dimension, which makes self-love into the earliest expression of *oikeiōsis* at the beginning of animal life; suggestive of this temporal reading of *primus* is the expression *simul et ortum est* which signifies the starting-point 'from the moment of birth'. In line with this, the first part of Antiochus' account contains a developmental aspect, which makes self-love an innate principle of 'protection' throughout a living being's life (*ad omnem vitam tuendam*).[46] Thus, self-love serves both mere preservation at the beginning of life but also the attainment of the best possible state (*optime secundum naturam affectum esse*) of the living being's nature, which follows up on the initial stage

---

[46] See also *On Ends* 5.33, where self-love is said to be the mechanism underlying an innate (*ingeneratum*) impulse which leads us to the pursuit of things appropriate to our nature: *illum appetitum rerum ad naturam accommodatarum ingeneratum putaverunt omnibus (sc. gravissimi philosophi), quia continentur ea commendatione naturae, qua se ipsi diligunt.*

manifested from the moment of birth onwards, as a perfection thereof. Loving oneself amounts in this case to desiring to be in the best possible state of oneself as member of a particular natural kind.

The developmental aspect of Antiochus' account becomes central in the second part of his *oikeiōsis* argument. Here, we find numerous markers which point to the idea that appropriation is manifested in living beings in different stages of development from the more primitive towards the more developed (*processit, progredi*). This progress gives clues as to how the initial self-love in the form of self-preservation gives way to a kind of self-love which underpins the pursuit of the *telos*. Here, again the Stoic influence is pervasive; the pursuit of the *telos* is associated with self-knowledge (*se agnoscere*, most probably translating the Greek *gnōthi sauton*), a counterpart to the Stoic term *syneidēsis*, and although reference to knowledge and intellectual activity (*agnoscere, intellegere*) point specifically to a kind of cognition which is peculiar to human beings, the account is meant to show how *oikeiōsis* is manifested in all animals.

Still, Antiochus' account deviates also in marked ways from Stoic theory: Contrary to the 'canonical' passage of Diogenes on Stoic *oikeiōsis* considered above, Antiochus suggests a process of appropriation which unfolds gradually (*sensim*), manifesting successive changes in the cognitive state of living beings.[47] Thus, from a first 'vague and uncertain' state whereby desire for self-preservation is not accompanied by any understanding of one's nature whatsoever,[48] we move gradually to a 'grasp' of things pertaining to oneself (*quicquid se attingat ad seque pertineat perspicere coepit*). The last, and most developed stage of development, which is connected with self-knowledge, manifests an understanding of the causes of one's desire of the mind (*seseque agnoscere et intellegere quam ob causam habeat ...... animi*

---

[47] Cf. also *On Ends* 5.41: *progredientibus autem aetatibus sensim tardeve potius quasi nosmet ipsos cognoscimus.*

[48] This is also repeated at *ibid.* 5.41: *itaque prima illa commendatio quae a natura nostri facta est nobis incerta et obscura est, primusque appetitus ille animi tantum agit ut salvi atque integri esse possimus.* Cf. also *ibid.* 5.58: *in primo enim ortu inest teneritas ac mollitia quaedam, ut nec res videre optimas nec agere possint.*

appetitum). At this stage a living being has access to what is an appropriate object of desire, i.e. to what constitutes its *telos*, *through* rational cognition. Its desires are, in this case, in full correspondence with what is (extensionally defined) as appropriate to its nature, so that it desires not only what it perceives *as* appropriate to him- or herself, but also what *is* appropriate to him- or herself (*coeptatque et ea, quae naturae sentit apta, appetere et propulsare contraria*).[49] The conclusion of the passage corroborates the idea that *oikeiōsis* is meant to offer an ultimate justification to a living being's pursuit of its *telos*: the object of desire (*illud quod appetit*), Piso concludes, is to be found in what is appropriate to a living being's nature (*naturae ... accommodatum*). The consequence of this is that all desires (both rational and non-rational) are conceived as in some sense pre-oriented with regard to their respective objects.[50] This is supposed to provide an independent standard for the teleological success of organisms, including human beings, who are meant to grasp appropriate objects of desire by means of their reasoning capacities.

The last part of the Antiochean passage introducing *oikeiōsis* brings this conclusion to bear on the conception of the *telos*; thus, the final end is conceived in Stoic manner as 'living according to nature' (*secundum naturam vivere*, translating the Greek *kata physin zēn*),[51] which is further glossed as 'living in the state which is the best possible one *and* the most appropriate to nature' (*ut optime affici possit ad naturamque accommodatissime*). The best possible state is thus the one which *corresponds* to what is most appropriate to the living being's nature according to the teleological structure that obtains in nature. This state is pursued by the ideal agent by means of rational understanding, i.e.

---

[49] At *ibid*. 5.41 this stage is connected with knowledge of the way we differ from other animals: *cum autem dispicere coepimus et sentire quid simus et quid <ab> animantibus ceteris differamus, tum ea sequi incipimus ad quae nati sumus*.

[50] This prompts Brunner (2014) 208 to characterise Antiochus' theory as 'quasi-Humean' in the sense that according to it the 'source of our motivations lies outside reason altogether, such that the basic direction and goal of the "natural desire" springing from this source cannot be altered or modified by virtue of any rational considerations whatsoever', see *ibid*. 208–09.

[51] The formula is, however, attested in Polemo as well. For discussion, see Chapter 2, *supra*.

knowledge of what is most appropriate to human nature. Antiochus interprets accordingly the Pythian maxim 'know thyself' in a way that fits his ideas: the aim of self-knowledge is the discovery of what is appropriate to our distinctively human nature, without any reference to an accommodation to the nature of the universe as found in the Stoic theory.

Both in the Stoic and the Peripatetic versions of *oikeiōsis* (as they have come down to us in Diogenes and Cicero respectively) human appropriation is embedded into a larger naturalistic framework which presents the attainment of a human being's peculiar *telos* as analogous to the appropriation of other animals (and even plants) towards their respective *telos*. The Stoics employed such an argument as part of a strategy which aimed at showing how god *qua* cosmos manifests itself, encompassing all life forms into a single teleological process of *oikeiōsis*; this may support a 'unitary' understanding of the *telos* formula, according to which 'living according to nature' amounts, for every living constituent of the cosmos, to living the life plan prescribed by the single cosmic *physis*, namely *logos*.

In Antiochus' account, *oikeiōsis* serves instead a distinctively Aristotelian type of teleology which focuses exclusively on the inherent *telos* of specific living organisms, without any reference to the premise of a universal, cosmic nature. Antiochus understands thus *oikeiōsis* as the process underpinning each organism's fundamental desire for achieving its *telos*, in accordance with each being's peculiar nature and inner power granted to it by nature.[52] This tallies with the advocacy of a species-specific teleology at *On Ends* 5.25–6, which contains the Aristotelien/Peripatetic version of the 'analogical argument' which is found in the Diogenes account in relation to Stoic *oikeiōsis*: whereas it is true, Piso asserts, that every animate creature has as its *telos* to reach the perfection of its nature (*finem quoque omnium hunc esse ut natura*

---

[52] In the Antiochean account we find many references to a congenital *vis* which underpins the *oikeiōsis* of living organisms, see e.g. *On Ends* 5.43 (with reference to human beings). On δύναμις as synonymous for soul and as a principle of motion, see Aristotle *On the Soul* 2.413a25–28: διὸ καὶ τὰ φυόμενα πάντα δοκεῖ ζῆν· φαίνεται γὰρ ἐν αὐτοῖς ἔχοντα δύναμιν καὶ ἀρχὴν τοιαύτην, δι' ἧς αὔξησίν τε καὶ φθίσιν λαμβάνουσι κατὰ τοὺς ἐναντίους τόπους and *Nicomachean Ethics* 1.1102a34.

expleatur),[53] the final end is different for animals belonging to different species (*extrema illa et summa ...... inter animalium genera distincta et dispertita sint*) and, thus, it cannot be expressed with a single formula.[54] The specific final end for different species of animals corresponds to 'what is appropriate and suited to the desire of each animal's peculiar nature' (*sua cuique propria et ad id apta quod cuiusque natura desideret*),[55] suggesting that different animals perceive different things as *oikeia* according to their *idia physis*.

This betrays the influence of an Aristotelian methodological principle according to which one seeks similarities (*koinon*) but also the special property of the species (*idion*) for the explanation of natural kinds.[56] Piso accordingly recognises that a proper understanding of the *telos* needs to take into account the peculiar nature of each living organism, and concludes that the final end is *analogous* for all kinds of organisms, albeit not the same for all of them (*necesse sit omnium rerum quae natura vigeant similem esse finem, non eundem*).[57] He does not thus assume a unifying principle of nature in his account but recognises the way each living form, analogously to all others, strives for the perfection of its own peculiar kind due to an inherent natural power which belongs to it.[58] The exposition of the way nature imposes on all living things an

---

[53] *On Ends* 5.25: *necesse est finem quoque omnium hunc esse, ut natura expleatur.* Cf. *ibid.* 5.26.

[54] *On Ends* 5.26: *quare cum dicimus omnibus animalibus extremum esse secundum naturam vivere, non ita accipiendum est, quasi dicamus unum esse omnium extremum.*

[55] *On Ends* 5.25. Cf. *Tusculan Disputations* 5.38.

[56] This is reflected in the so-called function argument of *Nicomachean Ethics* 1.1097b33–34: τὸ μὲν γὰρ ζῆν κοινὸν εἶναι φαίνεται καὶ τοῖς φυτοῖς, ζητεῖται δὲ τὸ ἴδιον. The same differentiation is used in a different context in *Politics* 3.1276b21–26: τῶν δὲ πλωτήρων καίπερ ἀνομοίων ὄντων τὴν δύναμιν (ὁ μὲν γάρ ἐστιν ἐρέτης, ὁ δὲ κυβερνήτης, ὁ δὲ πρωρεύς, ὁ δ' ἄλλην τιν' ἔχων τοιαύτην ἐπωνυμίαν) δῆλον ὡς ὁ μὲν ἀκριβέστατος ἑκάστου λόγος ἴδιος ἔσται τῆς ἀρετῆς, ὁμοίως δὲ καὶ κοινός τις ἐφαρμόσει πᾶσιν.

[57] *On Ends* 5.26; *ibid.* 5.40 makes the same point on the basis of a vine-human analogy (see Chapter 9, *infra*); cf. also *On Ends* 4.32. For the idea that human and animal faculties are analogous, see also *History of Animals* 588a28–31.

[58] The consequences that this has for a non-instrumental understanding of the *telos* of animals will be discussed in Chapter 9, *infra*.

analogously similar teleological structure and makes every living form strive for the *telos* that is peculiar to it concludes by focusing on the actual topic of the discussion, namely the human *telos*. Thus, in the case of human beings living according to nature consists in 'living according to human nature when it has been in all respects brought to perfection and lacks nothing further'.[59]

What transpires from the above is that Antiochus, while modelling his account very closely on a Stoic 'prototype', adapts the existing framework in a way that he sees fit in order to convey Aristotelian/Peripatetic ideas. Far from being a syncretist, if the latter amounts to a conscious aim to combine divergent views (in this case Aristotelian/Peripatetic and Stoic ones), he is carefully crafting his account in order to fit into it what he understands as most representative of the Aristotelian/ Peripatetic position on the *telos* and its foundation in nature. The philosophical agenda of providing a foundation of the *telos* by reference to the peculiar nature of each organism seems indeed to post-date Aristotle and the Peripatos, since grounding ethics in nature does not play a central role in the surviving treatises of the school; this does not mean, however, that there are no elements in the Aristotelian/Peripatetic (and Platonic, for that matter)[60] tradition which could have given support to the Antiochean project.

One may start with evidence which is pertinent to the link between *oikeiōsis* and the *telos*. Thus, the content of the human *telos* is linked in the so-called function argument at *Nicomachean Ethics* 1.7 to the concept of appropriate virtue (*oikeia aretē*), a line of argumentation which is tellingly prefigured in Plato's *Republic* 1 (352d–354a). According to Aristotle's argument, the good for a human being, namely *eudaimonia*, consists (primarily) in activity of the soul in

---

[59] *On Ends* 5.26: *ex quo intellegi debet homini id esse in bonis ultimum, secundum naturam vivere, quod ita interpretemur: vivere ex hominis natura undique perfecta et nihil requirente.*

[60] A link of the *oikeion* with the *agathon* is found already, in the context of the discussion of friendship, in Plato's *Lysis* 222d5: τὸ ἀγαθὸν καὶ τὸ οἰκεῖον ἂν ταὐτὸν φῶμεν εἶναι, ἄλλο τι ἢ ὁ ἀγαθὸς τῷ ἀγαθῷ μόνον φίλος.

accordance with virtue.⁶¹ The basis of Aristotle's argument is
that there is an *ergon* peculiar to human beings analogous to
the *ergon* of bodily parts and occupations; the implicit assumption is that human *eudaimonia* corresponds to the *ergon* that
humans have. Such an assumption, however, does not explain
why human beings strive after the 'highest good' which corresponds to their *ergon*; it seems that if the argument is to
provide an undisputable foundation for the 'good life' it
needs additional premises which would link the concept of
the *ergon* with human nature. Reading the main constituent
of *eudaimonia* as *oikeion*, along the lines that Antiochus suggests, offers both a metaphysical and a psychological grounding to the notion of *eudaimonia*: according to this, the final
good is pursued both because it is established as an appropriate
object of desire on the part of a teleological principle of nature
and because it is the kind of object that arouses our desire
towards its pursuit. The term *oikeion* is suitable to convey this
since it uniquely combines the meanings of both 'what is one's
own' (as the object of desire) and the 'appropriate' (as what is
normatively suited to our nature).⁶²

Another promising area where Antiochus could have found
material for crafting his Antiochean/Peripatetic theory of
oikeiōsis is the domain of natural science. Thus, precedents for
an argument from *oikeiōsis* could be found in the cases, when the
word *oikeios* relates to the desire of organisms for suitable things
in their environment; such desire is premised on the idea that each
living organism has an inherent *telos* which it strives to fulfil and
as a consequence of which it seeks things conducive to its fulfilment. Relevant examples include birds living by the sea whose

---

⁶¹ *Nicomachean Ethics* I.1098a12–18: εἰ δ' οὕτως, [ἀνθρώπου δὲ τίθεμεν ἔργον ζωήν τινα,
ταύτην δὲ ψυχῆς ἐνέργειαν καὶ πράξεις μετὰ λόγου, σπουδαίου δ' ἀνδρὸς εὖ ταῦτα καὶ
καλῶς, ἕκαστον δ' εὖ κατὰ τὴν οἰκείαν ἀρετὴν ἀποτελεῖται· εἰ δ' οὕτω,] τὸ ἀνθρώπινον
ἀγαθὸν ψυχῆς ἐνέργεια γίνεται κατ' ἀρετήν, εἰ δὲ πλείους αἱ ἀρεταί, κατὰ τὴν ἀρίστην καὶ
τελειοτάτην. *Oikeia aretē* is in *Nicomachean Ethics* I.7 related to the distinctive function
(*ergon*) of human beings, which is defined with analogy to the evaluative practices that
we apply in the exercise of skills and in the performance of bodily parts. This follows a
precedent in Plato's *Republic* I.352d–354a. No explicit link is drawn between *oikeia
aretē* and desire for happiness in the context of this particular chapter. But one may
assume such a link, as suggested by Barney (2008) 311.
⁶² The double meaning of *oikeios* is stressed in Szaif (2012) 230–31 as well.

nature has been equipped for their aquatic environment, and the way animals seek the food which is proper to them (*oikeia trophē*) in line with the kind of environment they grow up in.[63] The *oikeion* is prominent in the Theophrastean botanical treatises as well:[64] there, Theophrastus discusses the importance for a plant's development of the appropriate place (*oikeios topos*), in which he includes both air or seasonal occurrences and soil;[65] furthermore, the word stands there in close association with the *harmotton*, namely with what is suited to an organism and its peculiar 'power'.[66]

The discussion of desires for appropriate things which conduce to one's *telos* from the context of natural science may be supplemented by references to 'what is according to nature' in the treatises of the Aristotelian tradition. Like *oikeion*, the locution *kata physin* suggests that what an organism desires from the beginning of its life corresponds to the species-form of the particular organism. This again corresponds to a strong normative understanding of nature which reflects the perfected state of an organism. Extensive use of this strong notion of *kata physin* is made notably in the first book of Aristotle's *Politics*. There, it is explicitly stated that nature is an end (*telos*), 'since what we say the nature of each thing is, is what it is when its coming-into-being is perfected'.[67] The expression *kata physin* in Peripatetic texts also qualifies objects of desire which correspond to the 'natural state' of an organism. Thus, in the *History of Animals* (589a10) we read

---

[63] *History of Animals* 621b4–6: ἅπαντα δὲ καὶ τὰ πλωτὰ καὶ τὰ μόνιμα τούτους νέμεται τοὺς τόπους ἐν οἷς ἂν φυῶσι, καὶ τοὺς ὁμοίους τούτοις· ἡ γὰρ οἰκεία τροφὴ ἑκάστων ἐν τούτοις ἐστίν.

[64] See e.g. *On Ends* 5.10: *persecutus est Aristoteles animantium omnium ortus victus figuras, Theophrastus autem stirpium naturas omniumque fere rerum quae e terra gignerentur causas atque rationes.* Antiochus' knowledge of the Theophrastean botanical treatises, and especially of the *On the Causes of Plants*, is discussed in Chapter 2, *supra*.

[65] See e.g. *On the Causes of Plants* 1.9.3; 1.16.11; 2.3.7; 2.7.1; 3.6.6; 3.6.7.

[66] On the *Causes of Plants* 2.19.6.5–6: ἐκ τούτων γὰρ τὰ κοινὰ πάθη καὶ αἱ κατὰ γένη παραλλαγαὶ καὶ τὸ ἁρμόττον καὶ τὸ οἰκεῖον ἑκάστοις γίνεται φανερόν; however, the οἰκεῖον retains a more intimate connection with an organism's nature, see *ibid.* 2.16.8.5–7: διττῶς δὲ καὶ τὸ τῆς χώρας πρόσφορον· ἢ γὰρ τὸ οἰκεῖον τῆς φύσεως ἢ τὸ πρὸς ἰσχὺν καὶ δύναμιν ἁρμόττον. See also *ibid.* 1.16.13.9: ἐξ ὧν καὶ διαιρετέον ὥσπερ καὶ ἡ φύσις διῄρηται ἡμέροις καὶ ἀγρίοις ὁμοίως ἔν τε ζώοις καὶ φυτοῖς. ἑκατέροις γὰρ ἐστι πολλὰ φυσικὰ καὶ οἰκεῖα καὶ πρὸς σωτηρίαν καὶ πρὸς διαμονὴν καὶ πρὸς αὔξησιν καὶ βλάστησιν καὶ πρὸς τὴν τῶν καρπῶν γέννησιν.

[67] *Politics* 1.1252b32-33.

that all animals are said to pursue the pleasure appropriate to their nature.[68] Moreover, living things are said to do, in Aristotle's *On the Soul*, whatever they do 'in accordance with nature' because of a desire to 'partake of the everlasting and divine in so far as they can'.[69] This places the desires and actions of living organisms in a wider teleological context. In line with this approach, Antiochus places the foundations of ethical development within the wider context of natural science, and imports from it teleological assumptions which are missing in the ethical treatises of the Peripatetic tradition.

---

[68] Evidence for this use of the expression with regard to objects of desire is also found in one fragment of Theophrastus from Didymus' summary of Peripatetic Ethics, which states that one extreme opposed to the virtue of temperance is someone who 'like a stone does not desire even things which are natural' (τὸν μὲν γὰρ λίθου δίκην μηδὲ τῶν κατὰ φύσιν ὀρέγεσθαι), see Theophrastus *Fr.* 449A FHS&G. = Stobaeus *Selections* 2 141.6–7 Wachsmuth.

[69] *On the Soul* 2.415a26–b2: φυσικώτατον γὰρ τῶν ἔργων τοῖς ζῶσιν, ὅσα τέλεια καὶ μὴ πηρώματα ἢ τὴν γένεσιν αὐτομάτην ἔχει, τὸ ποιῆσαι ἕτερον οἷον αὐτό, ζῷον μὲν ζῷον, φυτὸν δὲ φυτόν, ἵνα τοῦ ἀεὶ καὶ τοῦ θείου μετέχωσιν ᾗ δύνανται· πάντα γὰρ ἐκείνου ὀρέγεται, καὶ ἐκείνου ἕνεκα πράττει ὅσα πράττει κατὰ φύσιν.

4

SELF-LOVE IN THE ANTIOCHEAN-PERIPATETIC ACCOUNT

Although self-love constitutes according to the Antiochean spokesperson a psychological principle rooted in nature, which is accessible to the senses and cannot be seriously doubted by anyone, Piso goes on at *On Ends* 5.27 to offer arguments (*rationes*) that justify it philosophically as well.[1] The defence of self-love in the Antiochean theory rests primarily on its role as the necessary motivational force for every impulse which is (analytically) directed at something perceived as good for the organism.[2] This conclusion is advocated by means of two *reductio* arguments at *On Ends* 5.28. The relevant passage reads as follows:

> But how could one conceive or imagine [*intellegi aut cogitari*] that there is some animal which hates itself? In fact (sc. in that case) two contrary things would happen at the same time [*res concurrent contrariae*]. For, given that an animal is hostile towards itself, such an impulse would deliberately [*consulto*] start drawing something harmful to it, but because it would be doing it for its own sake [*quoniam*[3] *id sua causa faciet*], it would be loving and hating itself at the same time [*et oderit se et simul diligent*], which is impossible. Furthermore, necessarily someone who is hostile towards oneself would think of goods as evils and evils as goods and would avoid what should be sought while seeking what should be avoided, something which without doubt would make life impossible [*quae sine dubio vitae eversio*]. (Cicero *On Ends* 5.28)

The main argument of Piso on this point could be reconstructed in the following way:

Premise 1 An animal which hates itself knowingly (*consulto*) has an impulse for things harmful to itself.

---

[1] *On Ends* 5.27: *quod quamquam dubitationem non habet (est enim infixum in ipsa natura comprehenditur<que> suis cuiusque sensibus, sic ut contra si quis velit non audiatur), tamen, ne quid praetermittamus, rationes quoque cur hoc ita sit adferenda puto.*

[2] Cf. Annas (1993):261.

[3] *quoniam* here is a conjecture of Madvig, whereas the MSS. give *cum*.

Premise 2 Every animal acts for its own sake (*id sua causa faciet*).

Premise 3 (Follows from Premise 2) Every animal in acting seeks what is beneficial to itself, that is (in the case of human beings) what conduces to its own happiness [Implied premise].

Premise 4 Seeking what is beneficial to oneself is equivalent to loving oneself.

Premise 5 In the case of acts of self-hate an animal both loves and hates itself.

Premise 6 But loving and hating oneself at the same time is a logical contradiction.

Conclusion Therefore, self-hate is impossible.

One may derive from the Antiochean account the principle that in order for x to desire y, x needs to have either the impression, or the belief, that y is good *for* x. This is, according to the defence of self-love provided in the Antiochean account, equivalent to the thesis that in order for x to desire y, x needs to love x. This argument rests on the analytical connection between impulse or desire and what is perceived as good for oneself, what in the Aristotelian tradition is called the 'seeming good' (*phainomenon agathon*). According to that, whatever one deems as an object of desire and, thus, as something to be sought, has to be conceived as good for oneself, even if it is not necessarily to be identified with the good *simpliciter.*

Antecedents for the position that all desires are for what is good could be found in other representatives of the Old Academic tradition Antiochus drew on, in a way that would confirm the Antiochean thesis of the unity of Plato's Academy and the Peripatos. Indeed, the view espoused by Antiochus bears echoes from the intellectualist position ascribed to the character Socrates in some Platonic dialogues. Thus, in the *Meno*, Socrates defends the thesis that no one seeks bad things because no one seeks to harm him- or herself and, as a consequence of this, not to be happy; and in the *Apology* Socrates defends himself against the charge that he has corrupted the youth by arguing that no one would intentionally do such a thing because that would run counter to one's self-interest.[4] It transpires from the above that Antiochus defended the impossibility of self-hate by trivialising self-love and making it a prerequisite of every impulse whatsoever, without which (voluntary) action would be impossible. Following the Socratic-Platonic tradition and its Aristotelian-Peripatetic counterpart, Antiochus claims that every voluntary action is premised on a desire for the agent's own good, something which, in his account, is re-conceptualised as self-love.

In the last part of the quoted passage from Piso's speech, the impossibility of self-hate is corroborated by the view that such an occurrence would make life impossible. The motif of an 'overthrow of life' (*vitae eversio*) accompanying the impossibility of hate for oneself in the passage discussed has a direct epistemological parallel at *Lucullus* 31:[5] there, the Antiochean Lucullus accuses those who deny the possibility of *katalēpsis* of 'ruining the foundations of the whole of life' (*totam vitam evertunt funditus*), since that would tear out 'the very tools and equipment of life' (*eripiunt vel instrumenta vel ornamenta vitae*). Someone unable to perceive something as true and choice worthy would never identify an object of attainment or avoidance. In the same way at *On Ends* 5, someone unable to experience love towards him- or herself, would never undertake any action whatsoever, thus making life and survival impossible.

A counter-argument to the universal application of self-love advocated by the Antiochean spokesman is the existence of self-destructive behaviour. Can someone who suffers deliberately, or even decides to commit suicide, be still considered a self-lover? The examples that Piso considers at *On Ends* 5.28–9 apply to such cases and aim at countering objections to the existence of a universal feeling of self-love, whilst at

---

[4] *Meno* 77c–78b; *Apology* 25e. For the defence of a desire for one's good as a principle of action, see also *Gorgias* 468b and *Protagoras* 358c–d. In Aristotle, see especially *Nicomachean Ethics* 8.1155b23–27, where the vocabulary of *philia* is employed with regard to the object of desire: δοκεῖ δὲ τὸ αὑτῷ ἀγαθὸν φιλεῖν ἕκαστος, καὶ εἶναι ἁπλῶς μὲν τἀγαθὸν φιλητόν, ἑκάστῳ δὲ τὸ ἑκάστῳ· φιλεῖ δ' ἕκαστος οὐ τὸ ὂν αὑτῷ ἀγαθὸν ἀλλὰ τὸ φαινόμενον. Cf. *ibid.* 5.1129b6.

[5] *Lucullus* 31: *ergo i qui negant quicquam posse comprendi haec ipsa eripiunt vel instrumenta vel ornamenta vitae, vel potius etiam totam vitam evertunt funditus ipsumque animal orbant animo, ut difficile sit de temeritate eorum perinde ut causa postulat dicere.*

the same time highlighting the Antiochean views on the passions. The relevant part of Piso's account reads as follows:

In fact nor should some, if found to have preferred the noose or other forms of departure from life, or the character in Terence, who said in his own words that 'he decreed that the more he suffers the less injustice he will be doing to his son', be considered to be hostile towards themselves [*inimicus ipse sibi putandus est*]. But some are driven by grief [*dolore*], others by lust [*cupiditate*], whereas many become insane by anger [*iracundia*] so that whereas they rush into disaster deliberately [*scientes*], they nonetheless think that in this way they are taking care of themselves in the best way [*se optime sibi consulere arbitrantur*]. So, they say without hesitation: 'This is what is right for me; you should do what is needed for you to do.' Those who would have declared war on themselves would like to be tortured day and night and, certainly, they wouldn't reproach themselves and say that they have not taken care of their own affairs in a good way [*quod se male suis rebus consuluisse dicerent*]; these accusations are rather the mark of people who care for and love themselves [*eorum ... qui sibi cari sunt seseque diligent*]. Therefore, whenever it is said that one does not value oneself [*male quis de se mereri*] and that one is an enemy and hostile towards oneself [*sibique esse inimicus atque hostis*], and that lastly one avoids life, we should have in mind that there is an underlying explanation for this stance [*aliquam subesse ... causam*], such as to make us understand that, even in those very cases, everyone is dear to themselves [*ut ex eo ipso intelligi possit sibi quemque esse carum*]. (On Ends 5.28–9)

Examples of self-destructive behaviour would seem *prima facie* to contradict the Antiochean view that human beings have a natural love for their own selves, something which is taken to be equivalent, as already shown, to a desire to be happy. Instead, what Piso demonstrates is that even such cases of self-destruction can be explained on the basis of the hypothesis that self-love supplies the necessary motivation for action. To that end, the Antiochean spokesman claims that self-punishment and self-destruction do not arise out of a feeling which runs counter to that of self-love but out of particular judgements that people make with regard to what they believe to serve best their own interests; if such judgements are false they result in reprehensible passions but the latter can still be shown to be motivated by self-love. Self-destructive behaviour can thereby be judged to serve as a means to the attainment of one's own good or happiness.

The Antiochean spokesman illustrates his point with an example from poetry. The example chosen is that of a character from one of Menander's comedies, the 'Self-Tormentor' (in Greek *Heautontimoroumenos*), translated into Latin by Terence. As the title betrays, the main character of the play is someone who deliberately punishes himself and may thus serve well as an example of a case where self-love is absent from the motivation of an agent. The example, by contrast, serves for Piso as a good one for the defence of the psychological primacy of self-love but also of the role of judgement for shaping one's desires. Instead of exhibiting self-hate, the character is shown to be driven to punish himself as the outcome of a conscious decision (*decrevit*) resulting from the belief that in this way he would pay off for the injustice he has committed against his son.[6] Piso claims that, as in the case of Menedemus, also in the case of licentious people driven by passions such as pain, anger or lust, their behaviour results from a belief that such a reaction is for the best interest of the agent (*tum se optime sibi consulere arbitrantur*), showing precisely that, even in those cases, self-love is the underlying cause of behaviour.[7] Thus, harmful or self-destructive reactions serve in some cases as a means for the achievement of the agent's good and rely on judgements of what is appropriate to do in the particular circumstances. The role of belief in those cases puts the stress on the responsibility of the agent and presents the action as an outcome of deliberation and decision-making. To make his point, Antiochus does not focus on incontinent action but speaks of people whose non-rational desires set the ends they pursue and the decisions they form: in accordance with that, base people seem to act voluntarily.

The impossibility of self-hate is corroborated in Piso's account by two further arguments. The first suggests that we cannot remain indifferent towards ourselves and towards what is perceived as good for ourselves, and the second defends the view that our own

---

[6] Cf. also *Tusculan Disputations* 3.65.

[7] *On Ends* 5.29: *intellegatur aliquam subesse eius modi causam, ut ex eo ipso intellegi possit sibi quemque esse carum.*

self, rather than other contesters, is the most fundamental object of care, and offers an ultimate explanation of human motivation. The first argument reads as follows:

Nor is it actually enough to say that nobody exists who could hate himself, but this also should be considered, that there is no one who could judge that it is of no interest to him in what condition he is found [*quomodo se habeat nihil sua censeat interesse*]. For that would abolish impulse [*tolletur ... appetitus animi*] if we were disposed towards our own affairs in the same way that we are disposed towards things that we consider to be of no interest to us in cases when we have no inclination for one thing or another [*neutram in partem propensiores sumus*]. (*On Ends* 5.30)

The implicit reasoning behind this argument suggests that indifference towards what appears good to us, and is thus an expression of self-love, would result in the withdrawal of impulse and, thus, in inactivity, since it is only through a representation of something as good for ourselves that we are moved towards it. What conduces to our own well-being would be equivalent in this case to an indifferent thing that is unable to stir our impulse and move us to action. The argument seems to be particularly addressed against those who advocated 'indifference' (*adiaphoria*) as a viable stance or, even, as a necessary means for achieving happiness. Among them, we find two groups of philosophers: the followers of Pyrrho who suggested that no distinction of value is necessary for the conduct of life and who advocated that nothing can be securely believed to be 'good'[8] and some dissident Stoics, like Aristo, who abolished distinctions of value other than virtue or knowledge.[9] This is at

---

[8] See e.g. the account from Eusebius, *Preparation for the Gospel*: 14.18.2–4: τὰ μὲν οὖν πράγματά φησιν αὐτὸν (sc. Πύρρων) ἀποφαίνειν ἐπ᾽ ἴσης ἀδιάφορα καὶ ἀστάθμητα καὶ ἀνεπίκριτα, διὰ τοῦτο μήτε τὰς αἰσθήσεις ἡμῶν μήτε τὰς δόξας ἀληθεύειν ἢ ψεύδεσθαι. διὰ τοῦτο οὖν μηδὲ πιστεύειν αὐταῖς δεῖν, ἀλλ᾽ ἀδοξάστους καὶ ἀκλινεῖς καὶ ἀκραδάντους εἶναι, περὶ ἑνὸς ἑκάστου λέγοντας ὅτι οὐ μᾶλλον ἔστιν ἢ οὐκ ἔστιν ἢ καὶ ἔστι καὶ οὐκ ἔστιν ἢ οὔτε ἔστιν οὔτε οὐκ ἔστιν. On Pyrrho, see also *Lucullus* 130: *Pyrrho autem ea ne sentire quidem sapientem, quae ἀπάθεια nominatur.*

[9] The doctrine of 'indifference' was first introduced, according to Cicero's *Lucullus* 130, by the pupil of Zeno, Aristo of Chios: *hos si contemnimus et iam abiectos putamus, illos certe minus despicere debemus: Aristonem, qui cum Zenonis fuisset auditor re probavit ea quae ille verbis, nihil esse bonum nisi virtutem nec malum nisi quod virtuti esset contrarium; in mediis ea momenta quae Zeno voluit nulla esse censuit. huic summum bonum est in is rebus neutram in partem moveri, quae ἀδιαφορία ab ipso dicitur.* Cf. *On Ends* 5.73: *Multa sunt dicta ab antiquis de contemnendis ac despiciendis rebus humanis; hoc unum Aristo tenuit: praeter vitia atque virtutes negavit rem esse ullam*

odds with the 'mainstream' Stoic position that certain 'indifferents' are preferred, i.e. have a selective value or priority.[10] These philosophers either questioned the assumption that the objects of desire to which we are drawn are 'goods' altogether (Pyrrho), or they radically restricted the scope of these 'goods' to only one object, namely the 'moral' good (*honestum*), granting no difference in value whatsoever between, say, health and disease or life and death (Aristo). Antiochus rejects the view of both these heterodox Stoics and Pyrrhonian sceptics that living is possible without committing oneself to the belief that certain things (to which one should include not only virtue and knowledge) are advantageous to oneself. This tallies well with his belief that we are drawn towards appropriate objects of desire by virtue of natural appropriation and on the basis of the teleological structure of nature. The second argument contained at *On Ends* 5.30 reads as follows:

And even that would be totally absurd, if someone would say that there is self-love but that this power of love is directed to another object [*ad aliam rem quampiam referatur*] and not to the actual person who loves himself. When this is said of friendship, duties or virtues, however it is said, this possible objection makes some sense [*intellegi*]; but in the case of our own selves such a thing, namely that we love ourselves for the sake of something else, e.g. for the sake of pleasure [*propter voluptatem*], cannot even be conceived. For we love pleasure for the sake of ourselves and not the other way round.

The argument is based on the impossibility of the instrumentalisation of love of the self in comparison to other motivations: thus whereas, Piso argues, virtue, friendship or pleasure can be conceived as means to some further end beyond themselves, self-love, being analytically tied to every desire, could never become instrumental for the achievement of something beyond itself. Rather

---

aut fugiendam aut expetendam; ibid. 5.23. See also Diogenes Laertius *Lives of Eminent Philosophers* 7.37 and *ibid.* 7.160.

[10] See also the critique of Cato at *On Ends* 3.50 against Aristo: *deinceps explicatur differentia rerum, quam si non ullam esse diceremus, confunderetur omnis vita, ut ab Aristone, neque ullum sapientiae munus aut opus inveniretur, cum inter res eas, quae ad vitam degendam pertinerent, nihil omnino interesset, neque ullum dilectum adhiberi oporteret.*

every other thing, like pleasure, gains its importance by reference to oneself, since we seek pleasure in order to experience it *ourselves*.[11] The fundamental character of self-love in comparison with pleasure is corroborated further on in Piso's account by reference to a desire to preserve ourselves even in situations of acute pain, as illustrated by the character Philoctetes in the homonymous play.[12] This serves as a proof for the view that self-love is prior and more fundamental than the desire to pursue pleasure.

Finally, Antiochus shows the primacy of self-love by means of a defence of the natural character of the *pathos* of fear of death. Thus, in opposition to the Stoa, which condemned all passions as excessive desires, the Antiochean spokesperson is keen to stress the difference between reprehensible passions and passions which are 'in accordance with nature'. The Antiochean thesis is that not all *pathē* are to be extirpated; certain *pathē* may reflect correct desires and, accordingly, be genuine expressions of our *oikeiōsis*. This becomes most obvious in Piso's discussion of fear of death at *On Ends* 5.31–32. The relevant part of Piso's account reads as follows:

> Yet what is more evident than the fact that not only are we dear to ourselves but we are ardently so? For who is there, even one, whose 'blood does not flee from fear and skin not turn pale from horror', when death approaches? Even if it is false [*in vitio*] to dread so strongly the dissolution of our nature – a similar fear of pain is also reprehensible – is it not the fact that for the most part we all feel the same, a sufficient argument [*satis argumenti est*] that our nature shrinks back from its destruction [*ab interitu naturam abhorrere*]? And the more some people react like that – though justly reprehended – the more they make us realize that these excessive cases [*nimia*] wouldn't have occurred if there were not a moderate [*modica*] (fear of death) (bestowed on us) by nature [*natura*]. Of course, I am not referring to those who fear death, because they believe that it will deprive them of the goods of life or because they dread some horrors in the

---

[11] A similar idea features in Seneca *Letters* 121.17: *primum sibi ipsum conciliatur animal; debet enim aliquid esse ad quod alia referantur. Voluptatem peto. Cui? mihi; ergo mei curam ago. Dolorem refugio. Pro quo? pro me; ergo mei curam ago. Si omnia propter curam mei facio, ante omnia est mei cura.*

[12] *On Ends* 5.32: *maxime autem in hoc quidem genere vis est perspicua naturae, cum et mendicitatem multi perpetiantur ut vivant, et angantur adpropinquatione mortis confecti homines senectute et ea perferant, quae Philoctetam videmus in fabulis. Qui cum cruciaretur non ferendis doloribus, propagabat tamen vitam aucupio, 'configebat tardus celeres, stans volantis', ut apud Accium est, pinnarumque contextu corpori tegumenta faciebat.*

other life or those who avoid death because they are afraid of dying in pain. For even small children, who don't reflect on those things, many times when we in fun threaten to throw them down from somewhere, they fear greatly. Even, as Pacuvius says, 'wild animals who lack the rational ability to protect themselves', they 'shake when seized with fear of death'. But who supposes regarding the sage himself [de ipso sapiente] other than that even when he has decided that he must die, he is still moved [moveatur] at parting from his family and abandoning the very daylight? But indeed in this case, the power of (our) nature [vis ... naturae] becomes manifest in the highest degree, since many people will endure being beggars so that they remain alive, and others weakened by old age are tormented at the approach of death and bear the sufferings of Philoctetes in the play; who though tortured by intolerable pains would nevertheless extend his life by fowling – 'slow and standing he pierced the swift that flew' as Accius says, to make coverings for his body by weaving their feathers together. (On Ends 5.31–32)

The above passage shows that the most fundamental proof for the existence of self-love is for Antiochus the existence of a universal *pathos* of fear of death.[13] Although, Piso claims, excessive fear of death is reprehensible, a moderate fear seems to be 'in accordance with nature'. The view that certain passions are 'in accordance with nature' by admitting due measure seems to correspond to the idea of 'moderation' (*mediocritas*, translating the Greek *metriotēs*) of passions, which is attributed elsewhere in Cicero to the Old Academy and is presented as an alternative to the Stoic view on passions.[14] According to this

[13] The fundamental desire to remain alive and preserve one's existence is also asserted by Aristotle who refers to a natural love of life in *Politics* 3.1278b27-30: δῆλον δ' ὡς καρτεροῦσι πολλὴν κακοπάθειαν οἱ πολλοὶ τῶν ἀνθρώπων γλιχόμενοι τοῦ ζῆν, ὡς ἐνούσης τινὸς εὐημερίας ἐν αὐτῷ καὶ γλυκύτητος φυσικῆς.

[14] See *Academic Books* 38 where the view of the 'ancients' on the moderation of passions is contrasted to the Stoic view of extirpation of these 'diseases of the soul': *cumque perturbationem animi illi (sc. superiores) ex homine non tollerent naturaque et condolescere et concupiscere et extimescere et efferri laetitia dicerent, sed ea contraherent in angustumque deducerent, hic* (sc. Zeno) *omnibus his quasi morbis voluit carere sapientem*. The idea of *mediocritas* is assigned to the Peripatetics at *On Appropriate Actions* 1.89, *Tusculan Disputations* 3.22 and *ibid.* 4.38–46; 57. Whereas Piso follows the view attributed to the 'ancients' in the passages above in ascribing to the sage passions, such as the fear of death, he seems not to admit in his account the dualistic psychology which is related to *metriopatheia*. Moderation of passions is associated with a dualistic psychology in Varro's account at *Academic Books* 39 (in a part which contrasts 'ancient' with Stoic theses): *cumque eas perturbationes antiqui naturales esse dicerent et rationis expertes aliaque in parte animi cupiditatem alia rationem collocarent, ne his quidem assentiebatur* (sc. Zeno). Brunner (2014) 199–202 rightly traces a discrepancy between the views on *metriopatheia* ascribed to the 'ancients' in *Academic Books* 38 and the Antiochean position in *On Ends* 5. He further proposes *ibid.* 194; 202, however, that Cicero's remarks in *Academic Books* 38 should be dismissed as

view, a moderate amount of certain *pathē* constitutes the 'natural' state of human beings and is useful for the conduct of life,[15] whereas only excessive passions are reprehensible. Suggestive of such Peripatetic views is a formulation we find in Stobaeus: the doxographer, using a later Peripatetic source, defines *pathos* as a movement which is 'liable to grow to excess' (*pleonastikē*);[16] this can be contrasted to the Stoic definition of *pathos* as an impulse *already* grown to excess (*hormē pleonazousa*).[17] For the Stoics, any passion is by its very nature excessive and therefore morally wrong; for the Peripatetics by contrast it is only liable to grow excessive and therefore dangerous, but as long as it remains within bounds it is legitimate and should not be eradicated.[18] Such an ideal by the time

---

evidence for Antiochus' view. By contrast, Fladerer (1996) 178–81 connects Piso's views on the naturalness of fear of death with a dualistic moral psychology evidence of which is, however, lacking in *On Ends*. He is followed on this by Bonazzi (2012) 327. Similarly Karamanolis (2006) 78–79 observes that 'it would be strange if Antiochus ascribed to Plato the view that the soul is reason only' based on the assumption that Varro's endorsement of a dualist psychology in the *Academic Books* applies to Piso's account as well. For the 'intellectualist' model of the soul advanced in Piso's account (possibly under the influence of views attributed to Socrates in Plato), see Chapter 5, *infra*. The adoption of a non-dualistic moral psychology on Antiochus' part (at least in the period represented in Piso's account at *On Ends*) may have given rise to Cicero's critique at *Lucullus* 135, which traces an inconsistency between Antiochus' views on passions and the Old Academic view of *metriopatheia* as represented by Crantor: *sed quaero quando ista fuerint ab Academia vetere decreta, ut animum sapientis commoveri et conturbari negarent. mediocritates illi probabant et in omni permotione naturalem volebant esse quendam modum. legimus omnes Crantoris veteris Academici de luctu.* This suggestion is endorsed by Görler (1994) 960. For an alternative reading of Cicero's attack against Antiochus in *Lucullus* 135 see Brunner (2014) 195, who reads in it 'a rhetorically overstated variation' of Cicero's objection to Antiochus' views on the sufficiency of virtue for a happy life.

[15] See *Tusculan Disputations* 4.43–46.

[16] Stobaeus *Selections* 2 38.18–24 Wachsmuth: πάθος δ' ἐστίν, ὡς μὲν Ἀριστοτέλης, ἄλογος ψυχῆς κίνησις πλεοναστική. (. . .) τὸ δὲ 'πλεοναστικόν' κατὰ τοῦ πεφυκότος ἐπιδέχεσθαι πλεονασμόν, οὐ κατὰ τοῦ ἤδη πλεονάζοντος· ποτὲ μὲν γὰρ πλεονάζει, ποτὲ δ' ἐλλείπει. Since no formal definition of πάθος can be found in Aristotle, the definition cited in the above text may derive from the post-Aristotelian Peripatos. Indeed, the doxographer applies the same definition in *ibid.* 39.4 Wachsmuth generally to the Peripatetics.

[17] Stobaeus *Selections* 2 39.4–7 Wachsmuth.

[18] See *Lucullus* 135: *sed quaero quando ista fuerint ab Academia vetere decreta, ut animum sapientis commoveri et conturbari negarent: mediocritates illi probabant et in omni permotione naturalem volebant esse quendam modum.* As part of a polemical strategy, which purports to present Antiochus as an adherent of Stoicism in all areas of philosophy, Old Academic views on passions are used by Cicero in this passage against the supposedly Antiochean view of ἀπάθεια.

of Seneca is taken to represent the standard Peripatetic view on *pathē*.[19]

In the second part of the quoted passage, Piso differentiates his conception of fear of death from cases whereby people fear death not because they believe that death, or destruction of themselves, is bad 'for its own sake' but because they either think that they will lose the goods of life or they believe in some horrors in the *post mortem* life or, finally, they are afraid of the pain that will accompany their death. The Antiochean spokesman, by contrast, suggests that a moderate fear of death is grounded in the very natural appropriation which orients our ethical development. The assertion is backed up with 'cradle arguments': even children who haven't yet reached a rational stage (*qui nihil eorum cogitant*) and irrational animals exhibit such a fear, a fact which shows that such a *pathos* has a source in our natural make-up.

Noteworthy in this regard is the further claim of Piso that the sage, even in the case he has decided to abandon life for the sake of a noble cause, e.g. in order to defend the freedom of his country, will still be moved (*moveatur*) not only at parting from his family but also at abandoning the very daylight. 'Being moved' here seems to suggest that the sage, despite his choice to stand his ground in battle, will still believe that life is something 'choice worthy for its own sake' and will be, accordingly, pained at the prospect of abandoning life. This suggests that the *pathos* of fear of death is, according to Antiochus, present even in the sage, who is motivated to act according to a moral principle. Piso's remarks on this point seem to reflect the Aristotelian view that the courageous person will experience fear when faced with life-threatening situations, even when deciding to act for the sake of the *kalon*.[20]

---

[19] See e.g. *Tusculan Disputations* 3.74 and Seneca *Letters* 85.3: *huic collectioni hoc modo Peripatetici quidam respondent, ut inperturbatum et constantem et sine tristitia sic interpretentur tamquam inperturbatus dicatur qui raro perturbatur et modice, non qui numquam. Item sine tristitia eum dici aiunt qui non est obnoxius tristitiae nec frequens nimiusve in hoc vitio; illud enim humanam naturam negare, alicuius animum inmunem esse tristitia; sapientem non vinci maerore, ceterum tangi; et cetera in hunc modum sectae suae respondentia.* Cf. also Diogenes Laertius *Lives of Eminent Philosophers* 5.31: ἔφη δὲ (sc. Ἀριστοτέλης) τὸν σοφὸν ἀπαθῆ μὲν μὴ εἶναι, μετριοπαθῆ δέ.

[20] *Nicomachean Ethics* 3.1115b7–13: ὁ δὲ ἀνδρεῖος ἀνέκπληκτος ὡς ἄνθρωπος. φοβήσεται μὲν οὖν καὶ τὰ τοιαῦτα, ὡς δεῖ δὲ καὶ ὡς ὁ λόγος ὑπομενεῖ τοῦ καλοῦ ἕνεκα.

The wish to avoid death will in this case not overcome the desire to perform the action which is in accordance with the *kalon*, something which would seem to turn the virtuous person into an incontinent. The painful state of the courageous person, manifested as the passion of fear, will be based not on the belief that 'standing one's ground is bad', but rather on the belief that 'losing one's life is bad'. Assuming that the virtuous person recognises the overriding appeal of the *kalon*, such a wish to preserve one's life can be conducive to the virtuous action by encouraging the person to seek the preservation of his or her life in the overall best way.[21]

After considering Antiochus' defence of self-love, it is worth examining briefly some ideas from the Aristotelian/Peripatetic tradition that Antiochus could be drawing inspiration from. Aristotle refers explicitly to a natural self-love as *philia pros heauton* in the second book of the *Politics*. This constitutes part of the critique that the philosopher advances against Plato's *Republic*: contrary to the strictly unitary model of the polis that Socrates put forward in the fifth book of the *Republic*,[22] Aristotle defends the value of diverse kinship relationships within the polis.[23] Those attachments constitute, according to him, the presupposition of political friendship, which sustains a healthy political community. Furthermore, Aristotle claims that abolishing the idea of perceiving something as one's own abolishes at the same time the desire to extend one's interest towards something, since 'there are two things that most cause human beings to care for and love each other: perceiving something as one's own and as beloved'.[24] Affective relationships, Aristotle seems to argue, are not possible if one does not perceive a relatedness with another person—but the very idea of relatedness (*oikeiotēs*) presupposes first of all a relationship with oneself. The extent to which this disagrees with Platonic views becomes clear when one considers

---

[21] For such an interpretation of the role of passions in Aristotelian virtuous action, see Curzer (2012) 59ff.

[22] See e.g. *Republic* 412d with regard to the guardians in the ideal state.

[23] See e.g. *Politics* 2.1262b14–22.

[24] *Ibid.* 1262b22–3: δύο γάρ ἐστιν ἃ μάλιστα ποιεῖ κήδεσθαι τοὺς ἀνθρώπους καὶ φιλεῖν, τό τε ἴδιον καὶ τὸ ἀγαπητόν.

a passage from *Laws* 5, where the speaker in a polemical remark attacks natural love for oneself as the source of the greatest evils for humankind.[25] Although Plato refers properly speaking to excessive self-love (*sphodra heautou philian*), he holds there the view that someone should act justly for the sake of a highest good that transcends one's own perceived good,[26] and that the good man will abolish any considerations and feelings with regard to his own self, for the sake of justice.[27] Contrary to Plato's strictly unitary model of the polis, Aristotle in *Politics* 2.5 defends the idea that private property has a psychological foundation in a natural feeling of self-love. The text reads as follows:

> Moreover, to regard something as one's own makes an untold difference to one's pleasure. For it may well be no accident that each individual himself loves himself [*tēn pros hauton philian*]; on the contrary, this is natural [*physikon*]. But selfishness [*to philauton*] is condemned, justly; this is not to love oneself, but to love more than one should – as in the case of love of money, too (since of course practically everybody does love each of the things of that sort). (*Politics* 2.1263a40–b5 (trans. Saunders 1995))[28]

In the above passage, the natural feeling of self-love is advanced as part of an argument in favour of the idea of private property. The latter not only guarantees the sustenance of all social relationships within the polis through generosity and reciprocity, but it is also necessary for the exercise of the virtue of liberality and the enjoyment of the pleasure associated with it. Furthermore, it is based on a natural feeling of love towards oneself implanted in us by nature (*physikon*). Aristotle uses to

---

[25] *Laws* 5.731d6–e5:πάντων δὲ μέγιστον κακῶν ἀνθρώποις τοῖς πολλοῖς ἔμφυτον ἐν ταῖς ψυχαῖς ἐστιν, οὗ πᾶς αὑτῷ συγγνώμην ἔχων ἀποφυγὴν οὐδεμίαν μηχανᾶται· τοῦτο δ' ἔστιν ὃ λέγουσιν ὡς φίλος αὑτῷ πᾶς ἄνθρωπος φύσει τέ ἐστιν καὶ ὀρθῶς ἔχει τὸ δεῖν εἶναι τοιοῦτον. τὸ δὲ ἀληθείᾳ γε πάντων ἁμαρτημάτων διὰ τὴν σφόδρα ἑαυτοῦ φιλίαν αἴτιον ἑκάστῳ γίγνεται ἑκάστοτε.

[26] Contrast to the above the reference to one's self as the 'most akin to nature and dearest' in *Laws* 9.873c2–d1. Plato alludes here to the natural character of self-love that he had rejected before and uses it, in this particular case, in order to condemn suicide.

[27] *Laws* 5.732a2–4: οὔτε γὰρ ἑαυτὸν οὔτε τὰ ἑαυτοῦ χρή τόν γε μέγαν ἄνδρα ἐσόμενον στέργειν, ἀλλὰ τὰ δίκαια, ἐάντε παρ' αὑτῷ ἐάντε παρ' ἄλλῳ μᾶλλον πραττόμενα τυγχάνῃ.

[28] ἔτι δὲ καὶ πρὸς ἡδονὴν ἀμύθητον ὅσον διαφέρει τὸ νομίζειν ἴδιόν τι. μὴ γὰρ οὐ μάτην τὴν πρὸς αὑτὸν αὐτὸς ἔχει φιλίαν ἕκαστος, ἀλλ' ἔστι τοῦτο φυσικόν. τὸ δὲ φίλαυτον εἶναι ψέγεται δικαίως· οὐκ ἔστι δὲ τοῦτο τὸ φιλεῖν ἑαυτόν, ἀλλὰ τὸ μᾶλλον ἢ δεῖ φιλεῖν, καθάπερ καὶ τὸ φιλοχρήματον, ἐπεὶ φιλοῦσί γε πάντες ὡς εἰπεῖν ἕκαστον τῶν τοιούτων.

that end one of his fundamental principles, i.e. that 'nature does nothing in vain'. To the extent that it serves nature's purposes, this feeling is legitimate and justified. Aristotle takes care to differentiate conceptually this feeling of love towards oneself from the vice of selfishness (*philautia*) resulting from an excessive adherence to oneself beyond the natural limits prescribed by nature (*to mallon ē dei philein*), a kind of passion which deserves reproach.[29] Even if it does not receive further analysis neither in the *Politics* nor in the Aristotelian ethical treatises, we can trace in Aristotle's remarks in *Politics* 2.5 the notion of self-love as a natural impulse, which, in its moderate form, is a necessary prerequisite of action. To that extent, the passage can be regarded as an antecedent of the views on self-love advanced by the Antiochean spokesman in *On Ends* 5.

The notion of Antiochean self-love may be associated not only with (narrowly understood) self-interested action, or merely with the preservation of one's bodily integrity, but also spans virtuous action; for love of the self may be also understood as the desire to fulfil the potential of one's soul, as a part of oneself, and even that of the highest part of one's soul, namely *nous*. Indeed, Antiochus suggests that children who act merely on the basis of self-love without a clear understanding of their nature strive not only for a good state of their body but also for the exercise of their mental faculties by e.g. showing an interest in learning and social activities (see especially *On Ends* 5.42–43), something which for Antiochus shows that they possess 'seeds of virtues'.

A conception of an 'elevated' self-love relating to the human *telos* is supported by passages in the *Nicomachean Ethics*, where Aristotle expounds on the relationship the virtuous person enjoys with himself:[30] for example at *Nicomachean Ethics* 9.1166a13–14 the good person is said to be 'of one mind with

---

[29] For a differentiation between the two notions of τὴν πρὸς ἑαυτὸν φιλίαν and φιλαυτία, see also Stobaeus *Selections* 2 143.11–16 Wachsmuth from Didymus' epitome of Peripatetic ethics.

[30] An Aristotelian influence from *Nicomachean Ethics* 8 and 9 on Antiochus' views on self-love is also suggested at Schmitz (2014) 34–35.

himself' and to desire the same things in his whole soul. Such a person wishes and does the good things for the sake of himself, i.e. for the sake of the best part in oneself, which is reason. Thus the *spoudaios* 'wishes himself to live and to be preserved, but he wishes this for his rational part more than for any other part of his soul'.[31] Aristotle devotes a whole chapter to virtuous self-love in *Nicomachean Ethics* 9.8. The chapter begins with the exposition of an *aporia* with regard to 'whether one ought to love oneself or someone else most of all'. What immediately follows is the challenge that Aristotle counters in the rest of the chapter: self-lovers are denounced as though self-love were something shameful, since they seem to act only with regard to their own interest. The good person instead acts, according to that position, for the sake of the fine (*kalon*) and for his friend's sake, disregarding his own interest.[32]

Aristotle's strategy in the remainder of the chapter consists in differentiating the self-love appearing in the 'many', and which is justly reproachable, from the self-love which the virtuous person experiences and which, far from being reproachable, is the most commendable. This is achieved by showing, contrary to his dialectical opponents, that the good person can act for the sake of the fine but without at the same time disregarding his own interest. The differentiation between the two types of self-love rests on the different objects of desire pursued in the 'popular' and the 'elevated' type, as also on the psychology of the person who experiences it. Thus, whereas the base self-lover desires things like money, honours and bodily pleasures by gratifying his appetites and in general his passions and the non-rational part of the soul,[33] the 'real' self-lover by contrast is led to action by obeying the reasoning part of his soul, accomplishing just and virtuous actions. This person 'awards himself what is finest and best of all and gratifies the most controlling part of himself (sc.

---

[31] *Nicomachean Ethics* 9.1166a13–9: οὗτος γὰρ ὁμογνωμονεῖ ἑαυτῷ, καὶ τῶν αὐτῶν ὀρέγεται κατὰ πᾶσαν τὴν ψυχήν· καὶ βούλεται δὴ ἑαυτῷ τἀγαθὰ καὶ τὰ φαινόμενα καὶ πράττει (τοῦ γὰρ ἀγαθοῦ τἀγαθὸν διαπονεῖν) καὶ ἑαυτοῦ ἕνεκα (τοῦ γὰρ διανοητικοῦ χάριν, ὅπερ ἕκαστος εἶναι δοκεῖ)·καὶ ζῆν δὲ βούλεται ἑαυτὸν καὶ σῴζεσθαι, καὶ μάλιστα τοῦτο ᾧ φρονεῖ.
[32] *Ibid.* 9.1168a27–35. [33] *Ibid.* 9.1168b19–21.

the reasoning part), obeying it in everything'.[34] The use of reflexive verbs in this last passage shows that the choice of the fine is not dissociated from a loving relationship with oneself. Indeed, such a person as desires the fine is called a self-lover in the highest degree (*Nicomachean Ethics* 9.1168b33–4). His form of self-love differs from the base kind 'as much as the life guided by reason differs from the life guided by passions, and as much as the desire for what is fine differs from the desire for what seems advantageous'.[35] In the case of the virtuous person, the fine coincides with what is perceived as good for oneself, since reason guides the irrational part of the soul, not giving rise to a conflict in the motivational make-up of the agent.[36] This allows even for the explanation of actions like self-sacrifice for one's country and friends, which one would intuitively describe as purely altruistic actions, in terms of both the *kalon* and *philia* towards oneself: in those cases self-love makes one want to do virtuous actions through a desire to 'acquire the fine for oneself' (*peripoioumenos heautōi to kalon*).[37] Aristotle concludes that the good person *should* be a self-lover, since he will both help himself and benefit others by doing fine actions.[38] In this way, the text achieves to differentiate clearly between this type of self-love and common selfishness. Considering the above, one may assume that Aristotelian remarks on self-love as a first-order psychological phenomenon and as the basis of an appropriate relationship with oneself (or with one's soul) lurk in the background of Antiochus' discussion of self-love as a primary manifestation of *oikeiōsis*.

---

[34] *Ibid.* 9.1168b28–31: δόξειε δ' ἂν ὁ τοιοῦτος μᾶλλον εἶναι φίλαυτος ἀπονέμει γοῦν ἑαυτῷ τὰ κάλλιστα καὶ μάλιστ' ἀγαθά, καὶ χαρίζεται ἑαυτοῦ τῷ κυριωτάτῳ, καὶ πάντα τούτῳ πείθεται.

[35] *Ibid.* 9.1169a3-6: διὸ φίλαυτος μάλιστ' ἂν εἴη, καθ' ἕτερον εἶδος τοῦ ὀνειδιζομένου, καὶ διαφέρων τοσοῦτον ὅσον τὸ κατὰ λόγον ζῆν τοῦ κατὰ πάθος, καὶ ὀρέγεσθαι ἢ τοῦ καλοῦ ἢ τοῦ δοκοῦντος συμφέρειν.

[36] For the agreement between good *simpliciter* and good for oneself in a virtuous disposition, see *Eudemian Ethics* 7.1237a1–3.

[37] See *Nicomachean Ethics* 9.1169a18–22; cf. *ibid.* 1169a25–6: τοῖς δ' ὑπεραποθνήσκουσι τοῦτ' ἴσως συμβαίνει· αἱροῦνται δὴ μέγα καλὸν ἑαυτοῖς and 1169a28–9: τὸ δὴ μεῖζον ἀγαθὸν ἑαυτῷ ἀπονέμει.

[38] *Ibid.* 9.1169a11–3: ὥστε τὸν μὲν ἀγαθὸν δεῖ φίλαυτον εἶναι (καὶ γὰρ αὐτὸς ὀνήσεται τὰ καλὰ πράττων καὶ τοὺς ἄλλους ὠφελήσει).

Still, Antiochus' account contains an equally strong emphasis on self-knowledge as the state characterising the ideal agent (especially at *On Ends* 5.44); self-love, which is manifested primarily in the first stages of our lives,[39] is transformed in this case into a rational attitude towards oneself characterised by knowledge about our nature, consisting primarily in knowledge of the virtues of the soul and the human *telos*.[40] The Antiochean account postulates thereby a correspondence between what is according to nature and object of our *oikeiōsis* and what is grasped as an intrinsically valuable object of choice on the part of the rational agent.[41] Thus, appropriate states and activities of our bodily and mental faculties are said to be desired as 'choice worthy for their own sake' (*per se expetenda*, translating the Greek expression *di'hauta haireta*) *because* there is a natural appropriation towards them. This correspondence features in Didymus' account of Peripatetic ethics as well: in one passage from the doxography, 'a natural goodwill and affection towards everybody' rooted in *oikeiotēs* is taken to reveal (*emphainousa*) a proper reason for action, namely what is according to right reason.[42] The account suggests that the rational agent comes to view the *kata physin* objects of desire as forming the content of appropriate actions,

---

[39] For the link between self-love and the first *oikeiōsis* (*prima commendatio*), see *On Ends* 5.46.

[40] At *On Ends* 5.58 a citation from Plato's *Laws* is used in order to show that such knowledge dawns on us at a later stage of our development (and only in the case of exceptional individuals): *virtutis enim beataeque vitae, quae duo maxime expetenda sunt, serius lumen apparet, multo etiam serius ut plane qualia sint intellegantur. Praeclare enim Plato: 'Beatum cui etiam in senectute contigerit ut sapientiam verasque opiniones assequi possit!'* The Stoic account at *On Ends* 3.73 also contains a reference to self-knowledge which implies, in this case, an understanding of the way human nature relates to the cosmic one: *nec vero potest quisquam de bonis et malis vere iudicare nisi omni cognita ratione naturae et vitae etiam deorum, et utrum conveniat necne natura hominis cum universa. quaeque sunt vetera praecepta sapientium, qui iubent tempori parere et sequi deum et se noscere et nihil nimis, haec sine physicis quam vim habeant (et habent maximam) videre nemo potest.*

[41] See *On Ends* 5.61: *hoc autem loco tantum explicemus haec honesta, quae dico, praeterquam quod nosmet ipsos diligamus, praeterea suapte natura per se esse expetenda.*

[42] Didymus *ap.* Stobaeus *Selections* 121.17–19 Wachsmuth: φανερὸν οὖν ὅτι πρὸς πάντας ἐστὶν ἡμῖν εὔνοια φυσικὴ καὶ φιλία τὸ δι' αὑθ'αἱρετὸν ἐμφαίνουσα καὶ τὸ κατὰ λόγον. Cf. also the way virtue is deemed συνῳδός . . . τῇ φύσει in *ibid.* 119.12–13 Wachsmuth: τὴν τῆς ἐπικρίσεως βέβαιον εἴδησιν ἐπεζητήσαμεν, ἣν καὶ συνῳδὸν εὑρόμενοι τῇ φύσει, διὰ τὸ τῆς ἐνεργείας μεγαλοπρεπὲς ἀρετὴν προσηγορεύσαμεν.

which may be grasped as such by reason. Thus, in their reconstruction of Aristotelian/Peripatetic ethics both sources stress the correspondence that obtains between the knowledge which forms the basis of action for the rational agent and what is (extensionally) appropriate to our human nature by virtue of natural teleology.

The importance of self-knowledge *qua* knowledge of our human nature is a motif that Antiochus seems to borrow from the Platonic tradition; it is for example a central theme in the *Alcibiades*, where we find Socrates exhorting the young politician to know himself according to the precept of the 'Delphic inscription'.[43] This is shown in the dialogue to amount exclusively to gaining knowledge about one's soul and its virtues through philosophical dialectic.[44] Antiochus uses in his account this motif and assigns a primary role to the psychic virtues as the object of our self-knowledge. He adds, however, the body as part of 'oneself' in his anthropology,[45] re-interpreting the Delphic maxim as implying that we should know the 'power' of each of the two aspects of our human nature, and especially that of our reason. Such a knowledge enables us to acquire and practise the virtues, which are the main constituents of human *eudaimonia*. In order to see more clearly how Antiochus' *oikeiōsis* account is structured around a conception of human nature as a composite of soul and body, we turn now to the discussion of the objects of Antiochean *oikeiōsis*.

---

[43] Ps. Plato *Alcibiades* 124a7–b2: ἀλλ', ὦ μακάριε, πειθόμενος ἐμοί τε καὶ τῷ ἐν Δελφοῖς γράμματι, γνῶθι σαυτόν, ὅτι οὗτοι ἡμῖν εἰσιν ἀντίπαλοι, ἀλλ' οὐχ οὓς σὺ οἴει; *ibid.* 129a2–4: πότερον οὖν δὴ ῥᾴδιον τυγχάνει τὸ γνῶναι ἑαυτόν, καί τις ἦν φαῦλος ὁ τοῦτο ἀναθεὶς εἰς τὸν ἐν Πυθοῖ νεών, ἢ χαλεπόν τι καὶ οὐχὶ παντός; cf. *ibid.* 132c9-10. The dialogue *Alcibiades* was believed up until the nineteenth century to have been authored by Plato; nowadays it is considered by the majority of scholars to be spurious and to belong to the post-Platonic Academy. On the authenticity of the dialogue, see Denyer (2001) 14–26. Also, Prost (2001) 249 alludes briefly to an influence of the *Alcibiades* on Antiochus.

[44] *Ibid.* 130e8–9: ψυχὴν ἄρα ἡμᾶς κελεύει γνωρίσαι ὁ ἐπιτάττων γνῶναι ἑαυτόν. On the importance of philosophical dialectic for self-knowledge, see *ibid.* 133b7-10, where there is reference to the way a soul cognises itself by looking at another soul and, in particular, at the part of it where virtue resides: – ἀρ' οὖν, ὦ φίλε Ἀλκιβιάδη, καὶ ψυχὴ εἰ μέλλει γνώσεσθαι αὑτήν, εἰς ψυχὴν αὐτῇ βλεπτέον, καὶ μάλιστ' εἰς τοῦτον αὐτῆς τὸν τόπον ἐν ᾧ ἐγγίγνεται ἡ ψυχῆς ἀρετή, σοφία, καὶ εἰς ἄλλο ᾧ τοῦτο τυγχάνει ὅμοιον ὄν.

[45] For another opinion expressed in the *Alcibiades* that the body is not part of oneself but 'belongs to oneself', see *ibid.* 131b10–11: οὐκοῦν πάλιν ὅστις αὖ σῶμα θεραπεύει, τὰ ἑαυτοῦ ἀλλ' οὐχ αὑτὸν θεραπεύει.

5

'CRADLE ARGUMENTS' AND THE OBJECTS OF
OIKEIŌSIS

Oikeiōsis towards the Bodily Virtues

After establishing that love of the self is the most fundamental
motivation underpinning all our desires and actions, the
Antiochean spokesman spells out the idea of a natural appropriation towards oneself on the basis of the distinction between body
and soul. According to the reasoning employed in the account our
self (understood generically as our human nature) consists of the
two aspects of body and soul.[1] Accordingly, our *oikeiōsis* towards
our nature is manifested in the way we are appropriated to our
body and, primarily, to our soul, which is the most valuable and
authoritative part of ourselves.[2] A manifestation of this appropriation is that we are drawn towards an appropriate state of our body
by means of non-rational impulses at the beginning of our lives but
also that, once we have acquired (complete) rationality, we regard
certain bodily and psychic states as choice worthy for their own
sake, i.e. as possessing an inherent value. What is appropriate for
human nature becomes in this case the standard of right reason.

Piso's argument contains markedly Aristotelian/Peripatetic features in that it stresses that the *oikeiōsis* towards our body and soul

---

[1] On Ends 5.34: *atqui perspicuum est hominem e corpore animoque constare, cum primae
sint animi partes, secundae corporis.* For a similar Platonic distinction of human nature
in these two aspects, see *Gorgias* 464a. Cf. also the 'third' view offered in *Alcibiades*
130a7–9: Μὴ οὐ τριῶν ἕν γέ τι εἶναι τὸν ἄνθρωπον.-Τίνων;- Ψυχὴν ἢ σῶμα ἢ
συναμφότερον, τὸ ὅλον τοῦτο. The view that a human being is a composite of body and
soul is dismissed, however, in the dialogue for the sake of the position that a human being
is to be identified merely with what leads the body, namely the soul (130c).

[2] See *On Ends* 5.37: *nam cui proposita sit conservatio sui, necesse est huic partes quoque
sui caras esse, carioresque quo perfectiores sint et magis in suo genere laudabiles.* Cf.
*ibid.: quo cognito dubitari non potest quin, cum ipsi homines sibi sint per se et sua sponte
cari, partes quoque et corporis et animi et earum rerum quae sunt in utriusque motu et
statu sua caritate colantur et per se ipsae appetantur* and *ibid.* 5.46. A similar reasoning
is found also in Didymus' account of Peripatetic ethics, see Stobaeus *Selections* 2 122.
11–13 Wachsmuth: εἰ γὰρ ὁ ἄνθρωπος δι᾽ αὑτὸν αἱρετὸς καὶ τὰ μέρη τοῦ ἀνθρώπου δι᾽
αὑτὰ ἂν εἴη αἱρετά, μέρη δ᾽ ἐστὶν ἀνθρώπου ὁλοσχερέστατα σῶμα καὶ ψυχή.

does not only encompass the possession of bodily and psychic features but also the 'use' and 'activity' of them. This invests the *oikeiōsis* argument with a metaphysical dimension, according to which the inherent natural desire to preserve ourselves corresponds also to an inherent desire to actualise the powers of all the parts of our body and soul. Accordingly, the *telos* is reconceptualised as a state in which the powers of all the parts of our body and soul have been perfected and have reached the state that is most appropriate to our natural kind.[3] Most conducive to this state is the knowledge of the inherent power of our body and soul, which Antiochus connects with the Pythian maxim 'know thyself' (*gnōthi sauton*).[4]

In the bodily domain Piso refers to an appropriate form and posture of the various parts of the body, such as of the forehead, the eyes and the ears, which is agreed upon by everyone.[5] The Antiochean spokesperson demonstrates this by making use of examples from the behaviour of children; thus, while newborn children lie still, as though they do not possess a soul, when their strength has a little increased and they can make use of their elementary mental and perceptual faculties, they 'strive to raise themselves up and bring their hands into use', showing that they have a natural inclination towards the appropriate posture of their body and the use of their bodily parts.[6] On the other hand, the Antiochean account stresses how ordinary people avoid bodily deformities and defects either by hiding them or by undertaking painful treatments in order to bring the body back to a 'natural state'; that this occurs independently of the utility of our bodily

---

[3] On the perfection of body and soul as constituents of human *eudaimonia*, see *On Ends* 5.37: *ex quo perspicuum est, quoniam ipsi a nobis diligamur omniaque et in animo et in corpore perfecta velimus esse, ea nobis ipsa cara esse propter se et in iis esse ad bene vivendum momenta maxima.*

[4] Cf. *ibid.* 5.44: *iubet igitur nos Pythius Apollo noscere nosmet ipsos; cognitio autem haec est una nostri, ut <vim> corporis animique norimus sequamurque eam vitam quae rebus iis perfruatur.*

[5] *Ibid.* 5.35: *corporis igitur nostri partes totaque figura et forma et statura quam apta ad naturam sit apparet, neque est dubium quin frons, oculi, aures et reliquae partes quales propriae sint hominis intellegatur.*

[6] *Ibid.* 5.42: *parvi enim primo ortu sic iacent tamquam omnino sine animo sint; cum autem paulum firmitatis accessit, et animo utuntur et sensibus conitunturque ut sese erigant et manibus utuntur et eos agnoscunt a quibus educantur.*

form is shown by the fact that such treatments at times impair bodily utility, but are still chosen nonetheless.[7]

Natural appropriation extends beyond the bodily form to the 'natural motions and uses' (*naturales motus ususque*, translating the Greek *kinēseis* and *chrēseis*) of bodily parts. The Antiochean spokesperson invites us to think of the 'unnaturalness' of the bodily action (*actio ... corporis*) of someone who walks with his hands or when walking goes backwards instead of forwards, in order to convey the point that nature has appropriated us to a certain use of our body.[8] Piso alludes also to the social recognition of bodily appropriateness by referring to the postures, movements and expressions of immodest and 'effeminate' men, which are 'against nature' (*contra naturam*) and are for this reason condemned. Moderate persons on the other hand are said to preserve propriety and make their bodily movements and uses comply with the standard set by nature.[9] The praise attached to such an attitude may serve as proof that an appropriate use of our body is recognised as such and valued by (right) reason.

---

[7] On Ends 5.46: *atque ut a corpore ordiar, videsne <ut> si quae in membris prava aut debilitata aut inminuta sint occultent homines? ut etiam contendant et elaborent, si efficere possint ut aut non appareat corporis vitium aut quam minimum appareat, multosque etiam dolores curationis causa perferant ut, si ipse usus membrorum non modo non maior verum etiam minor futurus sit, eorum tamen species ad naturam revertatur?*

[8] Ibid.: *est autem etiam actio quaedam corporis quae motus et status naturae congruentis tenet; in quibus si peccetur distortione et depravatione quadam aut motu statuve deformi, ut si aut manibus ingrediatur quis aut non ante sed retro, fugere plane se ipse et hominem ex homine exuens naturam odisse videatur.*

[9] Ibid. 5.35–36: *quam ob rem etiam sessiones quaedam et flexi fractique motus, quales protervorum hominum aut mollium esse solent, contra naturam sunt, ut etiamsi animi vitio id eveniat, tamen in corpore immutari hominis natura videatur. Itaque e contrario moderati aequabilesque habitus adfectiones ususque corporis apti esse ad naturam videntur.* The same point is made at On Ends 5.47 by means of a series of rhetorical questions which all point towards the idea that there is a universally recognised standard of decency with regard to 'carrying' one's body: *quid? in motu et in statu corporis nihil inest quod animadvertendum esse ipsa natura iudicet? quem ad modum quis ambulet sedeat, qui ductus oris, qui vultus in quoque sit, nihilne est in his rebus quod dignum libero aut indignum esse ducamus? nonne odio multos dignos putamus qui quodam motu aut statu videntur naturae legem et modum contempsisse?* The views presented here are in line with the defence of physical modesty (*verecundia*), which Cicero presents as a particularly Roman virtue, at On Appropriate Actions 1.126–9. On decency (εὐκοσμία) as a disposition which guards propriety in bodily movements and postures (κινήσεις καὶ σχέσεις), see also Didymus *ap.* Stobaeus Selections 2 147.12–14.

The good state and use of our bodily parts, which is in line with natural appropriation, is presented in the Antiochean account as connected with a series of other bodily virtues, such as beauty, health, freedom from pain and strength, which 'we choose for their own sake' (*propter se expetemus*) and not only for the sake of their utility (*non propter utilitatem solum*).[10] On the other hand, ugliness, infirmity, illness and pain suggest conditions which go against *oikeiōsis* and which for that reason are avoided.[11] The catalogue of bodily virtues offered in the Antiochean account corresponds to Didymus' Peripatetic doxography which survives in Stobaeus' *Selections*. Like Antiochus, Didymus connects *oikeiōsis* towards oneself with the desire to preserve one's body in the most appropriate state and lists a number of corresponding conditions.[12] The relevant passage reads as follows:

And first of all, humans desire existence as they have a natural appropriation towards themselves [φύσει γὰρ ᾠκειῶσθαι πρὸς ἑαυτόν]; that is why they also experience a suitable enjoyment among things according to nature and are annoyed at things which are contrary to nature. For they take care to preserve their health and they desire pleasure and strive for life, these things being according to nature and for their own sake choice worthy and good [κατὰ φύσιν καὶ <δι'> αὐθ'αἱρετὰ καὶ ἀγαθά]. Conversely, they reject and avoid illness,

---

[10] On Ends 5.47: *et quoniam haec deducuntur de corpore, quid est cur non recte pulchritudo etiam ipsa propter se expetenda ducatur? (. . .) Atque etiam valetudinem vires vacuitatem doloris non propter utilitatem solum sed etiam ipsas propter se expetemus.* Cf. also *ibid.* 5.18 (part of Antiochus' presentation of the *Carneadea divisio*): *ab iis alii quae prima secundum naturam nominant proficiscuntur, in quibus numerant incolumitatem conservationemque omnium partium, valetudinem, sensus integros, doloris vacuitatem, viris, pulchritudinem.* A catalogue of bodily virtues is contained also in Varro's exposition of Old Academic ethics, whereby bodily virtues are further divided into general ones and those pertaining to particular parts of the body, see *Academic Books* 19–20: *corporis autem alia ponebant esse in toto alia in partibus, valetudinem vires pulchritudinem in toto, in partibus autem sensus integros et praestantiam aliquam partium singularum, ut in pedibus celeritatem, vim in manibus, claritatem in voce, in lingua etiam explanatam vocum impressionem.* For an antecedent of the virtues which pertain to the body as a whole, see Plato *Laws* 1.631c1–4: ἔστι δὲ τὰ μὲν ἐλάττονα ὧν ἡγεῖται μὲν ὑγίεια, κάλλος δὲ δεύτερον, τὸ δὲ τρίτον ἰσχὺς εἴς τε δρόμον καὶ εἰς τὰς ἄλλας πάσας κινήσεις τῷ σώματι. Such goods are deemed in this passage 'human' as opposed to the 'divine' goods of the virtues of the soul.

[11] On Ends 5.47: *quoniam enim natura suis omnibus expleri partibus vult, hunc statum corporis per se ipsum expetit qui est maxime e natura, quae tota perturbatur, si aut aegrum corpus est aut dolet aut caret viribus.*

[12] Cf. also Varro's account in Cicero's *Academic Books* 22 which transmits Antiochean doctrine: *communis haec ratio, et utrisque hic bonorum finis videbatur, adipisci quae essent prima in natura quaeque ipsa per sese expetenda aut omnia aut maxima.*

suffering and destruction as they are against nature and in themselves to be avoided and evil. (Didymus *ap.* Stobaeus *Selections* 2 118.11–20 Wachsmuth)[13]

In a further catalogue which includes generally the 'bodily virtues', Didymus adds to health, pleasure and life itself the more specific bodily goods of strength and good functioning of the senses.[14] In addition to these, beauty is presented in Didymus' Peripatetic doxography as one of the major bodily goods towards which we experience an *oikeiōsis*; affinity towards beauty as something appropriate to us is shown by the fact that avoidance of ugliness appears as a reasonable course of action independently of its utility.[15]

Still, on one important point Antiochus departs from Didymus' Peripatetic account on bodily *oikeiōsis*. The reluctance to include (bodily) pleasure among the things to which we are appropriately attracted by nature is a characteristic feature of the Antiochean account in *On Ends* 5. Instead of highlighting the connection between the *oikeion* and the *hēdy*, the Antiochean spokesman dismisses the role of pleasure in his exposition of *oikeiōsis*, as something which makes no difference to his general argument: according to him, either pleasure does not belong at all to the catalogue of the 'first natural goods', which is presented in

---

[13] καὶ πρῶτον μὲν ὀρέγεσθαι τοῦ εἶναι, φύσει γὰρ ᾠκειῶσθαι πρὸς ἑαυτόν· διὸ καὶ προσηκόντως ἀσμενίζειν μὲν ἐν τοῖς κατὰ φύσιν δυσχεραίνειν δ' ἐπὶ τοῖς παρὰ φύσιν. Τήν τε γὰρ ὑγίειαν περιποιεῖσθαι σπουδάζειν καὶ τῆς ἡδονῆς ἔφεσιν ἔχειν καὶ τοῦ ζῆν ἀντιποιεῖσθαι τῷ ταῦτα μὲν εἶναι κατὰ φύσιν καὶ ⟨δι'⟩ αὕθ'αἱρετὰ καὶ ἀγαθά, κατὰ δὲ τ'ἀναντία τὴν νόσον καὶ τὴν ἀλγηδόνα καὶ τὴν φθορὰν διακρούεσθαι καὶ παρακλίνειν τῷ παρὰ φύσιν ὑπάρχειν καὶ δι' αὐτὰ φευκτὰ καὶ κακά. The text of Didymus follows Tsouni (2017).

[14] Didymus *ap.* Stobaeus *Selections* 2 122.20–123.1 Wachsmuth: ὥστε δι'αὐτὰ αἱρετὰ ἡμῖν εἶναι τὴν ὑγείαν, τὴν ἰσχύν, τὸ κάλλος, τὴν ποδώκειαν, τὴν εὐεξίαν, τὴν εὐαισθησίαν, καθόλου πάσας ὡς ἔπος εἰπεῖν ⟨τὰς σωματικὰς ἀρετάς⟩. A similar catalogue is contained in the Stoic ethical doxography with reference to indifferent things which are 'according to nature', see *ibid.* 2.79.20–80.1 Wachsmuth: κατὰ φύσιν μὲν οὖν τὰ τοιαῦτα· ὑγίειαν, ἰσχύν, αἰσθητηρίων ἀρτιότητα, καὶ τὰ παραπλήσια τούτοις.

[15] *Ibid.* 2 123.1–14 Wachsmuth: καὶ γὰρ ἄλλως οὐδεὶς ἂν εὖ φρονῶν δέξαιτο ἄμορφος καὶ λελωβημένος εἶναι κατὰ τὸ εἶδος, κἂν εἰ μηδεμία μέλλοι δυσχρηστία τὸ παράπαν ἐπακολουθεῖν διὰ τὴν τοιαύτην εἰδέχθειαν. Ὥστε καὶ δίχα τῆς δυσχρηστίας εὔλογον φυγὴν φαίνεσθαι τοῦ αἴσχους. Εἰ δὲ δι'αὐτὸ φευκτόν ἐστι τὸ αἶσχος καὶ τὸ κάλλος οὐ μόνον διὰ τὴν χρείαν αἱρετό, ἀλλὰ καὶ δι'αὐτό. Ὅτι γὰρ ἐξ αὐτοῦ προκλητικὸν ⟨τι⟩ ἔχει τὸ κάλλος ἐμφανές· πάντας γοῦν φυσικῶς οἰκειοῦσθαι τοῖς καλοῖς χωρὶς πάσης χρείας καὶ γὰρ πρὸς τοὺς εὖ ποιεῖν αὐτοὺς καὶ εὐεργετεῖν ἑτοίμως ἔχειν, ὅθεν δὴ καὶ δοκεῖν εὐνοίας εἶναι παρασκευαστικόν. Ὥστε καὶ κατὰ τοῦτον τὸν λόγον, τὸ μὲν κάλλος τῶν δι' αὐτὰ αἱρετῶν ὑπάρχειν, τὸ δ'αἶσχος τῶν δι' αὐτὰ φευκτῶν.

Cicero's account as the position most favoured by Antiochus, or, if it does, it should be merely reckoned as one of the bodily goods with no privileged place among them; this, as Piso claims, would not alter the gist of the Peripatetic theory of the *summum bonum* as it is presented in *On Ends* 5.[16] Antiochus' dismissal of the importance of pleasure is shown by the fact that in his catalogue of bodily virtues he opts for a 'negative' definition of pleasure as 'absence of pain' (*vacuitas doloris*) rather than for its 'positive' counterpart.[17] This may betray an influence of the Epicurean conception of pleasure and of the (New) Academic debates surrounding this notion and its identification with pleasure. Again, in Antiochus' discussion of the virtues, although there are references to the way a virtuous activity is pleasant to the one who exercises it,[18] mental pleasure as such does not play an explanatory role in the account but is presented as accompanying a mental activity which is desired for its own sake, even at the face of anguish and disadvantage.[19] Although there is no explicit argument available in his account, we may hypothesise that Antiochus held the view that pleasure is parasitical on the pursuit of the appropriate objects of desire which are chosen for their own sake; that would be in line with some remarks in Aristotle which suggest that the value of pleasure is supervenient on appropriate activities.[20] In this latter

---

[16] *On Ends* 5.45: *utrum enim sit voluptas in iis rebus quas primas secundum naturam esse diximus necne sit, ad id quod agimus nihil interest. Si enim, ut mihi quidem videtur, non explet bona naturae voluptas, iure praetermissa est; sin autem est in ea quod quidam volunt, nihil impedit hanc nostram comprehensionem summi boni. Quae enim constituta sunt prima naturae, ad ea si voluptas accesserit, unum aliquod accesserit commodum corporis neque eam constitutionem summi boni quae est proposita mutaverit.*

[17] *On Ends* 5.47. Cf. *ibid.* 5.73: *positum est a nostris in iis esse rebus quae secundum naturam essent non dolere.*

[18] See for example the reference to the pleasure deriving from learning (*ex discendo ... voluptatem*) at *On Ends* 5.49.

[19] See *On Ends* 5.50 for the idea that the mental pleasure which accompanies intellectual activities is independent of their utility and may even bring about pain and disadvantage for the agent: *atque hoc loco qui propter animi voluptates coli dicunt ea studia quae dixi non intellegunt idcirco esse ea propter se expetenda quod nulla utilitate obiecta delectentur animi atque ipsa scientia, etiamsi incommodatura sit, gaudeant.* A similar point is made at *ibid.* 5.57.

[20] On the 'supervenient' character of pleasure see *Nicomachean Ethics* 10.1174b31–33. Cf. also the anti-hedonistic line of argument employed at Diogenes Laertius *Lives of Eminent Philosophers* 7.86: ὃ δὲ λέγουσί τινες, πρὸς ἡδονὴν γίγνεσθαι τὴν πρώτην ὁρμὴν τοῖς ζῴοις, ψεῦδος ἀποφαίνουσιν. ἐπιγέννημα γάρ φασιν, εἰ ἄρα ἔστιν, ἡδονὴν εἶναι ὅταν αὐτὴ καθ' αὑτὴν ἡ φύσις ἐπιζητήσασα τὰ ἐναρμόζοντα τῇ συστάσει ἀπολάβῃ.

128

case, pleasure has no special explanatory role to play for our actions and desires and is not a constituent of the *telos* in its own right.

On this point we may also consider the dialectical context against which Antiochus proposed his reconstruction of Aristotelian/Peripatetic ethics: a stress on pleasure could invite a comparison with later members of the Peripatos who included pleasure into their conception of the final end alongside virtue, like Callipho and Dinomachus; such Peripatetics are 'excised' from the canon of the Old Academy in Antiochus' version of history of philosophy.[21] Not least, the stress on our natural appropriation towards pleasure would make the (polemical) project of the assimilation of Stoicism into the Old Academy, which Antiochus advertised, more difficult.[22]

In Didymus' epitome of Peripatetic ethics, by contrast, pleasure belongs to the 'first natural things' which are desired, like health and life itself, for their own sake.[23] This inclusion receives strong corroboration by Aristotelian evidence. The pleasant appears to be a universally accepted object of desire at *Nicomachean Ethics* and is sought, according to *NE* 3. 1119b5–7, primarily by children.[24] Furthermore, Aristotle links in his ethical works pleasure with activity (*energeia*) in accordance with a 'natural disposition';[25] such a link is explored by Peripatetics belonging to the next generation after Antiochus, who wished to construct alternative readings of an Aristotelian/ Peripatetic *oikeiōsis* theory.[26] The ambivalent stance towards the inclusion of pleasure in the catalogue of the 'first objects of

---

[21] See *On Ends* 5.21.

[22] On the Stoic exclusion of pleasure from the catalogue of 'first things according to nature', see e.g. *On Ends* 3.17: *in principiis autem naturalibus plerique Stoici non putant voluptatem esse ponendam.*

[23] Didymus *ap.* Stobaeus *Selections* 2 118.15–16 Wachsmuth. The difference between Antiochus and Didymus on this point is also commented upon by Hirzel (1882) 713–14.

[24] κατ' ἐπιθυμίαν γὰρ ζῶσι καὶ τὰ παιδία, καὶ μάλιστα ἐν τούτοις ἡ τοῦ ἡδέος ὄρεξις. See also *Nicomachean Ethics* 7.1152b19–20: ἔτι παιδία καὶ θηρία διώκει τὰς ἡδονάς.

[25] See *ibid.* 7.1153a12–14: διὸ καὶ οὐ καλῶς ἔχει τὸ αἰσθητὴν γένεσιν φάναι εἶναι τὴν ἡδονήν, ἀλλὰ μᾶλλον λεκτέον ἐνέργειαν τῆς κατὰ φύσιν ἕξεως. For the use of *oikeiousthai* in relation to pleasure in Aristotle see also *ibid.* 10.1172a19–21: μετὰ δὲ ταῦτα περὶ ἡδονῆς ἴσως ἕπεται διελθεῖν. μάλιστα γὰρ δοκεῖ συνωκειῶσθαι τῷ γένει ἡμῶν, διὸ παιδεύουσι τοὺς νέους οἰακίζοντες ἡδονῇ καὶ λύπῃ.

[26] See Alexander *Mantissa* 151.30–153.27 Bruns.

oikeiōsis' or *prima naturae* in Piso's account indicates thus that Antiochus felt free to select evidence in the Aristotelian-Peripatetic tradition which would fit his own philosophical agenda.

Oikeiōsis towards the Soul

Piso's account presupposes a hierarchy between the two aspects of human nature, namely the body and the soul. Accordingly, the *oikeiōsis* towards the soul and its virtues plays in the Antiochean account a far more significant role for the attainment of human *eudaimonia*.[27] When referring to our *oikeiōsis* towards the soul, Piso starts with the faculties of the various senses of which he admits that there can be a virtuous exercise. The virtues of the senses consist in the fulfilment of their function (*munus*, which may well translate the Greek *ergon*) through the perception of appropriate sensible objects without any impediment.[28] Antiochus' focus lies, however, almost exclusively on the intellectual aspect of the soul. Thus, the pre-eminence of the soul is based on its most valuable part, the *nous* (*mens*), which is the most authoritative and guiding principle of human nature and encompasses the distinctively human intellectual faculties of reason, inquiry,

---

[27] See *Fin.* 5.38. The Peripatetic doxography of Didymus also provides references to the most authoritative *oikeiōsis* towards the virtues of the soul. *Oikeiōsis* towards virtue is eloquently illustrated in one passage from Didymus' summary where virtue, after receiving its starting point from the pursuit of external and bodily goods, 'turns to view itself' and experiences an *oikeiōsis* towards itself and its proper virtues; the latter is deemed higher than the *oikeiōsis* experienced towards bodily goods. This is due to the fact that virtue, both theoretical and practical, is more valuable than all other goods, and more 'in accordance with nature', see 123.21–27 Wachsmuth: τὴν γὰρ εἴσοδον ἡ ἀρετὴ λαβοῦσα, καθάπερ ὑπεδείξαμεν, ἀπὸ τῶν σωματικῶν καὶ τῶν ἔξωθεν ἀγαθῶν καὶ πρὸς ἑαυτὴν ἐπιστρέψασα καὶ θεασαμένη, διότι καὶ αὐτὴν τῶν κατὰ φύσιν πολὺ μᾶλλον τῶν τοῦ σώματος ἀρετῶν, ᾠκειώθη πρὸς ἑαυτὴν ὡς πρὸς δι' αὐτὴν αἱρετὴν καὶ μᾶλλον γε πρὸς ἑαυτὴν ἢ πρὸς τὰς τοῦ σώματος ἀρετάς· ὥστε παρὰ πολὺ τιμιωτέρας εἶναι <τὰς> τῆς ψυχῆς ἀρετάς. The turn of the personified virtue towards its own self may signify that the appropriation of the soul towards its own virtue is an outcome of reflection. For a discussion of the passage see Szaif (2012) 251–52.

[28] *On Ends* 5.36: *atque in sensibus est sua cuiusque virtus, ut ne quid impediat quominus suo sensu quisque munere fungatur in iis rebus celeriter expediteque percipiendis quae subiectae sunt sensibus.* Cf. *ibid.* 5.59: *sensibus enim ornavit ad res percipiendas idoneis, ut nihil aut non multum adiumento ullo ad suam confirmationem indigerent.* On the virtues of the senses, cf. Plato *Republic* 1.353b–c.

(theoretical) understanding and *all* the virtues.[29] The intellect is also repeatedly called by the Antiochean spokesman the most 'divine element' in the human soul, an idea with clear Platonic and Aristotelian precedents.[30]

With regard to the virtues of the mind the Antiochean spokesperson draws a distinction between the 'non-voluntary' (*non voluntariae*) and the 'voluntary' (*in voluntate positae*) virtues.[31] The former comprise congenital cognitive capacities (*quae ingenerantur suapte natura*) which are inherited and do not depend on learning and experience, as for example aptness for learning (*docilitas*) or memory (*memoria*).[32] This category of intellectual virtues receives the generic name *ingenium* and translates in all probablility the Greek term for 'a good natural endowment' (*euphyia*).[33] Congenital cognitive capacities are differentiated in Piso's account from the 'properly called' virtues, namely the psychic virtues which imply perfected reasoning manifested in

---

[29] *On Ends* 5.34: *animum ita constitutum ut et sensibus instructus sit et habeat praestantiam mentis, cui tota hominis natura pareat, in qua sit mirabilis quaedam vis rationis et cognitionis et scientiae virtutumque omnium.*

[30] See e.g. (ps.) Plato *Alcibiades* 133c1–6:- Ἔχομεν οὖν εἰπεῖν ὅτι ἐστὶ τῆς ψυχῆς θειότερον ἢ τοῦτο, περὶ ὃ τὸ εἰδέναι τε καὶ φρονεῖν ἐστιν; – Οὐκ ἔχομεν. – Τῷ θεῷ ἄρα τοῦτ' ἔοικεν αὐτῆς, καί τις εἰς τοῦτο βλέπων καὶ πᾶν τὸ θεῖον γνούς, θεόν τε καὶ φρόνησιν, οὕτω καὶ ἑαυτὸν ἂν γνοίη μάλιστα and *Nicomachean Ethics* 10. 1177a13–17: εἴτε δὴ νοῦς τοῦτο εἴτε ἄλλο τι, ὃ δὴ κατὰ φύσιν δοκεῖ ἄρχειν καὶ ἡγεῖσθαι καὶ ἔννοιαν ἔχειν περὶ καλῶν καὶ θείων, εἴτε θεῖον ὂν καὶ αὐτὸ εἴτε τῶν ἐν ἡμῖν τὸ θειότατον, ἡ τούτου ἐνέργεια κατὰ τὴν οἰκείαν ἀρετὴν εἴη ἂν ἡ τελεία εὐδαιμονία.

[31] By contrast, in Varro's account at *Academic Books* 20 the differentiation is drawn between congenital virtues (*in naturam*) and those which pertain to moral character (*mores*): *animi autem quae essent ad comprehendendam ingeniis virtutem idonea, eaque ab his in naturam et mores dividebantur.*

[32] Cf. *Academic Books* 20, where things like aptness to learn and memory are reckoned among the 'natural' goods of the soul: *naturae celeritatem ad discendum et memoriam dabant, quorum utrumque mentis esset proprium et ingenii.*

[33] We may also find here a correspondence to Didymus' Peripatetic doxography in Stobaeus *Selections* 2. There we find the classification of virtues into 'perfected' and 'imperfect', the latter comprising the natural cognitive endowments (εὐφυΐα) and that of moral progress (προκοπή), see *ibid.* 131.15–17 Wachsmuth: τῶν ἀρετῶν τὰς μὲν ἔλεγον εἶναι τελείας, τὰς δὲ ἀτελεῖς· τελείας μὲν τήν τε δικαιοσύνην καὶ τὴν καλοκἀγαθίαν ἀτελεῖς δὲ τὴν εὐφυΐαν καὶ τὴν προκοπήν. On εὐφυΐα, cf. *ibid.* 136.16–18. A similar catalogue features in the Stoic doxography as well with reference to psychic 'preferred indifferents', see *ibid.* 80.22–81.4 Wachsmuth: τῶν δὲ προηγμένων τὰ μὲν εἶναι περὶ ψυχήν, τὰ δὲ περὶ σῶμα, τὰ δ' ἐκτός. Περὶ ψυχὴν μὲν εἶναι τὰ τοιαῦτα· εὐφυΐαν, προκοπήν, μνήμην, ὀξύτητα διανοίας, ἕξιν καθ' ἣν ἐπίμονοί εἰσιν ἐπὶ τῶν καθηκόντων καὶ τέχνας ὅσαι δύνανται συνεργεῖν ἐπιπλεῖον πρὸς τὸν κατὰ φύσιν βίον.

deliberation and choice;[34] such virtues are said to be a product of *voluntas*, a word which translates in Cicero the Greek *boulēsis*,[35] and stands for a rational desire premised on the grasping of a virtuous principle of action. Piso subsumes in this category the cardinal virtues, namely prudence, justice, courage, temperance and the species thereof.

Although 'proper virtues' are dependent upon the fully developed reasoning faculty of the mind, Antiochus goes to great lengths to show that even such virtues are anticipated by inclinations and representations which draw us from an early stage of our lives towards appropriate objects of pursuit. This is shown on the basis of 'cradle arguments', which draw on empirical observations of the behaviour of children.[36] It has been suggested that the rise of a developmental approach to ethics, with its emphasis on the non-rational stages of life, was linked to the empiricist methodology of the Epicurean school which focused on evidence delivered immediately to the senses and drew from such evidence normative conclusions; the Epicureans advocated the view that it is best to observe the behaviour of new-borns in order to draw conclusions about ethics, because such behaviour gives us testimony of a kind of value which is independent of judgements arising out of teaching or the influence of social norms.[37] The latter can lead to the formation of false beliefs, which are of no use for judging what is valuable in human life.[38]

---

[34] See *Fin.* 5.38.

[35] Cicero explicitly uses *voluntas* to translate the Stoic term βούλησις, see *Tusculan Disputations* 4.12: *id cum constanter prudenterque fit, eius modi adpetitionem Stoici βούλησιν appellant, nos appellemus voluntatem, eam illi putant in solo esse sapiente; quam sic definiunt: voluntas est quae quid cum ratione desiderat.* Antiochus seems here to adopt Stoic terminology, since he uses *voluntas* to denote all rational impulses, as equivalent to the Aristotelian term προαίρεσις. For βούλησις as a Stoic term, see Stobaeus *Selections* 2 87.14–22 Wachsmuth. For the special meaning that βούλησις has in Aristotle, see e.g. *Nicomachean Ethics* 3. 1111b19–29.

[36] The term is introduced in Brunschwig (1986) 113.

[37] See the Epicurean spokesperson's references to the 'uncorrupted' behaviour of children at *On Ends* 1.30: *idque facere nondum depravatum ipsa natura incorrupte atque integre iudicante.* For a discussion of Epicurean 'cradle arguments' see Brunschwig (1986) 115–28.

[38] *Ibid.* 1.71 (part of Torquatus' defence of Epicurean ethics): *si infantes pueri, mutae etiam bestiae paene loquuntur magistra ac duce natura nihil esse prosperum nisi voluptatem, nihil asperum nisi dolorem, de quibus neque depravate iudicant neque corrupte.*

In line with this development, Antiochus supplements his reconstruction of an Aristotelian-Peripatetic theory of *oikeiōsis* with 'cradle arguments', which purport to confirm the premise of an inherent desire of human beings towards their appropriate *telos*.[39] Such empirical examples serve in this case as *indications* of the kind of values, which are grasped by the rational agent as appropriate reasons for action; as Piso puts it at *On Ends* 5.61 nature is reflected in the behaviour of children 'as in a mirror' (*ut in speculis*). The Antiochean spokesperson even argues in *On Ends* 5.55 that 'all old philosophers, and most of all those of our school, visit the cradle with the belief that in childhood one can most easily discern the will of nature'.[40] The examples of children's behaviour that Antiochus cites serve to show specifically our primary natural appropriation towards the virtues, both theoretical and practical ones.

Thus, with regard to an inclination towards learning and the intellectual virtues, Antiochus cites the way children eagerly listen to stories and engage in playing, as also the way they examine inquisitively all that happens at home or show interest in learning the names of the people who take care of them.[41] There is a similar tendency observed towards the social virtues; according to the Antiochean spokesperson these are grounded in a natural propensity towards socialisation and participation in common endeavours, but also in the interest each child takes in winning contests and enjoying the recognition of others.[42]

The observation of impulses towards the theoretical and practical virtues, such as towards theoretical understanding, practical

---

[39] For an early example of a 'cradle argument' in Plato, see *Republic* 441a–b, where the behaviour of children is invoked in order to prove the existence of a special part of the soul, namely the spirited one (*thymos*).

[40] *quamquam enim vereor ne nimius in hoc genere videar, tamen omnes veteres philosophi, maxime nostri, ad incunabula accedunt, quod in pueritia facillime se arbitrantur naturae voluntatem posse cognoscere.*

[41] *On Ends* 5.42: *dantque se* (sc. *parvi*) *ad ludendum fabellarumque auditione ducuntur, deque eo quod ipsis superat aliis gratificari volunt, animadvertuntque ea quae domi fiunt curiosius, incipiuntque commentari aliquid et discere et eorum quos vident volunt non ignorare nomina.*

[42] *Ibid.: quibusque rebus* <*cum*> *aequalibus decertant* (sc. *parvi*) *si vicerunt efferunt se laetitia, victi debilitantur animosque demittunt.*

wisdom and courage,[43] is also linked for Antiochus to the idea of the existence of 'seeds' (*semina*) of virtue in children, which are available from the moment of birth and 'without teaching' (*sine doctrina*); alternative expressions provided to express this idea are those of 'semblances' (*simulacra*) or 'sparks' (*scintillae*) of virtues.[44] The biological metaphor of 'seeds of virtue' suggests the understanding of human ethical development as an organic process akin to the development of a plant from a seed; these seeds or, what are alternatively called first 'elements' (*elementa* or *principia*, translating the Greek *archai*), 'grow and blossom' into virtue.[45] Antiochus interprets this idea as supporting the conclusion that children already exhibit in a rudimentary form the virtuous behaviour of the fully developed agent. Thus, they are presented as possessing impulses and representations which, while not fully rational, pre-orient us towards the direction that is appropriate to our nature. This is ultimately grounded in a teleological outlook which postulates that nature supplies the organism with suitable equipment for its teleological success.[46]

The positive light into which children's behaviour is put in Antiochus' account does not seem to be matched in the Aristotelian ethical treatises: it is suggestive that children are excluded from the discussion on *eudaimonia* in *Nicomachean Ethics* 1, since they are not able to perform virtuous actions

---

[43] *On Ends* 5.43: *nam cum ita nati factique simus ut et agendi aliquid et diligendi aliquos et liberalitatis et referendae gratiae principia in nobis contineremus atque ad scientiam prudentiam fortitudinem aptos animos haberemus a contrariisque rebus alienos non sine causa eas quas dixi in pueris virtutum quasi scintillas videmus.*

[44] *Ibid.*: *ob eamque causam parvi virtutum simulacris, quarum in se habent semina, sine doctrina moventur*; *ibid.* 5.18: *cetera generis eiusdem, quorum similia sunt prima in animis, quasi virtutum igniculi et semina.* Cf. *On Ends* 4.17 (*iustitiae semina*) and Didymus *ap.* Stobaeus *Selections* 2 116.22 Wachsmuth which equates 'principles' with 'seeds': ὧν γὰρ ἐκ φύσεως ἀρχὰς ἔχομεν καὶ σπέρματα.

[45] *On Ends* 5.43: *sunt enim prima elementa naturae, quibus auctis virtutis quasi germen efficitur.* The metaphor is also used in Stoic theory with relation to the 'seminal principles' (σπερματικοὶ λόγοι) manifested in the primary appropriation of the living being towards itself, see e.g. Stobaeus *Selections* 2 47.12–17 Wachsmuth: ὑποτελὶς δ' ἐστὶ τὸ πρῶτον οἰκεῖον τοῦ ζῴου πάθος, ἀφ' οὗ κατήρξατο συναισθάνεσθαι τὸ ζῷον τῆς συστάσεως αὐτοῦ, οὔπω λογικὸν ὂν ἀλλ' ἄλογον, κατὰ τοὺς φυσικοὺς καὶ σπερματικοὺς λόγους, ὥσπερ τὸ θρεπτικὸν καὶ τὸ αἰσθητικόν, καὶ τῶν τοιούτων ἕκαστον ῥίζης τόπον ἐπέχει, οὐδέ πω φυτοῦ.

[46] *On Ends* 5.43: *quorum sine causa fieri nihil putandum est. Est enim natura sic generata vis hominis ut ad omnem virtutem percipiendam facta videatur.*

which are the primary constituents of a happy life.[47] The idea of
semina virtutum may, however, be linked to Aristotle's remarks
about 'natural virtue' (*physikē aretē*) at *Nicomachean Ethics* 6.13.
There, Aristotle seems to allow for the existence of virtuous
inclinations in children.[48] It is not clear, however, whether such
inclinations refer solely to certain exceptional individuals, or
whether Aristotle thinks that they are universal characteristics
which all children share and not only some gifted few. Still, the
emphasis of the Aristotelian passage is rather on reasoning as to
why these inclinations should not count as virtues 'properly speaking' and on highlighting the contrast between the imperfect abilities of children and those of a virtuous agent. This imperfection
seems to be particularly linked to the lack of practical wisdom
(*phronēsis*), which is the main topic of *Nicomachean Ethics* 6.
Lacking practical wisdom, children are unable to apply their
virtuous feelings in *particular* circumstances by making use of
deliberation and choice;[49] as a result of this, in some cases, their
actions might even produce damaging effects, such as when one
who is prone to liberality gives in particular cases resources to the
wrong kind of person. Accordingly, the idea of 'natural virtue'
never develops in Aristotle's *Nicomachean Ethics* into
a foundation for advanced, moral behaviour.

Antiochus, by contrast, treats natural virtuous inclinations as
indications, albeit rudimentary, of the perfected state of the
rational agent. He also takes such inclinations to be universal
dispositions shared to a certain degree by all and not just by
some gifted few.[50] A similar view is found in the context of
Aristotelian/Peripatetic natural science and in particular in
History of Animals 588a31–b3, where we read that we can detect
in children the 'traces and seeds' (*ichnē kai spermata*) of the

---

[47] See *Nicomachean Ethics* 1.1100a1–3. Cf. Brunschwig (1986) 119.
[48] Aristotle presents the idea that (moral) character is manifest from the moment of birth as
a 'common opinion', see *Nicomachean Ethics* 6.1144b4–6: πᾶσι γὰρ δοκεῖ ἕκαστα τῶν
ἠθῶν ὑπάρχειν φύσει πως καὶ γὰρ δίκαιοι καὶ σωφρονικοὶ καὶ ἀνδρεῖοι καὶ τἆλλα ἔχομεν
εὐθὺς ἐκ γενετῆς.
[49] See White (1994) 159.
[50] However, at *On Ends* 5.61, Piso notes that *oikeiōsis* towards the practical virtues is *most*
apparent in those endowed with the 'best natural dispositions': *atque ea in optima
quaque indole maxime apparent, in qua haec honesta, quae intelligimus, a natura
tamquam adumbrantur.*

dispositions that follow up later, alluding to the virtuous dispositions of the fully developed agent.[51] The continuation of the
passage which refers to similar characteristics in animals finds
again correspondences in the Antiochean account[52] and suggests
that Antiochus might be drawing from this context for the construction of his thesis. An additional source of inspiration for
Antiochus' thesis of 'natural virtues' could be drawn from
Plato's ideas in the *Republic* on the 'philosophical nature' and
the way the latter is manifested from early on in (some) children,
showing their innate tendencies towards virtue. Plato argues that if
such tendencies are supported by the right instruction, they lead to
the development of all virtues and illustrates this by using
a botanical analogy which is reminiscent of the Antiochean idea
of 'seeds of virtue'.[53] In the case of Antiochus, the favourable
view of children's behaviour as prefiguring the virtuous outlook of
the fully developed agent stresses the continuity between the first
and the most mature stages of ethical development and aims at
showing that reason ultimately serves goals for human nature that
are set up by a mechanism of natural appropriation.

There is also an epistemological dimension to the doctrine of
the 'seeds of virtue' in Antiochus' account, which suggests that
children possess 'elementary concepts of the most important
things' (*notitias parvas rerum maximarum*), and thus

---

[51] φανερώτατον δ' ἐστὶ τὸ τοιοῦτον ἐπὶ τὴν τῶν παίδων ἡλικίαν βλέψασιν ἐν τούτοις γὰρ
τῶν μὲν ὕστερον ἕξεων ἐσομένων ἔστιν ἰδεῖν οἷον ἴχνη καὶ σπέρματα, διαφέρει δ' οὐδὲν ὡς
εἰπεῖν ἡ ψυχὴ τῆς τῶν θηρίων ψυχῆς κατὰ τὸν χρόνον τοῦτον, ὥστ' οὐδὲν ἄλογον εἰ τὰ μὲν
ταὐτὰ τὰ δὲ παραπλήσια τὰ δ' ἀνάλογον ὑπάρχει τοῖς ἄλλοις ζῴοις. Already Dirlmeier
(1937) 55 draws attention to this text and to its significance for Peripatetic *oikeiōsis*.
In *Magna Moralia* 2.1206b23–26 we also find a reference to a natural impulse, or
passion, towards the *kalon*. The idea there seems to be that reason, which is acquired at
a later stage, agrees with this non-rational impulse towards noble action: ἴδοι δ' ἄν τις
τοῦτο ἐκ τῶν παιδίων καὶ τῶν ἄνευ λόγου ζῴων· ἐν γὰρ τούτοις ἄνευ τοῦ λόγου
ἐγγίνονται ὁρμαὶ τῶν παθῶν πρὸς τὸ καλὸν πρότερον, ὁ δὲ λόγος ὕστερος ἐπιγινόμενος
καὶ σύμψηφος ὢν ποιεῖ πράττειν τὰ καλά.

[52] See *On Ends* 5.38 for the idea that some animals possess 'a resemblance of virtue'
(*simile virtutis*). The passage is discussed in Chapter 9, *infra*.

[53] See esp. *Republic* 492a, where the idea of innate tendencies towards virtue is supplemented by the view that a 'good nature' which lacks the appropriate instruction will in
all likelihood develop into the extreme opposite of a bad character: ἦν τοίνυν ἔθεμεν τοῦ
φιλοσόφου φύσιν, ἂν μὲν οἶμαι μαθήσεως προσηκούσης τύχῃ, εἰς πᾶσαν ἀρετὴν ἀνάγκη
αὐξανομένην ἀφικνεῖσθαι, ἐὰν δὲ μὴ ἐν προσηκούσῃ σπαρεῖσά τε καὶ φυτευθεῖσα τρέφηται,
εἰς πάντα τἀναντία αὖ, ἐὰν μή τις αὐτῇ βοηθήσας θεῶν τύχῃ;

a rudimentary mental understanding of virtuous forms of behaviour without any instruction (*sine doctrina*).[54] Such a universal capacity to reach an understanding of virtue by means of innate mental resources is exemplified by Plato with the use of an 'experiment' in the *Meno* (82a–86c), where a slave without the use of instruction is able to follow abstract geometrical concepts; although the example is drawn from geometry, it is meant to be relevant for Socrates' and Meno's discussion on the teachability of virtue as well. Antiochus may have understood the Platonic idea of recollection, which is defended in the dialogues *Phaedo* and *Meno*, as supporting the view that all share innate 'rudimentary ideas' of the virtues.[55] One may speculate that he found in Plato an answer to contemporary epistemological debates for which little could be found in the resurrected Aristotelian treatises.[56]

---

[54] On Ends 5.59: *etsi dedit talem mentem quae omnem virtutem accipere posset, ingenuitque sine doctrina notitias parvas rerum maximarum et quasi instituit docere et induxit in ea quae inerant tamquam elementa virtutis.* Cicero translates with *notitia* the Stoic term ἔννοια, see *Lucullus* 22: *quod si essent falsae notitiae (ἐννοίας enim notitias appellare tu videbare).*

[55] In the *Phaedo* as well 'Ideas' are discussed as concepts (ἔννοιαι), i.e. as contents in one's soul or mind, and not as independently existing entities, see *Phaedo* 73c–d: ἆρα οὐχὶ τοῦτο δικαίως λέγομεν ὅτι ἀνεμνήσθη, οὗ τὴν ἔννοιαν ἔλαβεν; A passage from *Tusculan Disputations* 1.57, which is connected with quotations from Plato's *Phaedo* and *Meno*, makes use of very similar language to that found in the Antiochean account, making reference to *insitas et quasi consignatas in animis notiones.* However, in this passage the idea of 'innate concepts' in children is supplemented by a clear reference to the immortality of the soul: *quem locum multo etiam accuratius explicat in eo sermone, quem habuit eo ipso die quo excessit e vita; docet enim quemvis, qui omnium rerum rudis esse videatur, bene interroganti respondentem declarare se non tum illa discere sed reminiscendo recognoscere nec vero fieri ullo modo posse ut a pueris tot rerum atque tantarum insitas et quasi consignatas in animis notiones, quas* ἐννοίας *vocant, haberemus nisi animus, ante quam in corpus intravisset, in rerum cognitione viguisset.* An Antiochean pedigree for this text is defended by Bonazzi (2012) 323, who traces its similarities with Varro's account in *Academic Books* 32 (albeit not with *On Ends* 5.59).

[56] Cf. the idea of 'seeds of knowledge' in Seneca *Letters* 120.4: *nunc ergo ad id revertor de quo desideras dici, quomodo ad nos prima boni honestique notitia pervenerit. Hoc nos natura docere non potuit: semina nobis scientiae dedit, scientiam non dedit.* See also a doxographical fragment on Stoic epistemology which survives in the first book of Stobaeus' *Selections* 1 136.21 Wachsmuth = *SVF* 1.65 (possibly originating from the epistemological part of Didymus' doxography): Ζήνωνος καὶ τῶν ἀπ' αὐτοῦ. Τὰ ἐννοήματά φασι μήτε τινὰ εἶναι μήτε ποιά, ὡσανεὶ δέ τινα καὶ ὡσανεὶ ποιὰ φαντάσματα ψυχῆς· ταῦτα δὲ ὑπὸ τῶν ἀρχαίων ἰδέας προσαγορεύεσθαι. In this passage the 'ideas' (ascribed to the 'ancients') are explicitly identified with Stoic concepts. Varro may be following a similar strategy when referring to Platonic Ideas as *notiones* in *Academic Books* 32. Cf. Bonazzi (2012) 322.

Following again the lead of Plato (in dialogues such as the *Meno*), Piso suggests that it is through the guidance of philosophical reason that we come to acquire knowledge about ourselves. Thus, at *On Ends* 5.43 philosophical thought is the divine guide (*quasi deum ducem*) which kindles our natural 'sparks' for virtue and leads us to happiness.[57] The development sketched seems to be exclusively an intellectual one based on the exercise and fulfilment of our inherent reasoning capacities. Antiochus goes so far as to say that all virtues spring from reason (*ex ratione gignuntur*), also deemed the most divine element in human nature.[58] This is corroborated by other passages in the account, where the Stoic definition of virtue as the 'perfection of reason' (*rationis absolutio*) is defended as correct and is attributed to the 'ancients' as well.[59] Parallel to this, Antiochus endorses the model of expert knowledge (*ars*, translating the Greek *technē*) to describe the kind of method that is applicable to the discovery of the human *telos*.[60]

This goes against another picture of moral psychology which admits of a non-rational part of the human soul, found in both the Platonic and Aristotelian traditions. Making the virtues wholly dependent upon the mind seems rather to support the view that Antiochus advances in *On Ends* 5 an intellectualist reading of the virtues, according to which the latter amount exclusively to rational knowledge of the human good. This seems to be coupled by an 'internalist' view on motivation as well; according to this, all impulses to act spring from reason and there cannot be a conflict between what is prescribed by

---

[57] *On Ends* 5.43: *non sine causa eas quas dixi in pueris virtutum quasi scintillas videmus, e quibus accendi philosophi ratio debet, ut eam quasi deum ducem subsequens ad naturae perveniat extremum.*

[58] *Ibid.* 5.38: *virtutes voluntariae, quae quidem proprie virtutes appellantur multumque excellunt propterea quod ex ratione gignuntur, qua nihil est in homine divinius.*

[59] *Ibid.*: *in homine autem summa omnis animi est et in animo rationis, ex qua virtus est, quae rationis absolutio definitur, quam etiam atque etiam explicandam putant.*

[60] *Ibid.* 5.60: *sed virtutem ipsam inchoavit, nihil amplius. Itaque nostrum est (quod nostrum dico, artis est) ad ea principia quae accepimus consequentia exquirere, quoad sit id quod volumus effectum.* For Antiochus' endorsement of the expression τέχνη τοῦ βίου in relation to practical knowledge, see also *ibid.* 5.16: *sic vivendi ars est prudentia*; 5.18: *prudentia, quam artem vitae esse diximus.*

the reasoning faculty and an independent, non-rational centre of desire in the human soul.[61] Accordingly, Piso does not put any stress on the role of habituation for the development of virtue.

By contrast, Varro in his concise presentation of the ethics of the Old Academy in the *Academic Books* ascribes another division of the virtues to the 'ancients', which acknowledges the fundamental Aristotelian distinction between intellectual and ethical virtues; development of the latter ensues partly through the use of reason and partly through habituation of the non-reasoning part of the human soul.[62] An intellectualist reading of the virtues is ascribed, by contrast, in Varro's account to Zeno, as a distinctive doctrine of the Stoa.[63] Accordingly, the 'ancients', according to Varro, held that passions have a pre-rational basis in nature (*naturales ... et rationis expertes*) and should not be extirpated. The Stoics, on the other hand, made passions dependent upon judgement (*opinionisque iudicio*) and choice (*voluntarias*) and favoured the ideal of 'apathy'.[64]

The reason for adopting an intellectualist reading of the virtues in *On Ends* 5 may be readily explained as part of an Antiochean strategy which aims at offering Old Academic alternatives to Stoic theses. This may not, however, be

---

[61] This is corroborated by the view that all desires are for what is good, which Antiochus expounds in his discussion of the concept of self-love, see Chapter 4, *supra*. See also Brunner (2014) 199, who suggests that Antiochus shares the assumption that 'the wise person's emotional-motivational patterns are determined by her recognition of the presence or absence of good and bad things in her own life'. By contrast, Karamanolis (2006) 79 ascribes to Antiochus the view that *pathē* are generated in the non-rational part of the soul.

[62] *Academic Books* 20: *morum autem putabant studia esse et quasi consuetudinem, quam partim assiduitate exercitationis partim ratione formabant, in quibus erat ipsa philosophia.* This view is espoused by Didymus as well in his epitome of Peripatetic ethics, who refers to reason and passion as the two principles of the virtues. Accordingly, virtue is said to be in his account 'the harmony and concordance of the two principles of the soul, the one of them (*sc.* the rational part) leading to the right destination, the other (*sc.* the irrational part) following obediently', see 128.17–25 Wachsmuth. Cf. also *ibid.* 137.15–18 Wachsmuth.

[63] *Academic Books* 38: *cumque superiores non omnem virtutem in ratione esse dicerent sed quasdam virtutes quasi natura aut more perfectas, hic (sc. Zeno) omnis in ratione ponebat.*

[64] *Ibid.* 39.

'Cradle Arguments' and the Objects of *Oikeiōsis*

automatically interpreted as an outright adoption of a Stoic position on Antiochus' part. Antiochus could have taken here resort to a view which is attributed in some Platonic dialogues to Socrates, according to which virtue amounts to rational knowledge akin to the model of expert knowledge (*technē*).[65] Antiochus could have read similar views of the Stoics about the identification of virtue with rational knowledge and with a 'craft having to do with the things of life' (*technē peri tōn bion*)[66] as essentially anticipated by the 'Socratic' views. A similar strategy may be in play to explain Antiochus' endorsement of what appears to be a doctrine of the unity of virtues: thus, at *On Ends* 5.67 Antiochus seems to suggest that virtue is a single type of comprehensive practical knowledge which is differentiated solely with reference to its domain of application and the circumstances in which it is instantiated, e.g. courage is manifested in hardships and dangerous circumstances.[67] This is a view that is endorsed by the Stoics[68] but it finds also an antecedent in ideas put into the mouth of Socrates in the *Protagoras*.[69] In the source of Varro's account in the *Academic Books*, by contrast, Antiochus seems to have offered a view of Old Academic virtues, which entailed the distinction between the intellectual virtues and the virtues of character and, thus, a more complex

[65] For the parallelism between wisdom and *technē*, see e.g. *Euthydemus* 280b–d. For the Aristotelian critique of the Socratic identification of virtue with knowledge, see especially *Nicomachean Ethics* 6.1144b17–30.

[66] See e.g. Stobaeus *Selections* 2 66.19–67.2: τῷ γὰρ κατὰ λόγον ὀρθὸν ἐπιτελεῖν πάντα καὶ οἷον κατ' ἀρετήν, περὶ ὅλον οὖσαν τὸν βίον τέχνην, ἀκόλουθον ᾠήθησαν τὸ περὶ τοῦ πάντ' εὖ ποιεῖν τὸν σοφὸν δόγμα. Cf. Sextus Empiricus *Against the Professors* 11.200 = *SVF* 3.516.

[67] *nam cum ita copulatae conexaeque sint ut omnes omnium participes sint nec alia ab alia possit separari, tamen proprium suum cuiusque munus est, ut fortitudo in laboribus periculisque cernatur, temperantia in praetermittendis voluptatibus, prudentia in delectu bonorum et malorum, iustitia in suo cuique tribuendo.* The idea that Antiochus here endorses some version of the unity of virtue thesis is defended also in Annas and Woolf (2001) 140, n.47. Varro, by contrast, deviates from this thesis and presents it as the distinctive position of the Stoic school, see *Academic Books* 38: *cumque illi (sc. superiores) ea genera virtutum quae supra dixi seiungi posse arbitrarentur, hic (sc. Zeno) nec id ullo modo fieri posse disserebat.*

[68] See Diogenes Laertius *Lives of Eminent Philosophers* 7.125 = *SVF* 3.295: τὰς δ' ἀρετὰς λέγουσιν ἀντακολουθεῖν ἀλλήλαις καὶ τὸν μίαν ἔχοντα πάσας ἔχειν εἶναι γὰρ αὐτῶν τὰ θεωρήματα κοινά, καθάπερ Χρύσιππος ἐν τῷ πρώτῳ Περὶ ἀρετῶν φησιν.

[69] 348b–351b.

140

picture of moral psychology. This would tally with the hypothesis that Varro's account reflects a different phase in Antiochus' philosophical production, which contained more historically sensitive readings of the old tradition.[70]

[70] This would seem to confirm the suggestion made in Sedley (2012a) 84 that 'Antiochus did not operate throughout with a single historical model, and that in his version of philosophical history preserved in Cicero's *Academic Books* he was less syncretistic than in some other contexts'. See *ibid.* 101 for the view that Antiochus' later phase (to which Varro's account belongs) testifies to 'contemporary progress in the close study of canonical philosophical texts'. In this phase, Antiochus appears more open to emphasise 'signs of the diversity' of the old tradition, see *ibid.* 103. For an alternative view with regard to Antiochus' ethics see Brunner (2014) 189, who takes Varro's exposition of Old Academic ethics in the *Academic Books* not to be representative of Antiochus' views in ethics (as expressed in *On Ends* 5).

6

OIKEIŌSIS TOWARDS THEORETICAL VIRTUE

Prominent place in Piso's account is occupied by arguments and examples which purport to show our *oikeiōsis* towards the exercise of our theoretical *nous* (conveyed by the word *contemplatio*, translating the Greek *theōria*) and the corresponding virtue of understanding (*scientia*, translating the Greek *epistēmē*). Piso's account deserves special attention not only because it is the only one in the Ciceronian philosophical corpus conveying explicitly the Aristotelian/Peripatetic views on *theōria*; I shall claim in addition that some of the arguments in favour of *theōria* cited by Piso at *On Ends* 5.48–58 show signs of a protreptic to philosophy, which could have been based on a Peripatetic work of that genre, and perhaps stem from the *Protrepticus* itself, fragments of which survive in Iamblichus' homonymous work.[1]

The defence of our appropriation towards theoretical reason begins at *On Ends* 5.48 with a reference to an 'innate desire for knowledge and understanding' (*innatus cognitionis amor et scientiae*) present in all, which is reminiscent of the beginning of Aristotle's *Metaphysics* and the statement that 'all human beings by nature desire to know'.[2] This is shown first, in a characteristic Antiochean fashion, by the use of 'cradle arguments': thus, the way children investigate the world around them and are eager to watch games and other spectacles is taken to be a sign of our inherent tendency towards the exercise of our mental faculties, which are geared towards theoretical knowledge. Piso counters possible objections to the thesis of the inherent desirability of

---

[1] See also the concluding remarks of Piso at *On Ends* 5.74 commending Peripatetic philosophy to both intellectuals and politicians. Protreptic speeches were written not only by Aristotle, but also by, among other Peripatetics, Theophrastus and Demetrius of Phaleron, see Diogenes Laertius *Lives of Eminent Philosophers* 5.49 and *ibid.* 5.81.

[2] Aristotle *Metaphysics* 980a21: πάντες ἄνθρωποι τοῦ εἰδέναι ὀρέγονται φύσει. Cf. *On Ends* 4.18.

objects of knowledge by adding that children are devoted to 'theoretical' pursuits despite the fact that sometimes the latter incur disadvantages and pain, as when a child is punished or suffers hunger and thirst for the sake of his or her devotion to investigation.[3] This suggests that such pursuits are sought for their own sake independently of their utility.

Piso's discussion of *theōria* continues with an allegorical interpretation of an episode from the *Odyssey*.[4] Here, the desire for theoretical knowledge is represented by the long travels of Ulysses, who appears, not as forced to endure many adventures before arriving back to Ithaca, but as travelling for the sake of learning. In this way the hero is vindicated as an example of a wise man who devoted himself to the theoretical life and embarked upon journeys led by a desire for knowledge (*sapientiae cupido*). This relates to the traditional understanding of *theōria*, one form of which consisted in travelling abroad in pursuit of knowledge.[5] Accordingly Antiochus, following his Peripatetic source, explains the allurement that the Sirens exercised over the hero as primarily intellectual and not sensual: thus what allured the travellers was not the sweetness of the Sirens' voices (*vocum suavitate*) but the promise of knowledge which induced what Piso has shown to be the natural desire for learning (*discendi cupiditate*).[6] This allegorical interpretation of the Sirens' episode in Homer[7] finds a parallel in the introductory remarks to *Tusculan Disputations* 1, where mythical figures such as Prometheus or Cepheus are explained as the original *theōroi* whose activity was distorted by the 'fairy tales of myth'.[8]

The Odyssean model of the wanderer who embarks on the acquisition of knowledge serves in *On Ends* 5 as a mythical archetype. It initiates the examples of old authorities and famous people of the past

---

[3] *On Ends* 5.48: *videmusne ut pueri ne verberibus quidem a contemplandis rebus perquirendisque deterreantur? ut pulsi recurrant? ut aliquid scire se gaudeant? ut id aliis narrare gestiant? ut pompa, ludis atque eius modi spectaculis teneantur ob eamque rem vel famem et sitim perferant?*

[4] *Ibid.*: 5.49.   [5] See Nightingale (2004) 63–68.   [6] *On Ends* 5.49.

[7] The episode of which Cicero provides a Latin translation is from *Odyssey* 12.184–91. A Greek version of the allegorical interpretation appears in Sextus Empiricus *Against the Professors* 1.42.

[8] *Tusculan Disputations* 1.7–8.

who by devoting themselves to the 'contemplation of greater things' (*maiorum rerum contemplatio*) were led by the desire of understanding (*scientia*). This is followed up in the Antiochean account by concrete examples of wise men (*sophoi*), who may be said to have reached the highest theoretical wisdom. There, we find a reference to intellectuals from the Hellenistic period who devoted themselves to geometry, music and philology, represented by Archimedes, Aristoxenus and Aristophanes of Byzantium, but also to Pythagoras, Plato and Democritus as representatives of philosophy encompassing enquiry into the natural world and its principles. The relevant passage reads as follows:

> What can I say about Pythagoras, Plato and Democritus? Because of their desire for learning [*propter discendi cupiditatem*] they travelled to the remotest corners of the earth. Those who cannot understand this have never loved something lofty and worthy of knowledge. (On Ends 5.50)[9]

With regard to the great philosophers Pythagoras, Plato and Democritus, Piso makes use of the motif of journeys in search of knowledge; such journeys were attributed widely to early Greek thinkers and philosophers. According to competing evaluations of 'lives', old authorities were ascribed either a theoretical or a practical-political life.[10] Thus Pythagoras, Plato and Democritus appear as examples of wandering philosophers who travelled the world to acquire wisdom motivated by a desire for learning.[11] Pythagoras appears as an archetype of *theōria* already in Aristotle's *Protrepticus*, where he is ascribed the view that one is born to be a contemplator of nature (*theōros tēs physeōs*).[12] In Piso's account

---

[9] *Quem enim ardorem studi censetis fuisse in Archimede, qui dum in pulvere quaedam describit attentius, ne patriam <quidem> captam esse senserit! Quantum Aristoxeni ingenium consumptum videmus in musicis! Quo studio Aristophanem putamus aetatem in litteris duxisse!*

[10] Cicero testifies to this tradition at the beginning of *On the Republic* 1.12 in his attempt to eliminate doubts about taking part in public life.

[11] The emphasis on *cupiditas* may well mark an anti-Stoic point: at *Tusculan Disputations* 4.44, Cicero, expounding on the positive role of a *modicum* of natural emotions in Peripatetic theory, emphasizes, with the very same examples, the role of ἐπιθυμία for one's devotion to a noble pursuit.

[12] Iamblichus *Protrepticus* 51.6 Pistelli = B 18 Düring. This squares well with the anecdote about Pythagoras told by Heraclides of Pontus and cited at *Tusculan Disputations* 5.8–9. There, using a parable, Pythagoras describes the philosopher as someone who comes to a festival only for the sake of the spectacle (*visendi causa*).

(*On Ends* 5.87) he is assigned travels to Egypt and the Babylonian Magi,[13] and is invoked in defence of the view that a philosophical life can guarantee happiness. By contrast, Dicaearchus presented Pythagoras as a politically active man in southern Italy. This is in line with Dicaearchus' general practical orientation and his depiction of the Seven Sages as practical politicians.[14] Travels for the acquisition of theoretical knowledge are ascribed also to Democritus who for the same reason is praised and called a *sophos* in one of the fragments of Theophrastus.[15] Piso makes use of a biographical tradition which attempts to present Democritus as someone totally devoted to a life of study (*On Ends* 5.87), neglecting his paternal fortune and even putting out his own eyes in order to devote himself to the investigation of truth,[16] thus corroborating to the highest degree the Antiochean view that theoretical investigations are desired for their own sake independently of the utility they incur. The use of Democritus in this context is significant because he played an important role in the New Academic version of the history of philosophy, and served as model for the sceptical reading of Plato.[17]

Corresponding to the examples invoked in the above-mentioned passages, Antiochus' conception of *theōria* is presented primarily as inquiry into nature, originating in the practice of the Presocratics. This is shown by the fact that the observation of the movement of the celestial bodies and the understanding of the 'hidden realities' of nature (*quae naturae obscuritate occultantur*) are chosen as primary examples of theoretical pursuits at *On Ends* 5.51.[18] The word *occultus* used by Piso in this context translates the Greek *adēlon*, a term which comes to mean in Hellenistic philosophy everything that is not itself accessible to the senses but constitutes the underlying principle of perceptible

---

[13] Cf. Diogenes Laertius *Lives of Eminent Philosophers* 7.3.
[14] *Frs*. 33–4 Wehrli. Cf. *Fr*. 31 Wehrli, where Dicaearchus exalts the ancient wise men who 'did not philosophize in words and by creating pithy sayings (but rather) by the practice of noble deeds' (ἀλλ'εἶναι τὴν σοφίαν τότε γοῦν ἐπιτήδευσιν ἔργων καλῶν).
[15] *Fr*. 513 FHS&.G. = Aelian *Historical Miscellany* 4.20.
[16] Cf. Diogenes Laertius *Lives of Eminent Philosophers* 9.36.　　[17] See e.g. *Lucullus* 73.
[18] *Ipsi enim quaeramus a nobis stellarum motus contemplationesque rerum caelestium eorumque omnium quae naturae obscuritate occultantur cognitiones quem ad modum nos moveant.*

phenomena.[19] These are discovered through a process of reasoning which takes its starting-point in perception (*On Ends* 5.58); what Piso alludes to is the attainment of theoretical knowledge through the process of demonstration (*conclusio,* translating the Greek *apodeiksis*).[20]

However, alongside natural science, we meet in Piso's account a broader notion of intellectual activity which includes the personal study of subjects such as history or fiction;[21] these are said to be often pursued by people who do not aspire to any high position of power and, by virtue of this, they are shown to be desired quite independently of their utility.[22] This broader conception of learning addresses perhaps in particular a Roman audience, which, while interested in 'liberal' pursuits, does not approve the exclusive devotion to an intellectual life. Intellectual endeavours are construed in this case broadly enough to encompass leisure activities, pursued along with other practical or political actions, and are not limited to activities which require complete devotion to study and inquiry. Finally, Piso gives examples of uncultivated persons of lower social rank, who, while foreign to scientific pursuits or even to 'liberal' learning, seek to exercise their mental capacities by engaging in games or discussions with others. Highlighting our tendency towards such 'lower' intellectual pursuits helps to corroborate Antiochus' point that there is a universal natural tendency towards the exercise of the theoretical part of our mind independently of any practical utility, even among those who

---

[19] Cf. *ibid.* 1.30; Sextus Empiricus *Against the Professors* 10.250ff.; Lucretius 1.422–5. The use of the superlative *occultissimus* in *On Ends* 5 could suggest the cause least accessible to the senses, i.e. the first cause of the cosmos. By contrast, Bénatouïl (2009) 10 sees in the use of the word *occultus* the influence of the New Academy on Antiochus.

[20] In *Lucullus* 26 and *On Ends* 1.30 we find the metaphorical expression *involuta aperire,* which captures ἐκκαλύπτειν, used in Greek texts in connection with argument and definition. A definition of demonstration is provided by the Antiochean spokesman Lucullus at *Lucullus* 26 in the context of an attack on New Academic scepticism: *itaque argumenti conclusio, quae est Graece ἀπόδειξις, ita definitur: 'ratio quae ex rebus perceptis ad id quod non percipiebatur adducit'.*

[21] *On Ends* 5.51–52: *quid cum fictas fabulas, e quibus utilitas nulla elici potest, cum voluptate legimus? Quid cum volumus nomina eorum qui quid gesserint nota nobis esse, parentes, patriam, multa praeterea minime necessaria?*

[22] *Ibid.* 5.52: *quid quod homines infima fortuna, nulla spe rerum gerendarum, opifices denique delectantur historia? maximeque eos videre possumus res gestas audire et legere velle qui a spe gerendi absunt confecti senectute.*

may never reach the highest virtue of *scientia*, or even the status of a cultivated nobleman.

An Echo from the *Protrepticus*: The Pursuit of Learning in the Isles of the Blest

The dissociation of theoretical knowledge from utility, which finds in *On Ends* 5 its unique expression in the Ciceronian corpus, is firmly rooted in the Aristotelian/Peripatetic tradition. For example, at the beginning of *Metaphysics* Aristotle defends the disinterested character of knowledge, as something dissociated from the realm of need or use, being most akin to a free man as opposed to a slave.[23] But also in the fragments of the *Protrepticus*,[24] the superiority of the activity of philosophy is justified on the basis of a distinction between things 'necessary' (*anagkaia*) and 'goods in the strict sense' (*agatha kyriōs*). Proper goods, unlike necessary things, do not result in anything external to themselves.[25]

Piso's account contains an explicit testimony which suggests that the *Protrepticus* was one among the sources used for the construction of the account. The *per se* choice worthiness of theoretical activity is reinforced in the Antiochean account by the depiction of a fully blessed life, free from necessities, in the imaginary Isles of the Blest (*in beatorum insulis*).[26] The example is contained in the following passage:

> The old philosophers also depict how the life of wise men will be in the Isles of the Blest. Freed from every trouble [*cura omni liberatos*] and not needing to care or provide for any of the necessities of life [*nullum necessarium vitae cultum aut*

---

[23] See e.g. *Metaphysics* 982b19–21: ὥστ᾽ εἴπερ διὰ τὸ φεύγειν τὴν ἄγνοιαν ἐφιλοσόφησαν, φανερὸν ὅτι διὰ τὸ εἰδέναι τὸ ἐπίστασθαι ἐδίωκον καὶ οὐ χρήσεώς τινος ἕνεκεν.

[24] The idea that Iamblichus' *Protrepticus* contains many arguments from a homonymous Aristotelian work has been forcefully argued, after Bywater's first discovery in 1869, by Düring (1961), who offers a reconstruction and rearrangement of the chain of argumentation with a commentary. A new reading by Hutchinson and Johnson (2005) suggests that we find in Iamblichus pure blocks of quotation in a natural sequence as they appeared in Aristotle's original work, which had the form of a dialogue.

[25] Iamblichus *Protrepticus* 52.16–53.2 Pistelli = B 42 Düring.

[26] The similarity between the two passages has been already noted by Theiler (1930) 52 and Gigon (1988) 267; the latter attributes the relevant fragment in Iamblichus to the Aristotelian dialogue *On Philosophy*.

paratum requirentis], they think that they will do nothing else but spend all the time, investigating and learning, in the knowledge of nature [*naturae cognitione*]. (*On Ends* 5.53)

The poetic haven of heroes[27] is in *On Ends* 5.53 used in a way that serves the exhortation to theoretical knowledge: sages are depicted as free from trouble and necessities, spending their time in investigating and acquiring knowledge of the physical world.[28] This vision of the happiest possible life, even if relating to a *post mortem* existence, aims at promoting the value of theoretical activity in one's incarnate life. The implicit protreptic argument here is that one should engage in the exercise of theoretical virtue because it is the kind of activity which most resembles the happiest possible life enjoyed at the 'Isles of the Blessed'. A corroboration of this could come from the consideration that such engagement may bring with it the reward of a *post mortem* blissful existence.[29] Another implication of the passage is, however, that uninterrupted devotion to higher pursuits, such as natural science, is only possible when the intellect is enjoying an existence independent of the body; in our incarnate lives a concern for necessities and other provisions makes such an exclusive devotion impossible.

The depiction of an imaginary life devoted to the contemplation of nature is attributed in Piso's account directly to the 'ancient philosophers' (*veteres ... philosophi*) by whom one should understand, especially in *On Ends* 5, Aristotle and the

---

[27] Cf. Hesiod *Works and Days* 171.

[28] The *topos* of the Isles of the Blest as the dwelling place of the wise men after death featured also at the lost Ciceronian dialogue *Hortensius,* according to the testimony of Augustine in *On the Trinity* 14.12.

[29] The dimension of a reward for the ones who devote themselves to the exercise of their intellect is present in Aristotle at the end of *Nicomachean Ethics* 10.8, where it is being argued that granting that there is care of the gods for human affairs — a concession, I take it, to popular beliefs on Aristotle's part — then, even in this case, it seems reasonable to think that the wise person will be to the highest degree loved by the gods, see *Nicomachean Ethics* 1179a22–32: ὁ δὲ κατὰ νοῦν ἐνεργῶν καὶ τοῦτον θεραπεύων καὶ διακείμενος ἄριστα καὶ θεοφιλέστατος ἔοικεν. εἰ γάρ τις ἐπιμέλεια τῶν ἀνθρωπίνων ὑπὸ θεῶν γίνεται, ὥσπερ δοκεῖ, καὶ εἴη ἂν εὔλογον χαίρειν τε αὐτοὺς τῷ ἀρίστῳ καὶ συγγενεστάτῳ (τοῦτο δ' ἂν εἴη ὁ νοῦς) καὶ τοὺς ἀγαπῶντας μάλιστα τοῦτο καὶ τιμῶντας ἀντευποιεῖν ὡς τῶν φίλων αὐτοῖς ἐπιμελουμένους καὶ ὀρθῶς τε καὶ καλῶς πράττοντας. ὅτι δὲ πάντα ταῦτα τῷ σοφῷ μάλισθ' ὑπάρχει, οὐκ ἄδηλον. θεοφιλέστατος ἄρα. τὸν αὐτὸν δ' εἰκὸς καὶ εὐδαιμονέστατον· ὥστε κἂν οὕτως εἴη ὁ σοφὸς μάλιστ' εὐδαίμων.

Peripatetics.[30] Indeed, the passage constitutes an almost verbatim quotation from the *Protrepticus*. The example makes use of the same vocabulary as its original, as it has come down to us in Iamblichus' *Protrepticus*, where it serves likewise as a protreptic argument in favour of engaging in contemplation and intellectual activity. As in *On Ends* 5 theoretical activity, disconnected from the necessities of everyday life, is represented in the *Protrepticus* as being enjoyed by the wise outside the earthly realm, according to the existing myths of the afterlife:

> One might see that what we say is all the more true if someone transported us in thought, as it were, to the Isles of the Blessed [εἰς μακάρων νήσους], for in that place there would turn out to be no need of anything [οὐδενὸς χρεία] nor any benefit from anything else [οὐδὲ τῶν ἄλλων τινὸς ὄφελος], with only thinking and contemplating [τὸ διανοεῖσθαι καὶ θεωρεῖν] left remaining, which we say now too is a free way of life. (Iamblichus *Protrepticus* 53.2–7 Pistelli = B43 Düring (trans. Hutchinson and Johnson with small alterations))

Although the above-mentioned passage from Piso's account seems to contain a clear echo from the corresponding passage of the *Protrepticus*, we may note that the original appearance of the *topos* of the Isles of the Blest stems from Plato. In Book 7 of the *Republic* it features as the reason why the philosopher after coming into contact with the Ideas and practising dialectic will be reluctant to return back to the 'cave' and act for the benefit of society.[31] It is furthermore connected in Plato with the fate of the philosophical soul after the end of its earthly existence.[32] The appearance of the same motif in Platonic texts could function as a corroboration of the Antiochean reading of the old tradition, according to which Aristotle elaborated on Platonic philosophy and remained faithful to the same set of doctrines as Plato.

---

[30] The remark *ac veteres philosophi . . . fingunt* at *On Ends* 5.53 points to a direct quotation from an ancient philosophical source.

[31] *Republic* 519c: τοὺς δὲ ὅτι ἑκόντες εἶναι οὐ πράξουσιν, ἡγούμενοι ἐν μακάρων νήσοις ζῶντες ἔτι ἀπῳκίσθαι;

[32] *Ibid.* 540b: καὶ οὕτως ἄλλους ἀεὶ παιδεύσαντας τοιούτους, ἀντικαταλιπόντας τῆς πόλεως φύλακας, εἰς μακάρων νήσους ἀπιόντας οἰκεῖν. Cf. *Gorgias* 526c.

Oikeiōsis **towards Different Kinds of** *Actio*

After referring to the happiest possible life on the Isles of the
Blest, the Antiochean account turns to a new point which puts
centre stage the notion of 'activity' (*actio*, translating the
Greek *energeia*), with a view to establishing all the activities
which come up to constitute the happy life. The idea that the
happy life is a kind of *energeia* appears again to be a point of
particularly Aristotelian-Peripatetic origin.[33] Antiochus makes
use of it in order to show that the happy life consists of *both*
the activities of the theoretical and the practical virtues,[34]
whereby the former are deemed 'higher' than the latter. His
views seem to serve thereby an ideal of an 'inclusive' form of
life (*bios*) which is composed both of theoretical pursuits and
practical and social engagements. The method used by
Antiochus to this end seems to have been one of progression
from lower activities of the mind to the highest ones. The
implicit reasoning behind this aims to show that if we value
lower mental activities for their own sake, then *a fortiori* we
value the highest mental activities for their own sake as well.
The highest activities of theoretical and practical virtues comprise the constituents of a happy life and are inherently valued
by all those who have reached a correct understanding of the
human *telos*.

Starting with the lowest mental faculties Piso makes reference to the way the exercise of our senses, and in particular
perception, is valued for its own sake. The point is illustrated
by the example of the blind man Gnaeus Aufidius, a Roman
praetor, who is said to have missed the very daylight rather

---

[33] On *eudaimonia* as a kind of ἐνέργεια, see e.g. *Nicomachean Ethics* 1.1098a16. On the
Aristotelian credentials of this aspect of Antiochus' theory cf. Inwood (2014) 70.

[34] *Actio* is meant thereby to refer also to actions (the Greek πρᾶξις). This might be due to
the unavailability of a terminological distinction in Cicero's Latin between the Greek
notions of ἐνέργεια and πρᾶξις, or of the later distinction between *actus* and *actio*. For the
association of the two words in Aristotle, see *Nicomachean Ethics* 10.1176b6–9 where
actions in accordance with virtue are themselves ἐνέργειαι. Aristotle uses interchange-
ably in *Nicomachean Ethics* 10.6 the expression κατ'ἀρετὴν πράξεις and κατ'ἀρετὴν
ἐνέργειαι; cf. also Didymus *ap.* Stobaeus *Selections* 2 127.1–2 Wachsmuth and *ibid.*
130.3–4Wachsmuth, where πρᾶξις is said to be explicitly a species of ἐνέργεια: πᾶσαν
μὲν γὰρ πρᾶξιν ἐνέργειαν εἶναί τινα ψυχῆς.

than any practical advantage resulting from seeing.[35] This is corroborated by the example of sleep at *On Ends* 5.54. Piso claims there that we would consider sleep something contrary to nature, were it not providing to us rest for our bodies and a kind of remedy for our toils, because it deprives us of using our senses and also of any kind of activity, either practical or theoretical:

> Finally sleep: if it were not for the fact that it offers relaxation for our body and some sort of remedy for our toils, we would think that it is given to us contrary to nature [*contra naturam putaremus datum*]; for it deprives us of perception and of any kind of activity [*actionemque tollit omnem*].[36]

The Antiochean spokesperson corroborates this by using a thought-experiment in the form of a mythical example. Endymion was bestowed in ancient mythology immortality but was condemned to a state of eternal sleep. The Antiochean spokesperson appeals to widely shared intuitions suggesting that if we had the choice we would never opt to live forever like this, even if this state was accompanied by the most delightful dreams.[37] This is meant to show that we value as a happy life one characterised by the full exercise of our perceptual and mental faculties.

The invocation of sleep in order to show the intrinsic value of the kind of activity which constitutes the happy life has antecedents in Aristotle and writings of Peripatetic provenance. It is, for instance, on the basis of the example of sleep, among others, that Aristotle establishes in *Nicomachean Ethics* 10 that happiness involves some sort of *energeia*, and in particular the activity of *nous*.[38] We may adduce to the above some remarks from the *Protrepticus*, which point in the same direction as the one sketched in the

---

[35] *On Ends* 5.54: *equidem e Cn. Aufidio, praetorio, erudito homine, oculis capto, saepe audiebam, cum se lucis magis quam utilitatis desiderio moveri diceret.*

[36] *somnum denique nobis, nisi requietem corporibus et medicinam quandam laboris afferret, contra naturam putaremus datum; aufert enim sensus actionemque tollit omnem.*

[37] *itaque, ne si iucundissimis quidem nos somniis usuros putemus, Endymionis somnum nobis velimus dari, idque si accidat, mortis instar putemus.*

[38] See *Nicomachean Ethics* 10.1176a33–36. Cf. *ibid.* 10.1178b18-20, where the example of Endymion is used in relation to the life and *energeia* of the divine.

Antiochean account. Although the example of Endymion which features in Piso's account is missing in the text of the *Protrepticus*, sleep is condemned on similar grounds, despite being a most pleasant state (*hēdiston*). The argument is based, however, there on the idea that sleep and activity during sleep (e.g. the experience of dreams) fail to provide us secure epistemic access to truth. The relevant passage reads as follows:

> So on account of this too, though sleeping is extremely pleasant, it is not choice worthy, even if we were to hypothesise that all the pleasures were present to the sleeper, because the apparitions during sleep are falsehoods, while those of the waking are true [διότι τὰ ἐν καθ' ὕπνον φαντάσματα ψευδῆ, τὰ δ' ἐγρηγορόσιν ἀληθῆ]. For sleep and waking are no different from each other except that the soul of the person who is awake often tells the truth, but when sleeping is always misled, for the phantom in dream visions is actually a complete falsehood.[39] (Iamblichus *Protrepticus* 45.25–46.7 Pistelli = B 101 Düring (trans. Hutchinson/Johnson, with small alterations))

According to this passage, during sleep we experience highly pleasant states with, however, no truth value. Since we value truth higher than falsehood, we prefer being awake in that state in which we *may* have access to truth, than to remain in a state in which we are always deceived, even if such a state of deception is the most pleasant one. The rest of the argument that is implied here is that *nous* is ultimately the source of truth by passing authoritative judgement on the material that it receives from the senses and by enabling infallible knowledge, namely understanding (*epistēmē*). Hence the activity of *nous* is the most choice-worthy one.[40] The example shows that even if the *Protrepticus* functioned as one of the sources of the account to make the case for the intrinsic value of theoretical activity, Antiochus adjusted his sources as he saw fit; in this case, emphasis on the pleasantness

---

[39] διὰ δὴ τοῦτο καὶ τὸ καθεύδειν ἥδιστον μὲν οὐχ αἱρετὸν δέ, κἂν ὑποθώμεθα πάσας τῷ καθεύδοντι παρούσας τὰς ἡδονάς, διότι τὰ ἐν καθ' ὕπνον φαντάσματα ψευδῆ, τὰ δ' ἐγρηγορόσιν ἀληθῆ. διαφέρει γὰρ οὐδενὶ τῶν ἄλλων τὸ καθεύδειν καὶ τὸ ἐγρηγορέναι πλὴν τῷ τὴν ψυχὴν τότε μὲν πολλάκις ἀληθεύειν, καθεύδοντος δὲ ἀεὶ διεψεῦσθαι· τὸ γὰρ τῶν ἐνυπνίων εἴδωλόν ἐστι καὶ ψεῦδος ἅπαν.

[40] For truth as the function of the thinking part of the soul, see Iamblichus *Protrepticus* 41.24–43.5 and *ibid.* 43.27–44.26 Pistelli.

of Endymion's state, rather than on its epistemic inadequacies, could serve well an anti-Epicurean argument, in order to show that we would have reasons to reject the most pleasant life if it was not accompanied by characteristically human activities, such as that of theoretical thinking and virtuous actions. This serves the Antiochean point that we value such activities in and for themselves as constituents of the human *telos*. The specific epistemological rationale of the text of the *Protrepticus* could have been in this process abridged.

The 'intuitive' line in the defence of the intrinsic value of theoretical activity is further backed up in Piso's account by empirical observations from the behaviour of children ('cradle arguments') and animals; thus, the desire of the adult agent to engage in theoretical activities is anticipated by the inability of infants to keep still and by the natural inclination of somewhat older children to engage in 'toilsome games' even despite the threat of punishment.[41] Desire of activity (*cupiditas agendi*) is even present in wild animals, which, even if they are better fed when held captive, still miss roaming around freely in accordance with the capacities of their own nature.[42] Finally, the observation of ordinary agents who do not exhibit any special mental capacities, as the ones possessed by wise men and noblemen, whatsoever show that all human beings possess a natural desire to exercise their mind. Thus, even the laziest of people (*inertissimi homines*) are found in constant bodily and mental activity and, when they are not occupied with necessary tasks, they seek for 'lower' amusements such as games, pastimes or social gatherings.[43] People who possess advanced mental capacities come, on the

---

[41] On Ends 5.55: *videmus igitur ut conquiescere ne infantes quidem possint; cum vero paulum processerunt, lusionibus vel laboriosis delectantur, ut ne verberibus quidem deterreri possint, eaque cupiditas agendi aliquid adolescit una cum aetatibus.*

[42] Ibid. 5.56: *quin ne bestiae quidem quas delectationis causa concludimus, cum copiosius alantur quam si essent liberae, facile patiuntur sese contineri motusque solutos et vagos a natura sibi tributos requirunt.*

[43] Ibid.: *quin etiam inertissimos homines nescio qua singulari segnitia praeditos videmus tamen et corpore et animo moveri semper et, cum re nulla impediantur necessaria, aut alveolum poscere aut quaerere quempiam ludum aut sermonem aliquem requirere, cumque non habeant ingenuas ex doctrina oblectationes, circulos aliquos et sessiunculas consectari.*

other hand, to value and pursue 'higher' activities, among which the Antiochean spokesman identifies three in particular: the fulfilment of private practical tasks and business, the engagement with public affairs and government and, finally, the pursuit of theoretical science.[44]

---

[44] *Ibid.* 5.57: *nam aut privatim aliquid gerere malunt aut, qui altiore animo sunt, capessunt rem publicam honoribus imperiisque adipiscendis, aut totos se ad studia doctrinae conferunt.* A parallel for the choice between the 'highest' pursuits of the political and theoretical life can be found at Aristotle's *Politics* 7.1324a29–32, where those who choose the political or the theoretical life are characterised as φιλοτιμότατοι πρὸς ἀρετήν. But see already Plato's *Republic* 521b: ἔχεις οὖν, ἦν δ' ἐγώ, βίον ἄλλον τινὰ πολιτικῶν ἀρχῶν καταφρονοῦντα ἢ τὸν τῆς ἀληθινῆς φιλοσοφίας;

7

SOCIAL *OIKEIŌSIS*

After showing our *oikeiōsis* towards theoretical virtue, Piso goes on to claim that there is an equivalent *oikeiōsis* towards the practical virtues, such as the virtues of justice, practical wisdom, courage and temperance. These virtues are subsumed in Cicero under the 'honourable' (*honestum*, translating the Greek καλόν),[1] suggesting that their development essentially involves a social context.[2] Following the method of using 'cradle arguments' in order to make the thesis of a natural appropriation towards the *telos* plausible, the Antiochean spokesperson presents the practical virtues as being grounded in a natural propensity towards sociali-sation. Such an innate social feeling is shown in the interest children take in winning contests and enjoying the recognition by others. Thus, Piso stresses how children engage into contests with passion and the way they are overpowered by delight when they have won the victory, whereas they feel disgraced when they are defeated.[3] Such behaviour suggests that children value the opinion of others and are motivated from an early age onwards towards actions which incite the praise of the community they belong to.[4] Presenting this as sign of our *oikeiōsis* towards the practical virtues may well point to the view that the desire to excel and gain honour by others is a driving psychological force towards

---

[1] See *On Ends* 5.60: *itaque omnis honos, omnis admiratio, omne studium ad virtutem et ad eas actiones quae virtuti sunt consentaneae refertur, eaque omnia quae aut ita in animis sunt aut ita geruntur uno nomine honesta dicuntur.*

[2] Cf. *On Ends* 5.67: *igitur inest in omni virtute cura quaedam quasi foras spectans aliosque appetens atque complectens.*

[3] *Ibid.* 5.61: *quanta studia decertantium sunt! quanta ipsa certamina! ut illi efferuntur laetitia cum vicerunt, ut pudet victos!* Cf. *Ibid.* 5.42: *quibusque rebus <cum> aequalibus decertant* (sc. *parvi*) *si vicerunt efferunt se laetitia, victi debilitantur animosque demittunt.*

[4] *Ibid.* 5.61: *ut se accusari nolunt! quam cupiunt laudari! quos illi labores non perferunt ut aequalium principes sint!* On our *oikeiōsis* towards praise, cf. Didymus *ap.* Stobaeus *Selections* 2 122.2–4 Wachsmuth: ὥστε καὶ τὸν ἔπαινον εἶναι δι' αὐτὸν αἱρετόν· οἰκειοῦσθαι γὰρ ἡμᾶς πρὸς τοὺς ἐπαινοῦντας.

the development of the full-blown virtues. The implicit idea would be that the person who has acquired 'full virtue' comes to see the inherent value of a behaviour that was initially pursued for the sake of self-esteem. Thus, whereas the virtuous person would engage in the honourable action for its own sake, a more 'primitive' motivation may be connected to the desire to acquire fame (*gloria*).[5] Piso refers also to other indications of virtuous behaviour in children, such as the tendency to reciprocate kindnesses done to them.[6]

A natural propensity towards the social virtues is corroborated by appealing to a general moral sentiment which, according to Piso, may be observed not only in well-educated people and noblemen[7] but also in the 'uneducated crowd' (*vulgus*). This is shown in the way moral characters and actions receive approval and praise when one reads about them in fiction or when they are presented in dramatic plays.[8] To illustrate this Piso uses the applause of the audience in the theatre whenever a 'heroic' action is presented. Thus, when both Orestes and Pylades offer themselves to die rather than have either of them save his own life by saying that the other is Orestes (an example taken by Pacuvius' play *Orestes*), Piso refers to the unanimous admiration that this act of self-sacrifice incites in the theatre audience.[9] This is meant to show that the inherent value of moral characters and actions is generally acknowledged and praised, even among those who do not have a virtuous disposition themselves and are thus unable to act in line with the behaviour that they approve.

In the fully developed rational agent, *oikeiōsis* towards the social virtues takes the form of the 'full-blown' virtues. Piso

---

[5] Such a motivation is ascribed to those who have not advanced to the perfection of virtue at *On Ends* 5.69: *non perfecti autem homines et tamen ingeniis excellentibus praediti excitantur saepe gloria, quae habet speciem honestatis et similitudinem.*

[6] *Ibid.* 5.61: *quae memoria est in iis bene merentium, quae referendae gratiae cupiditas!*

[7] *Ibid.* 5.63: *quid loquor de nobis, qui ad laudem et ad decus nati suscepti instituti sumus?*

[8] *Ibid.* 5.62: *an obliviscimur quantopere in audiendo [in] legendoque moveamur cum pie, cum amice, cum magno animo aliquid factum cognoscimus?*

[9] *Ibid.* 5.63: *qui clamores vulgi atque imperitorum excitantur in theatris, cum illa dicuntur:'Ego sum Orestes', contraque ab altero: 'Immo enimvero ego sum, inquam, Orestes!' Cum autem etiam exitus ab utroque datur conturbato errantique regi, 'Ambo ergo †sunaneganum† precamur', —quotiens hoc agitur, ecquandone nisi admirationibus maximis? Nemo est igitur quin hanc adfectionem animi probet atque laudet, qua non modo utilitas nulla quaeritur, sed contra utilitatem etiam conservatur fides.*

makes particular reference to justice as the social virtue *par excellence* and shows how this disposition to 'assign everyone their due' is structured around a nexus of relationships which starts with the closest association between parents and children and extends so far as to encompass humanity as a whole. The relevant passage from the Antiochean account reads as follows:

> But in the whole domain of virtue that we are discussing, nothing is so noble as, or extends more widely than, the fellowship between human beings [*coniunctio inter homines hominum*] and a certain, as it were, association [*societas*] and interconnection of interests [*communicatio utilitatum*], and the very love for humankind [*caritas generis humani*]. This arises at birth [*a primo satu*], since children are loved by their parents and the whole house is united by the bonds of coupling and family [*coniugio et stirpe*], and then spreads gradually outwards [*serpit sensim foras*], first to blood relatives, then to kin by marriage, next friends, then neighbours, and then to fellow-citizens and to friends and allies in the public sphere. Finally, it embraces the whole human kind [*totius complexu gentis humanae*]. (*On Ends* 5.65)

Justice in the above passage is shown to manifest itself in the framework of a series of 'associations' (*societas*, translating most probably the Greek *koinōnia*) and 'friendships' (*caritas*, translating the Greek *philia*) with other human beings. The starting-point of a virtuous person's relationship with other human beings is the *philia* that parents have for their offspring. The second manifestation of social virtue is found in the household grounded in the union between man and woman.[10] This disposition extends gradually (*serpit sensim foras*) to relationships with other kin, friends, fellow-citizens and partners. Finally, Piso refers to a universal human bonding and to the community of the human race (*coniunctio inter homines hominum*).[11] In relation to the latter, we find in Antiochus' account the notion of a generalised love for humankind (*caritas generis humani*), which most probably translates the

---

[10] This becomes clearer in *On Ends* 4.17, where Cicero is wearing his Antiochean hat: *ut coniugia virorum et uxorum natura coniuncta esse dicerent, qua ex stirpe orirentur amicitiae cognationum.* Cf. also a very similar scheme at *On Appropriate Actions* 1.54. For Antiochus this could also be an expression of the definition of a human being as 'by nature disposed to live in pairs' (φύσει συνδυαστικόν), see *Nicomachean Ethics* 8.1162a17–19.

[11] See also *Academic Books* 21 (from Varro's Old Academic account): *hominem enim esse censebant quasi partem quandam civitatis et universi generis humani, eumque esse coniunctum cum hominibus humana quadam societate.*

Greek term *philanthrōpia*.[12] Antiochus claims that the virtuous attitude that applies to each of these associations reveals that other humans are desired 'for their own sake' (*propter se expetendi*) and not (merely) for the sake of utility.[13]

What is further envisaged in Antiochus' scheme of justice is a widening of the scope of one's social concern from more narrow to the widest possible associations. The gradual outward (*sensim foras*) movement of the associations of friendship suggests a widening of the scope of the application of justice and a corresponding 'loosening' in the intensity of the association from the strongest bond (the association between parents and offspring) down to the weaker one (the association with fellow human beings as such). The idea of justice envisaged here does not presuppose in every case strict equality but depends on the type of *philia* which it accompanies, its manifestation varying according to the relationship to which it applies. Further, justice is defined in the Antiochean account as a state of mind[14] 'which assigns to each person their due'[15] and preserves the association of human bonding by which is meant the complete range of relationships sketched in the previous part of the account. Antiochus goes further on to provide a list of virtues, which form species of justice:[16]

This state of mind [*animi adfectio*] which assigns to each person their due [*suum cuique tribuens*] and preserves with generosity and equity [*munifice et aeque*] this association of human bonding that I am talking about is called justice. Connected with it are piety, kindness, liberality, courtesy, friendliness and all of this kind.

---

[12] I propose this translation for φιλανθρωπία against Brink (1956) who identifies it with *humanitas*. The translation of φιλανθρωπία with *humanitas* can also be found in De Ruiter (1931).

[13] *On Ends* 5.67: *quando igitur inest in omni virtute cura quaedam quasi foras spectans aliosque appetens atque complectens, exsistit illud, ut amici, ut fratres, ut propinqui, ut affines, ut cives, ut omnes denique (quoniam unam societatem hominum esse volumus) propter se expetendi sint.*

[14] *Adfectio animi* here translates διάθεσις as opposed to ἕξις, the difference being that for the Stoics the former is incapable of increase or decrease. It is used in the summary of Peripatetic ethics in Didymus *ap.* Stobaeus *Selections* 2 128.11 Wachsmuth as well.

[15] This became the standard Stoic definition of justice (e.g. Stobaeus *Selections* 2 59.9–10, 84.15–16 Wachsmuth) but it appears also in the pseudo-Aristotelian *On Virtues and Vices*, see 1250a12: δικαιοσύνη δ' ἐστὶν ἀρετὴ ψυχῆς διανεμητικὴ τοῦ κατ'ἀξίαν.

[16] The species of justice mentioned here bear a resemblance to the catalogue of virtues offered in Didymus *ap.* Stobaeus *Selections* 2 146.15–18 Wachsmuth but also to the Stoic catalogue of virtues at Stobaeus *Selections* 2 60.22–24 Wachsmuth.

And while these belong especially to justice, they are common to the rest of the virtues as well. (*On Ends* 5.65)

The nexus of relationships in which our social *oikeiōsis* manifests itself receives more attention in Didymus' summary of Peripatetic ethics, which provides a fuller version of a Peripatetic model of social *oikeiōsis* than the one found in Antiochus' account, albeit with many similarities to the latter. In the relevant text, the recognition of the inherent choice worthiness of other human beings and the corresponding (appropriate) actions that ensue from such a recognition are grounded in an objective relatedness (*oikeiotēs*) and the social nature of human beings, showing that Didymus makes use, like Antiochus, of the idea of natural appropriation in order to ground virtuous behaviour towards others in human nature.[17] The following passage from Didymus' account contains his Peripatetic version of social *oikeiōsis*:

If there is such a love towards the children because of their being choice worthy for their own sake [κατὰ τὸ <δι'> αὐθ' αἱρετόν], necessarily also parents and brothers and one's wife and relatives and other close persons and fellow-citizens are loved for their own sake [ὡς δι'αὐτοὺς φιλίας τυγχάνειν]; for we have by nature certain kinds of relatedness with them too [ἔχειν γὰρ ἐκ φύσεως ἡμᾶς καὶ πρὸς τούτους τινὰς οἰκειότητας], since humans are social living beings with love for each other [φιλάλληλον γὰρ εἶναι καὶ κοινωνικὸν ζῷον τὸν ἄνθρωπον] (. . .) If love towards one's fellow citizens is choice worthy for its own sake, then so must be that towards people of the same nation or race, and therefore also that towards all human beings. For also all those who save (someone) have manifestly such a disposition towards their neighbours as to act in most of the cases not according to the merit (of each person) [κατ'ἀξίαν][18] but according to what is choice worthy for its own sake [κατὰ τὸ δι' αὐθ'αἱρετόν]. For who wouldn't rescue, if one could, someone who is seen being violated by a beast? Who wouldn't indicate the way to someone who is lost? Who wouldn't assist someone who is dying through lack of means? (Didymus *ap.* Stobaeus *Selections* 2 120.8–121.6 Wachsmuth)

---

[17] The use of the word *oikeiotēs* instead of *oikeiōsis* in this part of Didymus' account could signify that our appropriation is properly speaking towards developing the disposition of justice towards others. Since others are not strictly speaking a part of ourselves, there cannot be an *oikeiōsis* towards them but only an *oikeiotēs*, i.e. a relatedness. For the difference between *oikeiōsis* and *oikeiotēs* see Brink (1956).

[18] This is the reading that I propose against the mss. reading τὰς πράξεις and Wachsmuth's πρὸς ἀξίαν.

Like in the Antiochean account, the manifestation of social virtue is presented as starting from the relationship between parents and children and extending, by means of a series of hypothetical syllogisms, gradually to the relationship between relatives, friends, fellow-citizens, and people of the same nation to apply finally to humanity as as whole. Didymus takes these successive relationships to differ in their range and intensity.[19] The appropriate actions implied in each case differ accordingly, suggesting that different kinds of relationships present us with different normative claims. The reasonableness of acting for the sake of other human beings as such, even those outside one's immediate political context, is made plausible in the above text by means of rhetorical questions. These are meant to elicit intuitions which approve of helping people in need (with the proviso that one has the necessary means to provide the help), even independently of assessments of the utility of the action (expressed with the word *chreia* in the account) or the worth (*axia*) of the recipient of the virtuous action. Providing the basic help needed for sustenance to someone who is in great need or showing the way to someone who is lost can be regarded as widely accepted injunctions in Greek society, which in the account of Didymus receive a philosophical justification. Thus, the basic moral commitment that arises from these examples is that one ought to help those in need of assistance, when one can do so at little or no cost to oneself, even without the expectation that the act is going to be reciprocated by the recipient of the deed. Such an attitude is characteristic of the virtue of 'love of humanity' (*philanthrōpia*). By contrast, the virtue of 'beneficence' (*euergesia*) is acted on the implicit assumption that the beneficiary recognises the beneficence done and is expected to show gratitude to the beneficent.

The material provided by both Antiochus and Didymus offers important evidence on the way those later Peripatetics integrated the 'philanthropic' virtue into the list of the other Aristotelian virtues, with a view to updating Aristotle's theory. The new

---

[19] See for example the remark in Didymus *ap.* Stobaeus *Selections* 2 121.21–22 Wachsmuth that 'the choiceworthy for its own sake is much more obvious when it is directed towards intimate friends': πολὺ μᾶλλον πρὸς τοὺς ἐν συνηθείᾳ φίλους τὸ δι' αὐθ'αἱρετὸν φανερώτερον.

importance assigned to *philanthrōpia* seems to correspond (and provide an alternative) to Stoic ideas on the 'common fellowship' of humanity, which were, like in the case of Antiochus and Didymus, connected to natural appropriation. Thus, Porphyry attests that the Stoics viewed *oikeiōsis* as the starting-point of justice.[20] The Stoic account of *On Ends* 3 reflects also an attempt to accommodate the notion of *oikeiōsis* into the discussion of both the relationship of parents with their children and one's relationship to humanity as a whole. Thus, Cato attests that for the Stoics it is important to realise that parental love towards one's offspring arises naturally and that it constitutes the principle (*initium*) of the 'common association of the human race' (*communem humani generis societatem*).[21] Parental love is in this case justified as being embedded in the rational structure of the cosmos and as guaranteeing human survival.[22] Cato at *On Ends* 3.63 is further led to the conception of a universal fellowship with other human beings, based on the idea of a 'common natural appropriation' (*communis hominum inter homines naturalis commendatio*).[23] This is shown to be based explicitly on the common possession of reason, and is understood along the lines of civil and legal bonds.[24] Thus alongside the idea of a 'common humanity' we find the view that the universe is a single city and state shared by human beings and gods (*communem urbem et civitatem hominum et deorum*) and governed by a rational divine will.[25] Such views

---

[20] Porphyry *On Abstinence* 3.19: τὴν δὲ οἰκείωσιν ἀρχὴν τίθενται δικαιοσύνης οἱ ἀπὸ Ζήνωνος. Nowhere is the idea of οἰκείωσις ascribed *specifically* to Zeno; the expression οἱ ἀπὸ Ζήνωνος here need not mean anything more than 'the Stoics'.

[21] *On Ends* 3.62: *pertinere autem ad rem arbitrantur intellegi natura fieri ut liberi a parentibus amentur; a quo initio profectam communem humani generis societatem persequimur.*

[22] *Ibid.* 3.62: *neque vero haec inter se congruere possent, ut natura et procreari vellet et diligi procreatos non curaret.* Cf. Lee (2002) 117.

[23] For the Stoic understanding of how *oikeiōsis* grounds sociability, cf. Schofield (2012a) 178 and Gill (2016) 238–39.

[24] See *On the Nature of the Gods* 2.78, where Cicero uses the word *conciliatio*, translating the Greek οἰκείωσις: *nec solum animantes sed etiam rationis compotes inter seque quasi civili conciliatione et societate coniunctos.* Cf. *On Appropriate Actions* 1.149. On the emphasis on justice and city in Stoic theory with reference to a relevant syllogism by Cleanthes, see e.g. Stobaeus *Selections* 2 103.12-23 Wachsmuth = *SVF* 1.587.

[25] See *On Ends* 3.64: *mundum autem censent regi numine deorum eumque esse quasi communem urbem et civitatem hominum et deorum, et unum quemque nostrum eius*

show the metaphysical and cosmological premises of the Stoic idea of a common fellowship of human beings. They point, however, also to potential tensions in Stoic theory: the political model of humanity as sharing a single *cosmopolis* points to an egalitarian, impartial model of association, which does not seem to allow for a variety of intensity in the manifestation of justice, as when allowing special duties of justice between parents and offspring. In line with this, testimonies from Zeno's *Republic* suggest that the only relevant difference from the point of view of justice is that between wise man and fool, all other distinctions, such as the one between relatives and strangers, being arbitrary and morally irrelevant.[26]

Later Stoics seem to have granted more importance to the way our moral concern is manifested in diverse relationships. Suggestive of this is that the section of Didymus' account containing examples of appropriate actions towards humanity as a whole finds important parallels in Cicero's *On Appropriate Actions* 1, which relies on Panaetius and his treatise 'On Appropriate Action' (*Peri kathēkontos*) for much of its content. There, we encounter the view that one should supply even to a stranger something out of one's own abundance when that does not bring about harm for oneself; one of the examples provided is showing the way to someone who is lost, which is identical to one of the examples of *philanthrōpia* provided by Didymus.[27] Furthermore,

---

> *mundi esse partem; ex quo illud natura consequi ut communem utilitatem nostrae anteponamus.*

[26] See Diogenes Laertius *Lives of Eminent Philosophers* 7.33: πάλιν ἐν τῇ Πολιτείᾳ παριστάντα (sc. τὸν Ζήνωνα) πολίτας καὶ φίλους καὶ οἰκείους καὶ ἐλευθέρους τοὺς σπουδαίους μόνον, ὥστε τοῖς στωικοῖς οἱ γονεῖς καὶ τὰ τέκνα ἐχθροί· οὐ γάρ εἰσι σοφοί.

[27] See *On Appropriate Actions* 1.51–52: *ac latissime quidem patens hominibus inter ipsos, omnibus inter omnes societas haec est. In qua omnium rerum, quas ad communem hominum usum natura genuit, est servanda communitas, ⌊⌊ut quae descripta sunt legibus et iure civili, haec ita teneantur, †ut sit constitutum e quibus ipsis, cetera sic observentur,⌋⌋ ut in Graecorum proverbio est, amicorum esse communia omnia. Omnium autem communia hominum videntur ea, quae sunt generis eius, quod ab Ennio positum in una re transferri in permultas potest: 'Homo qui erranti comiter monstrat viam, Quasi lumen de suo lumine accendat facit. Nihilo minus ipsi lucet, cum illi accenderit.' Una ex re satis praecipit, ut quidquid sine detrimento commodari possit, id tribuatur vel ignoto. Ex quo illa communia: non prohibere aqua profluente, pati ab igne ignem capere, si qui velit, consilium fidele deliberanti dare, quae sunt iis utilia, qui accipiunt, danti non molesta. Quare et his utendum est et semper aliquid ad communem utilitatem afferendum. Sed quoniam copiae parvae singulorum sunt, eorum autem, qui his egeant, infinita est multitudo, vulgaris liberalitas referenda*

the second-century AD Stoic Hierocles, in a passage from a work *On Appropriate Actions*, presents an image of concentric circles representing the individual's inclusion into different relationships, which is strongly reminiscent of both Antiochus' and Didymus' presentation of successive types of *philia*.[28] The different circles extend from the centre (which is said to represent one's relationship with oneself) outwards and ultimately encompass humanity as whole.[29] Hierocles defends the view that one should strive, by making use of one's reason, to 'contract' the circles inwards and thus aim at the 'assimilation' (*exomoiōsis*) of the distance between oneself and others.[30] It is questionable, however, whether the assimilation that Hierocles refers to may be achieved in this way.[31]

That the Stoics were criticised on similar grounds already in antiquity is suggested by some remarks in an anonymous commentary on Plato's *Theaetetus*,[32] which, if we follow suggestions by some scholars,[33] may belong to the late first century BCE.[34] There, Anonymous, in his attempt to offer a 'correct' interpretation of Plato,[35] attacks the idea that there is an equal *oikeiōsis*

est ad illum Ennii *finem* 'nihilo minus ipsi lucet', ut facultas sit, qua in nostros simus *liberales*. Cf. the commentary at Dyck (1996): 170.

[28] Stobaeus *Selections* 4 671.3–673.11 Hense = LS 57G.

[29] *Ibid*. 671.24–672.2 Hense: ὁ δ' ἐξωτάτω καὶ μέγιστος περιέχων τε πάντας τοὺς κύκλους ὁ τοῦ παντὸς ἀνθρώπων γένους.

[30] *Ibid*. 672.17–673.1 Hense: ἀφαιρήσεται μὲν γάρ τι τῆς εὐνοίας τὸ καθ' αἷμα διάστημα πλέον ὄν· ἡμῖν δ' ὅμως σπουδαστέα περὶ τὴν ἐξομοίωσίν ἐστιν. ἥκοι μὲν γὰρ ἂν εἰς τὸ μέτριον, εἰ διὰ τῆς ἡμετέρας αὐτῶν ἐνστάσεως ἐπιτεμνόμεθα τὸ μῆκος τῆς πρὸς ἕκαστον τὸ πρόσωπον σχέσεως.

[31] As Annas (1993) 270 notes, Hierocles' scheme seems to result only 'in weak partiality, not in impartiality'. For a criticism of Hierocles' model of 'extended egoism', see also McCabe (2005) 424–26.

[32] Anonymous On Plato's *Theaetetus* col. 5.18–6.31 = LS 57H.

[33] Tarrant (1985) 67–69 and Sedley (1997) 117.

[34] Cf. Bastianini and Sedley (1995) 256. In col. 6.31 of the commentary there is reference to 'the people from the Academy' (οἱ ἐξ Ἀκαδημείας); those can with some security be identified with the New Academics and the circle of Carneades, since the example of the shipwreck employed is associated with Carneades in Cicero's *On the Republic* 3.30 and was addressed by Hecato according to *On Appropriate Actions* 3.90. As Sedley (1997) 118 notes, the anonymous commentator 'is still acutely conscious of the preceding tradition of Academic scepticism, and fights hard to recapture the authority of Plato from the sceptical camp'. For additional arguments for an early dating, see Tarrant (1985) 67–68.

[35] Part of the strategy of the commentator is also to show that the notion of οἰκείωσις was already introduced by Socrates and some sophists in Plato, see Anonymous On Plato's *Theaetetus* col. 7.20–25.

towards all human beings: addressing those who derive justice from *oikeiōsis*, i.e. the Stoics, he claims that, in order for justice to be guaranteed, the degree of *oikeiōsis* to oneself and to all other human beings, or, as it is put there, to the 'furthest Mysian', should be equal (col. 5.24–34). It is clear, however, it is further argued (col. 5.34–36), that by virtue of the self-evident (*enargeia*) and self-awareness (*synaisthēsis*) this is not the case, and that, thus, *oikeiōsis* admits of different degrees.[36] Anonymous uses as an additional argument against the Stoics the contention that, in case it is conceded that *oikeiōsis* admits of degrees, that would leave *philanthrōpia* intact, but not any longer justice (col. 6.17–20).[37] This may suggest that the anonymous commentator has in mind a dialectical context in which the Stoic notion of justice and the idea of *philanthrōpia* were juxtaposed. One may speculate that he could have drawn for the latter view on the Peripatetic accounts of Antiochus or Didymus.

It transpires from the above discussion that Antiochus (and Didymus, for that matter) were under the influence of Stoic ideas, when formulating their views on the way *oikeiōsis* is manifested when social virtues are fully developed. The passages cited by the Antiochean account contain some clear Stoic echoes; as it was shown, the idea of a 'common fellowship' of humanity, which Antiochus connects with *philanthrōpia*, was forcefully defended by the Stoics and embedded into their conception of a 'cosmic city'. Still, the way Antiochus explains the way justice is structured around diverse associations of *philia* is also compatible with an Aristotelian framework. Piso even refers to the Aristotelian dictum that humans are 'by nature political animals' at *On Ends* 5.66 to show his Aristotelian/Peripatetic credentials; the Aristotelian expression of humans as 'by nature political' (*physei politikon*)[38] animals is conveyed here as 'the innate civic and social character' (*ingenitum quasi civile atque populare*) of human nature, showing the way in which the original

---

[36] Anonymous On Plato's *Theaetetus* col. 5.22–24: ἐπιτείν]εται γὰρ καὶ ἀ[νίετ]α[ι] ἡ οἰκείωσις.

[37] εἰ δὲ καὶ α[ὐτ]οὶ φήσου|σι ἐπιτεί[ν]εσθα[ι] τὴν |οἰκείω[σιν, ἔσ]ται μὲν | φιλανθρ[ωπί]α.

[38] See *Politics* 1.1253a2–3: ὁ ἄνθρωπος φύσει πολιτικὸν ζῷον. Cf. *Nicomachean Ethics* 1.1097b11.

Aristotelian view is embedded into the Antiochean argument from natural appropriation. Political association in Aristotle contains non-political forms of *philia*, as the ones found within the household between husband and wife, and between parents and children, the types of *philia* which are presented at the start of Antiochus' account of justice.[39] Antiochus could even have found credentials for a defence of a universal *philanthrōpia* (translated by Cicero as *caritas generis humani*) in a passage belonging to the general observations (or *endoxa*) on *philia* at the beginning of Book 8 of *Nicomachean Ethics*.[40] The passage reads as follows:

> Again, parent seems by nature to feel love for offspring and offspring for parent, not only among humans but among birds and among most animals; it is felt mutually by members of the same race, and especially by human beings, whence we praise lovers of humanity [φιλανθρώπους]. We may see even in our travels how related and dear [οἰκεῖον (...) καὶ φίλον] every human being is to every other. (*Nicomachean Ethics* 8.1155a16–22)[41]

Without offering a neat classification of the types of *philia* under consideration, the Aristotelian passage above begins with a reference to the natural character of the reciprocal love between parents and children. Aristotle adds that the same applies to animals in relationship to their offspring and to the relationship between animals of the same species. This *philia* among members of the same species is said to apply 'especially among human beings'. The last sentence gives an empirical justification to this type of *philia*: there we find the idea of the *oikeion* as disconnected from literal kinship and referring to random encounters outside the civic context—the use of the word *planais* here is suggestive of the fact that Aristotle does not have in mind an institutionalised type of guest-friendship, i.e. *xenia*. Further, the direct analogy between

---

[39] See e.g. *Politics* 1.1253b1–8.
[40] For the Platonic background to this notion, see Socrates' portrayal as φιλάνθρωπος, i.e. as someone who freely and willingly engages in discussion with all people in *Euthyphro* 3d6–8: ἐγὼ δὲ φοβοῦμαι μὴ ὑπὸ φιλανθρωπίας δοκῶ αὐτοῖς ὅτιπερ ἔχω ἐκκεχυμένως παντὶ ἀνδρὶ λέγειν.
[41] φύσει τ' ἐνυπάρχειν ἔοικε (sc. φιλία) πρὸς τὸ γεγεννημένον τῷ γεννήσαντι καὶ πρὸς τὸ γεννῆσαν τῷ γεννηθέντι, οὐ μόνον ἐν ἀνθρώποις ἀλλὰ καὶ ἐν ὄρνισι καὶ τοῖς πλείστοις τῶν ζῴων, καὶ τοῖς ὁμοεθνέσι πρὸς ἄλληλα, καὶ μάλιστα τοῖς ἀνθρώποις, ὅθεν τοὺς φιλανθρώπους ἐπαινοῦμεν. ἴδοι δ' ἄν τις καὶ ἐν ταῖς πλάναις ὡς οἰκεῖον ἅπας ἄνθρωπος ἀνθρώπῳ καὶ φίλον.

animal and human behaviour with regard to attitudes towards their offspring and members of the same species underlines the natural foundation of this type of *philia*. It is striking, however, that whereas the *philia* between parents and children receives an extensive analysis in *Nicomachean Ethics* 8–9, the same is not the case for the *philia* towards other human beings as such, which is introduced in the above passage.[42]

Returning to the Antiochean views on justice, we may say that they can be taken to reflect a systematic scheme of Aristotelian types of *philia,* which includes the main human associations into a comprehensive scheme; similar comprehensive schemes can be found in the later Stoics Panaetius and Hierocles. Furthermore, the Antiochean account seems to reflect the key Aristotelian idea that justice 'accompanies' *philia;*[43] accordingly, Piso grants in his account of justice moral significance to partial claims, such as the ones raised by family ties.

---

[42] The only other instance where Aristotle refers to such a type of *philia* in his ethics is in the striking reference in *Nicomachean Ethics* 8.1161b5–6 that there can be a *philia* between master and slave to the extent that the latter is recognised as a fellow-human being, and not *qua* slave: ᾗ μὲν οὖν δοῦλος, οὐκ ἔστι φιλία πρὸς αὐτόν, ᾗ δ' ἄνθρωπος.

[43] See e.g. *Nicomachean Ethics* 8.1159b25–26: ἔοικε δέ, καθάπερ ἐν ἀρχῇ εἴρηται, περὶ ταὐτὰ καὶ ἐν τοῖς αὐτοῖς εἶναι ἥ τε φιλία καὶ τὸ δίκαιον and *ibid.* 1160a7–8: αὔξεσθαι δὲ πέφυκεν ἅμα τῇ φιλίᾳ καὶ τὸ δίκαιον, ὡς ἐν τοῖς αὐτοῖς ὄντα καὶ ἐπ' ἴσον διήκοντα.

8

THE ANTIOCHEAN CONCEPTION OF THE HAPPY LIFE

The Best Form of Life (*Bios*)

Piso's discussion of our *oikeiōsis* towards activity (*actio*) led to the identification of three major human activities: the (virtuous) pursuit of a private life, public engagement and the exercise of theoretical science. Accordingly, these three activities come up to build the content of Antiochus' conception of a happy life, understood as a life characterised by virtuous activity. The relevant text contains an evaluative sequence whereby theoretical activity comes first, as the most honourable type of activity, being followed by political and private virtuous action:[1]

It is evident then that we are born to be active [*ad agendum esse natos*]. There are many kinds of activity, however, so that one might lose sight of the highest ones amidst the less important.[2] As to the most important, it is my view and that of the thinkers whose system I am discussing that these are: the contemplation and knowledge of heavenly things, and of those which are by nature hidden and obscure and which our intellect can explore [*consideratio cognitioque rerum caelestium et earum quas a natura occultatas et latentes indagare ratio potest*]; then the administration of public affairs, or knowledge of its theory [*rerum publicarum administratio aut administrandi scientia*]; and lastly prudent, temperate, brave and just reasoning, and the rest of the virtues and the actions that are in accordance with them [*prudens, temperata, fortis, iusta ratio reliquaeque virtutes et actiones virtutibus congruentes*]. Those are called by the one word 'morality' [*honesta*]; when we are already mature, we are led to the knowledge and practice of them by nature's own guidance. (*On Ends* 5.58)

Contemplation and knowledge of physical phenomena and first principles appears in the above passage as the highest activity and, we may assume, it is considered the one which makes the biggest

---

[1] A parallel can be found in Didymus' summary of Peripatetic ethics, where it is stated that the βίος is measured by political, social and contemplative actions, see Stobaeus *Selections* 2 125.19–21 Wachsmuth: παραμετρεῖσθαι γὰρ τὸν βίον ταῖς πολιτικαῖς καὶ ταῖς κοινωνικαῖς πράξεσι καὶ ταῖς θεωρητικαῖς.

[2] Here, following manuscript S, I read *maiora minoribus* instead of *minora maioribus*.

contribution to happiness. Piso, as already suggested, aims with the example of the happiest possible life of the wise men on the Isles of the Blest at promoting *theōria* as an 'immortal' activity on earth, and accordingly makes reference three times in his account to the god-like character of human *nous*.[3] Furthermore, in his introductory remarks, he presents the similarity of theoretical activity to the activity of the divine as the main reason why the Peripatetics (i.e. both Aristotle and Theophrastus) thought that a life devoted to contemplation and study is the most worthy of the wise man.[4] The theme of the happiest possible life devoted to contemplation was explored, as Piso attests, in a 'glorious' treatise:[5]

> However, those men (sc. Aristotle and Theophrastus) gave the best approval to a quiet plan of living, devoted to the contemplation and knowledge of things [*quieta, in contemplatione et cognitione posita rerum*]. Since this was most similar to the life of gods, it seemed most worthy of the wise man [*quae quia deorum erat vitae simillima, sapiente visa est dignissima*]. And concerning these matters their treatise is both brilliant and glorious. (*On Ends* 5.11)

The above passage may well be an allusion to the last chapters of the *Nicomachean Ethics*. The superiority of a theoretical life, but also the difficulty for humans, as embodied beings, of experiencing it fully, features most prominently in Aristotle's *Nicomachean Ethics* 10.7, a text full of Platonic overtones on *theōria* and its association with the divine.[6] There, it is stated that a life devoted exclusively to *theōria* would be superior to a human one, since someone will live it not insofar as he is a human being but insofar as he has some divine element in him.[7] Such a life is further described in the same chapter as a divine life when compared to

---

[3] *On Ends* 5.38: *quod ex ratione gignuntur, qua nihil est in homine divinius*; 5.57: *optimaque parte hominis, quae in nobis divina ducenda est, ingenii et mentis acie fruuntur.*

[4] This seems to reflect *Nicomachean Ethics* 10.1178b21–23: ὥστε ἡ τοῦ θεοῦ ἐνέργεια, μακαριότητι διαφέρουσα, θεωρητικὴ ἂν εἴη· καὶ τῶν ἀνθρωπίνων δὴ ἡ ταύτῃ συγγενεστάτη εὐδαιμονικωτάτη.

[5] The *oratio* alluded to in this passage may well be a work of the protreptic genre, see Düring (1961) 167 or the work of Theophrastus Περὶ τῆς θείας εὐδαιμονίας referred to in Diogenes Laertius *Lives of Eminent Philosophers* 5.49.

[6] The connection between the advocacy of the theoretical life in *Nicomachean Ethics* 10 and the *Timaeus* is discussed by Sedley (1999) 324–28.

[7] *Nicomachean Ethics* 10.1177b26–28.

a human life, in the same way as *nous* is something divine when compared to the composite human being.[8] This makes the pursuit of a contemplative life an ideal,[9] but at the same time a paradox for humans, who would need to transcend their own human traits in order to achieve complete happiness consisting in contemplation.[10] Indeed Aristotle states that to the extent that one is a human being and lives in a community he or she will choose the actions in accordance with the (practical) virtues and will need them in order to live a human life (*anthrōpeuesthai*).[11]

In line with these latter ideas, Antiochus does not defend the view that *theōria* should be the *exclusive* component of a happy human life. Whereas he does not question the primacy of theoretical activity among the other forms of activity, he incorporates it into an inclusive ideal of human life, which includes both *theōria* and *praxis*. Perhaps this was yet another point where Antiochus could have found fundamental agreement between the Academy and the Peripatos: leaving aside the objects of Platonic contemplation (which are not restricted to the realm of the natural world) Antiochus' views could also reflect the Platonic admission that the philosopher who has made the ascent to the world of Ideas could have lived a happier life if he did not have to return to the 'cave' of ordinary human affairs.[12] Although, such a life would have been indeed happier, moral duty (or perhaps the necessity to guarantee the best arrangement in the polis) forces the philosopher to participate in politics after his philosophical education is completed. Thus, as depicted in *Republic* 540a–b,[13] the life of

---

[8] *Ibid.* 1177b28–31.

[9] The ideal state of such a life is expressed through the use of the superlative εὐδαιμονέστατος in *ibid.* 1178a8 and εὐδαιμονικωτάτη in *ibid.* 1178b23.

[10] Cf. also *ibid.* 10.1178a20–22 where, contrary to the life in accordance with the 'practical' virtues, life in accordance with *nous* is called not human but 'separated' (κεχωρισμένη).

[11] *Ibid.* 1178b5–7: ᾗ δ᾽ ἄνθρωπός ἐστι καὶ πλείοσι συζῇ, αἱρεῖται τὰ κατὰ τὴν ἀρετὴν πράττειν· δεήσεται οὖν τῶν τοιούτων πρὸς τὸ ἀνθρωπεύεσθαι.

[12] This is expressed as a question on the part of Glaucon to Socrates in *Republic* 519d: ἔπειτ᾽, ἔφη, ἀδικήσομεν αὐτούς, καὶ ποιήσομεν χεῖρον ζῆν, δυνατὸν αὐτοῖς ν ἄμεινον.

[13] γενομένων δὲ πεντηκοντουτῶν τοὺς διασωθέντας καὶ ἀριστεύσαντας πάντα πάντῃ ἐν ἔργοις τε καὶ ἐπιστήμαις πρὸς τέλος ἤδη ἀκτέον, καὶ ἀναγκαστέον ἀνακλίναντας τὴν τῆς ψυχῆς αὐγὴν εἰς αὐτὸ ἀποβλέψαι τὸ πᾶσι φῶς παρέχον, καὶ ἰδόντας τὸ ἀγαθὸν αὐτό, παραδείγματι χρωμένους ἐκείνῳ, καὶ πόλιν καὶ ἰδιώτας καὶ ἑαυτοὺς κοσμεῖν τὸν ἐπίλοιπον βίον ἐν μέρει ἑκάστους, τὸ μὲν πολὺ πρὸς φιλοσοφίᾳ διατρίβοντας, ὅταν δὲ τὸ μέρος ἥκῃ, πρὸς πολιτικοῖς ἐπιταλαιπωροῦντας καὶ ἄρχοντας ἑκάστους τῆς πόλεως ἕνεκα, οὐχ ὡς

philosopher–kings after the age of fifty consists in an *alternation* between preoccupation with philosophy and assuming office in the city.

An inclusive ideal of life is defended in Antiochus' account as well, where following the contemplative activity comes, as second in order, the knowledge and administration of public affairs.[14] Lastly, below political activity, comes virtuous reasoning and actions in accordance with the virtues. According to this last distinction, every virtuous action has two aspects, *cognitio* and *usus* (equal to the Greek terms *gnōsis* and *chrēsis*): the emphasis on the exercise of virtue as opposed to mere knowledge restates the practical aim of ethics, in accordance with Aristotelian theory.[15] Theoretical activity and knowledge are thus part of a life aiming at *eudaimonia*, but not the sole components of *eudaimonia*, as some of the Aristotelian statements in *Nicomachean Ethics* 10.7 seem to suggest.[16] This is also confirmed by Varro who, according to a testimony of Augustine,[17] asserted on the authority of Antiochus (*auctore Antiocho*) that of the three kinds of life, the theoretical, the practical and the 'mixed' one (*quod ex utroque compositum est*), the Old Academics preferred the third (*hoc tertium sibi placere adseverant*).[18]

The Antiochean views on the inclusive character of the happy life correspond to the idea of a 'composite life' (*synthetos bios*), which is presented in Didymus' epitome of Peripatetic ethics, in

---

καλόν τι ἀλλ' ὡς ἀναγκαῖον πράττοντας, καὶ οὕτως ἄλλους ἀεὶ παιδεύσαντας τοιούτους, ἀντικαταλιπόντας τῆς πόλεως φύλακας, εἰς μακάρων νήσους ἀπιόντας οἰκεῖν.

[14] In Aristotle political action falls under the activity of the practical virtues, see *Nicomachean Ethics* 10.1177b6–7.

[15] Cf. *Nicomachean Ethics* 10.1179b2–4.

[16] At *Nicomachean Ethics* 10.1177a16–7 complete happiness seems to be identified *simpliciter* with the activity of *nous*. It is telling that at *ibid.* 10.1177b1ff. Aristotle constructs an opposition between θεωρία and πρᾶξις by presenting political activity as unleisured and not choice worthy for its own sake but only for the achievement of a further result (e.g. 1177b16–18). However, a more conciliatory picture is drawn at Aristotle's *Politics* 7.1–3. The arguments there, rather than imposing a hierarchy on the two competing kinds of lives, aim at including both theoretical and practical actions in the conception of an ideal virtuous life.

[17] *City of God* 19.3.

[18] That Antiochus commended not only the theoretical but also the practical life may be also suggested by the fact that, according to Plutarch *Life of Cicero* 4.3, he encouraged Cicero to take up public office.

the section on forms of life (*peri biōn*) (143.24–145.10), as a doctrine of the Peripatos. Didymus attempts there to do justice to the natural dispositions of human beings towards both theoretical and practical pursuits.[19] As already suggested,[20] although the text is not dependent directly upon Antiochus, it conveys in some key points the same version of Peripatetic ethics as can be discerned in Piso's account in *On Ends* 5. In the part of the summary dealing with the question of the *bios*, the expression 'composed out of both' (*synthetos eks amphoin*) appears alongside the 'theoretical' and the 'practical',[21] designating a life which combines both political and theoretical activities.[22] Although this part of the summary is extremely compressed, it transpires that Didymus defended the ideal of a virtuous agent who will both 'do and contemplate fine things'. In case the wise man is prohibited by circumstances from doing both, it is argued that his life will be characterised by *alternate* periods of devotion to politics and intellectual activity. The former, beyond the traditional role of law-giving, involves ruling or living in the court of a king, whereas the latter is said here also to take the form of paid teaching. The relevant text reads as follows:

The virtuous man will choose a life that involves virtue, whether as a ruler himself, if the circumstances promote him to that status, or if he has to live in the company of a king, or even be a legislator or in any other way involved in politics. If nothing of the above befalls him he will turn to the way of life of the common citizen or to the contemplative life, or to teaching, which lies in the middle. For he will prefer both to do and contemplate fine things [καὶ πράττειν καὶ θεωρεῖν τὰ καλά]. In case he is hindered by circumstances from occupying himself with both, he will become engaged in one of the two, showing a preference for the contemplative life, but engaging himself also in political activities because of his social character [προτιμῶντα μὲν τὸν θεωρητικὸν βίον,

---

[19] This corresponds to the conception of perfect virtue as a 'composite' one (*synthetos*) consisting of all three kinds of activities: theoretical, practical and ethical ones. Such a conception of virtue is ascribed to Aristotle in Stobaeus *Selections* 2 51.1–5 Wachsmuth: ἡ δ᾽ ἀρετὴ ἕξις ἡ βελτίστη ψυχῆς· 'τελεία' δὲ τριχῶς, καὶ γὰρ ἡ σύνθετος ἐκ τῶν θεωρητικῶν καὶ πρακτικῶν καὶ ἠθικῶν (τρία γὰρ ὑποτίθεται γένη), ἣν ἂν εἴποις ἀρετὴν κατὰ σύνθεσιν.

[20] See Introduction, *supra*.

[21] Didymus *ap.* Stobaeus *Selections* 2 144.16–17 Wachsmuth: βίων δὲ τριττὰς ἰδέας εἶναι, πρακτικόν, θεωρητικόν, σύνθετον ἐξ ἀμφοῖν.

[22] Cf. *ibid.* 125.19–21 Wachsmuth: παραμετρεῖσθαι γὰρ τὸν βίον ταῖς πολιτικαῖς καὶ ταῖς κοινωνικαῖς πράξεσι καὶ ταῖς θεωρητικαῖς.

διὰ δὲ τὸ κοινωνικὸν ἐπὶ τὰς πολιτικὰς ὁρμῶντα πράξεις]. (Didymus *ap.* Stobaeus *Selections* 2 143.24–144.8 Wachsmuth)

We may infer from the text above that Didymus, like Antiochus, attributed to the Peripatos the view that *theōria* is the highest human activity, but at the same time held that it forms part of an inclusive way of life which acknowledges the fundamental social nature of human beings as well, and, concomitantly, the supreme value of political engagement and of the practical virtues more generally.[23]

The Components of the *Telos*

It transpires from the above that virtuous activity, conceived either as activity of the theoretical or the practical virtues, is the main constituent of the happy life. A further question concerns, however, the issue whether virtuous activity is sufficient to guarantee the happy life. An extreme view proposed by the Stoic school in the Hellenistic period suggested that virtue guarantees happiness[24] and that all conditions and circumstances within which action takes place (including even one's bodily condition) are 'indifferent' (*adiaphora*) with regard to the attainment of happiness. Following this, the Stoics maintained that the sage will be to the highest degree happy even 'on the rack'.[25] Philosophers who attempted to offer a reconstruction of the views of the 'ancients', like Antiochus and Didymus, were confronted with the challenge to offer the position of the old tradition on the issue of the sufficiency of virtue for happiness and on the role that bodily or external circumstances play for the attainment of *eudaimonia*. This was particularly challenging because no coherent view is expressed on this issue either in the writings of Plato or in the surviving works of Aristotle.

---

[23] Notice also the idea at Didymus *ap.* Stobaeus *Selections* 2 125.21–2 Wachsmuth that virtue, according to the Peripatetics, is not selfish (φίλαυτον) but social and political (κοινωνικὴν καὶ πολιτικήν).

[24] See *SVF* 3.49–67.

[25] See e.g. *On Ends* 3.42, 5.84. Aristotle explicitly rejects the Stoic view at *Nicomachean Ethics* 7.1153b19–21: οἱ δὲ τὸν τροχιζόμενον καὶ τὸν δυστυχίαις μεγάλαις περιπίπτοντα εὐδαίμονα φάσκοντες εἶναι, ἐὰν ᾖ ἀγαθός, ἢ ἑκόντες ἢ ἄκοντες οὐδὲν λέγουσιν.

The views expressed in some Platonic dialogues seem to point to the direction that the Stoics later followed, namely the idea that virtue is on its own (under any circumstances) sufficient for happiness. Cicero himself at *Tusculan Disputations* 5.34, perhaps echoing Antiochean views, traces the source of the Stoic thesis for the self-sufficiency of virtue for a happy life back to Platonic texts using citations from the *Gorgias* (470d–471a) and the *Menexenus* (247e–248a).[26] However, whereas in some passages Plato seems to defend the thesis that virtue is on its own sufficient for happiness,[27] in other passages he puts forward the view that the happy life is dependent upon a variety of goods which include, beyond virtue, bodily and external things as well.[28]

Aristotle's discussion of *eudaimonia* in *Nicomachean Ethics* I seems also to pull into different directions. On the one hand Aristotle includes into the discussion 'reputable opinions' (*endoxa*) which clearly stress the role of external and bodily goods for the happy life. Thus, Aristotle claims that no one considers happy someone who suffers misfortunes as bad as Priam's.[29] Elsewhere in the same book, it is suggested that noble actions are made possible, or at least facilitated, by external conditions; the latter either act as 'tools' for the fulfilment of good actions, or their absence 'puts a stain' on our happiness, something that suggests that certain external goods have an

---

[26] *Tusculan Disputations* 5.34: *et, si Zeno Citieus, advena quidam et ignobilis verborum opifex, insinuasse se in antiquam philosophiam videtur, huius sententiae gravitas a Platonis auctoritate repetatur.* The remarks against Zeno which feature in this passage suggest that it is part of an attempt to downgrade the originality of the Stoic school in favour of the ancient tradition (for this Antiochean strategy, see Chapter 2, *supra*). Cf. also the remarks of the 'sceptic' Cicero at *On Ends* 5.84: *cupit enim dicere nihil posse ad beatam vitam deesse sapienti. Honesta oratio, Socratica, Platonis etiam.*

[27] Cf. also *Crito* 48b3–10: ἀλλ', ὦ θαυμάσιε, οὗτός τε ὁ λόγος ὃν διεληλύθαμεν ἔμοιγε δοκεῖ ἔτι ὅμοιος εἶναι καὶ πρότερον·καὶ τόνδε δὲ αὖ σκόπει εἰ ἔτι μένει ἡμῖν ἢ οὔ, ὅτι οὐ τὸ ζῆν περὶ πλείστου ποιητέον ἀλλὰ τὸ εὖ ζῆν.- Ἀλλὰ μένει.-Τὸ δὲ εὖ καὶ καλῶς καὶ δικαίως ὅτι ταὐτόν ἐστιν, μένει ἢ οὐ μένει;- Μένει.

[28] See, for example, *Laws* 1.631b–d, which refers to the 'human' and 'divine goods' which comprise happiness; the former encompass health, beauty, strength and wealth, whereas the latter the leading goods of the soul's virtues.

[29] *Nicomachean Ethics* 1.1100a5–9: πολλαὶ γὰρ μεταβολαὶ γίνονται καὶ παντοῖαι τύχαι κατὰ τὸν βίον, καὶ ἐνδέχεται τὸν μάλιστ' εὐθηνοῦντα μεγάλαις συμφοραῖς περιπεσεῖν ἐπὶ γήρως, καθάπερ ἐν τοῖς Τρωικοῖς περὶ Πριάμου μυθεύεται·τὸν δὲ τοιαύταις χρησάμενον τύχαις καὶ τελευτήσαντα ἀθλίως οὐδεὶς εὐδαιμονίζει.

intrinsic value.[30] This results in calling 'happy' the one who is active according to perfect virtue and has a sufficient supply of external goods during a complete lifetime, this being the closest one gets to finding a *telos* formulation in Aristotle.[31] Still, Aristotle stresses in the same account that virtuous activity is the dominant constituent of the happy life,[32] suggesting that the contribution that virtue makes to happiness should not be put on a par with that of other goods. Aristotle's discussion, however, does not sufficiently determine how to understand the dominant role of virtuous action for the attainment of a happy life, while granting a contributory role to conditions which lie outside the virtuous activity itself, like people with whom we may interact, our bodily condition, and external means of subsistence.[33]

In his attempt to offer the position of the Old Academy on the issue of the sufficiency of virtue for the happy life, Antiochus makes use of the different categories of goods that he presents in his account as inherently desirable by means of *oikeiōsis*. These comprise the goods of the soul, namely the virtues, the goods of the body (e.g. health, freedom from pain and strength) and external goods, in particular other human beings who are the recipients of

---

[30] *Ibid.* 1.1099a31–b6: φαίνεται δ' ὅμως καὶ τῶν ἐκτὸς ἀγαθῶν προσδεομένη, καθάπερ εἴπομεν· ἀδύνατον γὰρ ἢ οὐ ῥᾴδιον τὰ καλὰ πράττειν ἀχορήγητον ὄντα. πολλὰ μὲν γὰρ πράττεται, καθάπερ δι' ὀργάνων, διὰ φίλων καὶ πλούτου καὶ πολιτικῆς δυνάμεως·ἐνίων δὲ τητώμενοι ῥυπαίνουσι τὸ μακάριον, οἷον εὐγενείας εὐτεκνίας κάλλους οὐ πάνυ γὰρ εὐδαιμονικὸς ὁ τὴν ἰδέαν παναίσχης ἢ δυσγενὴς ἢ μονώτης καὶ ἄτεκνος, ἔτι δ' ἴσως ἧττον, εἴ τῳ πάγκακοι παῖδες εἶεν ἢ φίλοι, ἢ ἀγαθοὶ ὄντες τεθνᾶσιν. Cf. *ibid.* 1099b25–28: συμφανὲς δ' ἐστὶ καὶ ἐκ τοῦ λόγου τὸ ζητούμενον εἴρηται γὰρ ψυχῆς ἐνέργεια κατ' ἀρετὴν ποιά τις. τῶν δὲ λοιπῶν ἀγαθῶν τὰ μὲν ὑπάρχειν ἀναγκαῖον, τὰ δὲ συνεργὰ καὶ χρήσιμα πέφυκεν ὀργανικῶς. Alternatively, an adequate supply of external goods is connected with the 'unimpeded' character of a happy life at *Nicomachean Ethics* 7.13 (1153b16–19); there, external goods are said to *enable* the activity in which happiness consists: οὐδεμία γὰρ ἐνέργεια τέλειος ἐμποδιζομένη, ἡ δ' εὐδαιμονία τῶν τελείων·διὸ προσδεῖται ὁ εὐδαίμων τῶν ἐν σώματι ἀγαθῶν καὶ τῶν ἐκτὸς καὶ τῆς τύχης, ὅπως μὴ ἐμποδίζηται ταῦτα.

[31] *Nicomachean Ethics* 1.1101a14–16.

[32] See e.g. *ibid* 1.1098b18–20 and *ibid.* 1.1102a5–6, whereby the chief good is identified with 'some activity of the soul in accordance with perfect virtue', but not with any other component of the happy life. For an explicit statement that 'activities in accordance with virtue' are primary (*kyriai*) for *eudaimonia*, see *ibid.* 1.1100b9–10: κύριαι δ' εἰσὶν αἱ κατ' ἀρετὴν ἐνέργειαι τῆς εὐδαιμονίας.

[33] Cf. Sharples (2010) 166. The tensions inherent in the Aristotelian discussion in *Nicomachean Ethics* 1 with regard to the different constituents of *eudaimonia* are well presented in Russell (2010) 144–56.

the social virtues (e.g. offspring, friends, fellow-citizens). He goes on to classify these goods into two categories: the goods of the soul/mind and the goods of the body come up to 'complete' the supreme good (*iis in quibus completur ... extremum*), whereas other human beings are deemed 'external' (*extrinsecus*) and are not regarded as constitutive of the happy life.[34]

The differentiation between goods which are constitutive of the *telos* and those which are not is based on Antiochus' conception of human nature as a composite of soul/mind and body. According to this understanding, the *telos* is conceived as the fulfilment of both aspects of human nature. Thus, at *On Ends* 5.26 Piso explains that what he means by a happy life is a life in accordance with human nature, whereby the latter has been perfected in all respects (*undique perfecta*) and lacks nothing (*nihil requirente*).[35] Accordingly, *eudaimonia* is explained at *On Ends* 5.37 as a life 'fully endowed with the excellences of soul and body'.[36] Although the soul/mind is shown to enjoy absolute pre-eminence, the body is deemed by Antiochus worthy to be part of the final end, even as an inferior aspect of human nature. This is meant to follow from our *oikeiōsis* towards the body and its parts shown in the way both children and adults avoid bodily conditions which are 'contrary to nature' and in the way all, even those who have reached virtue, experience fear of death. Antiochus' inclusion of the bodily aspect of human nature into the conception of the *telos* entailed an implicit critique

---

[34] *On Ends* 5.68: *ita fit ut duo genera propter se expetendorum reperiantur, unum quod est in iis in quibus completur illud extremum, quae sunt aut animi aut corporis; haec autem quae sunt extrinsecus, id est quae neque in animo insunt neque in corpore, ut amici, ut parentes, ut liberi, ut propinqui, ut ipsa patria, sunt illa quidem sua sponte cara, sed eodem in genere quo illa non sunt.*

[35] *Ibid.* 5.26: *ex quo intellegi debet homini id esse in bonis ultimum, secundum naturam vivere, quod ita interpretemur: vivere ex hominis natura undique perfecta et nihil requirente.* The two requirements of perfection (*teleion* in Greek) and self-sufficiency (what in Greek is rendered by the term *autarkeia*) reflect Antiochus' preoccupation with the Aristotelian criteria of *eudaimonia*. The finality criterion is fulfilled if happiness is choice worthy *on its own*, being the only thing that is desired for its own sake and never for the sake of something else, whereas the self-sufficiency criterion (*to autarkes*) implies the availability of all individual goods which constitute happiness. For the Aristotelian discussion of the two criteria of *eudaimonia*, see *Nicomachean Ethics* 1. 1097a15–97b21.

[36] *On Ends* 5.37: *ea enim vita expetitur quae sit animi corporisque expleta virtutibus, in eoque summum bonum poni necesse est, quandoquidem id tale esse debet ut rerum expetendarum sit extremum.*

of the Stoics. Thus, Antiochus wished to maintain, contrary to the Stoic thesis that one's bodily condition is, similarly to all other external factors, a mere 'indifferent' with regard to happiness, the view that one's survival and bodily well-being remains inherently valuable, even when one has reached wisdom, since it is an integral part of one's nature and not strictly speaking something external to it.

The peculiarity of the Antiochean position consists in the attempt to present the thesis about the inherent choice worthiness of one's bodily condition (due to the fact that the latter is part of one's nature) as compatible with the thesis that virtue is sufficient for happiness. According to the latter position, the exercise of virtue is both necessary and sufficient for a happy life. The rationale behind this seems to be that one can exercise the virtues of the mind, the most excellent part of oneself, under *all* circumstances,[37] even in cases of extreme adversity, such as illness and death. In the latter cases, for example, one can approach such circumstances with courage. Furthermore, one can as a result of virtue decide to sacrifice oneself and one's bodily integrity. Deciding to do so from the point of view of the virtuous agent does not seem to go against one's overall happiness. That seems to support the thesis that virtue is sufficient for happiness.

Still, Antiochus suggests that a good state of one's body contributes something to happiness, to the extent that we can say that one who enjoys both a virtuous state of mind (and exercises it accordingly) and a good bodily condition, characterised by e.g. health and freedom from pain, is living a life which is 'happy to the highest extent' (*vita beatissima*).[38] This seems to introduce degrees to the state of happiness, i.e. a lower degree of mere happiness (connected with a virtuous disposition) and a highest

---

[37] *On Ends* 5.71: *iam non dubitabis quin earum compotes homines magno animo erectoque viventes semper sint beati, qui omnis motus fortunae mutationesque rerum et temporum levis et imbecillos fore intellegant, si in virtutis certamen venerint.*

[38] *Ibid.* 5.71: *illa enim quae sunt a nobis bona corporis numerata complent ea quidem beatissimam vitam, sed ita ut sine illis possit beata vita existere.* Cf. *ibid.* 5.81. A variation of this thesis is presented in Varro's account of Old Academic ethics in *Academic Books* 22, whereby the *beatissima vita* also includes the external goods which are suitable for the 'use' of virtue: *itaque omnis illa antiqua philosophia sensit in una virtute esse positam beatam vitam, nec tamen beatissimam nisi adiungerentur etiam corporis et cetera quae supra dicta sunt ad virtutis usum idonea.*

degree of ultimate happiness (characterised by a virtuous disposition *plus* a good bodily condition).[39] This 'aggregative' approach
may be misleading if one concludes from it that the good bodily
condition contributes the *same* amount of happiness as the one
which is the outcome of a virtuous disposition. Antiochus goes
therefore to great lengths, by using illustrative analogies, to show
that the contribution of a good bodily condition is only *infinitesi-
mal* in comparison with the contribution made by the virtuous
condition of the soul;[40] accordingly, the mere presence or absence
of bodily goods does not result in happiness or wretchedness
respectively.[41] Although the value of favourable bodily conditions
approaches zero, Antiochus claims that it is contrary to the theory
of human nature that he sketches in *On Ends* 5 not to recognise that
the state of one's body has any intrinsic value at all, of the sort that
it can make some contribution to human happiness.

On the other hand, Antiochus claims that external goods make
no contribution to human happiness at all; in his ethical account at
On Ends 5 we find only reference to such external goods as have an
intrinsic value, leaving aside external goods which have only
instrumental value (among these he could count material resources
or political power).[42] To external goods with intrinsic value, he

---

[39] A passage in Aristotle's *Nicomachean Ethics* 1.1101a6–8 seems also to point to degrees
of happiness. There we read that the 'happy person' (*eudaimōn*) will not become
'miserable' (*athlios*) but will not be 'blessed' (*makarios*) either, if falling into the fate
of Priam (the king of Troy who saw the destruction of his city): εἰ δ' οὕτως, ἄθλιος μὲν
οὐδέποτε γένοιτ' ἂν ὁ εὐδαίμων, οὐ μὴν μακάριός γε, ἂν Πριαμικαῖς τύχαις περιπέσῃ.
If Antiochus relied on this passage for his thesis, then he clearly took the two terms
'happy' and 'blessed' not to be strictly synonymous, but to be introducing two different
degrees of happiness, that of mere happiness and supreme happiness respectively.
Karamanolis (2006) 75, Sharples (2010) 168, Russell (2010) 172 and Irwin (2012)
157 point to the same text for an explanation of Antiochus' 'two degrees of happiness'
thesis, as well. However, such a reading is not supported by the immediate context of the
passage quoted. Thus, only a few lines before this passage we find *makarios* used as
a synonym for *eudaimōn* (e.g. *Nicomachean Ethics* 1.1100b34). Cf. also Rowe and
Broadie (2002) 278 and Irwin (2012) 159.

[40] See e.g. *On Ends* 5.71, where the value added to the *telos* by the bodily goods, in
comparison with the significance of virtue, can 'barely be seen', just like the starlight in
the rays of the sun: *ita enim parvae et exiguae sunt istae accessiones bonorum ut,
quem ad modum stellae in radiis solis, sic istae in virtutum splendore ne cernantur
quidem*. Cf. the series of analogies at *ibid.* 5.91–92.

[41] This point is central in Cicero's critique of the Antiochean view of the *telos*, see e.g.
On Ends 5.86.

[42] Varro's speech at *Academic Books* 19 may have diverted from the theory that is
advocated by Piso, since in this passage external conditions, referred to in the account

counts other human beings who are the recipients of the social virtues, such as one's friends, family, and one's country. In this case, he suggests that the value that these relationships have for our *eudaimonia* resides exclusively in enabling us to discharge the appropriate actions which flow from the corresponding virtues.[43] Thus, even though, the recipients of our virtuous actions are in themselves choice worthy (something reflected in the motivation of the virtuous agent) their well-being is not a constitutive part of our *eudaimonia*. Piso raises in this context the concern that if that were the case, it would lead to the absurd conclusion that *eudaimonia* may never be realised.[44] This seems to be an answer to some considerations found in Aristotle about the way other human beings to whom we relate form part of our happiness.[45]

Taking into account the reconstruction of the Antiochean views above, we may understand Antiochus' position with regard to the constituents of the happy life as a reformulation of the Platonic and Aristotelian thesis that virtue is the dominant criterion of happiness in human life. The recognition of the contribution of goods which are not psychological in the Antiochean account is only restricted to the body, which is conceived as not strictly speaking 'external' but as part of oneself.[46] Again the latter's contribution is only understood by Antiochus as an 'add-on' above the happiness threshold which is

---

as *vita*, form part of the *telos* as well and complete a life which is in accordance with nature: *extremum esse rerum expetendarum et finem bonorum adeptum esse omnia e natura et animo et corpore et vita.* In *ibid.* 21, *vita* is explained as what contributes to the 'use' of virtue: *vitae autem (id enim erat tertium) adiuncta esse dicebant quae ad virtutis usum valerent.*

[43] *On Ends* 5.69: *quomodo igitur, inquies, verum esse poterit omnia referri ad summum bonum, si amicitiae, si propinquitates, si reliqua externa summo bono non continentur? Hac videlicet ratione, quod ea quae externa sunt iis tuemur officiis quae oriuntur a suo cuiusque genere virtutis. Nam et amici cultus et parentis ei qui officio fungitur in eo ipso prodest quod ita fungi officio in recte factis est, quae sunt orta <a> virtutibus.*

[44] *Ibid.* 5.68: *nec vero umquam summum bonum adsequi quisquam posset, si omnia illa quae sunt extra, quamquam expetenda, summo bono continerentur.*

[45] See especially *Nicomachean Ethics* 1.1097b7–11: τὸ γὰρ τέλειον ἀγαθὸν αὔταρκες εἶναι δοκεῖ. τὸ δ' αὔταρκες λέγομεν οὐκ αὐτῷ μόνῳ, τῷ ζῶντι βίον μονώτην, ἀλλὰ καὶ γονεῦσι καὶ τέκνοις καὶ γυναικὶ καὶ ὅλως τοῖς φίλοις καὶ πολίταις, ἐπειδὴ φύσει πολιτικὸν ὁ ἄνθρωπος. Cf. Schofield (2012a) 184.

[46] Cf. Schofield (2012a) 185: '[T]he fundamental reason why external goods are not for Antiochus constituents of the supreme good must simply be that they are not conceived by him as elements in human nature, nor consequently as perfections of human nature.'

guaranteed by a virtuous disposition. All other external goods are regarded as indifferent to human *eudaimonia*.

Antiochus' thesis that human happiness is completed by two types of goods may be compared to attempts on the part of other, almost contemporary with Antiochus, proponents of the old tradition who also attempted to offer an account of the Aristotelian/Peripatetic *telos*. Thus, in the late second-century BCE, Critolaus advanced the thesis that *all* three categories of goods, psychic, bodily and external, 'make up' the final end, using the word *symplērōma* to convey his thesis about the plural constitutive parts of *eudaimonia*. The thesis received criticisms by other interpreters of the Aristotelian/Peripatetic tradition; thus, in a passage which stems from the first part of the ethical doxography in Stobaeus' *Selections* 2.7,[47] we find a critique of some 'recent Peripatetics', glossed as the 'followers of Critolaus' (*apo Critolaou*), who seem to be targeted for not drawing exact distinctions in their definition of the *telos* and for presenting *eudaimonia* as an (undifferentiated) completion (*symplērōma*) of all different goods.[48] Didymus goes on in his epitome of Peripatetic ethics to offer a discussion against the Critolaan position with a view to offering a more nuanced formulation of the *telos*, which does justice to the primacy of virtuous activity in relation to the other goods. The relevant text reads as follows:

As virtue is far superior in respect of enablement and choice worthiness for its own sake [κατά τε τὸ ποιητικὸν καὶ κατὰ τὸ δι' αὕθ' αἱρετὸν] compared with bodily and external goods, it is reasonable that the final end is not jointly completed [συμπλήρωμα] by bodily and external goods, neither is it the acquisition of them, but rather living in accordance with virtue surrounded by bodily and external goods [τὸ κατ' ἀρετὴν ζῆν ἐν τοῖς περὶ σῶμα καὶ τοῖς ἔξωθεν ἀγαθοῖς], whether all of them or the majority and the most important of them. It follows that happiness is an activity in accordance with virtue expressed in actions, which are as primary as one would wish for [ὅθεν ἐνέργειαν εἶναι τὴν εὐδαιμονίαν κατ' ἀρετὴν ἐν πράξεσι προηγουμέναις κατ' εὐχήν]. On the other hand, the goods belonging to the body and external goods are said to enable happiness by contributing

---

[47] This is known as Doxography A, see Hahm (1990) 2945.

[48] Stobaeus *Selections* 2 46.10–13 Wachsmuth = Critolaus *Fr.* 19 Wehrli: ὑπὸ δὲ τῶν νεωτέρων Περιπατητικῶν τῶν ἀπὸ Κριτολάου 'τὸ ἐκ πάντων τῶν ἀγαθῶν συμπεπληρωμένον' (τοῦτο δὲ ἦν 'τὸ ἐκ τῶν τριῶν γενῶν'), οὐκ ὀρθῶς.

something [τῷ συμβάλλεσθαί τι] through their presence; those who believe that they jointly complete happiness are unaware that happiness is of a life [βίος], and life is constituted by actions [ἐκ πράξεως]. None of the bodily and external goods are either actions in themselves or an activity [ἐνέργειαν] at all. (Didymus *ap.* Stobaeus *Selections* 2 126.12–127.2 Wachsmuth)[49]

The doxographer stresses the primacy of virtue for the 'production' of happiness. He modifies accordingly the Critolaan thesis by saying that happiness is not jointly completed by virtue and the other goods; happiness rather amounts to a life according to virtue *among* the bodily and external goods (supplemented by the qualification 'either all or the most important among them'). This suggests that the non-psychological goods provide the necessary context for the activation of virtue but do not belong to the same category as the virtues of the soul. Didymus goes on to offer an ontological argument for his thesis. Life consists of actions or activities; however, neither bodily nor external goods are actions or activities.[50] Therefore, they cannot be taken to constitute the *telos* but they should be understood as the 'enabling conditions' within which the virtuous activity takes place.

Still, when formulating the *telos*, Didymus includes both virtuous activity and the circumstances within which it takes place into his definition. Thus, the formula of the final end favoured by the doxographer in this passage is that of virtuous activity manifested in actions which are 'as primary as one would wish for'. The word *proēgoumenos* in the definition

---

[49] ἐπειδὴ μεγάλη τῆς ἀρετῆς ἐστιν ὑπεροχὴ κατά τε τὸ ποιητικὸν καὶ κατὰ τὸ δι᾽ αὔθ᾽ αἱρετὸν παρὰ τὰ σωματικὰ καὶ τὰ ἔξωθεν ἀγαθά, κατὰ τὸν λόγον οὐκ εἶναι συμπλήρωμα τὸ τέλος ἐκ τῶν σωματικῶν καὶ ἐκ τῶν ἔξωθεν ἀγαθῶν οὐδὲ τὸ τυγχάνειν αὐτῶν, ἀλλὰ μᾶλλον τὸ κατ᾽ ἀρετὴν ζῆν ἐν τοῖς περὶ σῶμα καὶ τοῖς ἔξωθεν ἀγαθοῖς ἢ πᾶσιν ἢ τοῖς πλείστοις καὶ κυριωτάτοις. Ὅθεν ἐνέργειαν εἶναι τὴν εὐδαιμονίαν κατ᾽ ἀρετὴν ἐν πράξεσι προηγουμέναις κατ᾽ εὐχήν. Τὰ δὲ περὶ σῶμα καὶ τὰ ἔξωθεν ἀγαθὰ ποιητικὰ λέγεσθαι τῆς εὐδαιμονίας τῷ συμβάλλεσθαί τι παρόντα· τοὺς δὲ νομίζοντας αὐτὰ συμπληροῦν τὴν εὐδαιμονίαν ἀγνοεῖν, ὅτι ἡ μὲν εὐδαιμονία βίος ἐστίν, ὁ δὲ βίος ἐκ πράξεως συμπεπλήρωται. Τῶν δὲ σωματικῶν ἢ τῶν ἐκτὸς ἀγαθῶν οὐδὲν οὔτε πρᾶξιν εἶναι καθ᾽ ἑαυτὸ οὔθ᾽ ὅλως ἐνέργειαν.

[50] Szaif (2012) 175 comments that the criticism suggests a 'category mistake' on Critolaus' part. Cf. Stobaeus *Selections* 2 46.13–17 Wachsmuth, which explicitly corrects the Critolaan formulation of the *telos*: οὐ γὰρ πάντα τἀγαθὰ μέρη γίνεται τοῦ τέλους οὔτε γὰρ τὰ σωματικά, οὔτε τὰ ἀπὸ τῶν ἐκτός, τὰ δὲ τῆς ψυχικῆς ἀρετῆς ἐνεργήματα μόνης. Κρεῖττον οὖν ἦν εἰπεῖν ἀντὶ τοῦ 'συμπληρούμενον' 'ἐνεργούμενον', ἵνα τὸ χρηστικὸν τῆς ἀρετῆς ἐμφαίνηται.

stands for the (appropriately) favourable circumstances for the exercise of virtue.[51] Thus, despite underlining the ontological distinction between virtue and non-psychological conditions, the doxographer defends the view that such (appropriate) conditions are necessary means for the exercise of virtue.[52] Accordingly, their absence may ruin happiness.

On this point, Didymus seems to take a Theophrastean line which put emphasis on the importance of external circumstances for happiness; according to this view, virtue is insufficient for happiness.[53] Antiochus, by contrast, follows a more 'rigorous' line, which he traces back to Aristotle and, most probably, Plato as well, defending the view that virtuous activity guarantees happiness under *any* circumstances. In line with this, we find in the Antiochean accounts of *On Ends* 5 and in the *Academic Books* a heavy critique of Theophrastus on the importance he assigns to fortune for happiness.[54]

---

[51] See Didymus *ap.* Stobaeus *Selections* 2 132.8–10 Wachsmuth: «προηγουμένην» δὲ τὴν τῆς ἀρετῆς ἐνέργειαν διὰ τὸ πάντως ἀναγκαῖον ἐν τοῖς κατὰ φύσιν ἀγαθοῖς ὑπάρχειν. In Wachsmuth (1884), προηγούμενος is in Didymus' account systematically substituted with χορηγούμενος in order to comply with the surviving Aristotelian treatises on ethics and politics. Although the words are co-extensive in meaning, Wachsmuth misses the point that here Didymus adopts Stoic terminology in order to convey (what he believes to be) an Aristotelian idea. For the meaning of the expression *proēgoumenos* in Didymus' Peripatetic doxography, see Tsouni (2017) 7–10.

[52] The idea that external and material goods are necessary means to the performance of virtuous actions is defended more explicitly at Didymus *ap.* Stobaeus *Selections* 2 129. 19–130.12 Wachsmuth by the use of an analogy with the crafts.

[53] See Didymus *ap.* Stobaeus *Selections* 2 145.3–6: διαφέρειν δὲ τὸν εὐδαίμονα βίον τοῦ καλοῦ καθ' ὅσον ὃ μὲν ἐν τοῖς κατὰ φύσιν εἶναι βούλεται διὰ παντός, ὃ δὲ καὶ ἐν τοῖς παρὰ φύσιν καὶ πρὸς ὃν μὲν οὐκ αὐτάρκης ἡ ἀρετή, πρὸς ὃν δὲ αὐτάρκης and *ibid.* 132.10–12 Wachsmuth: ἐπεὶ καὶ ἐν κακοῖς ἀρετῇ χρήσαιτ' ἂν καλῶς ὁ σπουδαῖος, οὐ μήν γε μακάριος ἔσται καὶ ἐν αἰκίαις ἀποδείξαιτ' ἂν τὸ γενναῖον, οὐ μὴν εὐδαιμονήσει. The above text also suggests that the doxographer understood the words μακάριος and εὐδαίμων as synonymous. The expression 'middle life' (μέσος βίος), which is introduced in *ibid.* 133.10, is meant to express the state which occupies a middle space between complete happiness and unhappiness. That the 'Theophrastean line' with regard to the *telos* was also endorsed by the contemporary with Antiochus Peripatetic Staseas of Naples is attested at *On Ends* 5.75: *memini Staseam Neapolitanum, doctorem illum tuum, nobilem sane Peripateticum, aliquanto ista secus dicere solitum, adsentientem iis qui multum in fortuna secunda aut adversa, multum in bonis aut malis corporis ponerent.* The doctrine that virtue is insufficient to guarantee happiness is also attributed to Aristotle at Diogenes Laertius *Lives of Eminent Philosophers* 5.30: τὴν τε ἀρετὴν μὴ εἶναι αὐτάρκη πρὸς εὐδαιμονίαν· προσδεῖσθαι γὰρ τῶν τε περὶ σῶμα καὶ τῶν ἐκτὸς ἀγαθῶν, ὡς κακοδαιμονήσοντος τοῦ σοφοῦ κἂν ἐν πόνοις ᾖ κἂν ἐν πενίᾳ καὶ τοῖς ὁμοίοις.

[54] See *Academic Books* 33 and *On Ends* 5.12. For the way Antiochus represents the Theophrastean views on fortune as a deviation from the Old Academic tradition, see

The comparison between Didymus and Antiochus on their proposed views of the *telos* thus shows that some of the first attempts to offer a coherent position on how different elements of Aristotelian/Peripatetic ethics fit together could lead to divergent, and even incompatible, conclusions.

Chapter 2, *supra*. For all the evidence on Theopharstus' views on fortune, see *Frs.* 487–501 FHS&G.

9

ANIMALS AND PLANTS IN THE
ANTIOCHEAN-PERIPATETIC ACCOUNT

As shown in the previous chapters, Antiochus proposes a distinctively Aristotelian/Peripatetic theory of *oikeiōsis* according to
which all living organisms strive from birth onwards for the
telos that is appropriate to their nature on the basis of a fundamental feeling of self-love.[1] As in the case of the Stoic account of
oikeiōsis in Diogenes Laertius' *Lives of Eminent Philosophers*
7.85–86, the special account of human *oikeiōsis* is accompanied
in Antiochus by an analogical argument which presents *oikeiōsis*
as a phenomenon applying to all living organisms alike.
According to this, all living forms (even plants) share the common
aim to fulfil their nature and reach the best state which their natural
kind admits, even though the particular *telos* which they pursue is
peculiar to their species-specific nature. Thus, a 'life according to
nature' manifests itself differently in the case of, for example,
horses, oxen and human beings.[2]

The Antiochean-Peripatetic account of *On Ends* 5 expands on
the way animals experience an impulse for the objects they perceive as suited to their particular nature.[3] Piso's remarks on the
means by which animals pursue what is *oikeion* to them, which
supplement his account of human *oikeiōsis*, reveal a Peripatetic
stance on the intellectual and emotional faculties of animals,
which focuses on the overlapping areas between humans and
animals. This may be contrasted to the Stoic view, which proposes
clear boundaries between humans and animals in a sort of binary
opposition. Peculiar to the Antiochean account is also an interest
in plants, as the process of *oikeiōsis* is shown to take place in their

---

[1] *On Ends* 5.24. Cf. *ibid.* 4.32.
[2] *On Ends.* 5.26: *sic commune animalium omnium secundum naturam vivere, sed naturas esse diversas, ut aliud equo sit e natura, aliud bovi, aliud homini.*
[3] See e.g. *On Ends* 4.19: *an quod omne animal ipsum sibi commendatum, ut se [et] salvum in suo genere et incolume vellet;* cf. *ibid.* 4.25.

case as well. Antiochus uses even a striking analogy from agriculture in order to convey his views about human *oikeiōsis*. In this chapter, I will attempt to show how the Antiochean account explains the *oikeiōsis* of animals and plants, and how the account reveals the use of Peripatetic material from the domain of natural science for the construction of its thesis.

Oikeiōsis and Animals

Antiochus acknowledges that animals have an analogous end to that of human beings and fulfil the formula of a life according to nature (*secundum naturam vivere*) in accordance with the capacities of the species they belong to.[4] In some cases animals, resembling inanimate beings, seem to fulfil a merely bodily *telos*. Such is the case of the pig in the example of *On Ends* 5.38, where we find the idea that pigs seem to have a soul only for their bodily preservation and not for the exercise of any higher faculties. As Piso puts it:

And indeed of all the things that nature creates and sustains, for those which have no soul or hardly one, the supreme good is found in the body so that it seems to be well said about the pig that a soul was given to it instead of salt, to keep it from rotting.[5]

Piso by the use of this example picks up on popular assumptions about the mental abilities of pigs.[6] The same example was, however, used also by the Stoic school. A version of the example of the pig in Greek can be found in Porphyry's *On Abstinence* 3.20.1–3, where it is attributed to the Stoic Chrysippus, although the same example is attributed in another source to his predecessor Cleanthes:[7]

But that famous opinion of Chrysippus is convincing: that the gods made us for themselves and for each other, and the animals for us; horses to campaign with us,

---

[4] *Ibid.* 5.25.

[5] *etenim omnium rerum quas et creat natura et tuetur, quae aut sine animo sunt aut <non> multo secus, earum summum bonum in corpore est, ut non inscite illud dictum videatur in sue, animum illi pecudi datum pro sale, ne putisceret.*

[6] Cf. Porphyry *On Abstinence* 1.14 and the comments of Glaucon at Plato's *Republic* 372d4.

[7] Clement of Alexandria *Miscellanies* 7.6.33 Stählin = *SVF* 1.516

dogs to hunt with us, leopards and bears and lions to exercise our courage. And the pig (for that is the most delightful of these favours) was born for nothing else but to be sacrificed, and god added soul to its flesh like salt, to make it tasty for us.[8] (Translation Clark (2000), with alterations)

As part of the Stoic account of divine nature, the example of the pig is attributed again explicitly to Chrysippus at Cicero's *On the Nature of the Gods* 2.160: according to the Stoic spokesman there, Chrysippus claimed that the pig was given a soul as salt in order to benefit the food supply.[9] This is suggestive of the Stoic views on the instrumentality of animals. According to Stoic sources, animals exist only in order to serve the 'community of human beings and gods'.[10] The Stoic world-view is founded upon the premise that only human beings and gods by their use of reason live in accordance with justice and law, forming a single community. If that is true, then any being lacking reason like brute animals cannot claim just treatment and can be a mere instrument for the use of rational beings without injustice.[11]

Numerous examples of the instrumental understanding of animals within the Stoic theory are quoted also in Plutarch from Chrysippus' *On Nature*, where bugs are said to be 'useful in waking us up and mice in making us attentive about putting things away carefully',[12] whereas in a similar vein Cicero at *On the Nature of the Gods* 2.158 claims that sheep exist only for the sake of furnishing men with material for clothes. Similarly, for the Stoics animals which provide a beautiful spectacle, such as the

---

[8] ἀλλ' ἐκεῖνο νὴ Δία τοῦ Χρυσίππου πιθανὸν ἦν, ὡς ἡμᾶς αὐτῶν καὶ ἀλλήλων οἱ θεοὶ χάριν ἐποιήσαντο, ἡμῶν δὲ τὰ ζῷα, συμπολεμεῖν μὲν ἵππους καὶ συνθηρεύειν κύνας, ἀνδρείας δὲ γυμνάσια παρδάλεις καὶ ἄρκτους καὶ λέοντας. ἡ δὲ ὗς, ἐνταῦθα γάρ ἐστιν τῶν χαρίτων τὸ ἥδιστον, οὐ δι' ἄλλο τι πλὴν θύεσθαι ἐγεγόνει, καὶ τῇ σαρκὶ τὴν ψυχὴν ὁ θεὸς οἷον ἅλας ἐνέμιξεν, εὐοψίαν ἡμῖν μηχανώμενος.
[9] *sus vero quid habet praeter escam; cui quidem ne putesceret animam ipsam pro sale datam dicit esse Chrysippus; qua pecude, quod erat ad vescendum hominibus apta, nihil genuit natura fecundius.*
[10] *On the Nature of the Gods* 2.133: *ita fit credibile deorum et hominum causa factum esse mundum quaeque in eo mundo sint omnia.*
[11] The anthropocentric world-view of the Stoics finds its canonical expression in one passage from Cicero's *On the Nature of the Gods* 2.154: *omnia quae sint in hoc mundo, quibus utantur homines, hominum causa facta esse et parata.* Cf. Diogenes Laertius *Lives of Eminent Philosophers* 7.129 from Chrysippus' *On Justice*: ἔτι ἀρέσκει αὐτοῖς μηδὲν εἶναι ἡμῖν δίκαιον πρὸς τὰ ἄλλα ζῷα, διὰ τὴν ἀνομοιότητα, καθά φησι Χρύσιππος ἐν τῷ πρώτῳ Περὶ δικαιοσύνης καὶ Ποσειδώνιος ἐν πρώτῳ Περὶ καθήκοντος.
[12] Plutarch *Stoic Self-Contradictions* 1044d.

peacock when it opens its tail, are no less a sign of the anthropo-centric focus of creation: the peacock is created for the sake of its tail and in order to provide us with a manifestation of beauty.[13]

Such Stoic views were vehemently attacked by the Academic sceptics. One case of this dialectical exchange survives in Porphyry; the text shows how, using Stoic premises with regard to the relation of animals to humans, Carneades derived the evidently absurd conclusion that it is in the interest of the pig to be devoured by human beings.[14] He thereby juxtaposed the Stoic instrumental view of animals with a view that stresses the inherent desire of animals to pursue what is according to (their) nature.[15]

If anthropocentrism suggests that the value of other beings is defined with regard to their use by humans, then we can conceive of Antiochus' exposition of how animals primarily strive for their own *telos*, independently of their instrumental value to humans, at *On Ends* 5.25–6, as an alternative position to the Stoic one. According to this position, the final end of animals is not defined primarily by the way human beings use them, but with reference to their own capacities and their corresponding natural appropriation. This does not exclude the use of those animals by human beings for the purposes of domestic economy: some of the examples that Piso picks out refer to animals widely used in such a context, and their usefulness could not have been reasonably doubted. The distinctive Antiochean approach consists rather in regarding the use of animals as something which corresponds to an animal's peculiar nature, rather than to a cosmic design which creates animals *for the sake* of rational beings.

Suggestive of this approach is that to the example of the pig, which is indicative of the Stoic views on the instrumentality of

---

[13] Plutarch *Stoic Self-Contradictions* 1044d = *SVF* 2.1163.

[14] Porphyry *On Abstinence* 3.20.15–23 = Carneades *Fr.* 8*b* Mette: ὅτῳ δὴ ταῦτα δοκεῖ τι τοῦ πιθανοῦ καὶ θεῷ πρέποντος μετέχειν, σκοπείτω, τί πρὸς ἐκεῖνον ἐρεῖ τὸν λόγον ὃν Καρνεάδης ἔλεγεν·ἕκαστον τῶν φύσει γεγονότων ὅταν τοῦ πρὸς ὃ πέφυκε καὶ γέγονε τυγχάνῃ [τέλους], ὠφελεῖται. κοινότερον δὲ <τὸ> τῆς ὠφελείας, ἣν εὐχρηστίαν οὗτοι λέγουσιν, ἀκουστέον. ἡ δὲ ὗς φύσει γέγονε πρὸς τὸ σφαγῆναι καὶ καταβρωθῆναι·καὶ τοῦτο πάσχουσα τυγχάνει τοῦ πρὸς ὃ πέφυκε, καὶ ὠφελεῖται. See also the discussion in Sedley (2007) 236.

[15] *Ibid.* 3.20.32–6: εἰ δὲ οὐ πάντα φασὶν ἡμῖν καὶ δι' ἡμᾶς γεγονέναι, πρὸς τῷ σύγχυσιν ἔχειν πολλὴν καὶ ἀσάφειαν τὸν διορισμὸν οὐδὲ ἐκφεύγομεν τὸ ἀδικεῖν, ἐπιτιθέμενοι καὶ χρώμενοι βλαβερῶς τοῖς οὐ δι' ἡμᾶς, ἀλλ' ὥσπερ ἡμεῖς κατὰ φύσιν γεγενημένοις.

animals, Antiochus contrasts the disposition of certain animals towards a virtuous-like behaviour. This reveals their *oikeiōsis* towards aims conducive to the attainment of their peculiar *telos*, independently of the way they may serve human needs. The relevant passage reads as follows:

> But there are some animals in which there is some resemblance of virtue [*aliquid simile virtutis*], for example lions, dogs and horses; in those, unlike pigs, we observe some movements not only of the body, but in some degree also of the soul [*non corporum solum (. . .) sed etiam animorum aliqua ex parte motus quosdam*]. In humans, however, we find the completion of the soul and of reasoning, from which virtue springs, which is defined as the perfection of reasoning [*rationis absolutio*], a point that they (sc. 'the ancients') believed should be spelled out again and again. (*On Ends* 5.38)

The Antiochean spokesman does not go so far as to ascribe to animals full-blown virtues, but uses the expression 'resemblance of virtue' (*simile virtutis*) to denote the 'soul movements'[16] which, although deprived of reason, lead to behaviour which is virtuous-like. The wording of the Antiochean passage above is reminiscent of the opening chapter in *History of Animals* 588a19–25,[17] where most animals are said to possess 'traces of the characteristics to do with the soul (*ichnē tōn peri tēn psychēn tropōn*), the differences of which are more obviously present in human beings',[18] as also 'resemblances' (*homoiotētes*) of virtues like gentleness and courage, but also of practical wisdom.[19] Along these lines, certain animals are said to possess a sort of 'natural power' (*physikē dynamis*), which is analogous to human capacities such as expert knowledge and wisdom.[20]

---

[16] For a Greek equivalent, see the expression κατὰ ψυχὴν κίνημα in Sextus Empiricus *Against the Professors* 7.219.

[17] This follows the MSS. order as restored by Balme (1991) 56.

[18] Aristotle *History of Animals* 588a18–21: ἔνεστι γὰρ ἐν τοῖς πλείστοις καὶ τῶν ἄλλων ζῴων ἴχνη τῶν περὶ τὴν ψυχὴν τρόπων, ἅπερ ἐπὶ τῶν ἀνθρώπων ἔχει φανερωτέρας τὰς διαφοράς.

[19] *Ibid.* 588a21–25: καὶ γὰρ ἡμερότης καὶ ἀγριότης, καὶ πραότης καὶ χαλεπότης, καὶ ἀνδρία καὶ δειλία, καὶ φόβοι καὶ θάρρη, καὶ θυμοὶ καὶ πανουργίαι καὶ τῆς περὶ τὴν διάνοιαν συνέσεως ἔνεισιν ἐν πολλοῖς αὐτῶν ὁμοιότητες, καθάπερ ἐπὶ τῶν μερῶν ἐλέγομεν. Cf. *ibid.* 608a14–18. Even later Stoics conceded with similar examples that animals can possess courage (*fortitudo*) but they insisted strongly on the total absence of *ratio* among them, see e.g. Cicero *On Appropriate Actions* 1.50.

[20] Aristotle *History of Animals* 588a29–31: ὡς γὰρ ἐν ἀνθρώπῳ τέχνη καὶ σοφία καὶ σύνεσις, οὕτως ἐνίοις τῶν ζῴων ἐστί τις ἑτέρα τοιαύτη φυσικὴ δύναμις.

The motif of 'semblances of virtues' (*simulacra virtutum*) appears also at *On Ends* 2.110, with reference to certain species of birds, in an anti-Epicurean argument which borrows from Antiochean-Peripatetic premises: there, the similarity between animals and humans consists in the possession of certain signs (*indicia*) in animals of, among other things, knowledge (*cognitionem*), memory (*memoriam*) and passions, like grief (*desideria*).[21] In his introduction of *oikeiōsis* at *On Ends* 5.24 Piso similarly uses the verbs 'knowing' (*agnoscere*) and 'understanding' (*intellegere*) in relation to an animal's developed pursuit of what is *oikeion*, alongside the faculties of perception (*perspicere*) and impulse (*appetitus*).[22] The claim made seems to be that the animal's impulse (*appetitus*) for what is *oikeion* rests on some sort of understanding, and therefore entails cognitive elements.[23]

Piso refers, furthermore, to the way animals pursue what is appropriate to them by means of the different bodily parts given to them by nature. The relevant passage reads as follows:

> We can observe something similar in other animals. Those at the beginning do not move away from the place, where they were born, but then each is moved by its own desire [*suo quaeque appetitu movetur*]: we see snakes crawling, ducks

---

[21] *videmus in quodam volucrium genere non nulla indicia pietatis, cognitionem, memoriam, in multis etiam desideria videmus. ergo in bestiis erunt secreta e voluptate humanarum quaedam simulacra virtutum, in ipsis hominibus virtus nisi voluptatis causa nulla erit?*

[22] There is a parallel here to the Stoic account at *On Ends* 3.17, which appears to ascribe the ability to form 'cataleptic' impressions to children and animals as well. As Schmitz (2014) 63 notes, this contradicts the rest of Stoic evidence on the cognitive abilities of animals and is most probably an attempt to incorporate Peripatetic material into the Stoic account of *oikeiōsis*.

[23] Cf. also Plutarch's *On the Intelligence of Animals* 960e–f, where a Peripatetic version of an *oikeiōsis* argument is presented according to which animals necessarily have also a natural ability of calculation (λογίζεσθαί), judgement (κρίνειν), remembering (μνημονεύειν) and attending (προσέχειν), since these are necessary for the pursuit of the *oikeion*: ἡ γὰρ φύσις, ἣν ἕνεκά του καὶ πρός τι πάντα ποιεῖν ὀρθῶς λέγουσιν, οὐκ ἐπὶ ψιλῷ τῷ πάσχον τι αἰσθάνεσθαι τὸ ζῷον αἰσθητικὸν ἐποίησεν· ἀλλ' ὄντων μὲν οἰκείων πρὸς αὐτὸ πολλῶν ὄντων δ' ἀλλοτρίων, οὐδ' ἀκαρὲς ἦν περιεῖναι μὴ μαθόντι τὰ μὲν φυλάττεσθαι τοῖς δὲ συμφέρεσθαι. τὴν μὲν οὖν γνῶσιν ἀμφοῖν ὁμοίως ἡ αἴσθησις ἑκάστῳ παρέχει τὰς δ' ἑπομένας τῇ αἰσθήσει τῶν μὲν ὠφελίμων λήψεις καὶ διώξεις, διακρούσεις δὲ καὶ φυγὰς τῶν ὀλεθρίων καὶ λυπηρῶν οὐδεμία μηχανὴ <παρεῖναι> τοῖς μὴ λογίζεσθαί τι καὶ κρίνειν καὶ μνημονεύειν καὶ προσέχειν πεφυκόσιν. Peripatetics are the subject of the verb λέγουσι at the beginning of the passage. The Peripatetic credentials of this argument are corroborated by the reference in Plutarch's text to Strato, the pupil of Theophrastus, at *On the Intelligence of Animals* 961a2–4. The argument survives also in Porphyry's *On Abstinence* 3.21.28–39.

swimming, blackbirds flying, oxen using their horn, scorpions their sting. In short, we see that their proper nature guides them for living [*suam denique cuique naturam esse ad vivendum ducem*]. (*On Ends* 5.42)

According to the above passage, the initial state of *prōtē oikeiōsis* or *prima commendatio* gives way through experience to a more advanced state followed by understanding of the animal's own abilities. Antiochus thereby allows that experience plays a role in reinforcing and developing the primary desire for what is suited to the animal's nature through a process of learning which reveals to each animal its proper capacities.[24] Piso's remarks are matched by observations on the intentional behaviour of animals stemming from the Peripatetic tradition.[25] In Porphyry's *On Abstinence,* for example, the ability of animals to use parts of their body as the right means for their defence is taken as a token of the existence of some sort of reasoning ability, although not of *logos* in the strict sense. Among the examples Porphyry uses at *On Abstinence* 3.9 are the way oxen use their horns and scorpions their stings in order to defend themselves.[26] The similarity of the examples from Porphyry to those from *On Ends* 5.42 suggests a common source for the two accounts. Indeed, Porphyry attests that the 'ancients' had used many such similar examples in their treatises with the title *On Animal Wisdom* by stating:

The ancients collected many more such instances in their works on animal wisdom [*en tois peri zōōn phronēseōs*], and Aristotle, who took the greatest trouble over the question, says that all animals devise their home with regard to their means of living and their security.[27] (*On Abstinence* 3.9.18–10.1 (Translation, Clark 2000))

The passage seems to allude to Theophrastus, who wrote a treatise 'On the Wisdom and Character of Animals' (*Peri zōōn*

---

[24] Cf. *Metaphysics* 980a27–b28 and *Nicomachean Ethics* 7.1147b5 which ascribe to animals memory and experience, albeit not λογισμός.

[25] According to Dierauer (1977) 169, this kind of research was undertaken by Theophrastus. An antecedent of the notion of intentionality can be found in the word πρόθεσις in Plutarch's *On the Intelligence of Animals* 966b5.

[26] 3.9.3–7: πρῶτον μὲν ἕκαστον οἶδεν εἴτε ἀσθενές ἐστιν εἴτε ἰσχυρόν, καὶ τὰ μὲν φυλάττεται, τοῖς δὲ χρῆται, ὡς πάρδαλις μὲν ὀδοῦσιν, ὄνυξι δὲ λέων καὶ ὀδοῦσιν, ἵππος δὲ ὁπλῇ καὶ βοῦς κέρασιν, καὶ ἀλεκτρυὼν μὲν πλήκτρῳ, σκορπίος δὲ κέντρῳ.

[27] ἃ δὴ ἐπὶ πλέον συνῆκται τοῖς παλαιοῖς ἐν τοῖς περὶ ζῴων φρονήσεως, τοῦ ταῦτα πολυπραγμονήσαντος ἐπὶ πλέον Ἀριστοτέλους λέγοντος πᾶσι τοῖς ζῴοις μεμηχανῆσθαι πρὸς τὸν βίον καὶ σωτηρίαν αὐτῶν τὴν <οἴκησιν>.

phronēseōs kai ēthous).[28] Furthermore, what follows in the above text is most probably a reference to Aristotle's *History of Animals* 614b31–33.[29] In the latter we find numerous examples of the intentional activity of animals which reveal 'the precision of their intelligence' (*tēs dianoias akribeian*), as for example the swallow's nest-building;[30] such examples could very well support the idea of an animal *oikeiōsis* along Antiochean lines. This shows that Antiochus may well have incorporated into his account material on animal practical intelligence from Peripatetic sources, and more precisely from Theophrastean biological works and from the material contained in the *History of Animals*.

On the other hand, the Stoics also defended the view that animals manifest *oikeiōsis*.[31] Early Stoics, however, regarded the *oikeiōsis* of animals as a mechanism of the providential cosmic nature, rather than as an outcome of the animal's inherent abilities and peculiar nature.[32] Also, they did not think that animal *oikeiōsis* requires the existence of cognitive abilities beyond the faculty of *synaisthēsis*.[33] Accordingly, there is little stress in the early Stoic surviving evidence on the way animals develop their faculties

---

[28] See Diogenes Laertius *Lives of Eminent Philosophers* 5.49.

[29] The word οἴκησιν was added to the text of Porphyry by Victorius from Aristotle *History of Animals* 614b31, see Clark (2000) 169 n.428. *On Abstinence* 3.23.27ff. draws also on the example of pigeons from *History of Animals* 612b33–a3. Theophrastean writings on animals were already conflated with Aristotelian ones by Alexandrian scholars, such as Callimachus and Hermippus. For numerous stylistic characteristics of *History of Animals* 8 which hint at Theophrastus, see an overview at Regenbogen (1940) 1433, Dirlmeier (1937) 56 and Dierauer (1977) 164–65. The case for Theophrastean authorship of the last books of *History of Animals* has been made more recently by Huby (1985), who argues that some chapters in *History of Animals* 7 incorporate material from some biological works of Theophrastus. The opposite view, supporting the Aristotelian orthodoxy of the last books of *History of Animals*, has been defended by Balme (1991) 1–13.

[30] Aristotle *History of Animals* 612b18ff.

[31] See Diogenes Laertius *Lives of Eminent Philosophers* 7.86: οὐδέν τε, φασί, διήλλαξεν ἡ φύσις ἐπὶ τῶν φυτῶν καὶ ἐπὶ τῶν ζώων, ὅτι χωρὶς ὁρμῆς καὶ αἰσθήσεως κἀκεῖνα οἰκονομεῖ καὶ ἐφ᾽ ἡμῶν τινα φυτοειδῶς γίνεται. ἐκ περιττοῦ δὲ τῆς ὁρμῆς τοῖς ζώοις ἐπιγενομένης, ᾗ συγχρώμενα πορεύεται πρὸς τὰ οἰκεῖα, τούτοις μὲν τὸ κατὰ φύσιν τῷ κατὰ τὴν ὁρμὴν διοικεῖσθαι.

[32] This is coupled by the absence of Stoic empirical research aiming at the understanding of animal behaviour comparable, for example, to Aristotle's *History of Animals*. Even Posidonius, who was interested in natural science, did not discuss the animal world. The only exception seems to be a lost treatise of the Stoic Antipater whose dating is not secure, see Dierauer (1977) 224.

[33] On the explanation of animal behaviour in terms of *synaisthēsis*, see Seneca *Letters* 121.9: *ergo omnibus constitutionis suae sensus est et inde membrorum tam expedita*

through experience and response to their immediate environment.[34]

However, in later versions of Stoic ethics by Hierocles and Seneca,[35] which postdate Antiochus' account in Cicero, one may find a stronger interest in the way animals employ their capacities in order to pursue their natural *telos*. For Hierocles, the way animals use the parts of their body for self-defence is primarily a proof that they perceive upon birth their own selves through the special faculty of *synaisthēsis*: it is through the awareness of oneself and not through experience that 'knowledge' of how to use the parts of one's body comes about. One empirical example provided to that end by Hierocles is that of bulls using their horns against other bulls or animals of different species, which is reminiscent of the examples of animal *oikeiōsis* given in the Antiochean account.[36] This in all probability betrays an attempt on the part of later Stoics to incorporate into their version of *oikeiōsis* material of Peripatetic origin, without at the same time giving up the main assumptions of Stoic theory.

The *Oikeiōsis* of Plants

One of the most striking features of Piso's speech in *On Ends* 5 is the way observations about plants are integrated into his account of *oikeiōsis*. This corroborates the naturalistic framework of the Antiochean version of the *oikeiōsis* argument.[37] Thus, at *On Ends* 5.26 Piso asserts that plants, like all animals, pursue by nature what is appropriate to them by means of a mechanism of natural appropriation, asserting that 'even the things which grow from the earth' can be said to undertake a number of activities by their own power (*multa ... efficere ipsa*

---

tractatio, nec ullum maius indicium habemus cum hac illa ad vivendum venire notitia quam quod nullum animal ad usum sui rude est.

[34] Thus, Seneca claims that animals possess the full knowledge necessary to use their bodily parts from the moment of birth onwards, see *Letters* 121.6: *hoc edita protinus faciunt* (sc. *animalia); cum hac scientia prodeunt; instituta nascuntur* and *ibid.* 121.20: *ex quo quidem apparet non usu illa in hoc pervenire sed naturali amore salutis suae.* See also Dierauer (1977) 219 and Sorabji (1993) 35.

[35] *Letters* 121.24.   [36] Hierocles Ἠθικὴ στοιχείωσις col. 2.1–19.

[37] Cf. Inwood (2014) 67–68.

sibi per se) which conduce to their life and growth so that they reach the ultimate goal of their species (*ut in suo genere perveniant ad extremum*)'.[38] By focusing on the most characteristic example of the *oikeiōsis* of plants in the Antiochean account, the vine-human analogy at *On Ends* 5.39–40, I intend to show, on the basis of it, the Peripatetic credentials of Antiochus' theory, and to suggest that it transmits the views of the Peripatos on the relationship between nature and *technē*. Finally, I shall show how these views have a bearing on Antiochus' theory of *oikeiōsis*.

In the Antiochean account of *On Ends* 5 plants are separated from animate beings (*animantes*) and referred to collectively as 'things which grow from the earth' (*res quae gignuntur e terra*, translating the Greek *ta ek gēs phyomena*).[39] By virtue of not possessing an internal principle of impulse and locomotion, plants occupy in the Antiochean account an intermediate space between animals and non-organic physical entities, but are not explicitly assigned a soul along the lines of Aristotle's *On the Soul*.[40] Whereas in the case of animate beings, *oikeiōsis* is manifested through the impulse towards things recognised through perception as appropriate and according to nature, the pursuit of the *oikeion* in plants[41] is achieved through an analogous process of growth and nutrition which naturally excludes impulse and locomotion.

Antiochus may well have read the Peripatetic botanical treatises as anticipating the idea that *oikeiōsis* extends to plants as

---

[38] Cf. *On Ends* 5.39: *ex quo non est alienum, ut animantibus, sic illis et apta quaedam ad naturam putare et aliena.* See also the inclusion of plants in the Stoic 'canonical' account of *oikeiōsis* at Diogenes Laertius *Lives of Eminent Philosophers* 7.86, n.33 *supra.*

[39] See e.g. *Academic Books* 26; *On Ends* 4.13. The expression is meant to include different types of vegetative organisms, see *On Ends* 5.10. Cf. *History of Plants* 1.3.6: ἀλλ' ὅμως τοιαῦτα διαιρετέον· ἔχει γάρ τι τῆς φύσεως κοινὸν ὁμοίως ἐν δένδροις καὶ θάμνοις καὶ τοῖς φρυγανικοῖς καὶ ποιώδεσιν.

[40] The existence of natural things without a soul is referred to in *On Ends* 5.38: *etenim omnium rerum, quas et creat natura et tuetur, quae aut sine animo sunt aut <non> multo secus.* Plants share in the nutritive faculty of the soul (θρεπτικόν) according to *On the Soul* 2.413a32ff. The ambivalent position of plants between inanimate and ensouled beings is expressed at Aristotle *History of Animals* 588b7–11.

[41] *On Ends* 5.39: *ex quo non est alienum, ut animantibus, sic illis et apta quaedam ad naturam putare et aliena.*

well. In particular, such an idea is in line with Theophrastus' botanical theory in *On the Causes of Plants*,[42] where plants are said to be led, for instance, to the localities most appropriate (*oikeioi topoi*) for their growth.[43] The idea of an *oikeiōsis* of plants towards their peculiar end corresponds to many cases discussed in Theophrastus, whereby the nature of the plant itself manifests what is appropriate or harmful to it through certain procedures: for example with trees whose bark is stripped off, such as the vine or linden, the tree's own nature appears to point out what is useful by divesting itself of its bark and making it an alien thing (*allotrion*).[44] Similarly in the chickpea, salinity appears to be both appropriate to its nature (*oikeion*) and useful (*chrēsimon*), 'so that it is for the purpose of preservation that its nature brings in such substances as are akin to it'.[45] This is due to an inherent power (*dynamis*),[46] through which plants secure their nourishment in a way analogous to animals; thereby roots play in plants the role that the senses and parts of the body play in animate beings.[47] The inherent power of plants, however, is not straightforwardly in all cases equivalent to a tendency for a particular form or perfection. Even if plants exhibit a tendency towards survival and reproduction, namely the main functions of the 'nutritive soul', their generation and subsequent development depends far too much on external conditions and a complex set of circumstances which resist full teleological explanation.

At *On Ends* 5.33 the *vis* which causes the plant's growth and survival is said to come about in interaction with a greater and more divine cause (*maior causa atque divinior*) or in a spontaneous way (*fortuito*), a view attributed to *doctissimi viri*, i.e. the

---

[42] Knowledge of this Theophrastean treatise is alluded to in the catalogue of Peripatetic works cited by Piso at *On Ends* 5.10: *Theophrastus autem stirpium naturas omniumque fere rerum quae e terra gignerentur, causas atque rationes.* For a discussion of Piso's catalogue see Chapter 2, *supra*.

[43] *On the Causes of Plants* 2.7.1.9–11: καὶ γὰρ τὸ συγγενὲς τῆς φύσεως ἕκαστον ἄγει πρὸς τὸν οἰκεῖον ἐν ᾧπερ καὶ τὰ αὐτόματα φύεται.

[44] *On the Causes of Plants* 3.18.3.3–6. [45] *Ibid.* 6.10.5.6–10.

[46] Cf. *ibid.* 1.17.1.9; 1.18.5.9 and *On the Soul* 2.413a25-28. At *Tusculan Disputations* 5.37 there is reference to an interior movement (*interiore quodam motu*) of plants, which leads them to the perfection of their kind.

[47] Cf. *Republic* 468a9–12.

'ancients'.[48] The reference to a 'more divine cause' could be a reference to the agency of the sun which causes the regular sprouting of plants, whereas the 'spontaneous' could refer to all non-regular causes, such as air temperature, which can influence vegetative organisms in a complex way and cause spontaneous generation. The double scheme of causation at *On Ends* 5.33 appears also in Theophrastus' *Metaphysics*, in a passage where there is reference jointly to plants and inanimate things. At 10b26–11a1 Theophrastus states: 'The account that it is by spontaneity and through the rotation of the whole that these things acquire certain forms or differences from one another seems to have some plausibility.'[49] He argues that the question regarding the type of cause applying to this level is difficult to answer on the basis solely of the *hou heneka* principle, namely the principle of final causation, due to the great diversity of phenomena observed in such entities and the complicated way in which external circumstances influence the development of the vegetative organism.[50] This does not challenge the purposiveness of nature, since in those cases the internal principle of growth in plants interacts and 'collaborates' with external circumstances. Against this background, Antiochus may also presuppose a more complex picture of *oikeiōsis* in the case of plants, where we have to assume a more extended notion of nature, one which takes into account environmental parameters as well, like the influence of the sun or climate. This idea originates already in Plato, where the appropriate provision (*trophē*) with regard to locality and season has a bearing on plants' flourishing.[51]

---

[48] *On Ends* 5.33: *sive enim, ut doctissimis viris visum est, maior aliqua causa atque divinior hanc vim ingenuit, sive hoc ita fit fortuito, videmus ea, quae terra gignit, corticibus et radicibus valida servari, quod contingit animalibus sensuum distributione et quadam compactione membrorum.*

[49] ἦ καὶ ἔοικεν ὁ λόγος ἔχειν τι πιστόν, ὡς ἄρα τῷ αὐτομάτῳ ταῦτα καὶ τῇ τοῦ ὅλου περιφορᾷ λαμβάνει τινὰς ἰδέας ἢ πρὸς ἄλληλα διαφοράς.

[50] See e.g. *On the Causes of Plants* 2.16.2–3. Cf. van Raalte (1993) 323: '[I]n view of the diversity of form in organic nature Theophrastus tends to prefer an explanation in terms of efficient causation by the heavenly bodies, via the climate and other meteorological circumstances, to the idea of an inherent *logos* directed towards a particular form in terms of final causation.'

[51] *Republic* 491d: παντός, ἦν δ' ἐγώ, σπέρματος πέρι ἢ φυτοῦ, εἴτε ἐγγείων εἴτε τῶν ζῴων, ἴσμεν ὅτι τὸ μὴ τυχὸν τροφῆς ἧς προσήκει ἑκάστῳ μηδ' ὥρας μηδὲ τόπου, ὅσῳ ἂν ἐρρωμενέστερον ᾖ, τοσούτῳ πλειόνων ἐνδεῖ τῶν πρεπόντων· ἀγαθῷ γάρ που κακὸν ἐναντιώτερον ἢ τῷ μὴ ἀγαθῷ.

The 'Vine-Human Analogy': Nature and *Technē*

In accordance with the above, the Antiochean spokesman refers in his account to cases where certain plants are unable to fulfil their own *telos* by relying solely on their inherent 'power'; in this case something external, namely *technē*, completes what the nature of the plant is unable to do on its own. An example of such plants invoked at *On Ends* 5.39 is that of the vine, which has 'too little strength to secure for itself the best condition possible for its species', relying as a result of this on the craft of the vine keeper.[52]

The example betrays knowledge of the Theophrastean botanical treatises, which are referred to at the beginning of Piso's exposition as an important part of Peripatetic natural science:[53] there, the vine features as an organism unable on its own to reach its distinctive *telos*.[54] This is based on a fundamental distinction, which appears at the beginning of the second book of Theophrastus' *On the Causes of Plants* (2.1.1.5–12),[55] between wild plants which can survive without the aid of agriculture (*automata*)[56] and those domesticated ones (*tōn kata tas ergasias*) that cannot.[57] The former possess an internal principle (*archē*), whereas the latter grow with the additional assistance of an external principle, namely the *technē* of agriculture. At *On the Causes of Plants* 1.16.10.1–7 Theophrastus raises an *aporia* as to which

---

[52] *On Ends* 5.39: *et nunc quidem quod eam tuetur, ut de vite potissimum loquar, est id extrinsecus; in ipsa enim parum magna vis inest ut quam optime se habere possit, si nulla cultura adhibeatur.*

[53] See *On Ends* 5.10.

[54] One may juxtapose the use of the example with *On the Nature of the Gods* 2.35, where the vine features in the Stoic account. Contrary to Antiochus' account, the vine is used here as an example of the way nature strives by its own means in every compartment of life towards perfection: *neque enim dici potest in ulla rerum institutione non esse aliquid extremum atque perfectum. ut enim in vite ut in pecude, nisi quae vis obstitit, videmus naturam suo quodam itinere ad ultimum pervenire.*

[55] The distinction between nature and τέχνη is reflected in the structure of *On the Causes of Plants* as a whole: Books 1 and 2 deal with nature, either the distinctive nature of the plant or that of the environment within which it grows, whereas books 3 and 4 discuss the works of agriculture.

[56] Αὐτόματα here refers to all natural processes not involving the intervention of τέχνη. In the strict sense, the term applies to generation due to external circumstances. For a distinction between a stricter and a wider use of the term, see *History of Plants* 2.1.1.

[57] This distinction corresponds to that between wild and tame animals, see *On the Causes of Plants* 1.16.13.6–8.

195

kind of growth is natural (*kata physin*) and the related issue whether the nature of a given kind should be studied in its wild or domesticated form.[58] Whereas plants which grow unaided can properly be deemed *kata physin*, the domesticated ones needing an external principle could seem to fall under the category of *kata technēn* entities.[59]

The *aporia* is resolved with the statement that husbandry is also natural because it supplies the things that an organism lacks and helps the nature of the plant to reach its perfection (*teleiōsis*).[60] In the case of domesticated plants, this happens through internal modifications brought about by husbandry[61] in a way that makes the latter similar to an internal principle. Agriculture as the external principle of growth and nutrition rather *imitates* and enforces the internal natural processes, which in other organisms take place unaided. As a result of this, cultivated plants come to accept the internal modifications brought about by husbandry as though they were appropriate to their nature (*hōs an oikeia*).[62] Nature in this case functions for the better under the influence of something external, but auxiliary, to it.

Theophrastus puts special stress on the effects of human *technē* on domesticated plants. A long part of book 3 of *On the Causes of Plants* is dedicated to agricultural procedures specific to the vine,[63] whereby he lays stress upon the sort of things which increase the power of the tree and encourage good feeding. These involve 'pinching off the largest leaves throughout the summer' and 'pulling the branches to one side and lowering the vine to the ground',[64] which safeguard the plant from various diseases. That is particularly relevant for weak plants like the vine, which is, as it were, by its own nature (*ek tēs physeōs*) liable to be destroyed by blasting

---

[58] αὐτοῦ δὲ τούτου τάχ' ἄν τις πάλιν ἀπορήσειε κοινήν τινα ἀπορίαν καὶ καθόλου πότερα τὴν φύσιν ἐκ τῶν αὐτομάτων μᾶλλον θεωρητέον ἢ ἐκ τῶν κατὰ τὰς ἐργασίας καὶ ἐν ποτέροις τὸ κατὰ φύσιν. σχεδὸν δὲ τούτῳ ταὐτό, μᾶλλον δὲ μέρος τούτου [καὶ] πότερον ἐκ τῶν ἀγρίων ἢ ἐκ τῶν ἡμέρων.
[59] *Ibid.* 1.16.10.8–16.11.6.   [60] *Ibid.* 1.16.11.7–11; cf. 3.1.1.5.   [61] *Ibid.* 1.16.12.3–4.
[62] *Ibid.* 1.16.12.4–6.
[63] *Ibid.* 3.11.1.3–16.4. Theophrastus prescribes there the right training for both the young and the full-grown vine.
[64] *Ibid.* 5.9.11.

winds.[65] The vulnerability of the vine is highlighted in numerous other passages of the Theophrastean botanical treatises, where the plant is described as tender (*hapalon*) and weak (*asthenes*).[66] In line with the Theophrastean references to the vine, Piso stresses the importance of viticulture for the preservation of the plant. Although the agricultural craft is an external principle, the Antiochean spokesperson underlines that if, counterfactually, the vine were asked it would admit that this is the treatment that suits it best; thus, although the craft is external, it is in accordance with the organism's nature and supplements the latter.[67] The assumption that *technē* in the case of the vine supplements nature contains an expression of the Aristotelian principle according to which 'craft imitates nature'; the canonical expression of it is found in the second book of Aristotle's *Physics*,[68] where Aristotle states that occasionally craft brings to completion those things that nature is unable to accomplish on its own.[69] By acting in an *analogous* way to nature, *technē* highlights the way nature itself proceeds: according to the striking counterfactual example in *Physics* 2, if houses were natural substances, they would look no different than the houses that are the products of *technē*.[70] Thus, the way *technē* operates as a cause towards a final end confirms *a fortiori* that nature is a cause 'for the sake of something' and possesses purposiveness. Still, for Aristotle nature is prior to

---

[65] *Ibid.* 5.12.8.6–7: καὶ ἡ ἄμπελος δὲ ἔχει τινὰ αἰτίαν ἐκ τῆς φύσεως καὶ ἐκ τῆς ἑλκώσεως τῆς περὶ τὴν τομήν; cf. *History of Plants* 2.7.2. On viticulture, see also Wardy (2005) 81.

[66] *On the Causes of Plants* 5.17.5.1–4 and *Ibid.* 5.17.7.1–11. Cf. also Cicero's *On Old Age* 52, which expands on the nature and the agricultural procedures pertaining to the vine.

[67] *On Ends* 5.39: *ut ipsae vites, si loqui possint, ita se tractandas tuendasque esse fateantur.*

[68] *Physics* 2.194a21; cf. *Meteorology* 4.381b6 and *Poetics* 1.1447a16.

[69] *Physics* 2.199a15–17: ὅλως δὲ ἡ τέχνη τὰ μὲν ἐπιτελεῖ ἃ ἡ φύσις ἀδυνατεῖ ἀπεργάσασθαι, τὰ δὲ μιμεῖται. This is reminiscent of an analogy embedded into the anti-Stoic critique of Cicero at *On Ends* 4.34, where it is stated that the role of wisdom is equal to that of the sculptor who takes over an unfinished work and perfects it. Like the sculptor, wisdom receives human beings from nature in an incomplete state (*inchoatum*) and has to perfect them (*absolvere*) as if they were statues *by* looking at nature herself (*hanc . . . intuens*): *ut Phidias potest a primo instituere signum idque perficere, potest ab alio inchoatum accipere et absolvere, huic similis est sapientia; non enim ipsa genuit hominem, sed accepit a natura inchoatum; hanc ergo intuens debet institutum illud quasi signum absolvere.*

[70] *Physics* 2.199a12–15: οἷον εἰ οἰκία τῶν φύσει γιγνομένων ἦν, οὕτως ἂν ἐγίγνετο ὡς νῦν ὑπὸ τῆς τέχνης· εἰ δὲ τὰ φύσει μὴ μόνον φύσει ἀλλὰ καὶ τέχνῃ γίγνοιτο, ὡσαύτως ἂν γίγνοιτο ἢ πέφυκεν.

technē, which suggests that he excludes actual agency in nature's operations.

Antiochus follows the example of Aristotelian counterfactual analogies and goes a step further: through a powerful image he invites us to imagine the craft of agriculture residing in the vine itself, so that 'if the vines could speak they would say that this is the way they want to be treated and preserved'. This has again clear antecedents in Aristotelian writings: at *Physics* 2.199b28-30 Aristotle imagines the craft of shipbuilding not in the builder but in the timber itself. If that were the case, ships would grow naturally, he adds.[71] Aristotle takes such a thought experiment to illuminate in the best way how nature operates without at the same time blurring the distinction between craft and nature.[72] Nowhere does he, however, apply the example to living organisms; the fact that Antiochus does so may be a sign of the greater preoccupation of the post-Aristotelian Peripatos with the role of *technē* in living organisms.

At *On Ends* 5.40 the thought-experiment invites us, as the vine which has internalised its external principle of growth and nutrition is transformed first into an animal and then into a rational human being, to reflect upon the common way in which nature and purpose manifest themselves in different living forms by means of an internal principle which leads each living form towards what is appropriate to its natural kind. This is illustrated again by means of a counterfactual image, according to which a vine equipped with perception and impulse, and thus capable of locomotion, would pursue of its own accord what is appropriate to its nature. The relevant passage reads as follows:

But what if perception were added to the vine, so that it would have also some impulse and self-motion? What do you think it would do? Wouldn't it take care on its own of what was previously provided by the vine-keeper? And wouldn't you notice that it would have an additional concern to preserve also its senses and the whole impulse that derives from them and all the bodily members that may

---

[71] καὶ εἰ ἐνῆν ἐν τῷ ξύλῳ ἡ ναυπηγική, ὁμοίως ἂν τῇ φύσει ἐποίει· ὥστ᾿ εἰ ἐν τῇ τέχνῃ ἔνεστι τὸ ἕνεκά του, καὶ ἐν τῇ φύσει.

[72] Cf. Sedley (2007) 177: 'Even then what such thought experiments reveal, and conceivably are designed to concede, is that the craft-nature gap could never be closed altogether.'

have been added to it? So to the features it always had are attached the ones that were added later, so that the vine won't have the same end that the vine-keeper had, but it would want to live according to this nature that was added to it afterwards. In this way its ultimate good will be analogous to what it was before, but not the same; for it will not seek any more the good of a plant, but that of an animal. What if it has been given not only perception, but also a human soul. Necessarily, while all its former features will remain objects of its care, these added ones will be much more dear to it, the best part of the soul being the most dear of all, since the final and ultimate good consists in this fulfilment of nature, mind and reason being far superior to anything else. Thus that would be the end of all things desired; guided by the first natural oikeiōsis [*a prima commendatione naturae*] it has ascended many steps [*multis gradibus adscendit*] to reach the highest good, which is made complete by bodily integrity and by perfected reason [*quod cumulatur ex integritate corporis et ex mentis ratione perfecta*]. (*On Ends* 5.40)

The thought-experiment presents us three different life forms: (a) a vine with an internalised principle of growth and nutrition; (b) an animal capable of perception and locomotion; and (c) a human being capable of the highest cognitive capacities of reason. The three life forms discussed correspond to the model of three different types of soul-form which are sketched in the second and third book of Aristotle's *On the Soul*. There, we find a discussion of nutrition, which is the fundamental function of the soul of all living things, including plants.[73] Subsequently Aristotle discusses sensation and locomotion, the functions which are characteristic of animals.[74] To these functions is added in the case of human beings thought, which can be both theoretical and practical.[75] All these soul-forms manifest in the Antiochean account the different stages of the transformation of the vine-human.

The three stages form a hierarchical order and underline the sequential way in which nature advances from lower to more advanced life forms, whereby the latter encompass the faculties of the former.[76] According to the example employed in Piso's speech, the vine, which has (counterfactually) acquired senses

---

[73] *On the Soul* 2.415a20ff.   [74] *Ibid.* 2.416b30ff.   [75] *Ibid.* 3.427a15ff.

[76] The Stoic doxography at Diogenes Laertius *Lives of Eminent Philosophers* 7.86 equally involves three living forms (plants-animals-human beings): οὐδέν τε, φασί, διήλλαξεν ἡ φύσις ἐπὶ τῶν φυτῶν καὶ ἐπὶ τῶν ζῴων, ὅτι χωρὶς ὁρμῆς καὶ αἰσθήσεως κἀκεῖνα οἰκονομεῖ καὶ ἐφ' ἡμῶν τινα φυτοειδῶς γίνεται. ἐκ περιττοῦ δὲ τῆς ὁρμῆς τοῖς ζῴοις ἐπιγενομένης, ᾗ συγχρώμενα πορεύεται πρὸς τὰ οἰκεῖα, τούτοις μὲν τὸ κατὰ φύσιν τῷ κατὰ τὴν ὁρμὴν διοικεῖσθαι τοῦ δὲ λόγου τοῖς λογικοῖς κατὰ τελειοτέραν προστασίαν δεδομένου, τὸ κατὰ

and impulse, will strive not only for its growth and nutrition, but also for the preservation of the bodily parts that it has acquired and for the acquisition of things suited to its nature through locomotion. It will thus live according to the nature of an animate being and not according to that of a plant. Finally, transformed into a human being, through the acquisition of the capacity of reason, the vine will, in addition to the desire for the preservation of its bodily parts, strive for the perfection of the faculties of the mind, and indeed much more so, since reason is the leading part of human nature, and 'infinitely superior' to the body.[77] The passage concludes by referring to the human *telos* as involving primarily the perfection of reason and, secondarily, the preservation of immaculate bodily integrity.[78] The thought experiment thus offers, by the way of the image of the transformed vine, an inter-species comparison which highlights both the similarities but also the differences in the way different life forms pursue their *oikeiōsis*.

The thought-experiment may serve, however, as an image of intra-species development as well. Regarded in this way, the image describes the different steps ascended from the 'first *oikeiōsis*' (*prima commendatio*), characterised by the quasi-

λόγον ζῆν ὀρθῶς γίνεσθαι τούτοις κατὰ φύσιν· τεχνίτης γὰρ οὗτος ἐπιγίνεται τῆς ὁρμῆς. This corroborates the point that the Antiochean account is developed as an alternative to Stoic theses. Notice, however, that in the Stoic passage the different life forms are said to be 'administered' (*dioikeisthai*) by nature pointing to a stronger form of providential teleology.

[77] *On Ends* 5.40: *haec multo esse cariora quae accesserint, animique optimam quamque partem carissimam, in eaque expletione naturae summi boni finem consistere, cum longe multumque praestet mens atque ratio?* The same point is made with the use of a similar thought experiment in the Antiochean-inspired Stoic critique of Cicero at *On Ends* 4.38: as viticulture when residing in the vine protects and guides all other 'powers' of the plant for the sake of its end, reason in human beings takes under its protection the impulse for the 'first natural things' and the corresponding activity of the senses: *ut si cultura vitium, cuius hoc munus est ut efficiat ut vitis cum partibus suis omnibus quam optime se habeat – sed sic intellegamus (licet enim, ut vos quoque soletis, fingere aliquid docendi causa) – si igitur illa cultura vitium in vite insit ipsa, cetera, credo, velit, quae ad colendam vitem attinebunt sicut antea, se autem omnibus vitis partibus praeferat statuatque nihil esse melius in vite quam se; similiter sensus, cum accessit ad naturam, tuetur illam quidem sed etiam se tuetur; cum autem assumpta ratio est, tanto in dominatu locatur ut omnia illa prima naturae huius tutelae subiciantur.* The last clause is reminiscent of the activity of reason in the Stoic 'canonical' account of *oikeiōsis* in Diogenes Laertius *Lives of Eminent Philosophers* 7.86: τοῦ δὲ λόγου τοῖς λογικοῖς κατὰ τελειοτέραν προστασίαν δεδομένου, τὸ κατὰ λόγον ζῆν ὀρθῶς γίνεσθαι τούτοις κατὰ φύσιν· τεχνίτης γὰρ οὗτος ἐπιγίνεται τῆς ὁρμῆς.

[78] *Ibid.* 5.40.

instinctive urge for self-preservation, to the perfection of reason and the acquisition of virtue. Thus, the different stages of the thought-experiment may serve to display the gradual development of human beings themselves from quasi-inanimate creatures in the cradle[79] to beings who have rational impulses and, ideally, wisdom. In line with this, the vine's dependence on *technē* may also serve the idea that the fulfilment of the human *telos* requires the 'straightening' of our initial, pre-rational impulses. Human beings, according to Antiochus, follow the perfecting of their nature through many stages and through a gradual development of their reasoning faculties. Against this background, the vine and its relation to husbandry could be viewed as an apt example for illustrating the method by which human beings attain their *telos*. Just as the vine needs the aid of the skill of husbandry for the attainment of its *telos*, humans, although possessing a natural inclination towards virtue, can attain it only through a process of gradual learning. The role of *technē* in the case of humans is assumed by wisdom and philosophy, which cause the flourishing of our innate tendency towards virtue.[80] In line with this, human development is explained by means of the metaphor of 'cultivation' (*cultura*) at *Tusculan Disputations* 2.13, with philosophy assuming the role of the cultivator who 'pulls out' (*extrahit*) the vices and 'sows' (*serit*) in it seeds which, when fully grown, bring the most abundant fruits (*quae adulta fructus uberrimos ferant*).[81] The idea originates in Plato, where it appears in connection with the right instruction of children's nature through education.[82]

---

[79] See *ibid*. 5.42: *parvi enim primo ortu sic iacent, tamquam omnino sine animo sint.*

[80] *Ibid*. 5.60: *itaque nostrum (quod nostrum dico, artis est) ad ea principia quae accepimus consequentia exquirere, quoad sit id quod volumus effectum.*

[81] *atque, ut in eodem simili verser, ut ager quamvis fertilis sine cultura fructuosus esse non potest, sic sine doctrina animus; ita est utraque res sine altera debilis. cultura autem animi philosophia est; haec extrahit vitia radicitus et praeparat animos ad satus accipiendos eaque mandat is et, ut ita dicam, serit, quae adulta fructus uberrimos ferant.*

[82] See esp. *Republic* 492a: ἥν τοίνυν ἔθεμεν τοῦ φιλοσόφου φύσιν, ἂν μὲν οἶμαι μαθήσεως προσηκούσης τύχῃ, εἰς πᾶσαν ἀρετὴν ἀνάγκη αὐξανομένην ἀφικνεῖσθαι, ἐὰν δὲ μὴ ἐν προσηκούσῃ σπαρεῖσά τε καὶ φυτευθεῖσα τρέφηται, εἰς πάντα τἀναντία αὖ, ἐὰν μή τις αὐτῇ βοηθήσας θεῶν τύχῃ; cf. *ibid*. 497b. Cf. *Laws* 766a: ἄνθρωπος δέ, ὥς φαμεν, ἥμερον ζῷον, ὅμως μὴν παιδείας μὲν ὀρθῆς τυχὸν καὶ φύσεως εὐτυχοῦς, θειότατον ἡμερώτατόν τε ζῷον γίγνεσθαι φιλεῖ, μὴ ἱκανῶς δὲ ἢ μὴ καλῶς τραφὲν ἀγριώτατον, ὁπόσα φύει γῆ. ὧν ἕνεκα οὐ δεύτερον οὐδὲ πάρεργον δεῖ τὴν παίδων τροφὴν τὸν νομοθέτην ἐᾶν γίγνεσθαι.

EPILOGUE

This study has offered an analysis of key aspects of Antiochus of Ascalon's philosophical activity with a special focus on his views as an historian of philosophy and his engagement with the Aristotelian/Peripatetic tradition in the domain of ethics. Chapter 1 attempted to present Antiochus' philosophical movement in its larger historical and social context, showing how it represents an episode in the process of cultural appropriation that took place between Rome and the Greek world in the late Republic. Antiochus' interest in the revival of the philosophy of the 'ancients' was shown to be partly motivated by the educational needs that arose in the new Roman context in which he operated. On the other hand, Cicero's appreciation of Antiochus is testimony to his interest in philosophical *auctoritas* but also serves as a medium at his attempt of making philosophy an accessible educational tool for the Roman elite.

Chapter 2 presents Antiochus' views on the history of philosophy. It was suggested that Antiochus adopts an original inclusive reading, according to which the Academy and the Peripatos have jointly contributed to the most 'complete' philosophical system. This allows for a more relaxed attitude towards Platonic authority, allowing for the elaboration of Plato's views through his successors. In the domain of ethics, Antiochus turns primarily to the authority of the Peripatos and its leading members, Aristotle and Theophrastus. Piso's account attests that the Antiochean reconstruction of the ethics of the Old Academy was based on surviving writings of the two authorities, which gained new attention in the first century BCE. On the other hand, Antiochus presents the post-Theophrastean phase of the Peripatos as degenerate and heterodox. The school of the Stoa is shown to be part of the same Old Academic tradition in the Antiochean reconstruction of the history of philosophy. Towards the Stoa Antiochus adopts an ambivalent stance which oscillates between the attribution of innovation and that of redundancy: in the domain of ethics the Stoics are said to be merely repeating the doctrines of the 'ancients' with new terminology, while in the domain of epistemology Antiochus allows for genuine innovations on their part.

The remaining chapters concentrate on the ethical side of Antiochus, analysing the main themes that emerge from the Antiochean ethical account at *On Ends* 5. Chapter 3 is dedicated to the reconstruction of the *oikeiōsis* argument ascribed to the Peripatos. It is thereby shown that this argument responds to a Stoic argument from appropriation but also to a rich dialectical context which involved both Epicureans and Academic sceptics. It was suggested that Antiochus offers an original Aristotelian/Peripatetic version of *oikeiōsis* which presents the inherent desire of human nature to fulfil its bodily and psychic capacities as the metaphysical foundation of *eudaimonia*. Chapter 4 offers an analysis of the Antiochean arguments for self-love as the main psychological mechanism of natural appropriation, along with a discussion of Aristotelian passages which may have served as an inspiration for these views.

Antiochus gives an account of the bodily and psychic goods which are constitutive of the 'best life', giving special emphasis on the theoretical and practical virtues. Most probably under the influence of the Epicurean school and with the use of both Platonic and Aristotelian/Peripatetic resources, Antiochus also develops an original set of 'cradle arguments' which purport to offer empirical proofs of the way natural appropriation is manifest in humans from the moment of birth. Children are said thereby to possess 'seeds of virtue', which 'flourish' under the influence of reason. Such a view was also shown in Chapter 5 to be linked to an intellectualist reading of the virtues which is Platonic (or 'Socratic') in origin.

The analysis of our natural appropriation towards the perfection of our psychic capacities shows Antiochus' commitment to theoretical virtue as the highest kind of excellence; his ideas were shown in Chapter 6 to be echoing lines of argument from Aristotle's *Protrepticus* which defend the inherent desirability of theoretical inquiry. The available evidence on social *oikeiōsis* on the other hand, which was discussed in Chapter 7, showed how our appropriation towards justice is structured around diverse associations (*philiai*). The furthest such association was shown to encompass humanity as a whole in the form of the virtue of *philanthrōpia*.

While Antiochus presents intellectual activity as the highest kind of activity he also includes political action and the social virtues in his account of *eudaimonia*. Chapter 8 contains a discussion of the sufficiency of virtue for the attainment of the 'best life'; it was shown that while Antiochus recognises the overriding primacy of virtue for the attainment of a happy life, defending even the view that virtue is sufficient for happiness, at the same time he suggests that bodily goods make up the 'best possible life'. Antiochus' views on the relative importance of the components of the *telos* were further compared to other Peripatetic attempts to offer a satisfactory account of Aristotelian/Peripatetic *eudaimonia*. Finally Chapter 9 suggested links between Antiochus' remarks about animals and plants at *On Ends* 5 and Aristotelian and Theophrastean natural science. Special emphasis was given thereby to the recognition of cognitive features in animal behaviour as also to the botanical example of the vine, which highlights the interaction between nature and *technē* in living organisms. This helps us appreciate better how Antiochus places ethics within a wider naturalistic context, designed to show the sequence of species-specific life forms on the basis of their respective participation in natural appropriation.

We may reflect now on the wider implications of the picture that emerges from this study. Antiochus challenges our classifications of ancient Greek philosophy into discrete schools of thought with competing agendas. It is accordingly difficult to pin down his philosophical identity by ascribing to him labels like 'Stoic', 'Platonist' or 'Peripatetic', precisely because his philosophical project eschews such labels and enjoys the freedom of constructing its thesis across a wide variety of sources from the schools of the Academy and the Peripatos (e.g. 'Socratic' ideas about the intellectual character of the virtues are combined in his account with an Aristotelian type of teleology); furthermore, the influence of the Stoic philosophical agenda is pervasive throughout his thought and is reflected in the major topics discussed and the terminology used to express them (see e.g. the use of *oikeiōsis*). The Antiochean account in *On Ends* 5 even shows the influence of Epicurean methodology (with its use of 'cradle arguments').

Although from our (historically sensitive) point of view this seems like a pick-and-mix attitude (which appears to justify the label of an 'eclectic' or a 'syncretist'), that may not be an accurate description of what Antiochus himself was involved with. From *his* point of view what he offered was a faithful philosophical picture of the Academy, if one considers two peculiar Antiochean premises: (a) the Academic tradition is unified around certain primary 'consensual' points (e.g. natural teleology and preeminent role of virtue for a happy life) and (b) the structure of an Academic system should correspond to an Hellenistic (especially Stoic) agenda. In the domain of ethics this allows for the construction of an account which is largely based on the Aristotelian/Peripatetic tradition (which offers the main insights on natural teleology), while borrowing motifs from the Platonic tradition as well (with regard to the sufficiency of virtue for a happy life). The demand to construct an equivalent account to that offered by the Stoa justifies the abundant use of Stoic terminology as also the range of topics discussed (most prominently, the natural foundation of the *telos*). For sure, Antiochus does not seem aware of the limitations of his hermeneutic assumptions and of his 'projections' onto the 'ancients'. But these are modern concerns which postulate criteria of historical correctness and a corresponding methodology.[1] Antiochus is one of the first figures in the history of philosophy who, by their very activity, put at centre stage such hermeneutical questions on the interpretation of the texts of ancient authorities, even though the methodology that he pursues with regard to such questions is never itself made transparent.

We may speculate about the conditions which made possible such a uniquely inclusive project. There is no doubt that Antiochus' schooling in the New Academy, where the diverse philosophical views were discussed *in utramque partem* for the

---

[1] Still, the topic of the 'Platonism' of Aristotle receives attention even in modern scholarship, see e.g. Gerson (2004) on Aristotle's Platonism in the domain of ethics.

sake of refutation, contributed to his exposure to different philosophical currents and to a certain openness across school boundaries. This attitude of philosophical freedom was supported by the fact that Antiochus could express his views without the fear of the charge of 'heresy'. This again was granted to him by the special historical circumstances of the time: because the Academy and the Peripatos had ceased to operate as institutions, Antiochus was free to explore widely and present his ideas as a recovery of the thought of the 'ancients' without opposing existing institutional authorities on both camps. All this contributed to his developing novel philosophical readings of the ancient tradition.

It has also emerged as a consequence of this study that Antiochus developed in the domain of ethics a distinctive approach in comparison with his activity in other areas; while in his epistemology (as reflected in the *Lucullus*) he is shown almost wholeheartedly to endorse Stoicism (perhaps due to the lack of corresponding material in the ancient tradition, especially in the Peripatos), his reconstruction of the ethics of the old tradition attests a willingness to engage with the old material *in its own right*, recognising its distinctive approach and contribution. This shows the primary importance of ethics in Antiochus' philosophical project but is also indicative of different phases in Antiochus' philosophical production.

The new philosophical insights that this picture offers are also worth considering in their own right with regard to their merits. Especially promising areas offered by Antiochus' account, in my view, include the idea that our pursuit of *eudaimonia* has a grounding in our species-specific human nature and its capacities, as also the discussion of the *telos* of animals and plants alongside the *telos* of human beings, as part of a naturalistic ethical theory. Not least, Antiochus is among the first philosophers to offer an explicit defence of the importance of self-love for human flourishing, a topic which is worth considering further for its implications.

Finally, we may reflect on the influence of Antiochus on subsequent philosophers. It is not surprising that such a reading of the 'ancients' as attempted by Antiochus provoked reactions and motivated a renewed study of the original texts of the old authorities. Although a dogmatic interpretation of Plato was universally adopted, there was strong resistance to the attempt to read Plato *through* later philosophers.[2] Philosophers in the generations which followed after Antiochus explicitly fashioned themselves as 'Platonists' or 'Peripatetics' (as opposed to the inclusive term of an 'Academic' espoused by Antiochus).[3] It is suggestive that two of Antiochus' pupils, Aristo of Alexandria and Cratippus of Pergamum, are said to have defected from the Academy and to have become 'Peripatetics'. The evidence is contained in the *History of the Academy* written by the first-century BCE Epicurean Philodemus.[4] This might suggest that Antiochus' pupils turned their attention exclusively to the study of Peripatetic texts, and rejected the Antiochean thesis of a doctrinal unity between Plato's Academy and the Peripatos.[5] Furthermore, the approach of the next generation of Platonists and Peripatetics was much more text-based than Antiochus' own and led to the development of elaborate exegetical tools in order to account for inconsistencies in the texts of the two major authorities.[6] The thesis of an 'agreement' between Plato and Aristotle became a dominant idea in the subsequent philosophers from the third to the sixth century CE,

---

[2] Atticus (belonging to the so-called Middle Platonists), for example, explicitly opposed the attempt to read Plato through a Peripatetic lens, see Atticus' *Frs.* 1–9 Des Places from *Against Those Who Undertake to Interpret Plato's Doctrines through Those of Aristotle* (Πρὸς τοὺς διὰ τῶν Ἀριστοτέλους τὰ Πλάτωνος ὑπισχνουμένους). The content and the addressee of Atticus' polemical treatise is discussed in Karamanolis (2006) 150–57. For a list of works of later Platonists on the relation between Platonic and Aristotelian philosophy, see *ibid.* 337–38.

[3] For a sketch of this development, see Glucker (1978) 206–25.

[4] Antiochus *T*3 = Philodemus *History of the Academy* (*PHerc.* 1021) c. xxxv.11–15: Ἀρίστων [μὲν] καὶ Κράτ[ιπ]πος ε.[......] να[......ακουσαντε[ς] ζῆλον ε[.. .... ἐγένοντο Περιπατη[τικοί. The text follows Blank (2007) and Blank's revised readings in Sedley (2012b). For an alternative reading of the text, see Sharples (2010) 12. For the designation 'Peripatetic' in the next generation after Antiochus, see also τοὺς ἀπὸ τοῦ Περιπάτου in Alexander *Mantissa* 152.16.

[5] Karamanolis (2006) 82 speculates that 'Antiochus' students found Aristotelianism to be the best interpretation or development of Plato's philosophy in the sense that it offered a complete and systematic dogmatic philosophy.'

[6] For example, the anonymous commentator to Plato's *Theaetetus* focuses on the *ipsissima verba* of Plato's text, see Sedley (1997). Plutarch, on the other hand, applies in his Platonic treatise *On the Creation of the Soul according to the Timaeus* the principle of reading 'Plato from within Plato', a hermeneutical rule borrowed from Homeric scholarship, see, for instance, 1015f4–16a1: ἡ μὲν οὖν διάνοια τοιαύτη, κατά γε τὴν ἐμὴν δόξαν, τοῦ Πλάτωνος· ἀπόδειξις δὲ πρώτη μὲν ἡ τῆς λεγομένης καὶ δοκούσης αὐτοῦ πρὸς ἑαυτὸν ἀσυμφωνίας καὶ διαφορᾶς λύσις. For the exegetical activity of Peripatetics like Xenarchus, see Falcon (2012) 21–25.

Epilogue

although the primacy of Plato (the 'divine' philosopher) over Aristotle was strongly established and acknowledged in a way that is not yet visible in Antiochus.[7]

One thing, surely, did not change from the time of Antiochus onwards and until the last days of the tradition we may call 'ancient philosophy': meaningful philosophical activity was understood by all major philosophers, following Antiochus, primarily as an attempt to offer a correct understanding of the 'ancients'.

---

[7] As Karamanolis (2006) 4 notes, '[I]t is not the case that some Platonists from the third to sixth century AD studied Aristotle's philosophy for its own sake. Rather, Aristotle was appropriated by Platonists because they found his philosophy, if properly studied, a prerequisite for, and conducive to, an understanding of Plato's thought.'

BIBLIOGRAPHY

Primary Texts (Editions and Translations)

Alexander of Aphrodisias

Bruns, I. (ed.) (1887). *Alexandri Aphrodisiensis praeter Commentaria, Scripta Minora: De Anima liber cum mantissa.* Academiae Litterarum Regiae Borussicae, vol. 2, parts 1–2. Berlin.

Sharples, R.W. (transl.) (2004). *Supplement to On the Soul.* London.

Sharples, R.W. (2008). *De Anima libri mantissa.* Berlin/New York.

Anonymous Commentary on Plato's Theaetetus

Bastianini, G., and Sedley, D. (eds) (1995). *Corpus dei papiri filosofici greci e latini,* vol. 3. Florence, 227–562.

Aristotle

Balme, D.M. (ed. and transl.) (1991). *History of Animals. Books VII-X.* Aristotle Vol. XI. Loeb Classical Library 439. Cambridge, MA.

Barnes, J. (ed.) (1984). *The Complete Works of Aristotle. The Revised Oxford Translation.* 2 vols. Princeton, NJ.

Bywater, I. (ed.) (1894). *Aristotelis ethica Nicomachea.* Oxford.

Düring, I. (1961). *Aristotle's* Protrepticus. *An Attempt at Reconstruction.* Göteborg.

Hamlyn, D.W. (transl.) (1993). *De Anima. Books II and III.* Oxford.

Hicks, R.D. (ed.) (1907). *De Anima.* Cambridge.

Hutchinson, D.S., and Johnson, M.R. (eds and transl.) (2016). [Aristotle] *Protrepticus* or *Exhortation to Philosophy.* (Draft accessed from www .protrepticus.info (November 2016))

Irwin, T. (transl.) (1999). *Nicomachean Ethics.* Indianapolis/ Cambridge.

Kraut, R. (transl.) (1998). *Politics. Books VI and VIII.* Oxford.

Pakaluk, M. (transl.) (1998).*Nicomachean Ethics. Books VIII and IX.* Oxford.

Bibliography

Rowe, C. (transl.) (2002). *Nicomachean Ethics*. Introduction and Commentary by S. Broadie. Oxford.

Saunders, T. (transl.) (1995). *Politics. Books I and II*. Oxford.

Susemihl, F. (ed.) ([1935]1969). *Oeconomica and magna moralia*. Trans. G.C. Armstrong. Cambridge, MA.

Walzer, R.R., and Mingay, J.M. (eds) (1991). *Ethica eudemia*. Oxford.

Cicero

Annas, J. (ed.) and R. Woolf (trans.) (2001). *Cicero. On Moral Ends*. Cambridge.

Brittain, C. (transl.). (2006). *On Academic Scepticism*. Indianapolis/ Cambridge.

Dyck, A. (1996). De Officiis. *A Commentary*. Ann Arbor, MI.

Graver, M. (transl.) (2002). *Cicero on the Emotions. Tusculan Disputations 3 and 4*. Chicago/London.

Griffin, M.T., and Atkins, E.M. (eds) (1991). *Cicero. On Duties*. Cambridge Texts in the History of Political Thought. Cambridge.

Gigon, O. and Straume-Zimmermann, L. (1988). *Über die Ziele des menschlichen Handelns*. Munich/Zurich.

Keyes, C.W. (transl.) (1928). *De Re Publica. De Legibus*. Cicero Vol. XVI. Loeb Classical Library 213. Cambridge, MA.

Madvig, N. (1876³). *M. Tulli Ciceronis De Finibus Bonorum et Malorum. Libri Quinque*. Hauniae (Copenhagen).

Plasberg, O. (1922). *Academicorum reliquiae cum Lucullo*. Leipzig.

Powell, J.G.F. (ed. and transl.) (1990). *On Friendship and The Dream of Scipio*. Warminster, UK.

Powell, J.G.F. (ed.) (2006). *De Re Publica. De Legibus. Cato Maior De Senectute. Laelius De Amicitia*. Oxford Classical Text. Oxford.

Rackham, H.(transl.) ([1914] 1931²). *Cicero, De Finibus Bonorum et Malorum*. Cicero Vol. XVII. Loeb Classical Library 40. Cambridge, MA.

([1933] 1951). *De Natura Deorum. Academica*. Cicero Vol. XIX. The Loeb Classical Library 268. Cambridge MA.

(1942). *On the Orator Book 3. On Fate. Stoic Paradoxes. Divisions of Oratory*. Cicero Vol. IV. Loeb Classical Library 349. Cambridge, MA.

Reid, J.S. (1883). *M. Tulli Ciceronis De Finibus Bonorum et Malorum. Libri Quinque*, vol. 3. Cambridge.

Reid, J.S. (ed.) (1885). *Academica*. London.

Reynolds L.D. (ed.) (1998). *De Finibus Bonorum et Malorum. Libri Quinque*. Oxford Classical Texts. Oxford.

Schäublin, C., Bächli, A., and Graeser, A. (1995). *Akademische Abhandlungen. Lucullus*. Hamburg.

Shackleton Bailey, D.R. (ed. and transl.) (1999). *Letters to Atticus*. 4 vols. Cambridge.

Bibliography

Straume-Zimmermann, L., Broemser, F. and Gigon, O. (1990). *Hortensius. Lucullus. Academici Libri.* Munich/Zurich.

Zetzel, J. (trans.) (1999). *On the Commonwealth* and *On the Laws.* Cambridge.

[Arius?] Didymus

Fortenbaugh, W.W. (ed.) (2017). *Arius Didymus on Peripatetic Ethics, Household Management and Politics.* Critical Edition and Translation by Georgia Tsouni. Rutgers University Studies in Classical Humanities. Vol. 20. London.

Diogenes Laertius

Dorandi, T. (ed.) (2013). *Lives of Eminent Philosophers.* Cambridge Classical Texts and Commentaries 50. Cambridge.

Hicks, R.D. (transl.) (1925). *Lives of Eminent Philosophers*, vols. 1–2. Loeb Classical Library 184. Cambridge, MA.

Epictetus

Hard, R. (transl.) (2014). *Discourses, Fragments, Handbook.* With an Introduction and Notes by Christopher Gill. Oxford.

Eusebius

Mras, K. (ed.) (1954–1956). *Die Praeparatio evangelica.* Berlin.

Hierocles

Bastianini, G., and Long, A.A. (eds and transl.) (1992). *Elementa moralia. Corpus dei Papiri filosofici Greci e Latini*, vol. 1.1.2. Florence.

Ramelli, I. (2009). *Elements of Ethics, Fragments and Excerpts.* David Konstan (transl.). Writings from the Greco-Roman World 28. Atlanta.

Iamblichus

Pistelli, H. (ed.) (1888). *Iamblichi Protrepticus.* Leipzig.

Bibliography

Philodemus

Dorandi, T., (ed. and transl.) (1991). *Storia dei Filosofi. Platone e l' Academia (PHerc. 1021 e 164)*. Naples.

Plato

Burnet, J. (1900). *Platonis Opera*, vols. 1–5. Oxford.

Cooper, J.M. (1997). *Plato. Complete Works*. Indianapolis/Cambridge.

Denyer, N. (2001). Plato *Alcibiades*. Cambridge Greek and Latin Classics. Cambridge.

Plutarch

Cherniss, H. (1976). *On Stoic Self-Contradictions. Against the Stoics on Common Conceptions*. Loeb Classical Library 470. Cambridge, MA.

Polemo

Gigante, M. (ed.) (1976). *Polemonis Academici Fragmenta. Rendiconti dell'Accademia di Archeologia Lettere e Belle Arti di Napoli* 51, 91–144.

Porphyry

Bouffartigue, J., and Patillon, M. (1977–1995). *De l' abstinence*, vols. 1–3. Paris.

Clark, G. (transl.) (2000). *On Abstinence from Killing Animals*. London.

Seneca

Inwood, B. (transl.) (2007). *Selected Philosophical Letters*. Oxford.

Sextus Empiricus

Annas, J., and Barnes, J. (transl.) (1994). *Outlines of Scepticism*, Cambridge.

Bett, R. (ed. and transl.) (2005). *Against the Logicians. (Against the Professors Book 7)*. Cambridge Texts in the History of Philosophy. Cambridge.

Bury, R.G. (transl.) (1935). *Against the Logicians (Against the Professors Book 7)*. Sextus Empiricus Vol. II. Loeb Classical Library 291. Cambridge, MA.

Bibliography

Bury, R.G. (transl.) (1936). *Against the Physicists. Against the Ethicists.* Sextus Empiricus Vol. III. Loeb Classical Library 311. Cambridge, MA.

Speusippus

Parente, M.I. (1980). *Frammenti.* Naples.
Taran, L. (1981). *Speusippus of Athens.* Leiden.

Stobaeus

Hense, O. (1894–1909). *Ioannis Stobaei Anthologii. Books 3 and 4.* Berlin
Meineke, A. (ed.) (1860–1864). *Ioannis Stobaei Eclogarum Physicarum et Ethicarum Libri Duo.* Leipzig.
Wachsmuth, C. (ed.) (1884). *Ioannis Stobaei Anthologii. Books 1 and 2.* Berlin.

Theophrastus

Einerson, B. and Link, G.K. (transl.) (1976–90). *De Causis Plantarum.* 3 vols. Loeb Classical Library 475. London.
Hort, A. (1916). *Historia Plantarum* (Enquiry into Plants). 2 vols. Loeb Classical Library 70 Cambridge, MA, and London.
Huby, P. (1999). Theophrastus of Eresus. *Sources for His Life, Writings, Thought and Influence.* Commentary volume 4: Psychology. Leiden.
  (2007). *Theophrastus of Eresus. Sources for His Life, Writings, Thought and Influence. Commentary volume 2: Logic.* Leiden.
Sharples, R.W. (1998). *Theophrastus of Eresus. Sources for His Life, Writings, Thought and Influence.* Commentary volume 3.1: Physics. Leiden.
van Raalte, M. (ed. and transl.) (1993). *Metaphysics.* Leiden.

Xenocrates

Parente, M. I., and Dorandi T. (eds) (2012). *Testimonianze e Frammenti.* 2nd edn Pisa.

Secondary Literature

Algra, K. (1997). 'Chrysippus, Carneades, Cicero: The Ethical *divisiones* in Cicero's *Lucullus*' in B. Inwood and J. Mansfeld (eds), *Assent and Argument. Studies in Cicero's Academic Books* Leiden, 107–39.
Annas, J. (1993). *The Morality of Happiness.* New York/Oxford.

Bibliography

(2007). 'Carneades' Classification of Ethical Theories' in A.I. Ioppolo and D.N. Sedley (eds), *Pyrrhonists, Patricians, Platonizers. Hellenistic Philosophy in the Period* 155–86 B.C. Tenth Symposium Hellenisticum. Naples, 189–223.

Arnim von, H. (1926). *Arius Didymus' Abriß der Peripatetischen Ethik. Akademie der Wissenschaften in Wien, Philosophisch-historische Klasse, Sitzungsberichte Bd.* 204. 3. Abhandlung. Wien.

Balsdon, J.P.V.D. (1960). 'Auctoritas, Dignitas, Otium'. *The Classical Quarterly* 10.1: 43–50.

Barnes, J. (1985). 'Cicero's *De Fato* and a Greek Source' in J. Brunschwig, C. Imbert and A. Roger (eds) *Histoire et Structure. À la memoire de Victor Goldschmidt.* Paris, 229–39.

(1989). 'Antiochus of Ascalon' in J. Barnes and M. Griffin (eds), *Philosophia Togata I.* Oxford, 51–96.

(1997). 'Roman Aristotle' in J. Barnes and M. Griffin (eds), *Philosophia Togata II.* Oxford, 1–69.

Barney, R. (2008). 'Aristotle's Argument for a Human Function'. *Oxford Studies in Ancient Philosophy* 34: 293–322.

Bees, R. (2004). *Die Oikeiosislehre der Stoa I. Rekonstruktion ihres Inhalts.* Würzburg.

Bénatouil, T. (2009). 'Θεωρία et vie contemplative du stoicisme au platonisme' in M. Bonazzi and J. Opsomer (eds), *The Origins of the Platonic System. Platonism of the Early Empire and its Philosophical Context.* Leuven, 1–20.

Blank, D. (2007). 'The Life of Antiochus of Ascalon in Philodemus' *History of the Academy* and a Tale of Two Letters'. *Zeitschrift für Philosophie und Epigraphik* 162: 87–93.

(2012). 'Varro and Antiochus' in D. Sedley (ed.), *The Philosophy of Antiochus* Cambridge, 250–89.

Bonazzi, M. (2009). 'Antiochus' Ethics and the Subordination of Stoicism' in M. Bonazzi and J. Opsomer (eds), *The Origins of the Platonic System. Platonism of the Early Empire and Its Philosophical Context.* Leuven, 33–54.

(2012). 'Antiochus and Platonism' in D. Sedley (ed.), *The Philosophy of Antiochus.* Cambridge, 307–33.

Boys-Stones, G.R. (2001). *Post-Hellenistic Philosophy. A Study of Its Development from the Stoics to Origen.* Oxford.

(2012). 'Antiochus' Metaphysics' in D. Sedley (ed.), *The Philosophy of Antiochus.* Cambridge, 220–36.

(2014). 'Unity and the Good: Platonists Against οἰκείωσις' in B. Collette-Dučić and S. Delcomminette (eds), *Unité et origine des vertus dans la philosophie anciennes.* Brussels, 297–320.

Brink, C.O. (1956). 'Οἰκείωσις and οἰκειότης. Theophrastus and Zeno on Nature in Moral Theory'. *Phronesis* 1.2: 123–45.

Bibliography

Brittain, C. (2001). *Philo of Larissa. The Last of the Academic Sceptics.* Oxford.

(2012). 'Antiochus' Epistemology' in D. Sedley (ed.), *The Philosophy of Antiochus.* Cambridge, 104–30.

Brunner, Á. (2010). Totas Paginas Commovere? Cicero's Presentation of Stoic Ethics in *De Finibus* Book III. PhD thesis. Central European University, Budapest.

(2014). 'On Antiochus' Moral Psychology'. *Rhizomata* 2: 187–212.

Brunschwig, J. (1986). 'The Cradle Argument in Epicureanism and Stoicism' in M. Schofield and G. Striker (eds), *The Norms of Nature. Studies in Hellenistic Ethics.* Cambridge, 113–44.

Bywater, I. (1869). 'On a Lost Dialogue of Aristotle'. *Journal of Philology* 2: 55–69.

Catana, L. (2008). *The Historiographical Concept 'System of Philosophy'. Its Origin, Nature, Influence and Legitimacy.* Brill's Studies in Intellectual History 165. Leiden.

Chiaradonna, R. (2013). 'Platonist Approaches to Aristotle: From Antiochus of Ascalon to Eudorus of Alexandria (and Beyond)' in M. Schofield (ed.) *Aristotle, Plato and Pythagoreanism in the First Century BC.* Cambridge, 28–52.

Couissin, P. (1983). 'The Stoicism of the New Academy' in M. Burnyeat (ed.), *The Skeptical Tradition.* Berkeley, 31–63 (English Translation of the 1929 article of P. Couissin 'Le Stoicisme de la Nouvelle Académie' in *Revue d'histoire de la philosophie* 3: 241–76).

Cole, E. B. (1992). 'Theophrastus and Aristotle on Animal Intelligence', in W. Fortenbaugh and D. Gutas (eds), *Theophrastus, His Psychological, Doxographical and Scientific Writings.* RUSCH 5, 43–62.

Cooper, J. (1995). 'Eudaimonism and the Appeal to Nature in the Morality of Happiness: Comments on J. Annas, The Morality of Happiness'. *Philosophy and Phenomenological Research* 55.3: 587–98.

Corbeill, A. (2013) 'Cicero and the Intellectual Milieu of the Late Republic' in C. Steel (ed.), *The Cambridge Companion to Cicero.* Cambridge, 9–24.

Crawford, M.H. (1978). 'Greek Intellectuals and the Roman Aristocracy in the First Century B.C.' in P.D.A Garnsey and C.R. Whittaker (eds), *Imperialism in the Ancient World.* Cambridge, 193–207.

Curzer, H.J. (2012). *Aristotle and the Virtues.* Oxford.

De Ruiter, S.T. (1931). 'De vocis quae est φιλανθρωπία significatione atque usu'. *Mnemosyne* 59.3: 271–306.

Dierauer, U. (1977). *Tier und Mensch im Denken der Antike.* Amsterdam. 1977.

Dillon, J. (1977). *The Middle Platonists. 80 B.C. to A.D. 220.* New York.

(2003). *The Heirs of Plato. A Study of the Old Academy (347–274 BC).* Oxford.

Dirlmeier, F. (1937). *Die Oikeiosis-Lehre Theophrasts.* Philologus Supp. Bd. 30.1: 1–100.

Bibliography

Donini, P. (1988) 'The History of the Concept of Eclecticism' in J. Dillon and A.A. Long (eds), *The Question of 'Eclecticism'. Studies in Later Greek Philosophy*. Berkeley, 15–33.

Dyroff, A. (1897). *Die Ethik der alten Stoa*. Berlin.

Engberg-Pedersen, T. (1986). 'Discovering the Good: *Oikeiōsis* and *kathēkonta* in Stoic Ethics' in Schofield M. and Striker G. (eds), *The Norms of Nature*. Cambridge, 145–83.

(1990). *The Stoic Theory of Oikeiosis*. Aarhus.

Falcon, A. (2012). *Aristotelianism in the First Century BCE. Xenarchus of Seleucia*. Cambridge.

Ferrary, J.-L. (2007). 'Les Philosophes grecs a Rome (155–86 av. J.C.)' in A.M. Ioppolo and D. Sedley (eds), *Pyrrhonists, Patricians, Platonizers. Tenth Symposium Hellenisticum*. Naples, 19–46.

Fladerer, L. (1996). *Antiochos von Askalon. Hellenist und Humanist*. Grazer Beiträge. Supplementband VII. Graz.

Fortenbaugh, W.W. (1984). *Quellen zur Ethik Theophrasts*. Amsterdam.

Frede, M. (1999). 'Epilogue' in K. Algra, J. Barnes, J. Mansfeld and M. Schofield (eds), *The Cambridge History of Hellenistic Philosophy*. Cambridge, 771–97.

Gerson, L. (2004). 'Platonism in Aristotle's Ethics'. *Oxford Studies in Ancient Philosophy* 27: 217–98.

(2013). *From Plato to Platonism*. Ithaca and London.

Gigon, O. (1988). 'The Peripatos in Cicero's *De Finibus*' in W. Fortenbaugh and R.W. Sharples (eds), *Theophrastean Studies*. RUSCH 3, 259–71.

(1989). 'Theophrast in Cicero's *De Finibus*' in W. Fortenbaugh and P. Steinmetz (eds), *Cicero's Knowledge of the Peripatos RUSCH* 4, 159–85.

Gildenhard, I. (2007). *Paideia Romana. Cicero's Tusculan Disputations*. Proceedings of the Cambridge Philological Society. Supplementary Volume 30. Cambridge.

Gill, C. (2006). *The Structured Self in Hellenistic and Roman Thought*. Oxford.

(2016). 'Antiochus' Theory of Oikeiōsis' in J. Annas and G. Betegh (eds), *Cicero's De Finibus. Philosophical Approaches*. Cambridge, 221–47.

Giusta, M. (1964–1967). *I dossografi di Etica*, vols. 1–2. Turin.

(1990). 'Antioco di Ascalona e Carneade nel libro v del *De Finibus Bonorum et Malorum* di Cicerone'. *Elenchos* 11: 29–49.

Glucker, J. (1978). *Antiochus and the Late Academy*. Hypomnemata 56. Göttingen.

(2002). Book review of L. Fladerer: *Antiochos von Askalon. Hellenist und Humanist* (Graz, 1996) in *Gnomon* 74: 289–95.

Göransson, T. (1995). *Albinus, Alcinous, Arius Didymus*. Göteborg.

Görgemanns, H. (1983). '*Oikeiosis* in Arius Didymus' in W. Fortenbaugh (ed.), *On Stoic and Peripatetic Ethics: The Work of Arius Didymus*, RUSCH 1, 165–89

Bibliography

Görler, W. (1989). 'Cicero und die "Schule des Aristoteles"' in W.W. Fortenbaugh and P. Steinmetz (eds), *Cicero's Knowledge of the Peripatos*, RUSCH 4, 246–63.

(1990). 'Antiochos von Askalon über die Alten und über die Stoa. Beobachtungen zu Cicero, *Academici posteriores* I 24-43' in P. Steinmetz (ed.), *Beiträge zur hellenistischen Literatur und ihrer Rezeption in Rom*. Stuttgart, 123–39.

(1994). 'Älterer Pyrrhonismus, Jüngere Akademie, Antiochus aus Askalon' in H. Flashar (ed.), *Überweg. Grundriss der Geschichte der Philosophie. Die Philosophie der Antike*, Bd. 4: *Die Hellenistische Philosophie*. Basel, 717–989.

(1998). 'Theophrastus, the Academy, Antiochus and Cicero. A Response to John Glucker and an Appendix' in J. M. van Ophuijsen and M. van Raalte (eds), *Theophrastus. Reappraising the Sources*. RUSCH 8, 317–29.

(2011). 'Cicero De finibus bonorum et malorum Buch 5. Beobachtungen zur Quelle und zum Aufbau'. *Elenchos* 32: 329–54.

Gottschalk, H.B. (1987). 'Aristotelian Philosophy in the Roman World from the Time of Cicero to the End of the Second Century AD'. *ANRW* 36.2, 1079–1174.

Griffin, M. (1989). 'Philosophy, Politics and Politicians at Rome' in J. Barnes and M. Griffin (eds), *Philosophia Togata I*. Oxford, 1–37.

Hahm, D. (1983). 'The Diaeretic Method and the Purpose of Arius' Doxography' in W. Fortenbaugh (ed.), *On Stoic and Peripatetic Ethics. The Work of Arius Didymus*, RUSCH 1, 15–37.

(1990). 'The Ethical Doxography of Arius Didymus'. *ANRW* 36.4, 2935–3055.

(2007). 'Critolaus and Late Hellenistic Peripatetic Philosophy' in A.M. Ioppolo and D. Sedley (eds), *Pyrrhonists, Patricians, Platonizers. Tenth Symposium Hellenisticum*. Naples, 49–101.

Hatzimichali, M. (2011). *Potamo of Alexandria and the Emergence of Eclecticism in Late Hellenistic Philosophy*. Cambridge.

(2012). 'Antiochus' Biography' in D. Sedley (ed.), *The Philosophy of Antiochus*. Cambridge, 9–30.

(2013). 'The Texts of Plato and Aristotle in the First Century BC' in M. Schofield (ed.), *Aristotle, Plato and Pythagoreanism in the First Century BC*. Cambridge, 1–27.

Heinze, R. (1925). 'Auctoritas'. *Hermes* 60.3: 348–66.

Hirzel, R. (1882).*Untersuchungen zu Cicero's Philosophischen Schriften*,Vol. 2. Leipzig.

Huby, P. (1983). 'Peripatetic Definitions of Happiness' in W. Fortenbaugh (ed.), *On Stoic and Peripatetic Ethics. The Work of Arius Didymus*. RUSCH 1, 121–34.

Bibliography

(1985). 'Theophrastus in the Aristotelian Corpus, with Particular Reference to Biological Problems' in A. Gotthelf (ed.), *Aristotle on Nature and Living Things*. Pittsburgh/Bristol, 313–25.

Hutchinson, D.S., and Johnson, M.R. (2005). 'Authenticating Aristotle's Protrepticus'. *Oxford Studies in Ancient Philosophy*.29: 193–259.

Inwood, B. (1984). 'Hierocles: Theory and Argument in the Second Century AD'. *Oxford Studies in Ancient Philosophy* 2: 151–84.

(1985). *Ethics and Human Action in Early Stoicism*. Oxford.

(2012). 'Antiochus on Physics' in D. Sedley (ed.), *The Philosophy of Antiochus*. Cambridge, 188–219.

(2014). *Ethics After Aristotle*. Cambridge, MA.

(2016). 'A Later and (Nonstandard) Aristotelian Account of Moral Motivation' in I. Vasiliou (ed.), *Moral Motivation: A History*. Oxford, 65–86.

Irwin, T. (2012). 'Antiochus, Aristotle and the Stoics on Degrees of Happiness' in D. Sedley (ed.), *The Philosophy of Antiochus*. Cambridge, 151–72.

Johnson, M.R. (2005). *Aristotle on Teleology*. Oxford.

Joly, R. (1956). *Le thème philosophique des genres de vie dans l' Antiquité Classique*. Académie Royale de Belgique. Classe des lettres et des sciences morales et politiques. Mémoirs, Ser. II, Tome LI. Brussels.

Kahn, C. (1983). 'Arius as a Doxographer' in W. Fortenbaugh (ed.), *On Stoic and Peripatetic Ethics. The Work of Arius Didymus. RUSCH* 1, 3–13.

Karamanolis, G. (2006). *Plato and Aristotle in Agreement? Platonists on Aristotle from Antiochus to Porphyry*. Oxford.

Klein, J. (2016). 'The Stoic Argument from oikeiōsis'. *Oxford Studies in Ancient Philosophy* 50: 143–200.

Lee, C-U. (2002). *Oikeiosis. Stoische Ethik in naturphilosophischer Perspektive*. Freiburg/München.

Lévy, C. (2012). 'Other Followers of Antiochus' in D. Sedley (ed.), *The Philosophy of Antiochus*. Cambridge, 290–306.

Long, A.A. (1967). 'Carneades and the Stoic Telos'. *Phronesis* 12.1: 59–90.

(1983). 'Arius Didymus and the exposition of Stoic Ethics' in W.W. Fortenbaugh (ed.), *On Stoic and Peripatetic Ethics. The Work of Arius Didymus, RUSCH* 1, 41–65.

(1988). 'Socrates in Hellenistic Philosophy'. *Classical Quarterly* 38.1: 150–71.

(1993). 'Hierocles on Oikeiōsis and Self-Perception' in K.J. Boudouris (ed.), *Hellenistic Philosophy* 1. Athens, 93–104.

(1995). 'Cicero's Plato and Aristotle' in J.G.F. Powell (ed.), *Cicero the Philosopher. Twelve Papers*. Oxford, 37–61.

Luck, G. (1953). *Der Akademiker Antiochus*. Noctes Romanae 7. Bern/Stuttgart.

Lueder, A. (1940). *Die philosophische Persönlichkeit des Antiochos von Askalon*. Göttingen.

Lynch, J. P. (1972). *Aristotle's School. A Study of a Greek Educational Institution*. Berkeley.

Bibliography

McCabe, M.M. (2005). 'Extend or Identify: Two Stoic Accounts of Altruism' in R. Salles (ed.), *Metaphysics, Soul, and Ethics in Ancient Thought*. Oxford, 413–43.

MacKendrick, P. (1989). *The Philosophical Books of Cicero*. London.

Mette, H.J. (1984). 'Zwei Akademiker heute: Krantor von Soloi und Arkesilaos von Pitane'. *Lustrum* 26: 7–93.

(1985). 'Weitere Akademiker heute: Von Lakydes bis zu Kleitomachos'. *Lustrum* 27: 53–148.

(1986). 'Philon von Larissa und Antiochos von Askalon'. *Lustrum* 28: 9–63.

Momigliano, A. (1975). *Alien Wisdom: The Limits of Hellenization*. Cambridge.

Moraux, P. (1973). *Der Aristotelismus bei den Griechen. Von Andronikos bis Alexander von Aphrodisias Bd. I*. Berlin.

Moss, J. (2012). *Aristotle on the Apparent Good: Perception, Phantasia, Thought, and Desire*. Oxford.

Müller, R. (1968). 'Βίος Θεωρητικὸς bei Antiochos von Askalon und Cicero', *Helicon* 8: 222–37.

Nightingale, A. (2004). *Spectacles of Truth in Classical Greek Philosophy*. Cambridge.

Nikolsky, B. (2001). 'Epicurus on Pleasure'. *Phronesis* 46.4: 440–465.

Pembroke, S.G. (1971). '*Oikeiōsis*' in A.A. Long (ed.), *Problems in Stoicism*. London, 114–49.

Philippson, R. (1932). 'Das erste Naturgemäße', *Philologus* 87: 445–66.

Pohlenz, M. (1940). *Grundfragen der stoischen Philosophie*. Göttingen.

(1959⁵, 1978). *Die Stoa. Geschichte einer geistigen Bewegung*. Göttingen.

Polito, R. (2012). 'Antiochus and the Academy' in D. Sedley (ed.), *The Philosophy of Antiochus*. Cambridge, 31–54.

Powell, J.G.F. (1995). 'Cicero's Translation from Greek' in J.G.F. Powell (ed.), *Cicero the Philosopher. Twelve Papers*. Oxford, 273–30.

Primavesi, O. (2007). 'Ein Blick in den Stollen von Skepsis: vier Kapitel zur frühen Überlieferung des Corpus Aristotelicum'. *Philologus* 151: 51–77.

Prost, F. (2001). 'L' Éthique d'Antiochus d' Ascalon'. *Philologus* 145: 244–68

Raalte, M. van (1988). 'The Idea of the Cosmos as an Organic Whole in Theophrastus' Metaphysics' in W. Fortenbaugh and R.W. Sharples (eds), *Theophrastean Studies. RUSCH* 3, 189–215.

Rawson, E. (1985). *Intellectual Life in the Late Roman Republic*. London.

Regenbogen, O. (1940). 'Theophrastos' in W. Kroll and K. Mittelhaus (eds) *Paulys Real-encyclopädie der klassischen Altertumswissenschaft*, Supp. VII. Stuttgart, cols. 1354–1562.

Runia, D.T. (1989). 'Aristotle and Theophrastus Conjoined in the Writings of Cicero' in W. Fortenbaugh and P. Steinmetz (eds), *Cicero's Knowledge of the Peripatos. RUSCH* 4, 23–38.

Russell, D. (2010). 'Virtue and Happiness in the Lyceum and Beyond'. *Oxford Studies in Ancient Philosophy* 38: 143–85.

Bibliography

Sandbach, F.H. (1985). 'Aristotle and the Stoics'. *Proceedings of the Cambridge Philological Society*, Supplementary Vol. 10. Cambridge.

Schmitz, P. (2014). *Cato Peripateticus-Stoische und Peripatetische Ethik im Dialog*. Berlin/Boston.

Schofield, M. (1995). 'Two Stoic Approaches to Justice' in A. Laks and M. Schofield (eds), *Justice and Generosity: Studies in Hellenistic Social and Political Philosophy*. Cambridge, 191–212.

(1999). *The Stoic Idea of the City*. 2nd edn. Cambridge.

(2008). 'Ciceronian Dialogue' in S. Goldhill (ed.), *The End of Dialogue in Antiquity*. Cambridge, 63–84.

(2012a). 'Antiochus on Social Virtue' in D. Sedley (ed.), *The Philosophy of Antiochus*. Cambridge, 173–87.

(2012b). 'The Neutralizing Argument: Carneades, Antiochus, Cicero' in D. Sedley (ed.), *The Philosophy of Antiochus*. Cambridge, 237–49.

(2013). 'Writing Philosophy' in C. Steel (ed.), *The Cambridge Companion to Cicero*. Cambridge, 73–87.

Sedley, D. (1989). 'Philosophical Allegiance in the Greco-Roman World' in M. Griffin and J. Barnes (eds), *Philosophia Togata I. Essays on Philosophy and Roman Society*. Oxford, 97–119.

(1992). 'Sextus Empiricus and the Atomist Criteria of Truth'. *Elenchos* 13: 19–56.

(1997). 'Plato's *auctoritas* and the Rebirth of the Commentary Tradition' in M. Griffin and J. Barnes (eds), *Philosophia Togata II. Plato and Aristotle at Rome* Oxford, 110–29.

(1999). 'The Ideal of Godlikeness' in G. Fine (ed.), *Oxford Readings in Philosophy. Plato Vol. 2 Ethics, Politics, Religion, and the Soul*. Oxford, 309–28.

(2002). 'The Origins of Stoic God' in D. Frede and A. Laks (eds), *Traditions of Theology. Studies in Hellenistic Theology, Its Background and Aftermath*. Leiden, 41–83.

(2003). 'Philodemus and the Decentralisation of Philosophy'. *Cronache Ercolanesi* 33: 31–41.

(2007). *Creationism and its Critics in Antiquity*. Berkeley.

(2012a). 'Antiochus as Historian of Philosophy' in Sedley D. (ed.), *The Philosophy of Antiochus*. Cambridge, 80–103.

(2012b). 'A Guide to the Testimonies for Antiochus' in D. Sedley (ed.), *The Philosophy of Antiochus*. Cambridge, 334–46.

Sharples, R.W. (2010). *Peripatetic Philosophy 200 BC to AD 200. An Introduction and Collection of Sources in Translation*. Cambridge Source Books in Post-Hellenistic Philosophy. Cambridge.

Sorabji, R. (1993). *Animal Minds and Human Morals. The Origins of the Western Debate*. London.

Strache, H. (1909). *De Arii Didymi in Morali Philosophia Auctoribus*, Diss. Göttingen.

Bibliography

(1921). *Der Eklektizismus des Antiochus von Askalon*. Berlin.

Striker, G. (1983). 'The Role of *oikeiosis* in Stoic Ethics'. *Oxford Studies in Ancient Philosophy* 1: 145–67.

(1991). 'Following Nature: A Study in Stoic Ethics'. *Oxford Studies in Ancient Philosophy* 9: 1–73.

Szaif, J. (2012). *Gut des Menschen. Untersuchungen zur Problematik und Entwicklung der Glücksethik bei Aristoteles und in der Tradition des Peripatos*. Berlin/Boston.

Tarrant, H. (1985). *Scepticism or Platonism? The Philosophy of the Fourth Academy*. Cambridge Classical Studies. Cambridge.

(1987). 'Peripatetic and Stoic Epistemology in Boethus and Antiochus'. *Apeiron* 20.1: 17–37.

(2007). 'Antiochus: A New Beginning?' in R.W. Sharples and R. Sorabji (eds), *Greek and Roman Philosophy* 100 *BC*-200 *AD*, vol. 2. London, 317–32.

(2013). Review of David Sedley (ed.): *The Philosophy of Antiochus*, (Cambridge: 2012) *Sehepunkte* 13.3 [15.03.2013], URL: http://www.sehepunkte.de/2013/03/21482.html (accessed on 21 March 2016).

Theiler, W. (1930). *Die Vorbereitung des Neuplatonismus*. Berlin/Zurich.

Tsouni, G. (2012). 'Antiochus on Contemplation and the Happy Life' in Sedley D. (ed.), *The Philosophy of Antiochus*. Cambridge, 131–50.

(2016). 'Peripatetic Ethics in the First Century BC: The Summary of Didymus' in Falcon A. (ed.), *The Brill's Companion to the Reception of Aristotle in Antiquity*. Leiden, 120–37.

Wallace-Hadrill, A. (2008). *Rome's Cultural Revolution*. Cambridge.

Wardy, R. (2005). 'The Mysterious Aristotelian Olive'. *Science in Context* 18.1: 69–91.

White, S. (1994). 'Natural Virtue and Perfect Virtue in Aristotle'. *Proceedings of the Boston Area Colloquium in Ancient Philosophy* 8: 135–68.

(2004). 'Lyco and Hieronymus on the Good Life' in W. W. Fortenbaugh and S.A. White (eds), *Lyco of Troas and Hieronymus of Rhodes. Text, Translation and Discussion. RUSCH* 12, 389–409.

Wright, M.R. (1995). 'Cicero on Self-Love and Love of Humanity in *De Finibus* 3' in J.G.F. Powell (ed.), *Cicero the Philosopher. Twelve Papers*. Oxford, 171–95.

Zeller, E. (1856–1868). *Die Philosophie der Griechen in ihrer geschichtlichen Entwicklung*. Tübingen.

INDEX LOCORUM

Indented passages are cited with emboldened page references.

Index Locorum

GENERAL INDEX

229

General Index

Callipho, 64, 129

Carneades, 1, 26, 38, 64, 70, 90, 91, 96, 186

  his division of ethical positions (*carneadea divisio*), 60, 70, 90, 91, 93

  polemical strategies, 70

cataleptic impression, 65

Cato, Marcus Porcius, 22, 25, 33, 87, 161

choiceworthy for its own sake (Lat. *per se expetendum* = Gr. *haireton di'hauto*), 28, 87, 115, 121, 123, 126, 128, 147, 159, 179

Chrysippus, 82, 184, 185

  On Ends (*Peri Telōn*), 80

  On Nature, 185

Cicero, Marcus Tullius

  and Academic scepticism, 30–31

  and Antiochus, 2–5

  and *auctoritas*, 32–35

  philosophical works

    see also Index locorum

    Academic Books, 3, 4, 37, 40, 41, 42, 43, 44, 45, 47, 48, 53, 58, 63, 65, 66, 67, 68, 71, 72, 139, 140, 181

    Lucullus, 2, 5, 64, 65, 107, 206

    On Appropriate Actions, 162

    On Ends, 3, 4, 6, 8, 9, 10, 11, 12, 14, 21, 22, 23, 25, 26, 27, 28, 29, 31, 32, 33, 37, 41, 43, 45, 48, 50, 51, 53, 54, 55, 56, 57, 58, 59, 63, 64, 69, 70, 71, 72, 74, 78, 86, 87, 88, 89, 94, 99, 105, 107, 111, 112, 118, 127, 128, 133, 138, 139, 140, 142, 143, 145, 147, 148, 151, 161, 164, 171, 175, 177, 181, 184, 186, 188, 189, 191, 193, 194, 195, 198

    On the Nature of the Gods, 34, 35, 185

    On the Orator, 38

    Timaeus, 69

    Tusculan Disputations, 28, 29, 33, 34, 143, 173, 201

commentarii (of Aristotle and Theophrastus), 22, 53, 56

concept (Lat. *notio* = Gr. *ennoia*), 136

contemplation (Lat. *contemplatio* = Gr. *theōria*), 142, 143, 144, 145, 149, 167, 168, 169, 172

courage (Lat. *fortitudo* = Gr. *andreia*), 52, 132, 134, 140, 155, 176, 187

cradle arguments, 115, 124, 133–134, 142, 153, 155, 203, 205

Crantor, 48, 49, 52

Crates of Athens, 48

Cratippus, 207

criterion of truth, 1, 3, 20

Critolaus, 58, 63, 64, 179

  balance metaphor, 63

  on *eudaimonia*, 63, 179

decentralisation (of philosophical activity), 19

Demetrius of Phaleron, 30

Democritus, 144, 145

demonstration (Lat. *conclusio* = Gr. *apodeixis*), 146

diadochē, 59

diaphōnia, 70

Dicaearchus, 145

Didymus (Arius?), 126, 160, 163, 164, 171, 172, 180, 181, 182

  epitome of Peripatetic ethics, 10–13, 121, 126, 127, 129, 159, 162, 170, 179

Diodorus of Tyre, 59, 60, 61, 64

doxography, 1, 12, 13, 47, 78, 121, 126

eclecticism, 13, 14, 205

elements (Lat. *elementa* or *principia*= Gr. *stoicheia*), 54, 67, 68

elenchus, 38, 41

Endymion

  example of, 151, 152, 153

Epicureanism, 32

Epicurus, 46, 61, 62, 93

expertise (Lat. *ars* = Gr. *technē*), 44, 138, 140, 187, 192, 195, 196, 197, 198, 201, 204

  imitates nature, 195, 196, 197

fortune (its influence on happiness), 58, 181

function (Lat. *munus* = Gr. *ergon*), 130

86, 87, 88, 89, 90, 92, 94, 96,
97, 99, 111, 112, 115, 120,
121, 125, 126, 127, 129, 133,
136, 159, 161, 164, 165, 174,
186, 200, 203, 204, 205
Antiochean/Peripatetic argument from,
94–104
developmental aspects of, 90, 91, 96
Epicurean version of, 92–93
of animals, 99, 184–191
of plants, 99, 191–194
social, 155–166, 203
Stoic argument from, 80
towards oneself, 123, 126
towards the body, 127, 175
towards the soul, 130
towards the *telos*, 155
towards the virtues, 133
towards theoretical virtue, 142–154
oikeiotēs (relatedeness), 159

pain, 93, 109, 112, 126, 143, 174
fear of, 113, 115
Panaetius, 162, 166
pathos= Lat. *perturbatio* (passion or
emotion), 108, 109, 112, 113,
114, 115, 116, 118, 119,
139, 188
Peripatos, 4, 5, 8, 10, 13, 15, 21, 23, 32, 39,
53, 55, 56, 57, 58, 59, 61, 62,
64, 71, 78, 101, 129, 169, 171,
172, 192, 198, 202, 203,
204, 206
school treatises, 53
Philo of Larissa, 19, 20, 21, 24, 37, 38, 40
Piso, 3, 4, 5, 6, 8, 9, 11, 14, 23, 26, 27, 37,
53, 54, 55, 56, 57, 58, 64, 94,
99, 100, 105, 107, 108, 109,
111, 112, 113, 115, 124, 125,
128, 130, 133, 138, 142, 143,
144, 145, 146, 147, 148, 149,
150, 152, 153, 156, 164, 166,
168, 171, 175, 178, 183, 184,
186, 188, 189, 195, 197, 199
Plato, 6, 7, 9, 26, 28, 32, 33, 36, 38, 39, 40, 41,
42, 43, 44, 45, 46, 47, 48, 49, 52,
65, 68, 78, 117, 136, 137, 138,
144, 145, 149, 163, 172, 173,
181, 194, 201, 202, 206, 208

forms or 'ideas', 7, 68, 137, 149, 169
his authority, 7, 46
philosophical works
see also Index locorum
Alcibiades, 122
Apology, 39, 42, 106
Gorgias, 173
Laws, 117
Menexenos, 173
Meno, 106, 137, 138
Phaedo, 137
Protagoras, 140
Republic, 101, 116, 136, 149, 169
Theaetetus, 163
Timaeus, 49, 65, 67, 68
Platonism, 6, 8, 13, 14
pleasure (Lat. *voluptas* = Gr. *hēdonē*), 52,
61, 62, 92, 93, 104, 111, 112,
117, 127, 128, 129
Polemo, 45, 48, 49, 50, 51, 52
power (Lat. *vis* = Gr. *dynamis)*, 66, 67,
99, 100, 103, 124, 187,
193, 195
practical wisdom (Lat. *prudentia* = Gr.
phronēsis), 132, 134, 135,
155, 187
preferred indifferents (Lat. *praeposita* =
Gr. *proēgmena*), 72, 74, 111
Pyrrho, 110, 111
Pythagoras, 28, 35, 144, 145

reason (Lat. *ratio* = Gr. *logos*), 34, 35,
80, 84, 85, 86, 93, 99, 119,
120, 122, 123, 125, 130, 138,
139, 161, 185, 189, 199,
200, 201
life according to, 85, 86

sage (Lat. *sapiens*= Gr. *sophos*), 115, 144,
145, 148, 162, 171, 172
seeds (Lat. *semina* = Gr. *spermata*) sc. of
the virtues, 118, 134, 135,
136, 203
self-awareness, 82, 83, 88, 96, 97, 164,
190, 191
self-evidence (Lat. *perspicuitas* = Gr.
enargeia), 164
self-hate, 105, 106, 109
impossibility of, 107, 109

For EU product safety concerns, contact us at Calle de José Abascal, 56–1°, 28003 Madrid, Spain or eugpsr@cambridge.org.

www.ingramcontent.com/pod-product-compliance
Ingram Content Group UK Ltd.
Pitfield, Milton Keynes, MK11 3LW, UK
UKHW020324140625
459647UK00018B/1995